# RAILS TO PORTPATRICK

H. D. THORNE

G C Books, Wigtown - Scotland's National Book Town

To
Siu Wa Chow and Siu Kwan Chow,
My friends at the other side of the world.

鄒 小 華

鄒 小 群

"An auld wife she sat down to sew,
As wi' her specs she luik-ed through;
She saw a train come cross the Dee,
Oh! what a woners thing, said she."

"Rambles in Galloway"
Malcolm McL Harper,
3rd edition 1908

Copyright 2005
H D Thorne
2nd Edition

ISBN 1- 872350- 63- 1

Typeset & published by:
John Carter
Botany, Wigtown
Scotland DG8 9JG
Tel: 01988 402188

# INTRODUCTION TO THE SECOND EDITION OF "RAILS TO PORTPATRICK".

Half a century has gone by since I looked for the first time at a map of part of the province of Galloway and wondered at the single-track railway that seemed to follow a rather aimless course over a kind of countryside that deserved the term 'wilderness' better than any I had yet seen depicted on a large-scale map. What could possibly be the purpose of the station beside a desolate loch, approached only by a seeming footpath over the moor from the nearest road several miles away? Yet this railway could not have been easy to build, and the viaducts shown on the map told me that it must have been considered worthwhile to spend money on it. Here was a mystery, the answer to which could hardly fail to be interesting, and well worth the seeking.

It was only very shortly before this that I had established that Galloway is Scottish territory, not Irish, and it remained "a far-off country of which I knew little". Now, however, I began to remedy this disgraceful situation by purchasing a copy of Sir Herbert Maxwell's book about Dumfries and Galloway, published in 1896 in the County Histories of Scotland series, and the detailed and attractive map that accompanied it, provided by the house of Bartholomew of honoured memory, enabled me swiftly to remedy my ignorance of local geography and topography. Needless to say, I quickly informed myself of the whole course of the railway whose presence in the wilds around Loch Skerrow had so intrigued me. I saw that the main line ended at a pier in the little town of Stranraer (which also I had but lately learned to place in Scotland and not in Ireland), though a branch line wandered off several miles to the west to a modest-looking village named Portpatrick, where, curiously, it seemed trains must have finished their journeys facing the direction from which they had come. Truly an interesting and unusual railway, and light might well be shed on its purpose by the broken lines on the map indicating shipping routes on Loch Ryan and across the North Channel. Could communication with Ireland have been uppermost in the minds of the promoters of the railway? Clearly, for several reasons the railway whose existence I had discovered almost by accident deserved exploration, and I resolved that it would form part of what would be my first railway journey into Scotland.

For various reasons this resolution was not kept, and my first entry into Scotland by rail was made by means of the Border Counties branch, up the North Tyne valley from Hexham to join the Waverley Route at Riccarton Junction and so on to Hawick. "Few are the trains," read a guide-book published in the Victorian heyday of our railways, 'and few indeed are the passengers that use this single

# Rails to Portpatrick

line of railway that winds its lonely way through the Border hills." There are those who have told us that at the tiny station of Deadwater **(1)** the Border actually crossed the single platform, and that the engine of a north-bound train might be in Scotland and its carriages in England; however, this attractive claim is not quite accurate, though the Border Line did cross the track only just beyond the station. This was a Scottish railway, belonging to the North British Company, and the engine salvaged from the Tay after the disaster of 1879 worked here for a while, being stabled in the little shed at Reedsmouth, until misgivings about it among Scottish railwaymen had abated sufficiently to allow it to go north again and resume the kind of duties for which it had been intended.

My travels in the Border Country revived my interest in Galloway, and my first visit there was not much longer deferred. The "rot" on the railway scene had begun well before that time, with the end of the passenger service between Stranraer and Portpatrick in February 1950 and lifting the track beyond Colfin, the "stump" to Colfin surviving till 1959 to serve the creamery. I would never be able to ride Wheatley's Railway, the passenger trains on the Wigtownshire branch having been withdrawn in September 1950. However, I was in time to become fairly well acquainted with the main line, where only minor modifications had been made, like the closure of Palnure to passengers in May 1951 and reduction of Parton and Gatehouse of Fleet to unstaffed halts. The "Paddy" expresses still attracted passengers, but the stopping trains reminded me of those whose acquaintance I had made on the Border Counties line, where passenger services ceased in October 1956 and complete closure took place in September 1958. But the Transport Act of 1962 proposed much more than closure of branch lines, and it was resolved to close the main line completely from Dumfries to Challoch Junction. Stranraer and its steamers were to be served only by the railway from Ayr and Girvan; the London "Paddy" was to go that way in future, at the cost of over 40 extra miles between Dumfries and Stranraer. This drastic decision took effect at mid-June, 1965. The WR line had closed completely in October 1964 and the track been lifted remarkably quickly; the same feat was not attempted on the main line, where demolition was deferred till 1967-8.

This period should not be passed over without mentioning the offer of the enginemen at Dumfries shed to give up some of their rest-days, without payment, to provide a regular weekday service of two diesel trains in each direction between Dumfries and Stranraer. Not surprisingly, this remarkable offer did not gain acceptance, but it surely deserves to be remembered as a late example of the spirit of service that characterised Galloway's railwaymen.

(1)   "A Lilliputian station" that must be, so wrote J. Logan Mack in "The Border Line", his account of a remarkable walk from the Solway to the North Sea in the 1920s, "one of the least important in the British Islands, serving as it does so sparsely populated a district. No proper roadway leads to it, access being obtained by a footpath across a field. It is under the charge of one female official, who is empowered to issue tickets to six stations and no more."

# Rails to Portpatrick

About a year following closure of the main line, I paid a visit on a summer's day to the neighbourhood of Dromore, mounting the railway embankment from Viaduct Cottage and crossing Big Fleet. I continued some way beyond, then turned about and, re-crossing the viaduct, followed the track up the 1 in 76 to Gatehouse station. As I neared the station the figure of a man of middle height appeared from the building and walked purposefully towards the end of the down platform. His cloth cap was pushed back off his forehead; his shirt-sleeves were rolled up and his waistcoat unbuttoned. For a moment or two he peered down the track, seeming, I thought, not to be interested in me, possibly even not to be aware of me, but to be looking well beyond me, farther down the line. Then, his reconnoitre abruptly terminating, he turned on his heel and returned to the station building as briskly as he had come. Reaching it myself a little later, I found it deserted. Such was my brief encounter with the Mystery Man of Gatehouse Station.

I spent a little while standing close by in the sunshine, enjoying the panoramic view with the noble viaduct in the distance, the Clints of Dromore rising behind it. For a brief space of time there seemed to be total silence, with an atmosphere of perfect peace. The experience was all the pleasanter for knowing how different conditions could be here. Then I found myself recalling another genial occasion, though under less idyllic weather conditions, when, approaching on foot from Gatehouse Town, my arrival at the station coincided with that of an east-bound train. I had a minute or two's conversation with the driver and fireman of the 'Black Five' engine, then watched as their train drifted away into the wilds. I had already made my first journeys as a passenger on the railway, and I think it was now that I began to feel the strong wish to explore 'in depth' its history and the part it had played in the life of the province over the years.

Big Fleet Viaduct has defied the misgivings of many admirers for some time and survived fairly intact, but its condition is fragile, so that though it now belongs to Sustrans no public access is allowed. The Wee Fleet Viaduct has been demolished for a good while. Sustrans have tried to negotiate access to Loch Ken Viaduct, which also is still 'in situ', but have not been able to arrange terms with the owners. It was saddening to have it described to me a few days ago by someone living near it as "a very rickety old bridge". The viaduct at Stroan Loch survives, and so does public access; the same applies at Glenluce. Though the greater part of Graddoch Viaduct has gone, two of its eight arches have been carefully restored and preserved, with a commemorative plaque. This gives it the name Cairnsmore - by which it is marked on the map in Sir Herbert Maxwell's book that I mentioned earlier. Piltanton remained for some years after complete closure of the Portpatrick branch in 1959, an impressive object striding its valley as seen from the main Stranraer to Portpatrick road, but eventually had to be demolished; however, a few remains, more than negligible, survive near Lochans.

Several station buildings, or parts of them, survive as private houses, including Gatehouse and the next station to the west, Creetown. In the Epilogue to

# Rails to Portpatrick

our first edition, Mr K. Andrew painted a dismal picture indeed of the latter as he found it in 1974 - the erstwhile "trim little building" had become "a depressing ruin of broken glass, gaping floorboards, weeds and crumbling stone". It is now transformed, by restoration and enlargement, as Railway House. From nearby Spittal to Muirfad the path of the railway, here belonging to Sustrans, has been made into a very good route for walkers and cyclists by the Regional Council, providing a much needed refuge from the A75 trunk road. At Portpatrick, part of the single-storey building remains as a private residence, but the platform was demolished in 1995 in connection with the adjoining Loreburn Housing Association development. This necessitated the removal and relocation of the Scissors Stone.

The Scissors Stone commemorates a tragic event at Portpatrick on 3rd July, 1909. Four special trains had brought about 2,000 girls from the Ferguslie Thread Mills in Paisley for their yearly excursion. Accompanied by the Ferguslie brass and fife bands they marched to Dunskey Glen, which had been opened to them by Lady Orr-Ewing, owner of the Dunskey estate as she was of the new Portpatrick Hotel. A field had been set apart for catering and also for sports, but the latter had hardly been started when the weather broke, torrential rain sending the vast crowd of visitors rushing to the shelter of the village, where the church, trinity hall, workmen's club, and also numerous private houses, were made available to them. They remained very good-humoured in spite of appalling weather, had tea at the drill hall and then set off to the accompaniment of the bands to the station for their journey home. Two trains had received their complement of passengers and steamed away, when a girl of 18, Rachel Douglas, tried to get on the third as it was shunting backward; falling on the rails, she was crushed to death by the carriage passing over her. The local shopkeepers sent a beautiful wreath for her grave; a more lasting memorial was provided in the form of a stone, carved with a pair of scissors, built into the edge of the single platform at the station. When after the greater part of a century the platform came to be dismantled, the stone was saved, and given a new home in front of the new primary school building in Portpatrick, accompanied by a short length of rail. An inscription reads: 'Dedicated to the memory of Rachel Douglas of Paisley who died tragically near this spot 3rd July 1909. Aged 18 years." **(2)**

The decline of the railway was accompanied by a contrasting rapid increase in the importance of the sea-crossing. This had been hindered in the later '50s by lack of adequate carrying capacity, but the latter was remedied by the building of the *Caledonian Princess*, a particularly fine ship, planned to meet all the requirements of this route, which came into service at the end of 1961. She was so successful in improving patronage that in 1966 the *Stena Nordica,* a French-built, Swedish-owned vessel, had to be chartered at a high fee to assist, a duty which she performed with distinction. This handsome ship, the first 'drive-through'

**(2)** I am very grateful to Mr C. Monteith, Stranraer, for drawing my attention to the story of the Scissors Stone, and for the photograph of it in its present home.

## Rails to Portpatrick

vessel on the passage, introduced a name which, as the century wore on, would become intimately associated with it. *Caledonian Princess* survives at this day, still impressive in appearance but in a vastly changed capacity, some dozen miles from where I write - renamed *Tuxedo Princess* and moored to a quay in Gateshead, she does duty as a floating night-club.

By the mid-'70s over 200,000 vehicles and 680,000 passengers were being carried annually, and the years following saw great, and very expensive, improvements to terminal and harbour facilities. In 1992 SeaCat came on the scene with a stirring new development in the novel and impressive shape of a catamaran, with which they began a service that made possible business and pleasure visits to Dublin and back again the same day, with immediate success. They were not long in making Troon their Scottish terminal, but Stena Line, who had bought Sealink on privatisation and as yet still traded under that name, introduced a catamaran on the Belfast passage, spending very large sums on a new port and terminal at Belfast and on their facilities at Stranraer. In July 1996 they brought the *Stena Voyager* to Stranraer. This huge ship, the product of a vast amount of planning and experimentation through the company's High-speed Sea Service (HSS) 1500 project, is proudly claimed by her owners to be "the smoothest, largest fast ferry in the world". With a cruising speed of 40 knots, she is propelled by water-jets, providing greater efficiency at high speed, greater manoeuvrability and greatly reducing draught; she has satellite navigation systems and precision docking. The crossing-time of the *Stena Voyager* is approximately 1 hour and 45 minutes; she is supported by two super-ferries, the *Stena Galloway,* built in 1980, and the *Stena Caledonia,* built in 1981, multi-purpose vessels whose crossing-time is approximately 3 hours and 15 minutes.

The service to Larne is now provided by P&O Ferries, and from Cairnryan, not Stranraer. There, were numerous plans in the 1830s to 1850s to use the harbour at "the Cairn" as a cross-Channel port, but they foundered on the large sums of money spent on Portpatrick, and Cairnryan continued a long time as a tiny country village. **(3)**

In 1892 the JC found it expedient, in a dispute with Stranraer Town Council over the Railway Pier there, to threaten to transfer activities to Cairnryan as their port for Ireland, but the threat proved effective, and it took many years and the exigencies of war to bring about a change. Fear of great ports such as Glasgow and Liverpool being crippled by enemy action led to the creation of extensive facilities at this tiny port on Loch Ryan between 1941 and 1943, with the Cairnryan Military Railway, just over seven miles long, marshalling yards at the junction near Stranraer and at Leffnoll, and a multiplicity of sidings at Cairnryan Point, where

**(3)** "Cairnryan is a picturesque little village, consisting of a row of cottages running along the public shore road and facing the beach. It has a tidy and thriving appearance, and in the season is a favourite resort of sea-bathers. There is an excellent little inn." M.McL. Harper"

.... on a bright warm day in the middle of June...... the whitewashed cottages and gardens, decked with roses and poppies, of the present inhabitants of Cairnryan, shone out in their modest glory." C.H. Dick.

## Rails to Portpatrick

was the deep-water port. After the war, with the "raison d'etre" of all this gone, activity languished. There was some ship-breaking, including several warships, outstanding being the *Ark Royal* in 1980, but hopes for expansion of this, and of ship-repairing, were not realised and the yard closed in 1988.

Fortunately however by this time the prosperity of the port was assured through establishment of the kind of activity that had eluded it in the past, viz. as a cross-Channel port. This had commenced in July 1973, when European Ferries started a drive-on, drive-off service for vehicles and passengers to Larne, in direct competition with Sealink from Stranraer. Later that year they acquired the whole of the share capital of Larne Harbour Ltd. Their service was purchased in 1992 by P&O Ferries, who built a new terminal at Cairnryan. Four years later, to meet competition from the Stena HSS, they introduced their *Jetliner*, which, with a top speed of 35 knots, could make the crossing to Larne in about an hour. In March 2000 she was replaced by their fast craft, the *Super Star Express*, in service from March to October, more hugely expensive new facilities having been built at Cairnryan in preparation. Their conventional ferry, *European Causeway*, introduced in August 2000, crosses in 1hr 45mins - the fastest conventional crossing of the Irish Sea.

No such success attended the railway, though the remarkable progress of the ferry service during the later 1960s suggested that had the P P & W main line stayed open it would likely have received a substantial increase in goods traffic. The diversion of trains to and from Carlisle and beyond by Ayr and Mauchline involved over 40 additional miles between Stranraer and Carlisle, and of course a considerable increase in journey times, and though the "London Paddy" survived by following this route it was not very consistent with the idea of an Inter-City service in the later '60s and the '70s, and it is hardly surprising that patronage declined. For a short time the diverted service was steam-hauled, and in the magazine "Modern Railways" Mr T. Russell gave details of a journey on the down "Paddy" in autumn 1965 with a train of 15 carriages. Hauled by a Brittania Pacific locomotive, with a 'Black Five' as pilot, the train achieved impressive timings. The exceptionally heavy load, totalling well over 500 tons, was due to a national seamen's strike which left Stranraer to Larne as the only passage to Ireland still available. The performance of the engines, and of their drivers and firemen, on the part of their journey south of Girvan was particularly impressive, but speed fell to a minimum of 18 m.p.h. at Pinmore, and though not at all surprising in the circumstances this yet served to underline the unsuitability of the route for an Inter-City service. Before long, the Annbank/Mauchline diversion was itself closed, and trains to Carlisle from Stranraer had to make an even longer diversion by Kilmarnock, so going within 25 miles of Glasgow on their way. Patronage of the London trains declined steadily and the London carriages came to be attached to other trains, their routes varying; the service came to an ignominious end in the latter part of 1990, having not even been advertised during its last year.

# Rails to Portpatrick

About two years ago in Stranraer, I talked with a young man, a resident, who, after asking me how Stranraer had come to lose its direct rail links with the south, inquired where was the nearest place to join a through Inter-City train for London. When I told him Glasgow, he remarked how ridiculous that was and that "You'd be better off getting the overnight bus". He went on to say that however important road transport had become it could never entirely replace rail, and that there would always be something missing from Stranraer's relationship with the rest of the world so long as it lacked a proper rail link with London. In the account of the opening of the P P R in the third chapter of our story, I quote Viscount Dalrymple's reference to an old saying, "Out of the world, into Kirkcowan," and his comment that this could have been "Out of the world, into the county of Wigtown", but with the coming of the railway this was no longer applicable. Despite all that has changed, in the world of transport as elsewhere, since 1861, it is surely arguable that there is a real sense in which there can be no fully adequate substitute for a rail link, and that the severing of the long-established connection with London has reintroduced an element of isolation into Galloway's status in Britain which only the restoration of that service, in a fully adequate contemporary form, could remedy. **(4)**

Little more than a year after closure of the P P R line, diesel haulage replaced steam on trains using the diversion to and from Stranraer; diesel multiple-units, Inter-City type, had provided the Glasgow service for some seven years previously. In 1988 the ubiquitous 'Sprinter' trains were introduced - not Inter-City type. These also provide a through service to and from Newcastle (the journey taking far longer than that from Newcastle to London), one being derailed near New Luce due to a 'wash-out' of the track-bed, causing 16 people having to be taken to hospital in Stranraer; this ominous incident occurred ten days before Hatfield.

The station at Stranraer Harbour survives as Galloway's only working railway station. It is a bleak affair, giving the impression that it and the railway it serves are only just managing to survive. There have been plans to improve the railway terminal as part of a general scheme of improvement of public transport. In 1992 was published "Stranraer Seafront Strategy", a combined effort of the regional council, Dumfries & Galloway Enterprise and Wigtownshire district council, which recommended that "the railway station be relocated or an additional "halt" provided nearer the town. Along with a new bus/coach station and a designated taxi stance, this could provide a fully integrated public transport interchange of around 4,000 square metres for all modes of travel and assist in the better co-ordination and management of traffic in the locality". This has so far borne no fruit. Arrangements at the bus terminus in Stranraer remain thoroughly primitive. And it is surely not irrelevant here to mention that, at the similar facility in Newton Stewart, I saw last year an elderly woman, in attempting what should surely have been the simple andperfectly safe operation of crossing from a bus (of the 'box-on-wheels' type,

**(4)** We may compare the comment of Mr V. Dodd, chief executive of Cumbria Chamber of Commerce, on learning of the serious setbacks to the upgrading of the West Coast main line. "It means the perception of Cumbria as a place remote from London will continue".

# Rails to Portpatrick

incidentally) arrived from Wigtown to the connecting vehicle for Stranraer, very narrowly escape being run down by an arrogant, hurrying motorist ignoring the prohibition on driving between the stances. Nor were her troubles yet over - the driver of the Stranraer bus (in which I was a passenger), having closed the doors, disapproved of having to open them again, and informed her that she was "lucky" to be granted admission. Galloway has much pleasanter bus drivers, but this incident was a disagreeable reminder of how, around 40 years back, many people who would otherwise have been in no hurry to go in for private transport became car-owners chiefly on account of the unreliability of public transport and the incivility of its employees.

Restoration and re-opening of the Town Station in Stranraer have been suggested recently. It has been closed since March 1966, apart from a few days in the winter of '73 when it was reopened due to some explosives having been found at the Harbour Station. Previously a railway engineering depot, it is now a joiner's shop. There were also, quite recently, hopes of getting rolling-stock from Edinburgh to Glasgow (via Falkirk) trains, refurbished, for the Stranraer service; this would certainly have been welcome, but these hopes also have proved abortive. Hope has proved eternal where restoration of the P P R main line is concerned: less than three years after closure the Government, having reaffirmed their confidence in the Short Sea Route, declared in a Commons statement that restoration of the railway was one of two options they promised by way of support for their guarantee. If this proposal, or one of others mooted during these years, could have been acted on, it might well have been successful, with sufficient goods traffic to keep the railway a going concern and fewer problems with the A75 road. However, these hopes too were not fulfilled, and of course with the passage of time restoration of "the Paddy Line" became increasingly less practicable a proposition. Yet some advocates ought certainly to be credited with a degree of ingenuity as well as of persistence in the way they have striven to adapt their plans to the changed circumstances. A local newspaper referred a few weeks since to "current speculation and consideration of a future station in the Dunragit area and the (Dumfries & Galloway) Council's refusal to consider that the Dumfries to Stranraer line has gone forever".

The second of the options whereby the Board of Trade offered to prove their confidence in the Short Sea Route was a new road to serve it on the Scottish side. Here also promise has not been matched by performance. Two years ago a group was formed representing business, particularly the ferry companies, and politics in Galloway to press for improvement of the A75 and A77 (to Cairnryan) roads, and the President of Stena Line and Chairman of Dumfries & Galloway Enterprise joined in an earnest plea for Government commitment. **(5)**

---

**(5)** We hear of an intention eventually to make Cairnryan the sole terminal for the cross-Channel ferries. If this is to come about, improvement of the A77 road will be a matter of inescapable necessity.

# Rails to Portpatrick

Returning to the mid-1960s, the Transport Minister had stipulated that if the P P & W main line were closed, there must be an alternative bus service from Dumfries to Stranraer with facilities for heavy luggage. What were somewhat laughingly called express buses were the result, three daily, connecting with the trains at Dumfries and the steamers at Stranraer. I recall stirring in my sleep now and again at dead of night while a guest at Mr J. Girotti's very pleasant Douglas Arms Hotel in Castle Douglas, to hear the Stranraer bound bus hurrying down King Street, as previously I had been pleasantly disturbed by the sound of the "Night Paddy" steaming out of the station at "the top of the town". The bus had the liberal allowance of 2¾ hours for its full journey, with only a few intermediate stops; however, some of this should probably be regarded as a kind of 'recovery time', as the bus could be badly delayed by the late arrival of the train in Dumfries: I remember a wait of over half-an-hour at Castle Douglas. The journey time (reduced somewhat after a while) compared with the 3¾ hours of the tedious stage-carriage service. The black-and-white buses were not very long on the A75 road; they ran only with the aid of a subsidy, and after six years British Rail refused to continue this, and the service ceased abruptly in June 1971.

My recollections of bus travel in Galloway about that time are not particularly pleasant, especially its slowness and the age and poor maintenance of many of the vehicles. I recall the remark of a fellow-passenger that the company should pay people for using their buses and not vice versa. I recall also making the journey from Girvan to Stranraer in a superannuated double-decker of the 'low-bridge' type with uncomfortable bench-type seats upstairs, and finding that an aperture in the low roof immediately above me afforded a glimpse of the sky. There were numerous double-deckers on Galloway's main bus routes in those days, and they certainly did not contribute to a comfortable journey. My experience in the later '70s was that things had much improved, and some of my most enjoyable journeys in the province were made then. Returning recently after my long absence I have of course seen some consequences of deregulation, and my impressions are mixed. There are more buses than I expected to find - especially in view of the extensive need for subsidies - with very welcome accelerations getting rid of a lot of the old tedium; services seem to have been re-planned with real effort to meet the needs of prospective customers. There is something like a tolerable bus service between Dumfries and Stranraer. On most routes the vehicles themselves are something of a 'lucky dip': you may get a good one that gives you a comfortable journey; you may not. Some give the impression that they were never meant to provide for passenger comfort and convenience. They may confront even the fairly agile with hazards of ingress and egress. In my own part of the country, the present state of public transport falls far short of what is needed to tempt people away from their

**(6)** Some years ago this company, in the folder advertising their summer day-excursions, were at pains to assure prospective customers that their excursion buses bore no comparison to those they saw operating their daily stage-carriage services.

private cars. People in Galloway tell me that the same applies in their province.

We have nowadays the frequent menace of the narrow seat. During the war years of the 1940s, the main bus company in my area included with the stickers on the windows of their vehicles warning against careless talk, coughs and sneezes, etc., a cheerful one assuring their customers that "We are trying to get you a wider seat". In course of time this was accomplished; but now, nearly 60 years on, that company's successors operate many buses with seats so narrow that it does not require an obese person on the inside for him or her on the outside to ride in constant danger of precipitation into the gangway. What a confession of failure! **(6)** And we are reminded of how in years gone by transport operators, in providing ventilation in their vehicles, sometimes had the courtesy to provide also directions as to how to avoid draughts. Nowadays buses and trains alike have adopted a type of ventilator which can hardly be used at all without causing a mighty draught and, therefore, inviting mischievous or arrogant misuse.

The Sprinter trains boast luggage-racks so high that even a tall person finds them sufficiently difficult to reach. I recall my first journey on one of these trains, from Newcastle to Dumfries, in 1988. A little two-coach affair, it became quite hideously overcrowded; beyond Carlisle the surly conductor abandoned attempts to collect fares, and the refreshment service, provided by a trolley that had done good business but appeared to me to cause such an obstruction as to be a constant potential cause of an accident, had also to be discontinued. A group of young people left the train at Dumfries, loudly rejoicing at the fact that they had travelled from Carlisle without payment. And a vivid recollection of the journey is how an elderly man thought to fling a folded garment up on to the rack; unfolding, it flopped merrily down, to cover neatly the head of the passenger in a nearby seat. I was heartily glad that my own journey ended at Dumfries, but at the station there it was deeply depressing to contrast my latest experience with memories of travel to the Queen of the South in the trains of yesteryear. Shortly after, I had a conversation with a man who had to drive the new 'Pacer' trains for shorter journeys, with very austere bus-type bodies. "It seems," he remarked to me, "all they could afford was something cheap and nasty - and that's exactly what they've got!" "The trains are squalid and decrepit and the fares are high," was the comment on a television news programme a few months ago of a businesswoman, a regular passenger on part of the Tyne Valley line between Newcastle and Carlisle.

When the enormously expensive (£280m. at the prices of over 20 years ago) Tyne & Wear Metro, a rapid-transit-system, was opened in 1980, widely-distributed leaflets admitted that, the seating arrangements consisting mainly of pairs of facing seats, patrons might not enjoy sitting "eyeball to eyeball" and recommended, therefore, that they carry a newspaper, etc., wherewith to obscure the view of their fellow passenger opposite. This "showpiece system", "the envy of the world," to quote its operators, has been much troubled by ills characteristic of our in some respects very nasty society, including ugly incidents which the operators have tried to fight with a variety of expedients. A short time ago, a train window was smashed a mile from where I write by a stone flung from the lineside - cf. the narrative, and my comment, below, page 83.

When the shortcomings of vehicles are considered, along with the way in which, over a long period of time, many rail and bus stations have been allowed to become unpleasant and even intimidating places, and also how in numerous quite populous locations there is no attempt at a bus station, and passengers may have to wait in uncomfortable and even dangerous conditions, we cannot help acknowledging that people who want to use public transport, who may actually depend upon it, are regarded in our society as second-class citizens with no right to higher aspirations and who should be glad that any kind of provision is made for them at all. The extremely slow progress - sometimes lapsing into total lack of it - with schemes of improvement reflects the same attitude. In the area where I live, enthusiastic hopes have lately been voiced for the reopening of stations and restoration of passenger services on mineral railways still known as the Blyth & Tyne lines, after the prosperous, go-ahead little company that created them in early Victorian days. This, it is claimed, will do much for the prosperity of the district. But a similar scheme was eagerly mooted in the 1970s.

Under the new scheme, a condition of any passenger service is that it must be self-supporting. This implies distinctly the danger that trains and stations will be 'basic', with fares high for the standard of the facilities provided. A train service of this kind will be unlikely to entice people from their private cars. More probably it will attract some who have hitherto been patrons of the local bus services, leading quickly to the latter being reduced, to the discomfort of numerous people to whom the new trains are less convenient. A similar situation could well come about in the Scottish border country, where Government have told the promoters of the hoped for restored Waverley Route that all the capital must come from private sources; clearly, the proposed half-hourly passenger service between Edinburgh and Galashiels would have to be self-supporting, implying the same prospect of limited achievement. (Incidentally, the likely cost of restoration as far as Galashiels, about 35 miles, was officially stated to be about £80m.; it was curious to be told by the promoters, with television publicity, that they expected the total cost of complete restoration of the route, about 100 miles, to be around £70m.)

When the Tyne & Wear Metro, mentioned earlier, was created over 20 years ago, at great expense, it was assumed that it would. have the benefit of subsidies, and for a considerable time it did; however, patronage declined rather than increased: then, in 1988, it was made known that the subsidy was to be gradually eliminated. The operators appeared to accept this quite cheerfully, and to be confident that it could be successfully 'taken on board'. Fares, of course, were increased annually, and passenger numbers continued to decrease, the decline having been slightly relieved very recently only by introducing very low fares at certain times.

# Rails to Portpatrick

During this time, the Wear district had not been served by the Metro at all, in spite of its name and the fact that people in the Sunderland area contributed to it, and there was understandable resentment over this. In March this year, however, the Sunderland Extension was at last opened, at a cost of £100m. But it has been 'too long a-comin''; people are too accustomed to other means of transport, and the Metro trains, at current fares, are not an attractive enough alternative: the number of passengers using them has been below half that expected. (It is surely ironic that the same edition of a local newspaper that carried the bold headline, "Is the Metro about to hit the buffers?" carried also a Motoring Supplement of 32 pages.)

The RMT union claim always to have said that the extension could not pay, and must be operated on a social need basis and, as such, subsidised.. They add that funds for the extension were forthcoming only on condition of the operators "demonstrating self-sufficiency", a requirement that has been shown to be "absolute folly". The Metro faces a debt in the coming year of £7m. to £9m.

The news of this was quickly followed by the announcement of steep increases in concessionary fares on trains and buses for pensioners and disabled people; all fares on the Metro trains will be increased, when there is a desperate need for more passengers; services may well be reduced and jobs lost. Bus services are likely to be affected also, particularly those subsidised by the transport authority, while if the higher concessionary fares discourage elderly people from travelling, this will be another source of loss to the bus companies. Mr M. Harris, commercial director of one of the largest bus operators in the Tyne & Wear area, said the other week that recent changes in the concessionary fares scheme would cost his company nearly £400,000 in lost subsidy, and they may have to reduce services.

We have in this disaster a deeply disconcerting example of a very large scheme of improvement in public transport that is having the opposite effect to what was intended. But serious doubts had been expressed previously about the very limited area that it covered, and whether the huge amount of money spent on it would not have been better used in improving public transport generally over a wider area. Public authorities have to try to balance the needs of all road and transport users, with limited resources. The confusion and profusion of interests, opinions and prejudices involved are thoroughly daunting. But what is quite certain is that matters cannot be allowed to "drift".

We are faced, now, with the inescapable fact of the failure, overall, of rail and bus privatisation. One of their unwelcome achievements has been to produce

---

(7)   On a dark, rainy June evening last year, a friend and I sought rest and shelter at one of the inns in Portpatrick. As we chatted about railways, a man sitting nearby asked if he might join in the conversation, giving us the welcome information that he is a train driver. In the days of British Rail, he said, working for the same 'outfit' gave men something solid they had in common, that they were glad of because it helped them to have a certain sense of unity. Wherever you went as a driver - it might be a long way, as far as Penzance even - there was that bond between you and other drivers you met. "But now that's gone, it's finished, it just doesn't exist any more."

extensive fragmentation, one of the curses of our society. **(7)** Private profit has consistently taken precedence over the public interest, a policy guaranteed to defeat plans to provide the nation with efficient public transport. Mr. D. Foster, MP, Liberal Democrat transport spokesman, referring to Railtrack, spoke of "the obscene conflict between passenger safety and shareholder profit"; we are reminded of the phrase coined by a capitalist prime-minister in the early 1970s, when he referred to "this ugly, unacceptable face of capitalism". The state of affairs of which this forms part is a deep tragedy for our nation. We hear our railways compared with those of Third World Countries, to the disadvantage of ours. Behind the problems of recent creation lie the effects of many years of inadequate investment and continual political interference. Serious problems on our railways will be with us for a substantial time to come.

In 1969 there took place a large extension of bus nationalisation, involving spending large sums of public money, with the creation of the National Bus Company. At the time, I was very critical and apprehensive, but I was to prove mistaken; the NBC was an example of successful nationalisation. Since privatisation, bus patronage has steadily declined, which is not surprising when profit has, all too often, quite glaringly come before service. Not the least undesirable consequence is the decline in job satisfaction among employees, with frequent complaints of an unhappy working environment.

Matters have reached a critical stage on our roads, with the grave problems - loss and distress through accidents, delays, financial loss, injury to health by stress and pollution, etc. - owing to the degree of congestion now widespread on Europe's most overcrowded roads. Predicted increasing levels of car ownership menace the future. Numerous are the households who believe use of at least two cars to be vital for survival. Young people take for granted the right to own and drive a car, an object conflicting with the concern for environmental problems often accredited to them (deservedly in the case of some). I learned earlier this year of the death of Sir Colin Buchanan, reminding me of how, back in 1963, in his report "Traffic in Towns", he urged the need to come to terms with the increase in vehicle ownership and its implications for the quality of our urban life. His very timely appeal went unheeded of course, and significant action to combat the ever-growing problems on our roads has been constantly deferred over the years, Very strong vested interests played their part in this, just as they share responsibility for the neglect of our railways. New Labour's half-hearted initiative quickly melted away in face of public hostility, while a weapon which politicians of both parties had found it convenient to claim was useful in the battle against over-use of the car - and might even increase by half the number of people going by train (!) - received a notable blow in the fuel-tax protests of September 2000.

Mr C. Moyes, deputy chief executive of one of the better public transport companies to emerge from privatisation, wrote recently that "courageous and initially unpopular decisions about rationing road space and giving unhindered access for buses" will have to be taken. Perhaps the fairly wide area of agreement

## Rails to Portpatrick

- or at least of acquiescence - that has greeted Mayor Livingstone's proposals for Central London is a hopeful sign; admittedly this may well reflect the desperate stage matters have reached in the capital, but they are bad enough elsewhere and will deteriorate in places that have escaped so far if the problems arising from increased car ownership go unremedied.

Mayor Livingstone has just received an invitation to the city of Durham as a guest of the County Council, highly delighted as they are with the conspicuous initial success of their imposition of a toll on the steep and narrow road, of medieval origin, leading from the market place to the cathedral and castle. Up to 17,000 pedestrians use this road daily, and there were regularly 1,500 to 2,000 vehicles between 10 a.m. and 4 p.m. weekdays. From October 1$^{st}$ 2002, a toll of £2 per vehicle has been charged between these hours, unless the driver has an exemption permit, with a £30 fine in default. Vehicle numbers have diminished to between 300 and 400 daily; in the first three weeks only about 12 motorists have refused to pay. Some of the toll money will be used to subsidise the shuttle bus plying between Durham's rail and bus stations and car-parks and the castle and cathedral.

The excellent initial success of the Durham scheme will be welcome news to everyone really concerned about the problems on our roads, and no doubt encouraging to other local authorities contemplating similar measures to reduce traffic congestion. However, such measures on a larger scale will be acceptable, and have a prospect of success, only if there are improvements in public transport of a kind of which there is no certain sign as yet. It will need to be reliable, and to provide means of travel, by road and rail, that offer a degree of real comfort - including, perhaps particularly, at busy times. The disastrous policy of reduction of subsidies must be reversed, with fares low enough to draw people away from their cars. The customer, actual and potential, must be the main consideration. Of course this means much greater investment in public transport. Otherwise, there can be no hope whatever of the changes that are necessary to protect our environment and safeguard the quality of our society and, indeed, our civilisation, being acceptable and, therefore, successful.

In conclusion a suitable observation might be that if progress in the right direction is to be sustained, greater consideration for the pedestrian will be desirable, indeed essential, than that which is all too common at present. On this subject, how welcome it is to make Galloway once more my scene and to say what a pleasure it was, returning to Stranraer after my long absence, to be able to walk on pavements uncluttered with the parked vehicles and other varied impedimenta now so general elsewhere. Professor Buchanan saw the true state of our civilisation as being revealed in that of the environment in our towns; by his standard, the little town by Loch Ryan sets an excellent, if sadly rare, example.

I had decided to revisit in Stranraer the North West Castle, where I had

**(8)** C.H. Dick.

stayed several times while researching my book. Here it was my pleasure to meet once again Mr. H. C. Macmillan, whom I remembered over the years working with great industry and enthusiasm to improve and extend the hotel he had created from the handsome, if somewhat austere, mansion on the sea-front, built in the 1820s by Rear-Admiral Sir John Ross, who named it in commemoration of his voyages of exploration in the Canadian Arctic. The following day, I did as I had done several times on those earlier visits and walked over the Rhinns to Portpatrick by the Old Port Road - "old, precipitous, and delightful" **(8)** - and in a book I looked at in a shop there found a reference to Mr Carter, bookseller in Wigtown. On my return to the hotel, there was a message waiting for me from Mr McMillan, asking where he could obtain copies of my book as he would like to place a copy in each of the five hotels that his family firm now own in Galloway. His request sent me next day to Wigtown and Mr Carter, from whom I received the welcome news that my book, long out-of-print, is still appreciated and in demand, and that he would like to add a second edition of "Rails to Portpatrick" to the numerous titles with a Galloway connection that he has published, under his imprint "G.C. Book Publishers Ltd".

The main narrative of the first edition closed with the comment on the P P & W, "It was practically a family concern". This had been said. to me by Mr Peter Seggie, as we chatted in his home in Lockerbie one sunny spring afternoon in 1973. Mr Seggie grew up on the PP&W at its moorland outpost of Loch Skerrow; he attended the village school at Mossdale, near New Galloway station. He was a man of remarkable courtesy. As we strolled in the Lockerbie streets, though old enough to be my father he would make a point of walking on the outside. One other friend stands out in my memory as having shown me the same courtesy; he was Mr. Douglas Brunton, my tutor at college, whose career was tragically cut short by a road accident in 1952. He was educated at Winchester and at Wadham College, Oxford. Mr Seggie was also a man of extreme modesty, a quality which prevented him from receiving in the first edition the kind of acknowledgment that he deserved. It is surely permissible, indeed essential, now to make some degree of amends, and say of Mr Seggie that his opinions, comments and reminiscences (he was known among his friends on the railway as "the Memory Man") were invaluable; our story would have been much the poorer without his generous and expert help. Nothing could be more fitting than that in the new edition he should once again have "the last word".

H.D. THORNE,<br>
Whitley Bay,

April, 2005.

# Rails to Portpatrick

## Contents

**Introduction** ............ 5

**Section One:**
- Portpatrick Railway .......... 23
- A Grand Junction .......... 25
- The Line is built .......... 32
- Early Days .......... 48
- An Advantageous Alliance .......... 62
- Slow Progress .......... 68
- Better Times .......... 86

**Section Two:**
- Wigtownshire Railway .......... 109

**Section Three:**
- Portpatrick & Wigtownshire Joint Railways .......... 139
- Sale and Transfer .......... 140
- The New Broom .......... 154
- The Trains, 1892-1914 .......... 173
- The Steamers, 1892-1914 .......... 199
- Wind and Snow .......... 217
- Poorly Paid and Worried .......... 226
- Parting .......... 246

**Appendices** .......... 261
- The Building of Lock Ken Viaduct .......... 262
- The Stranraer-Drummore Bus .......... 263
- Motive Power on the P.P.&W .......... 268
- Track Lifting (Dr Brewster) .......... 271
- The Last Day (Dr Brewster) .......... 274
- Freight Train Operations on the Wigtown Branch .......... 277

**Illustrations:**   Part One   Between pages 32 & 33
                    Part Two:  Between pages 192 & 193

## List of Abbreviations

| | |
|---|---|
| A&W | Ayrshire & Wigtownshire Railway. |
| CR | Caledonian Railway |
| GN | Great Northern Railway (of England). |
| G&PP | Girvan & Portpatrick Junction Railway. |
| GSW | Glasgow & South Western Railway |
| JC | Joint Committee. |
| L&C | Lancaster & Carlisle |
| LMS | London, Midland & Scottish. |
| LNW | London & North Western Railway. |
| L&Y | Lancashire & Yorkshire Railway. |
| MR | Midland Railway. |
| NB | North British Railway. |
| NER | North Eastern Railway. |
| PPR | Portpatrick Railway. |
| PP&W | Portpatrick & Wigtownshire Joint Railways. |
| SC | Larne & Stranraer Steamship Joint Committee. |
| WR | Wigtownshire Railway |

## RAPID SERVICES
### BETWEEN STATIONS IN ENGLAND AND BELFAST,
*Via Stranraer and Larne.*

Sleeping Accommodation on Board Steamers, See Page 139.

Sleeping Accommodation on Board Steamers, See Page 139.

THE ROYAL MAIL AND SHORTEST SEA ROUTE.

Open Sea Passage, 80 Minutes.  Port to Port, 2 Hours.

| | Hours about | | Hours about |
|---|---|---|---|
| Birmingham | 11¼ | Middlesborough | 10 |
| Bishop Auckland | 9½ | Newcastle-on-Tyne | 7 |
| Bradford | 9¼ | Rugby | 11¼ |
| Crewe | 9¼ | Scarboro' | 12 |
| Darlington | 9 | Sheffield | 10½ |
| Derby | 10½ | South Shields | 9½ |
| Durham | 8½ | Stafford | 10 |
| Harrogate | 11 | Stockton | 10 |
| Leicester | 10½ | Sunderland | 9½ |
| Liverpool | 9½ | West Hartlepool | 10½ |
| London | 12 | York | 10 |
| Manchester | 9¼ | | |

NEWCASTLE-ON-TYNE AND DUBLIN ABOUT .................. 13 HOURS.

ONE SERVICE DAILY all the year round (Sundays excepted) and TWO SERVICES DAILY 2nd June to 30th September.

Through Carriages between Stranraer Harbour and London and Newcastle.

For Times of Trains consult Time Tables of L. and N.W., Midland, N.E., and B. & N.C Companies.

(1) Advertisement for the Short Sea Route in 1902 with GSW locos 87 & 88.
(Tours in Galloway)

SECTION ONE

# THE PORTPATRICK RAILWAY

(2) The tenth Earl of Stair, the first Chairman of the PPR.

# Rails to Portpatrick

**CHAPTER ONE**

A Grand Junction

THE Portpatrick Railway was, as Lord Dalrymple said in after times, "started" by himself and Sir William Dunbar: our story begins in 1856-7. Lord Dalrymple, Lord Lieutenant of Wigtownshire, was heir to the aged ninth Earl of Stair, one of the greatest landowners in the south of Scotland and head of a family that had played a very prominent part in national as well as in local affairs since the seventeenth century. Sir William Dunbar, the seventh baronet of Mochrum, also a very large landowner, became M.P. for Wigtown Burghs in 1857, a position which he held for the next 23 years. He played a leading part in the development of railways in Fife; at the time the Portpatrick scheme was started he was a member of the managing committee of the Edinburgh, Perth and Dundee and Scottish Central Railways, while by 1862 he was deputy-chairman of the Edinburgh, Perth and Dundee Co., and was referred to as "greatly esteemed" by the people of St. Andrew's "for the deep interest he has always taken in the Fife local railways, which owe much of their success to his unwearied efforts on their behalf".

By 1856 the Glasgow & South Western Company's main line from Glasgow to Carlisle by Kilmarnock and Dumfries had been open throughout for six years; now local promoters obtained an Act of Parliament for a line from Dumfries to Castle Douglas - the first railway penetration of Galloway. In this same year, if suitable rail connections were made. the Government undertook to restore the Royal Mail route between Britain and Ireland by the Short Sea Passage from Portpatrick to Donaghadee, started in 1662, promoted to a daily service in 1790 but abandoned in 1849. This was in response to a petition to the Treasury, presented by the Marquis of Londonderry, Lieutenant of County Down, and signed by 24 peers and over 800 landowners, merchants and others from all parts of Ireland. Galloway's principal line of railway was built as part of a plan, the chief aim of which was to bring greater prosperity to Ireland.

At the county meeting at Wigtown on 30th April 1856, a letter was read from Lord Dalrymple as Lord Lieutenant to the County Convener, Stair H. Stewart of Physgill, suggesting immediate steps to ascertain the support, "local and otherwise", for a railway through the county. The meeting resolved that it would be "of great local benefit as well as national importance" to complete "the chain of communication between the principal railways in Britain and the Irish Channel by a junction with the projected line between Dumfries and Castle Douglas". An interim committee was appointed, which was to "communicate with parties likely to be interested in both counties" - in the Stewartry of Kirkcudbright, that is, as well as in Wigtownshire. The Earl of Stair or his factor, George Guthrie, was to be convener of this committee; the secretary was Alexander Ingram, writer, of Stranraer, law and political agent to the Earl of Stair. Sir William Dunbar was to find out the terms on which the firm of B. & E. Blyth, 135 George Street, Edinburgh, would undertake the engineering of the projected line.

By June 1856, enough money had been raised to make it possible to go ahead with the scheme. At a public meeting held at Newton Stewart on the 13th, chaired by Stair Stewart, George Guthrie reported that a memorial to the Government "in favour of promoting a railway communication by Portpatrick, as the shortest sea passage" had been signed by all the noblemen in the North of Ireland; while there was a strong likelihood of support, including financial support, from the Glasgow & South Western and Lancaster & Carlisle Railway Companies. Several resolutions, proposed by Provost Caird of Stranraer and seconded by Provost McHaffie of Wigtown, were carried unanimously.

Dunbar's arrangement with Messrs. Blyth was approved, and they were to make a survey. A copy of the resolutions was to be sent to Lord Dufferin and the Belfast Chamber of Commerce.

At a further meeting at Newton Stewart on 19th September, with Dalrymple as chairman, E. Blyth, C.E., was present, exhibiting a chart of the line and answering questions. He had originally suggested that at its western end the line should follow a direct course between Glenluce and Portpatrick, via Genoch, Stranraer being served by a branch. Dunbar, however, reported that the G S W were strongly in favour of the main line serving Stranraer. "We must look to them for support in the undertaking", he said, "and ought to give their opinion the greatest weight". His proposal, seconded by Provost Caird, that the main line should go by Stranraer, was unanimously agreed to. The meeting was told that a good many proprietors had undertaken to accept the agricultural value of their land, with only severance damages. It was intended to take land and construct bridges for double track, though the line would be single for the time being. District committees were to be formed to raise subscriptions and win support generally. A prospectus was to be published of the projected company, under the noble title of "The British and Irish Grand Junction Railway".

During the ensuing autumn, there was great activity in seeking subscriptions, both in Galloway itself and wherever else in the U.K. there were people who, whether from loyalty to the province, commercial motives, or a combination of the two, might be persuaded to invest in the new undertaking. By the end of October, £103,900 had been raised in £10 shares; the Earl of Galloway subscribed £10,000. A month later, the total had risen to £150,000, and it was reported that Sir William Dunbar and George Guthrie had "got a considerable number of shares taken" in Liverpool and Manchester. A few years later Guthrie thus described their expedition:

"We went begging almost from door to door in Liverpool, Manchester and

London. We went to the then Mayor of Manchester (Ivie Mackie, Esq.), on whom we considered we had some claim, as he had a sister married in the county. He gave us £1,000 and told us if that would not do he would give more. Sir William Dunbar and myself went together begging for the railway, and we, of course, endeavoured to appeal to the patriotism of the parties we met-for we generally managed to have some claim on them either by birth or marriage in the county. On that occasion we got some £10,000 or £12,000, which I consider was begging to some purpose ... I do not know any man who could have done more than Sir William Dunbar for the railway."

A balance of £90,000 remained to be raised by the end of the year, and in early December district meetings were held at Portpatrick, GlenIuce, Kirkcowan, Newton Stewart, Wigtown, Garliestown, Whithorn and Portwilliam. Dunbar, recalled a correspondent in the *Wigtownshire Free Press* many years later:

".... traversed the whole county, and addressed meetings in every town, village and populated corner of the county, advocating the claims, and soliciting support for the railway."

By the middle of the month the amount still required was down to £35,000. The urgency was due to the condition made by the railway companies interested in the development of the Portpatrick line, that if they were to contribute funds, at least £240,000 must have been raised before the end of the year by the promoters themselves.

The Great Northern Company were offering £160,000. It was a remarkably large offer and, needless to say, they expected a good deal in return. They hoped to establish a new trunk route to Scotland, to a great extent under their control, by cultivating good relations with the "Little North Western" Company, owners of the Skipton-Lancaster line, and encouraging the building of a link between the latter company's branch to Ingleton and the Lancaster & Carlisle main line at Low Gill. Now the Portpatrick scheme gave a prospect of a new route to Ireland also, and the Great Northern made it a condition of their offer that through traffic to and from England by the new route should, as far as possible, pass over their system. The G S W had promised £60,000. The Belfast and County Down Company would give £15,000 if they received similar help with their extension from Newtownards to Donaghadee to complete the rail link with the mail route on the Irish side. Dunbar now announced that if another £20,000 could be raised locally at once, the companies would not insist on the remainder being obtained by the end of the year. The Earl of Stair undertook to increase his subscription by a third if other landowners would give "a proportional contribution".

The subscription lists give ample proof of the enthusiasm of the people of Galloway for the railway scheme, those in humble circumstances as well as landowners and more prosperous tenants-many people bought from one to five

£10 shares. By the time the bill for the railway was before Parliament £188,000 had been raised in local subscriptions. Robert Stewart, the "Laird of Cairnsmore", however, struck a heavily jarring note with his prediction that the railway would never pay for the grease for the wheels of the engines, while the only benefit it would confer would be to carry lunatics to the Crichton Institution at Dumfries. Not surprisingly, this comment - surely one of the most crudely disparaging ever made about a projected railway - was long remembered, and several times quoted.

More than half the year 1857 was spent in "long and anxious negotiation" in connection with the Act of Parliament. The G S W disapproved of the managing committee's understanding with the Great Northern, and sought instead to steer them toward the Lancaster & Carlisle Company and London & North Western Company. When the G N required the G S W and the County Down Company to be parties to the agreement about Portpatrick line traffic using their system, the G S W refused, expressing the view that the directors of "the Portpatrick Company" should not enter into any such agreement. The result was that, "at a very advanced stage of the bill", having failed to get the approval of Parliament for clauses in it advantageous to themselves, the G N withdrew their promise of £160,000. (Also withdrawn was a related offer of £20,000 from the "Little North Western.") Faced now with a real danger of having to abandon the bill, the committee of management applied to the Lancaster & Carlisle Company. The latter had previously promised a rebate on traffic passing along their line to and from Ireland. With difficulty, it was agreed that they would contribute £40,000 and take permissive powers to contribute a further £60,000 in lieu of this rebate. The G S W agreed to take permissive powers to contribute £40,000 "in addition to their subscription of £60,000" if £52,000 came "from other sources", which were to include the County Down Company. "All present pecuniary difficulties" were "thus removed", and the bill, which the Commons Committee described as "of manifest public utility", passed both Houses and received the Royal Assent on 17th August. The company was to be called "the Portpatrick Railway Company", its earlier splendid title being quietly forgotten. The coat-of-arms chosen for it, however, displayed the rose, shamrock and thistle, symbolic of the greater prosperity, and closer and happier union, that the railway was expected to help to bring.

The Act described the main line as commencing "by a junction with the railway authorised to be constructed by 'The Castle Douglas and Dumfries Railway Act 1856' near the commencement of the same railway at Castle Douglas in the Parish of Kelton and Stewartry of Kirkcudbright; it was to terminate "near Dinvin Mill, near the town and in the said Parish of Portpatrick" This was on the hillside above Portpatrick, a little beyond the last houses passed on leaving the village by the main road. There were to be two branches to the harbours of Stranraer and Portpatrick. Stranraer was always intended to be the port for heavy goods to and from Ireland. Facilities were lacking at Portpatrick, and the working of heavy goods on the harbour branch there, with its ferocious 1 in 35 gradient, would have involved prohibitive difficulties. The managing committee had tried to avoid the commitment to build the Portpatrick harbour branch, but the County Down Company had insisted, threatening opposition to the bill in the Lords, so the committee, fearing the loss of the bill, gave way. On an assurance from the Treasury that money would be made available for the necessary improvements to the harbours of Portpatrick and Donaghadee, they agreed also to a clause binding the Portpatrick Company to complete the railway to Portpatrick within five years.

On 10th November, at Stranraer, the first ordinary general meeting of the company was held and the original directors elected: Lord Dalrymple, chairman; Sir William Dunbar, Bart., M.P., of Mochrum, vice-chairman; Sir Andrew Agnew, Bart, M.P., of Lochnaw; Sir John McTaggart, Bart., of Ardwell; Stair H. Stewart, Esq., of Physgill; Horatio G. Murray Stewart, Esq., of Cally; Col. James McDouall, of Logan; James Newall Esq., of Goldielea; George Guthrie, Esq., of Appleby (near Whithorn); Wellwood Maxwell, Esq., of Glenlee; Lieut. Col. H. D. Maclean, Lazonby Hall, Penrith; W. N. Hodgson, Esq., Newby Grange, Carlisle; Sir Andrew Orr, of Harviestoun, Glasgow; James McClelland, Esq., Glasgow; and W. N. Wallace, Esq., Downpatrick. Maclean and Hodgson represented the Lancaster & Carlisle Company, Orr and McClelland the G SW Company and Wallace the Belfast and County Down Company. Ingram was appointed secretary and law agent at a salary of £300 per annum. He was to receive a payment of £500 for his services so far.

A few months later the directors were able to report that "the landed proprietors, farmers, merchants and others interested in the undertaking", to the number of more than 800, had subscribed £202,000; other railway companies had entered into obligations to contribute £115,000, and £143,000 was still to be raised. These remaining shares were to be offered to the general public, "in the confident expectation that they will be taken up by capitalists as a sound and profitable investment". The whole of the line between Castle Douglas and Newton Stewart was "set out on the ground", and detailed sections and plans were far advanced, so that contracts might be entered into immediately. All the landowners and tenants on the Loch Skerrow and Creetown contracts gave permission without statutory notices being necessary, with one exception. The reader will doubtless swiftly identify this exception. In March 1859, the directors considered a letter from him, stating his conditions for accepting their offer of compensation and agreed to these.

Controversy arose, however, from the route the line was to take between Castle Douglas and Creetown. The Act of Parliament prescribed a path northward from Castle Douglas to Boat of Rhone, there turning west, crossing Loch Ken and heading through the moors to Creetown and so to Newton Stewart. Not surprisingly, there was considerable public demand for a line that might serve the little towns, of Kirkcudbright and Gatehouse of Fleet, and thence follow a path similar to that of the main road, now A75, by the splendid coastal route to Creetown. The supporters of this "deviation line", as it was called, got a favourable report on it from Professor Rankin, of Glasgow. Blyth, however, made an unfavourable report on it to the directors. At the company's second ordinary general meeting on 26th February 1858, Mr. Neilson, of Queenshill, asked for Blyth's report to be read to the meeting. The exact route to be taken by the deviation line is not detailed, but while it was much the same length as the "Parliamentary line", Blyth described it as much more undulating; gradients and curves were alike more severe; and the works involved would be much heavier and more expensive - there would be more and bigger viaducts, a tunnel 500 yards long, more rock cutting would be needed, and the earthwork would be more than double what it would be on the Parliamentary line. The deviation line would cost £70,000 more, and though admittedly it would pass through richer country, the additional traffic thereby gained could not compensate for this extra cost.

Neilson in reply did not dispute Blyth's comparison of the two routes, but he urged the importance of attracting as much local traffic as possible, which he believed would go far to meet the increased cost. Sir William Dunbar then spoke strongly against the deviation route. The company's line was to be a through line, getting much of its traffic by connecting the North of Ireland with England and Scotland; "though we cannot go to Gatehouse and Kirkcudbright, they can soon come to us". A double line of track would soon be needed, making the additional cost of the deviation line much more than £70,000. Furthermore, the proposal had been made at the last moment, by which time the landowners of the Glenkens district, understanding that the new railway was to serve that area, had subscribed to it "most liberally"; they had lodged a protest against the deviation line, threatening "every legal obstruction" of it. One of their arguments was that the deviation route would bring the railway too much into competition with the steamers serving the ports along the coast, with the result that railway rates would be forced down and revenue diminished. Dunbar concluded that, on every consideration, the company must abide by Blyth's report.

Neilson said he would not divide the meeting. Dunbar in thanking him remarked that though the Portpatrick line could not go to Kirkcudbright, a branch must soon be made to link the two, and this might "ultimately form part of a great main line to Ayrshire and the north". Col. Maclean, one of the Lancaster & Carlisle representatives on the Portpatrick board, said he had been in favour of the route by Gatehouse at first, but was now convinced that it ought not to be taken; the factor of sea competition was clearly one of his strongest reasons for this conclusion. The other Lancaster & Carlisle representative, W. N. Hodgson, M.P., reinforced Dunbar's emphasis of the importance of through traffic, describing the Portpatrick line as "a great national line, having at each end the means of bringing a large traffic". If it had not had "such a good head and tail" his board would not have taken such an interest in it.

A different comment on this subject was made by a contributor, J. Stewart,

# Rails to Portpatrick

in the *Kirkcudbrightshire Advertiser* in November 1922, who blamed the railway's bypassing Gatehouse on Murray Stewart, of Cally - a director of the company - "and the other local lairds", who wanted to prevent disturbance of their estates. This probably represents what some people in the district had always thought, and there is possibly some truth in the theory; but however this may be, Gatehouse was left to be served by a moorland station near the farmhouse of Dromore, six miles north of the town. When the railway was built, there was not an adequate road to link town and station, and after hearing a statement from Murray Stewart, the directors agreed to pay one-sixth of the cost of making a road, up to a maximum of £100.

Meanwhile, they had been advertising for tenders for four of the eight contracts into which the building of the line from Castle Douglas to Portpatrick was to be divided. Firstly, the Loch Skerrow contract, from Boat of Rhone to Dromore, and the Creetown contract, Dromore to Palnure, were let, to McNaughton and Waddell and James Gowans, respectively. They offered the second lowest combined tenders - £95,841.2.0 for Loch Skerrow and £39,403.1.1 for Creetown. They were "highly recommended to the directors for the satisfactory manner in which they have executed similar works on other lines", and "showed confidence in the undertaking" by taking part payment in stock-£8,000 in the case of McNaughton and Waddell, £3,000 in that of James Gowans. Secondly, the Crossmichael (Castle Douglas - Boat of Rhone) and Newton Stewart (Palnure - Kirkcowan) contracts were let to Thomas Telford Mitchell and McDonald and Grieve, who, at their request, were associated as joint contractors. They had submitted the lowest tenders, £26,000 (including £2,000 in stock) for Crossmichael and £46,895 for Newton Stewart. This had been done by the close of 1858. The other contracts, except that for the Stranraer - Portpatrick section, were let a few weeks later: the separate contract for the viaduct over Loch Ken at Boat of Rhone - in itself a major task - to Thomas Nelson, who made the lowest offer of £12,288.13.0; and the Glenluce and Stranraer contracts (Kirkcowan - Stranraer) to James Falshaw, who submitted the lowest tender - Glenluce £41,788.3.7 and Stranraer £28,974 - while applying to work the contracts jointly, and to associate Thomas Brassey with him, both of which requests the board welcomed. The directors were sufficiently well pleased with the progress made to announce to the ordinary general meeting in March 1859 that there was "every prospect of the line being opened to Stranraer before the end of next year".

It was doubtless a heartening prospect; but before it could be made reality, there was much hard work to be done.

## CHAPTER TWO

### The Line is Built

IN Galloway, as in other thinly populated districts with a stable, slow-paced traditional life, the coming of the railway builders must have had, in numerous ways, a greatly disturbing effect. The presence of the much travelled navvies, with their unconventional way of living, would inevitably have an unsettling influence, more especially on some of the younger people, and no doubt in its more subtle effects it would be a good number of years before this influence had altogether spent itself. While, however, the people living near the route of the new line must certainly have felt a good deal of apprehension at the impending upheaval, in some respects many can hardly have failed to welcome it, especially considering the relative poverty of the province. The prospect would open opportunities of employment for local men and boys as labourers on the works, while a wide range of local tradesmen with their special skills; carriers, and people able to provide and to service horses; farmers, innkeepers, shopkeepers and others offering food and drink for sale, anyone able and willing to take in lodgers - not a few in each of these various sections of the local community must have reaped a good harvest of profit from the temporary increase in the population, activity and prosperity.

The path the railway was to follow lay for the most part outside the gentlest and more productive districts of Galloway. Much of the country through which the line was to pass was an upland region of moor, loch, river and stream, treeless or almost so, with large tracts of bracken and heather, the ground mossy in many places and often also stony, strewn about with granite rock and boulder: the edge of the Galloway Highlands. Except for a few miles near Castle Douglas and Stranraer, almost the whole route was a difficult one from the point of view of the railway engineer.

On the loneliest sections of the line, far from any village, navvy settlements were established. The wildest country of all was on the Loch Skerrow and Creetown contracts. In the words of C. H. Dick:

"Between New Galloway station and Creetown the railway crosses one of the most desert tracts of moorland in Scotland, and I have seen travellers, to whom such scenery is distasteful, shudder at the recollection."

Near the site of New Galloway station Mossdale huts were built. Between here and Loch Skerrow were Airie huts; there was a store hereabouts belonging to the contractors, McNaughton and Waddell, from which a workman stole provisions and tobacco and departed to Glasgow, where, however, he was arrested for the offence.

# Illustrations 1

"The years of creation & operation."

## List of Illustrations
## The years of creation and operation

(1) Advertisement for the Short Sea Route in 1902    Page 22
(2) The tenth Earl of Stair, the first Chairman of the PPR    Page 24
(3) Robert Mirray, first station-master at Stranraer Harbour
(4) F. W. Hutchinson, P P & W Traffic Manager
(5) William Grafton, P P R Traffic Manager
(6) 12th March, 1861, Stranraer to Castle Douglas Section
(7) 28th August, 1862, the opening of the Portpatrick Section
(8) Scene west of Newton Stewart on Sunday, 10th February 1895
(9) Portpatrick in 1860's
(10) Another view from the outer harbour wall of the same scene
(11) Portpatrick Station with train to Stranraer circa 1935
(12) "Chinnaman's Brig", Wauphill
(13) Loch Ken Viaduct circa 1904
(14) Glen Luce Viaduct circa 1900
(15) A late 19th century view of the Inner Harbour at Portpatrick
(16) The steam motor bus
(17) Royal Mail steamer Princess May entering Larne Harbour
(18) The Princess Maud alongside Larne
(19) The Princess Louise at the railway pier
(20) The Princess Beatrice, leaving Larne for Stranraer with the mails
(21) A fully operational station at Newton Stewart circa 1900
(22) The same station brought to a halt by heavy snow circa 1910
(23) The "Scissors Memorial"
(24) The dedication stone to Rachel Douglas.

(3) Robert Mirray, first station-master at Stranraer Harbour and station-master at Newton Stewart, 1892-1923, and Mrs Mirrey. (Dr. J. R. Mirrey)

(4) F. W. Hutchinson,
P P & W Traffic Manager
(Wigtownshire Free Press)

(5) William Grafton,
was P P R Traffic Manager
(Wigtownshire Free Press)

## OPENING FOR TRAFFIC

NOTICE IS HEREBY GIVEN, that the Directors of the Portpatrick Railway have Resolved to OPEN THE LINE for PASSENGER and GOODS TRAFFIC between CASTLE-DOUGLAS and STRANRAER, on TUESDAY, the 12th day of March next, when Trains will be despatched as under, viz.:—

### Up Trains. FROM STRANRAER TO CASTLE-DOUGLAS.

| STATIONS. | 1 1, 2, & Parly. | 2 1, 2, & Parly. | FARES FROM STRANRAER. ||||| 
|---|---|---|---|---|---|---|---|
| | | | SINGLE JOURNEY. ||| RETURN. ||
| | | | 1st Class. | 2d Class. | 3d Class. | 1st Class. | 2d Class. |
| Trains will not leave | A.M. | P.M. | S. D. | S. D. | S. D. | S. D. | S. D. |
| STRANRAER before...... | 7 25 | 2 15 | | | | | |
| GLENLUCE ............... | 7 48 | 2 41 | 1 8 | 1 2 | 0 8½ | 2 9 | 1 11 |
| KIRKCOWAN ............ | 8 11 | 3 7 | 3 2 | 2 4 | 1 5 | 5 3 | 3 11 |
| NEWTON-STEWART.... | 8 28 | 3 26 | 4 4 | 3 2 | 1 11 | 7 2 | 5 3 |
| CREETOWN ............... | 8 47 | 3 45 | 5 7 | 4 0 | 2 5½ | 9 3 | 6 8 |
| NEW GALLOWAY ...... | 9 30 | 4 25 | 8 4 | 6 0 | 3 8½ | 13 10 | 10 0 |
| PARTON .................... | 9 37 | 4 34 | 8 8 | 6 3 | 3 10½ | 14 5 | 10 5 |
| CROSSMICHAEL ......... | 9 47 | 4 44 | 9 3 | 6 8 | 4 1½ | 15 5 | 11 1 |
| Or arrive at | | | | | | | |
| CASTLE-DOUGLAS before...... | 9 57 | 4 55 | 10 0 | 7 3 | 4 5 | 16 8 | 12 1 |

| Trains are advertised to arrive at | A.M. | P.M. |
|---|---|---|
| Dalbeattie about............ | 10 14 | 5 14 |
| Dumfries ...................... | 10 55 | 5 50 |
| Glasgow ....................... | 3 55 | — |
| Carlisle ........................ | 12 30p | 7 15 |
| | P.M. | |
| Liverpool ..................... | 5 15 | 12 0 |
| London (Euston Square) .. | 9 50 | 5 30 |

### PARCEL REGULATIONS.

PARCELS to be forwarded by Passenger Trains must be at the respective Stations 15 minutes before the advertised hour of the Train's departure, otherwise they will be detained till the following Train.

It is requested that a full and proper Address be put on all parcels, as delay and losses occur from imperfect Addresses. The name of the Station should at all times be put on the Address.

GAME and other Perishable Goods not specially addressed to be sent by Luggage Trains, will be sent by Passenger Trains and charged accordingly.

### Down Trains. FROM CASTLE-DOUGLAS TO STRANRAER.

| Trains are advertised to leave | P.M. | A.M. |
|---|---|---|
| London (Euston Square) about..... | 9 0 | — |
| Liverpool ........................... | 1 15a | — |
| | A.M. | |
| Carlisle ............................... | 3 36 | 11 0 |
| Glasgow ............................. | — | 7 20a |
| Dumfries ............................ | 8 0 | 3 30 |
| Dalbeattie ........................... | 8 38 | 4 8 |

NO. 1 TRAIN.

The departure of the 9 A.M. Train from Castle-Douglas is contingent on the arrival of the South Mail. If that train is forward at Castle-Douglas by 9, 10 A.M., the train will proceed; if not, it will be detained till 10 A.M. and will then be started.

| STATIONS. | 1 1, 2, & Parly. | 2 1, 2, & Parly. | FARES FROM CASTLE-DOUGLAS. ||||| 
|---|---|---|---|---|---|---|---|
| | | | SINGLE JOURNEY. ||| RETURN. ||
| | | | 1st Class. | 2d Class. | 3d Class. | 1st Class. | 2d Class. |
| Trains will not leave | A.M. | P.M. | S. D. | S. D. | S. D. | S. D. | S. D. |
| CASTLE-DOUGLAS before ... | 9 0 | 5 0 | | | | | |
| CROSSMICHAEL ............... | 9 11 | 5 11 | 0 8 | 0 6 | 0 3½ | 1 0 | 0 10 |
| PARTON .......................... | 9 22 | 5 22 | 1 3 | 0 11 | 0 6 | 2 1 | 1 6 |
| NEW GALLOWAY ............ | 9 30 | 5 30 | 1 8 | 1 2 | 0 8½ | 2 9 | 1 11 |
| CREETOWN ..................... | 10 8 | 6 8 | 4 4 | 3 2 | 1 11 | 7 2 | 5 3 |
| NEWTON-STEWART ......... | 10 26 | 6 26 | 5 7 | 4 0 | 2 5½ | 9 3 | 6 8 |
| KIRKCOWAN ................... | 10 45 | 6 47 | 6 9 | 4 11 | 3 0 | 11 3 | 8 2 |
| GLENLUCE ...................... | 11 8 | 7 12 | 8 4 | 6 0 | 3 8½ | 13 10 | 10 0 |
| Or arrive at | | | | | | | |
| STRANRAER before ........... | 11 30 | 7 30 | 10 0 | 7 3 | 4 5 | 16 8 | 12 1 |

Goods will be received for transmission by this Railway at all Stations on the Line between the hours of 7 A.M. and 5 P.M. No Live Stock will be received for transmission on any day unless sent to Newton-Stewart and Creetown Stations before 12:30 P.M., and to the other Stations before 1:30 P.M. No Live Stock can at present be received at Parton Station.

By Order of the Board,

AL. INGRAM, Secretary.

Stranraer, 6th March, 1861.

(6) 12th March, 1861, the opening of the Stranraer to Castle Douglas Section.
(Wigtownshire Free Press)

## PORTPATRICK RAILWAY.

### OPENING OF THE PORTPATRICK SECTION

ON THURSDAY, 28th AUGUST, this Section of the Portpatrick Railway will be Opened for Public Traffic, viz.:—Passengers, Live Stock, Goods and Minerals.

The Trains, all of which carry 1st, 2d, and 3d Class Passengers, will run as under:—

|  | Mixed—Passenger and Goods. |  | Passenger. |
|---|---|---|---|
| From | A.M. |  | P.M. |
| Stranraer | at 9.30 |  | 3.45 |
| Colfin | 9.46 | and | 3.58 |
| Portpatrick arrive about | 9.56 |  | 4.6 |

* The 3.45 P.M. Train is in connection with the 11 A.M from Carlisle, 7.20 A.M. from Glasgow, and 12.15 P.M from Dumfries.

|  | Mixed—Passenger and Goods. |  | Passenger. |
|---|---|---|---|
| From | A.M. |  | P.M. |
| Portpatrick | at 10.30 |  | 5.20 |
| Colfin | 10.45 | and | 5.30 |
| Stranraer arrive about | 10.57 |  | 5.40 |

| Leave | Goods. | Passenger. |  |
|---|---|---|---|
|  | P.M. | P.M. | P.M. |
| Stranraer | at 12.15 | 1.0 | 6.0 |
| Dumfries arrive | 7.30 | 4.30 | 9.55 |
| Glasgow | 4.0 A.M. | 8.50 | — |
| Carlisle | 9.30 P.M. | 7.30 | 11.50 |
| London | — | 5.50 A.M. | 9.40 A.M |

### FARES:—

**SINGLE JOURNEY.**

|  | 1st Class. | 2d Class. | 3d Class |
|---|---|---|---|
| Portpatrick to Stranraer | 1s 3d | 10d | 7½d |
| Portpatrick to or from Colfin | 0s 7d | 4½d | 3d |
| Colfin to Stranraer | 0s 9d | 6d | 4d |

**RETURN.**

|  | 1st Class. | 2d Class. |
|---|---|---|
| Portpatrick to Stranraer, | 2s 1d | 1s 4½d |
| Portpatrick to or from Colfin, | 1s 0d | 0s 7½d |
| Colfin to Stranraer, | 1s 3d | 0s 10d |

By Order.
**WILLIAM GRAFTON, Manager.**
Manager's Office, Stranraer,
20th August, 1862.

(7) 28th August, 1862, the opening of the Portpatrick Section. (Wigtownshire Free Press)

(8) Scene west of Newton Stewart on Sunday, 10th February 1895
(Dr J R Mirrey)

(9) Portpatrick in 1860's, showing the inner harbour for the mail service and the Harbour Branch railway.
(Stranraer Public Library)

(10) Another view from the outer harbour wall of a similar scene.
(Wigtownshire Free Press)

(11) Portpatrick Station with train to Stranraer circa 1935.
(British Rail)

(12) "Chinnaman's Brig" between Kirkinner and Whauphill. Reputed to have been built by Chinese workmen employed on the construction of this section. (John Carter)

(13) Loch Ken Viaduct circa 1904.
(Tours in Galloway)

(14) The P P & W local train, from Stranraer to Newton Stewart,
crossing the Glen Luce Viaduct circa 1900.
(Stranraer Public Library)

(15) A late 19th century view of the Inner Harbour at Portpatrick showing the development of the infrastructure.
(Stranraer Public Library)

(16) The steam motor bus operated by the Portpatrick & Wigtown Joint Committee between Stranraer and Drummore 1907-08.
(Tours in Galloway)

(17) Royal Mail steamer Princess May entering Larne Harbour.
(Ulster Museum)

(18) The Princess Maud alongside Larne.
(National Library of Ireland)

(19) The Princess Louise at the railway pier, the first harbour station built in 1878 Stranraer.
(Stranraer Public Library)

(20) The Princess Beatrice, leaving Larne for Stranraer with the mails.
(Stranraer Public Library)

(21) A fully operational station at Newton Stewart circa 1900.
(Dr. J. R. Mirrey)

(22) The same station brought to a halt by heavy snow circa 1910.
(Dr. J. R. Mirrey)

(23) The "Scissors Memorial" with a length of rail recalling the tragedy in 1909. (see introduction).
(Colin Monteith)

(24) The dedication stone to Rachel Douglas.
(Colin Monteith)

# Rails to Portpatrick

A report prepared in November 1860 by William Gordon, surveyor, of Gatehouse, for G. A. Schneider, factor to H. G. Murray Stewart, of Cally, in connection with the latter's claim as landowner for damages against the Portpatrick Railway Company, gives us a detailed account of the buildings erected between Loch Skerrow and Dromore:

"There is erected on the estate by the contractors the following buildings constructed of stones, bricks, turf and wood and covered with slate, tiles, felt and wood; and at the north end of Loch Skerrow two ranges of houses 80 feet by 42 feet and 100 feet by 27 feet, all of wood.

"At Oak Clints a house built of stone 21 feet by 17 feet, from which it appears the roof has been carried away.

"On the east side of the Little Water of Fleet, near the viaduct, there is a range of houses and stables 122 feet by 18 feet, 82 feet being stone and slate and 40 feet turf and straw.

"On the west side of the Little Water of Fleet, near the viaduct, there is a range of houses built of turf and covered with felt 92 feet by 24 feet.

"At Corse Burn there are four ranges of houses built of stone and covered with slate 53 feet by 17 feet, 35 feet by 19 feet, 68 feet by 14 feet and 218 feet by 58 feet. Also a smithy 20 feet by 17 feet. There is also a powder magazine of stone and slate near the viaduct over the Big Water of Fleet."

Also in connection with Murray Stewart's claim, William Laurie, quarryman, of Gatehouse, aged 51, deposed that before construction of the line began he was employed by the contractors in making a road from the Big Water of Fleet to near Loch Skerrow - a distance of some 3½ miles. There was already a road of sorts over the moors from the south, past the farm of Grobdale and providing access to Loch Skerrow from the Gatehouse to Laurieston road. This Gordon described as "very much cut up and injured – by the cartage of material to the line". It is more than likely that, in such a country as this, the navvies would supplement the diet obtainable from the contractors' stores with the proceeds of poaching, on moor, in loch, and in stream. Gordon reported that the contractors had "opened peat holes at certain points along the line" and sold peats to the workmen: "It is generally reckoned that 3 cubic yards of wet moss when cut would form a cart-load of peats." William Laurie had "heard the navvies say that they paid sometimes 2/- and sometimes 2/6 a cart-load for peats".

In the spring and summer of 1859, weather conditions were excellent.

Of these the contractors took full advantage, the only exception being at the extreme east end of the line, at Castle Douglas. Here a start was delayed for many months. To make room for their Castle Douglas station, adjoining that of the Castle Douglas & Dumfries Company, the Portpatrick Company needed to divert the main road from Dumfries, now A75, from its then straight course on entering the town. This led to a prolonged dispute with the Stewartry road trustees, and it was late autumn 1859 before the contractor could begin operations. The company subsequently came to an agreement with the Castle Douglas Company for use of their station, which made the dispute seem very futile, and the road diversion, with its awkward bends at each side of the bridge over the railway, specially regrettable. Elsewhere, however, in early September, Blyth was able to report to the directors that conspicuous progress had been made.

## THE CROSSMICHAEL CONTRACT

7¼ miles. Castle Douglas - Boat of Rhone.

The works were well advanced on the southern half of this contract;

About ¾ mile of permanent way was already laid and about 2½ miles were expected to be down in a few weeks. The going was particularly easy between the villages of Crossmichael and Parton by the level meadows of the Dee. Here the river is very wide, and the view across it is beautiful, especially when the hills and trees of the opposite shore are reflected in the water. From Parton to Boat of Rhone cuttings were necessary, but mainly through gravel, so that the contractor was reserving them for winter work.

## LOCH KEN VIADUCT

Half a mile north of Parton the line turned west and crossed the southern end of Loch Ken, here about 300 feet wide and 36 feet deep. This was done by a viaduct 500 feet long, with three main bowstring girder spans, supported by stone piers, two of which, being in deep water, were partly built in iron cylinders; on each bank were two small stone arches. Blyth described the work here so far as "most satisfactorily carried on"; there was very good progress with the superstructure – "in some cases carried up to its full height", while the staging had been completed across the loch for some time. Much of the iron work of the girders was complete, and about 40 tons already laid on the ground.

## LOCH SKERROW CONTRACT

11½ miles. Boat of Rhone - Dromore.

Almost immediately on leaving Loch Ken, a scene typical of this contract was encountered – the "heavy rock cutting in the steep bank of the Dee". At the hamlet of Mossdale was the site for the station to serve the little town of New Galloway, six miles to the north. The line now climbed into the hills on a gradient of 1 in 80. In a mile it approached the cold, solitary beauty of Stroan's Loch and, passing its southern shore, crossed the aptly-named Black Water of Dee by the four-arch Stroan Viaduct, the largest span being 50 feet. Nearly three miles more, much of it on the same gradient, by Airie Braes, and Loch Skerrow was reached, its tiny islets, with their birch and alder trees, a welcome sight amid the barren scenery all around. Over five miles of scarcely inhabited land lay between Loch Skerrow and the site of the little station of Dromore, which marked the summit of the Portpatrick Railway, 495 feet above sea level. Two large ravines, the valleys of the Wee and the Big Water of Fleet, obstructed the way. They were crossed by viaducts built of granite from nearby cuttings and quarries; granite was used also in building an embankment at the Wee Water of Fleet. Wee Fleet Viaduct was of nine arches, and its maximum height was 51 feet. From it there was an attractive view of the softer, rich country downstream, towards Gatehouse. Big Fleet Viaduct had 20 arches, with a maximum height of 70 feet. Near this bridge to the west rose the massive precipices of the Clints of Dromore, where the mountain foxes must have been disturbed at this time by many an unaccustomed sound. The summit point was about 1¼ miles from the viaduct, and the line climbed up to it at a gradient of 1 in 76.

On this contract, well over half the earthwork was reported complete, over 200,000 cubic yards having been moved during the summer. Drainage works were almost finished, the smaller bridges and culverts being far advanced, while in the case of the three viaducts, the foundations of many of the abutments and piers were laid, and a large quantity of stone had been dressed and was ready to be placed. About a mile of permanent way was laid, more than a mile was ballasted and ready for the rails.

THE CREETOWN CONTRACT

7¾ miles. Dromore - Palnure.

This consisted almost entirely of the long descent from the summit to the Palnure Burn, mainly at 1 in 80. The line used the valley of the Moneypool Burn, with the hills above Gatehouse, principally Pibble and Cambret Hills and Cairnharrow to the south, and Craig Hill and Cairnsmore of Fleet, one of Galloway's highest and most prominent hills, to the north. In about 2½ miles the Culcronchie Burn was spanned by a four-arch low level viaduct, and about two miles farther came the site of Creetown Station, up on the hillside, on the opposite side of the Moneypool Burn to the village. A striking change of scenery now revealed a splendid view of far-spreading Wigtown Bay, and beyond it the genial countryside of the Machars (i.e. plains - not to be taken too literally) and Wigtown itself, with the Martyrs' Monument on Windy Hill a graceful landmark and memorial of an heroic chapter in Galloway's history. 2¼ miles on was Graddoch Viaduct, of eight sandstone arches, below Cairnsmore House, and a little farther the Palnure Burn was crossed by a girder bridge, the three spans supported by sandstone piers.

Blyth described this contract as having been "pushed on with the utmost vigour". Nearly three-quarters of the earthworks were finished, and drainage works almost completed. Only one bridge, over a road, was not yet begun; the others were "far advanced towards completion". About 1½ miles of permanent way were laid.

## THE NEWTON STEWART CONTRACT
9½ miles. Palnure - Kirkcowan.

From Palnure Viaduct the line crossed a mile of marshy ground to the River Cree, where it entered Wigtownshire. The river, fairly wide and tidal, was crossed by Cree Viaduct, of girders supported by timber piers. A mostly steep climb followed to Newton Stewart Station, up above the town on its west side - an excellent vantage ground, in fact, from which to see the neighbourhood. Turning west and away from the magnificent view of Caimsmore of Fleet and the hills above Glentrool, the route now lay across the moorland country between here and Glenluce. Though less rugged than the scenery east of the Cree these moors had still their problems for the railway builders. The line continued to be steeply graded in places. It followed an undulating course to Kirkcowan; 1½ miles short of the village, at Shennanton, it crossed the River Bladnoch by a single-span bowstring girder bridge.

Early in June 1859, the local press reported that work was going on day and night at the Cree Viaduct and at the heavy rock cutting at Nether Barr, between it and Newton Stewart. Two months later, a start was made with the foundations for the Bladnoch Viaduct, the workmen having a lot of trouble with water bursting in on them, so that pumps had to be kept going constantly. Blyth (early September) described upwards of 100,000 cubic yards of earth as having been moved on the contract, nearly half of the whole. Almost all the necessary excavations had been made for Newton Stewart Station, and the goods shed was nearly finished. Numerous bridges had been begun, and some almost completed. About half a mile of permanent way was laid, and nearly one mile ballasted "and ready to receive the rails".

## THE GLENLUCE AND STRANRAER CONTRACTS
17¾ miles. Kirkcowan - Stranraer.

It was some 4¼ miles from Kirkcowan to the summit point between Newton Stewart and Stranraer, at Cairn Top. The gradients on this section were not steeper than 1 in 100. On the way the line crossed the Tarf Water, a tributary of the Bladnoch, by a bridge of two arches. The fall from Cairn Top to Glenluce (about 3¾ miles) and Luce Bay (5½ miles) was steeper, most of it being on gradients varying between 1 in 90 and 1 in 83. At Glenluce the moors were left behind; the Water of Luce was crossed by an eight arch stone viaduct, 47 feet above the main road running alongside the river, and a little farther there opened up the fine, extensive view of Luce Bay, on its far side the Rhins peninsula tapering into the distance, the tiny projection at its extremity marking the lighthouse on the Mull of Galloway, Scotland's most southerly point. Ahead, the line passed over the isthmus between Luce Bay and Loch Ryan, by Dunragit and Castle Kennedy to Stranraer, nearly nine miles from Glenluce. This is a cultivated landscape, with numerous woods, and for the most part the going was as easy as the country is pleasant; in more characteristic fashion, however, the line ended its course thus far with a run at 1 in 86 down the last mile to Stranraer.

The works on these contracts had been carried on only since May, but already Blyth could report excellent progress on the Glenluce contract. Nearly half of all the earthwork was completed, while the Luce Viaduct, "the only heavy piece of masonry", was "considerably advanced; two out of the three water piers are far advanced towards completion, and the foundations of the third are expected to be completed this month". The contractors had concentrated on this section, as the light works of the Stranraer contract could be "pushed" during winter. At mid-August a shipload of rails and another of chairs had arrived at Stranraer, and a few days later the Albion, the Glasgow to Stranraer steamer, brought a more spectacular indication of progress - a locomotive. Weighing 10¾ tons it was got on shore only after much strenuous human exertion, no crane powerful enough being available. Mr. Morkill, Brassey & Falshaw's manager, personally superintended the unloading. Mounted on "a stout wagon", drawn by ten horses, the engine was taken out of the town, the streets "crackling" under its weight. Its progress was soon interrupted, however; the present main road between Stranraer and Castle Kennedy, through Aird Moss, was then new and there the wagon stuck, a wheel firmly embedded in the road. Two days' delay ensued; then the engine was taken on a bumpy, yet surer, passage over the old road by Limekiln, and reached Glenluce, its intended scene of operations, without further mishap.

Two groups among the local people who could expect a considerably increased demand for their services, with very little, however, by way of increased remuneration, through the coming of the railway builders, were doctors and the police. Serious accidents were regularly, though not frequently, reported in the press, with references to the attention given by local doctors, though there were doubtless occasions when skilled medical aid could not be available as quickly as the circumstances necessitated, or at all. There is no evidence of any special provision made by the Railway Company. The nearest hospitals would be at Dumfries and Ayr. As for the police, they were very few in number, even had conditions been normal. In Wigtownshire in 1861 there was a total of 15 policemen, with four in Stranraer, where one was town crier and "others attend to various other duties". By an Act of 1838 magistrates could appoint special constables in areas where public works were in building and charge the cost to the promoters of the works; a power which is said to have been "little used". On the Portpatrick line, the Steward-Substitute of Kirkcudbright appointed a constable at Crossmichael and one at Creetown; the company unsuccessfully requested their withdrawal and had to pay £102.5.6 for police between July 1859 and July 1860; from July 1860 to January 1861 they paid £25.10.5. A final payment of £220.17.9 to 31st January 1863 is recorded.

For the most part the evidence suggests that the navvies on the Portpatrick line were orderly and law-abiding. The *Free Press* mentioned in July 1859 "the great influx" of Irish labourers into the Stranraer district, but its only comment on this was that they may have had a subduing effect on the local Orangemen, whose "annual glorification" had been "waived". Certainly there is no report of major trouble between Catholic and Presbyterian, though minor incidents of the kind there must have been. The Rev. G. Wilson, of Glenluce, speaking at what is termed a "soiree", held in Glenluce School in August 1859 by Sir James Dalrymple Hay, of Dunragit House, for the railway workers employed on his estates, commented, "I can honestly say that on the whole the men working on this contract are quiet and peaceable". About 170 workmen came to the entertainment, Sir James himself greeting them at the door. Mr. Wilson obviously went to a good deal of trouble to encourage the men to save. The local bank agent, he explained, was not allowed to keep a savings bank, but let him keep a separate account for the "workmen's savings bank", and had promised an extra ½% in interest. He went on:

"I take the money in the school house near the pay office, and shall be there till nine o'clock on Saturday night. But I shall be glad to see you at any time in my own house. I take any sum, however small, and give stamped receipts. The average of the deposits I have got is £2.10.0."

In the course of a kindly homily on thrift, he gives us an account of a noteworthy man:

"Some of you spend all your wages in a way I can hardly find fault with. I had a talk with an Irishman working with a pick and shovel on this line, who told me he spent all his money in visiting old castles, battlefields and famous places. He once went from Edinburgh to London mainly to see the Tower where Sir William Wallace was executed. The jaunt cost him £3. Another time he went to work on a railway in France because he wanted to see some famous places there."

There were, nevertheless, occasions when the task of the few police available was sufficiently strenuous, exacting and dangerous. One such occasion was at Newton Stewart in June 1859, involving some men on the Creetown contract. According to the *Free Press*:

"On the Sabbath, having been supplied with whisky from some quarter at present unknown, a number of them sat down in Wigtown Street, measuring it out in a tea-cup, till they became inebriated, and then a fight took place. Another party in a house in the same street were fighting, and the police had to be sent for, who had to apply his baton to the belligerents at last for his own protection. In another respectable house, two more of them insulted the inmates, and physical force had to be applied to turn them out."

The report went on to urge the need for more police - "The idea that one policeman is sufficient for the district is not correct" - and for a lock-up at Newton Stewart. It added, however, that the large company of navvies who had come up to Newton Stewart the previous day, Saturday, "on the whole behaved themselves".

The Monday following, 13th June, there was a disturbance at Palnure, with 15 navvies fighting, "and the individuals in the neighbourhood much alarmed for their safety". The driver of Mr. McEwan's bread van brought word to the police at Newton Stewart, "who at once set out to quell the disturbance, but before their arrival they were dispersed". The correspondent added that "The monthly pay for the men on this section takes place on Saturday first, and we hope for improved morals". The system of monthly payment of wages was often regarded as the source of a great deal of harm among navvies, and it is interesting to come across this expectation that the pay would be followed by better, and not worse, behaviour. A month later it was reported from Newton Stewart that there had been no rioting or fighting on the day of the pay, and less "public drunkenness" than previously. "A large staff of the police" had been in attendance from Saturday to Tuesday; cases of crime would be much diminished were the local force to be permanently augmented by one or two good officers, while though a lock-up was now available, it was "not at all suitable".

By far the ugliest incident involving the navvies reported in the press took place on Dergoals Moor, three to four miles above Glenluce, in February 1860. On the morning of Friday, 10th, two men, John Merry and William McCaffrey, got their time from the timekeeper in Glenluce and drew their pay at the office. They then went up on to the moor, where forty men were working under a ganger named Daniel Brown. They approached Brown and demanded their time. Told they must see the timekeeper they felled Brown with "a pick shaft or iron bar", kicked him, and struck him with a pick shaft. A workman called William Crawford, of Glenluce, very courageously intervened, felling one of the assailants with a pick shaft. Two-thirds of the other men present now attacked him, with stones and other missiles, and he fled. Merry and McCafrrey also made off, calling on the rest to be avenged on Crawford (who was reported to have been repeatedly threatened since). Mr. Campbell, the Glenluce policeman, was told, and at once got help and set out in pursuit of Merry and McCaffrey. They were caught in a field near Kirkcowan, and taken to Stranraer jail. Brown was reported to be "in bed, badly injured".

As the press reporter commented, there was "obviously a made-up plot, otherwise two men would never have dared to make an unprovoked attack upon one man in open day in the presence of forty others". On the Monday following the attack, a number of the gang were paid off. Trouble was expected, and the Chief Constable himself came to GlenIuce with several constables, but the men who were sacked left the village immediately.

Even without such an occurrence as this, places like Dergoals Moor would be grim indeed for the railway builders by this time. After the glorious summer of 1859 they had no more luck with the weather. The ensuing winter was exceptionally severe, with a great deal of frost, so that all the work, but particularly masonry, was seriously delayed. Blyth reported in March 1860 that on the Crossmichael contract the earthwork and bridges were going on satisfactorily, but the greater part of the mason work had yet to be done. About three miles of permanent way were laid, nearly half the whole. Loch Ken Viaduct, said Blyth, was going on well: here the masonry was almost complete; some of the small cast iron girders had been placed; all the wrought iron for the large girders was on the ground, and the fitters would be at work in a few days. "Notwithstanding the difficulty of this work", he continued, "arising from the depth of the foundations of the piers below water, one of which is founded 32 feet and the other 36 feet below the lowest summer level. all has been accomplished successfully".

On the Loch Skerrow contract most of the earthworks had been done; the arches of Stroan Viaduct would very soon be in progress; on Wee Fleet Viaduct the abutments and six of the eight piers were ready for the arches, while all the piers and the abutments of Big Fleet Viaduct were "progressing rapidly". On this contract the rigours of the winter had had their greatest effect, the masonry in Big Fleet having been particularly badly delayed. About five miles of permanent way had been laid, nearly half the whole. The bad weather had had less effect on the Creetown contract, since so much progress had been made previously. The most urgent work had been on the rock cuttings and these were now almost finished. The extensive drainage works on this and the Loch Skerrow contract, mostly completed before winter, had stood the test of the bad weather well. Only 2¼ miles of permanent way were laid so far out of 7¾, but the greater part was ballasted.

There was a serious mishap on the Newton Stewart contract in December, when the combined effects of a very high tide and a lot of floating ice caused serious damage to the wooden piers of the viaduct over the Cree. The wood was recovered, but the piers had to be rebuilt, and this work was delayed by difficulty in getting the necessary long creosoted piles. Some of the wrought iron girders for the viaduct were on the ground. About a third of the 9½ miles of permanent way was now laid, and several parts ballasted.

On the Glenluce and Stranraer contracts, about three-quarters of the earthworks were finished, and most of the bridges in progress. The Luce Viaduct was "completed to the springing line of the arches" and was expected to be finished within three months. 9¾ miles out of a total of 17¾ miles of permanent way had been laid, most of it west of Glenluce.

Blyth reported the earthworks for most of the stations to be far advanced, though little had been done as yet towards the buildings.

This was not a prosperous time for the navvies and other workmen, but even so there were probably more than a few, especially on the Wigtownshire moors and in the rugged country between Creetown and Loch Ken, who threw up their jobs during the grim winter of 1859-60 and trudged away to search for less disagreeable conditions elsewhere. And a dismal, wet summer followed. In August

1860 the directors noted that Blyth expected the line to be open from Castle Douglas to Stranraer by the end of October, and they urged him to press the contractors to finish the works. In his report the following month, he stated that completion was prevented by the bad weather of the spring and summer, but that most, though not all, of the contractors deserved the greatest credit for their efforts during the trying season.

Earlier, the men near Glenluce had been reported working day and night to get the line open to Stranraer by 1st July. Sir J. D. Hay gave another entertainment in Glenluce parish room for the navvies on his estates - a farewell party. The attendance was affected by poor weather and the pressure of work, but 165 came, "of all grades -from the knipper who carries the workman's tools to the smithy, up to the head man among the masons". After the tea, wrote the *Free Press*:

"Sir James, in a few sentences, expressed the satisfaction it gave him to meet them all again in this friendly way before finally leaving the district. He bore testimony to their general good conduct during their stay about Glenluce, and assured them that they carried with them the best wishes of the inhabitants of the place. The hearty cheers which greeted his address testified how much the navvies appreciated the interest which Sir James and his family have all along taken in their welfare."

By the end of August many of the navvies had left Glenluce. Brassey & Falshaw had now made a junction with McDonald & Grieve. There had been serious delay at Dergoals, tons of material being poured, over a period of months, into the moss, "originally a lake of considerable extent", with only very gradual effect. There was a similar experience on the Newton Stewart contract, where the contractors had excavated the moss - described as "having been evidently a floating bog" – in some places to a depth of 15 feet. The Cree Viaduct was nearly finished - a triumph for the man in charge, Mr. Turnbull, foreman blacksmith with McClelland & Co., Glasgow, but his stay in Galloway was marred by tragedy, for his small child had died through falling into a boiling pot. A short distance east of the viaduct, near the farm of Parkmaclurg, was a small bridge over the stream called the Lane; over £200 worth of timber had to be used in establishing the foundations of this bridge. Men had for some time been working night and day on the Newton Stewart contract, but progress was constantly hindered by wet weather.

In the wilds farther east the last arch of Big Fleet Viaduct was closed on 8th September. A boy working on the travelling crane there had just had a narrow escape when he fell from the top of the crane to the ground, about 80 feet. Rather than use the ladder provided, he had tried to jump into a descending bucket, and missed. He landed on a gravel bank, and got away with only two broken ribs - and, no doubt, an unforgettable experience.

Nearly everywhere on the line where this remained to be done, ballasting and tracklaying were in progress. William Carrol, aged 35, of Laurieston, who worked as a navvy on the Portpatrick line throughout its construction, mainly

# Rails to Portpatrick

between Loch Skerrow and Stroans Loch, described seeing wagon load after wagon load of sand and ballast taken from pits beside Loch Skerrow and sent down to a part of the line nearer Stroans Loch. On the Newton Stewart contract, a locomotive was anxiously awaited for several weeks, to assist with the ballasting. It was a 12-ton tank engine. Made in Glasgow by George Neilson & Company, it came by rail to Castle Douglas. On the morning of the 11th September there was much excitement in Castle Douglas, as with great effort the engine was loaded on to a truck and hauled away by twelve first-rate horses. It got safely down King Street, the main street of the town, but at the foot of Queen Street the wheels of the truck sank deep into the road. Next day, truck and load were hauled into the middle of the road, Mitchell, the contractor, personally superintending the operation. The locomotive was then dismounted, "divided into three or four portions", and sent on to Newton Stewart a section at a time. The various sections, it seems, joined in a triumphant entry to Newton Stewart. Said the *Free Press*:

"The body, even in its dilapidated aspect, had a formidable appearance, and was drawn by nine powerful horses, three abreast, to the Path Brae, where it was halted for about an hour. Four additional horses were then brought, and at three o'clock the "iron horse" was brought up at full gallop. The route up the old Glenluce Road was then taken in grand style, and in less than half an hour the huge monster was safely got into the works at the station, a crowd following and cheering at the successful arrival. On Tuesday the engineer had the wheels fixed to the engine and it was placed on the rails, and in a few days he hopes to have it ready for working."

It was presumably this engine which hauled several wagon loads of excursionists from Newton Stewart to Creetown on 31st October, making five return trips in all, in complete safety. Mr. Newall, of Goldielea, director of the Portpatrick Company, a bank agent at Newton Stewart and very highly thought of in the district, rode on the engine on the first trip. The occasion was a bazaar at Creetown, to pay off the debt of the Free Church there, but needless to say there were also many who "went along for the ride". The train was welcomed by the people of the neighbourhood at many points along the line, and on reaching Newton Stewart station on its return from its last trip, long after dark, it was greeted with cheering. There was general appreciation of the trouble the contractors had gone to, which included effort and expense to have the line ready, and their notable "goodwill gesture" naturally encouraged people to look forward to the early opening of the line.

By this time, the end of all the puzzling and striving was, indeed, clearly in sight. In early October, the rails were continuous from Stranraer to Kirkcowan, and Dalrymple, Dunbar, Ingram and others went over the line with a locomotive, going on to see the viaducts over the Bladnoch and Cree. A fortnight later, the works in the Newton Stewart district were subjected to a severe unofficial test in the form of torrential rain, and emerged with triumph. At mid-November an engine set out from Castle Douglas station and "loudly cheered by the inhabitants, everyone seeming much delighted to see the welcome stranger", went by Crossmichael and Parton, passed over Loch Ken Viaduct, and steamed on as far as Mossdale Huts. Beyond here there was a short break in the permanent way. Early in December, a locomotive from Castle Douglas got as far as Big Fleet, beyond which, for half a mile, was the last remaining break in the permanent way between Castle Douglas and Stranraer, due to a shortage of sleepers. By this time, the first two of the Portpatrick Company's own engines had arrived at Castle Douglas - of these more later. The line was completely open throughout by Boxing Day, when large crowds gathered at the station to see Galloway's first train of passenger coaches - an engine hauling some of the company's new carriages to Stranraer. More carriages were taken to Stranraer the following day.

Severe weather, and the need to complete some minor works along the line, combined to delay the opening date, which the directors now hoped would be the beginning of February. The bad weather continued, however, with the worst frost in memory at Newton Stewart. A thaw caused the Cree to flood, with ice "flows" eight or nine inches thick, and there were fears for the safety of the viaduct. On 31st January 1861 the company's engine No. 1 ran from Castle Douglas to Stranraer, with Blyth and numerous others. Blyth inspecting the chief works on the line preparatory to his final report. The engine returned to Castle Douglas next day, taking Dalrymple and others to a meeting there. The train left Stranraer station to the accompaniment of loud cheers. The Board of Trade inspection, under Captain Tyler, R.E., took place in mid-February and lasted three days, Government sanction to the opening of the line being given very soon after. On 21st, McNaughton, the contractor, was entertained to dinner in the Douglas Arms at Castle Douglas, where he heard the following eulogy from the chairman, Samuel Cavan, of Kirkcudbright:

"Our guest belongs to a class who are the greatest benefactors of modern times, and to whose persevering and indomitable energy we are indebted for our medium of communication and other works, both ornamental and useful, in all parts of the country. It is impossible to overestimate the services rendered by such men in these respects."

The engines that had come to Castle Douglas by the end of 1860 had been designed by J. E. McConnell, locomotive superintendent with the L N W, and built by Sharp, Stewart & Company at their Atlas Works in Manchester. Numbered 1 and 2, they were 0-4-2 inside cylinder mixed traffic locomotives. A report in the *Kirkcudbrightshire Advertiser* describes them as incorporating Giffard's patent self-acting injector, then a recent invention. A third locomotive, identical with its predecessors, had arrived by March 1861.

The directors had ordered passenger carriages from Wright & Son, Saltley Works, Birmingham, There were six composites, with two first class and two second class compartments, seating 12 first class and 20 second class passengers; four second class carriages, each with four compartments "without cushions", each compartment to seat ten passengers; and five third class "carriages with breaks" – "guard's van, with luggage compartment next to engine and three third class compartments". From the same firm the company obtained also fifty open goods trucks, thirty cattle trucks, three goods brake vans, four horse boxes, three carriage trucks and six covered wagons.

The directors had also to appoint their chief officers, and in March 1861 they chose Alex Walker as locomotive superintendent, at a salary of £200, plus £25 for acting as P.W. inspector for the time being. Walker, who had previously been locomotive superintendent on the Edinburgh, Leith and Granton section of the Edinburgh, Perth and Dundee Railway, was not to stay very long at Stranraer, but during the time he was there, he gave ample evidence of enthusiasm for his job and of a very pleasant personality. In October 1860, William Grafton was appointed traffic manager. Formerly an assistant superintendent on the Caledonian at Glasgow, he had been manager of the Peebles Railway since February 1858. His salary there was £130, plus a bonus of £15 per half year latterly for his attention to the company's interests; he was to get £225 with the Portpatrick. Grafton was to stay with the Portpatrick Company, apart from one short interval not of his choosing, throughout its existence, and to serve it well. During the next few months, station masters, porters, guards, etc., were chosen, most of these appointments being made by George Guthrie, the Earl of Stair's factor.

The directors decided that movement of trains should be controlled solely by telegraph. In March 1859 the Castle Douglas & Dumfries Company had suggested that the Portpatrick Company join them in an agreement with the Magnetic Telegraph Company to erect wires along the line, but the Portpatrick Company decided to seek information from various other railway companies. A year later, they invited the Magnetic & Electric and the International Telegraph Companies to tender for the construction, maintenance and working of a line of telegraph along the railway, and accepted that of the Magnetic Company. A few weeks before the opening, Grafton was instructed to get the necessary fittings for telegraph offices at New Galloway, Creetown, Newton Stewart, Kirkcowan and Glenluce, the stations which marked the sections into which the line was to be divided for train working purposes.

The making of the new road to complete the link between Gatehouse of Fleet and the railway near Dromore caused the directors occasional concern, especially in September 1860, when they threatened to withdraw their offer of £100 towards its cost unless the balance were raised by the following Whitsuntide. Robert Hannay, of Rusko, however, now took a keen interest in the subject. He asked the company to pay £200 towards the cost of the road, and in return offered assurances about the building and fencing of the road by local parties, which clearly met with their approval, for they not only agreed to contribute the £200, but on condition of getting a further assurance that the work on the road would be done within six months, they undertook also to go ahead with the construction of a station at Dromore. A newspaper report early in June 1861 described "great activity" in building the road, and at the end of the same month pronounced it "excellent".

However, works of greater importance to the directors at this time than the making of the road to their moorland summit station were the new pier and harbour branch at Stranraer. These were to serve the bulk of the company's goods traffic to and from Ireland, Portpatrick being expected to become the main terminal for passengers. The directors entered into negotiations with Stranraer Town Council, and reached agreement with them for the building of "a low water pier in connection with the railway, at which steamers drawing from 10 to 12 feet of water can arrive and depart at all states of the tide". The Town Council advertised for the sum of £20,000, offering as security "the ordinary harbour revenue from tonnage on vessels" and the annuity of £1,100 that the Portpatrick Company would pay the Town Council in commutation of the harbour dues and petty customs on goods carried by or intended for the railway. Plans were drawn up with the help of Captain Hirste, the L N W's marine superintendent from Holyhead, and tenders invited. The proposed pier was to be "about 800 feet in length, constructed chiefly of timber". The engineer in charge was James Leslie, of Edinburgh. The contract for the pier, and for the branch of railway that was to lead down to it from the main line a little east of Stranraer station, was given to Thomas Nelson & Company, the capable builders of the Loch Ken Viaduct. In May 1861, the *Free Press* reported vigorous progress with the harbour works.

In the angle between main line and harbour branch were erected the company's workshops, with engine shed, turntable and superintendent's office. The tender for these also was awarded to Thomas Nelson, and to Sharp, Stewart went the tender for workshop tools viz., double face plate wheel turning lathe (£605), breakbed or gap lathe (£122), self-acting slide and screwcutting lathe (£48), self-acting vertical drilling machine (£116) and self-acting planing machine (£135). In March 1861 it was reported that the commencement of the workshops had been delayed by severe weather and long continued frost, but that a large force was now at work.

All things considered, the launching of the Portpatrick Company and the construction of the greater part of their main line had been done well and in good time and the directors could feel justifiable pride, relief and satisfaction at the progress that had been made. This was tempered, however, by anxiety, which was certainly equally justified, over two problems to neither of which was there an easy remedy.

The first of these was financial. The great enthusiasm for the railway among the people of the province, and the strenuous efforts of Sir W. Dunbar and others, had produced large subscriptions towards the necessary capital, but it had never been imagined that the line could be built without help from established companies that could expect to benefit from its completion. We saw that by the company's Act of Parliament, the L & C contributed £40,000 and took powers to contribute £60,000 more, while the G SW, who had contributed £60,000, took powers to give another £40,000, provided there were further contributions from elsewhere, including the County Down Company. The Act also gave the G S W powers to make an agreement with the P P R to work their line. At a G S W board meeting in August 1859, George Guthrie and Alex. Ingram urged the directors to make their farther contribution of £40,000. The latter agreed, on the following stringent conditions: the L & C were to give their £60,000; the Belfast and County Down Company were to give £20,000 (in addition to the £15,000 they had previously contributed), and the P P R directors were to raise an additional £12,000 to £13,000 from new shareholders.

After considerable negotiation, and with support for the P P R from the L NW, who at this juncture were in the process of taking a lease of the L & C, the latter agreed to take the additional £60,000 in stock. It was now (December 1859) reported that the G S W would take their £40,000 of stock, and that they were also willing to work the line. The P P R directors recorded that "the present feeling of the board is in favour of working their own line", but appointed a deputation to meet the G SW board. They were very understandably doubtful about the prospect of getting any further contribution from the County Down Company: in February 1860, they declined the latter's offer of preference stock in lieu of this. They claimed that at a meeting in Edinburgh in January, the forthcoming payment by the G S W of the £40,000 had been confirmed, with no reference to the additional contribution from the County Down, which "was known to be hopeless". In March, a G S W shareholders' meeting approved the contribution of a further sum not exceeding £40,000 to the P P R. The P P R directors said that the £60,000 from the L & C, which had been "paid with great promptitude", would "only just cover the company's claims", and again appealed to the G S W. They had also given the contract for the construction of the line from Stranraer to Portpatrick to Thomas Nelson - who had submitted the lowest tender, £55,886.1.9 - on faith of getting the additional contributions from both the L & C and the G S W. By July, however, they were complaining that the G S W were again insisting on their condition that the County Down Company contribute £20,000, and were "making the unwarranted assumption that they were to work the line".

We shall see that the G S W's terms for working the P P R were very high, and there can be little doubt that they were now unscrupulously bringing pressure to bear on the P P R directors to accept these terms. The latter recorded that they "regret(ted) extremely that matters seem(ed) tending to a final alienation from their early friends the G & S W Company" and proposed "an ultimatum" to "prevent, if possible, any separation of interests". In fairness, the claim on the County Down should be restricted to £10,000. If they did not take that amount in additional stock, the P P R directors would try to increase the additional capital to be raised by local shareholders from £12,000 to £20,000. In November they offered to raise a total of £23,000 in additional local subscriptions, in two years, if the G S W would contribute the £40,000, but after receiving a deputation, the G S W board declined these terms. Correspondence ensued between Dalrymple and Sir Andrew Orr, chairman of the G S W; this was submitted to the P P R general meeting in March 1861 and published in the *Free Press*. It included a letter to Dalrymple, supporting the P P R, from the Marquis of Chandos, chairman of the L N W. Dalrymple told his shareholders that lack of the £40,000, though "attended with great inconvenience", need not "make any material or, at least, permanent financial embarrassment", but in spite of these reassurances, the company's experience of their powerful neighbour had been a most unpleasant one, and had left them in a decidedly difficult situation.

The second problem was very different, though hardly less worrying. The P P R, always intended as a trunk line, had been promoted on the clear understanding that the Government would restore the Royal Mail route between Britain and Ireland by the shortest sea-passage, and that in connection with this they would carry out the improvements necessary to make the harbours of Portpatrick and Donaghadee suitable and safe, and maintain the harbours in the future. As time passed and construction of the railway went forward, however, there was no sign of a start being made with the very considerable works that would be needed at Portpatrick. In September 1859, the directors remonstrated with the Admiralty over the absence of progress, drawing attention to the need for an understanding between the harbour and the railway engineers before the railway works, which the company had undertaken to finish by August 1862, could be contracted for. They noted that in the last session of Parliament, £20,403 had been voted "for extending and improving the harbour of Portpatrick", and £10,000 for Donaghadee. A full year later, the directors reported that while on the Portpatrick contract, awarded to Thomas Nelson earlier in the year, the works were "well advanced and under excellent management", and the County Down Company's line to Donaghadee was "far advanced", the harbour works had still not been commenced.

The Admiralty had assured the directors that the works would be "proceeded with immediately"; they gave the same assurance six months later. Now, however, they could say that a contract deed for the works had been entered into, and the directors decided to go ahead with the harbour branch at Portpatrick, keeping the gradient of 1 in 35 formerly proposed. On 28th March 1861, the *Free Press* was able to report that "Mr. Greenhill, the contractor for Portpatrick harbour, has arrived from London, and commenced operations on Tuesday"- that would be the 26th. So at last a start was being made; but it had been a disconcerting story, and the dilatory behaviour of the Government was not encouraging for the future.

Serious however, though these difficulties were, both at the time and in their implications for the future, they were happily unable in any way to mar the general rejoicing at the public opening of the company's line.

## CHAPTER THREE

### Early Days

THE opening of the Portpatrick Company's line took place on Monday, 11th March 1861, when a special train for directors and shareholders left Stranraer at 9 a.m. for Castle Douglas. Hauled by locomotives 1 and 2, which were decorated with flags and evergreens, it steamed through the wintry morning, amid the enthusiastic demonstrations of the people, and, having called at Glenluce, Newton Stewart and New Galloway, reached Castle Douglas without mishap at 11.30.

Here the party were met by a large, cheering crowd and the firing of guns. W. H. Maxwell, of Munches, welcomed them. One of the most benevolent figures in nineteenth century Galloway he had been the chief promoter of the Castle Douglas and Dumfries Railway, of which he was chairman until it amalgamated with the G S W in 1865. He and his fellow directors entertained the P P R directors to lunch at the Douglas Arms Hotel, after which they joined them on their return journey as far as Newton Stewart, where a stop of nearly three hours was made for dinner. About sixty gentlemen sat down to this meal in the assembly rooms. Lord Dalrymple took the chair and in addition to Maxwell, of Munches, and numerous directors of the two companies, there were present "a large number of the leading agriculturists of Wigtownshire". Dalryrmple expressed his hope that the railway would end the comparative isolation of Galloway. There was, he remarked, an old saying, "Out of the world, into Kirkcowan", which might have been altered to "Out of the world, into the county of Wigtown"; but it was now no longer applicable. Urging the shareholders to send and receive goods by rail, he declared his confidence that they would get good dividends. Finally, he proposed "Success to the Portpatrick Railway", to great applause.

The train left Newton Stewart at 5 p.m., and after making calls at Kirkcowan and Glenluce, totalling fifteen minutes, arrived safely at Stranraer within the hour.

Ten days later, there was a public dinner at New Galloway, with Wellwood Maxwell, of Glenlee, in the chair, and MacNaughton, the contractor, among the guests. "The huge, old punch bowl, as large as a bushel, belonging to the burgh, was brought in nearly filled with steaming toddy, and the chairman called for a bumper to 'Success to the Portpatrick Railway'." Maxwell described his fellow directors of the P P R as favourable to an extension of seven miles from New Galloway to Dalry, along the side of Loch Ken and passing between the Loch and Kenmure Castle. He had had a survey made, and appealed for the greatest possible support to make the plan a reality. He added that he thought a line should be built from New Galloway Station to Sanquhar, as the best means of direct communication with Glasgow and Edinburgh.

*Herapath's Railway Magazine*, commenting on the opening of the P P R, said, "We are amazed at the economy exercised in expenditure of an unproductive character. It is estimated that in most railways about half of the capital is productive and half unproductive"; in the case of the P P R, however, of nearly £400,000 spent on the line, most "seems to have gone in substantial works and purchases, materials, and fittings. £3,742 has been spent in preliminary, law, and parliamentary agency. Then there is £2,056 for engineering, for survey, parliamentary plans, etc., making together £5,798 as the whole preliminary expense ... And since the Act has been obtained, and the line has been in course of construction, the whole sum spent in law appears to be £71, of which not a penny was spent last half-year". The line, it concluded, bade fair to be "a very economical and cheap one". There can be no doubt that so far the directors had succeeded very fully in their aim to practise strict economy, and much of the credit for this was due to Ingram as secretary.

The public service began on Tuesday, 12th March. At first, there were only two trains each way, daily, except Sundays, between Stranraer and Castle Douglas, with intermediate stations at Glenluce, Kirkcowan, Newton Stewart, Creetown, New Galloway, Parton and Crossmichael. In April, the "Glenluce Market Train" was put on. This ran every Friday at 4.15 p.m. from Stranraer to Glenluce, for the benefit of people who had been to Stranraer market. On Glenluce cattle market days, a second-class passenger carriage was to be attached to the midday goods train from Stranraer, returning from Glenluce at 3 p.m. In May, it was decided to run a market train on Wednesdays, leaving Castle Douglas at 5.20 p.m. for New Galloway, whence it was to return empty to Castle Douglas. A week or two later, permission was given for this train to carry passengers on its return journey. From the end of April, the through passenger service from Castle Douglas was augmented by the attachment of a second-class carriage to the 11.45 a.m. goods for Stranraer. A month after, the departure time of this train was changed to 1.45 p.m.; it was to carry one composite and one second-class carriage, and first- and third-class fares were to be charged. In June, the people of Portwilliam and "the lower districts of Wigtownshire" were petitioning for another train from Stranraer to Newton Stewart, but the company would provide this only "when they find it will be for the interest of the public and shareholders".

The stations of Castle Kennedy, Dunragit and Palnure were opened in July; the site for Duinragit Station was chosen by Sir J. D. Hay, of Dunragit House, who accepted payment for the land in shares. Dromore, for which Sir William Maxwell, of Cardoness, gave the land free, followed in September. At first, the passenger accommodation at the company's stations was very limited indeed: in September, even Newton Stewart was among a list described as "not having waiting rooms" and for which wooden sheds were to be ordered. In November, Blyth submitted drawings of small booking-offices and waiting-rooms for Palnure, Dunragit and

Castle Kennedy, but it was not until June 1862, however, that the directors ordered the taking of tenders for these, and also for a ladies' waiting-room at Castle Kennedy. A booking-office and waiting-room were also to be provided at Crossmichael, where, until now, temporary wooden buildings had been in use. It was July 1862 before east-bound passengers at Newton Stewart got any shelter on the platform - a wooden veranda about thirty feet long being provided.

From 1st October 1861, the through service - Stranraer to Castle Douglas - was increased to three trains in each direction every week-day, and on the same day what was described as a "large" reduction in second-class fares came into force - these were to be on a basis of 1³⁄₈d. per mile. Long-distance passengers could now take advantage of the refreshment room at Castle Douglas Station, opened in August by Mr. Payne, owner of the Douglas Arms Hotel. Numerous bus services were established by hotel proprietors - Payne was an example - between various towns and villages and the trains at the nearest station; and by 1864, the company were paying Robert Dalziell, of Gatehouse, £40 a year in guarantee for his twice-daily bus to and from Dromore Station.

THE STRANRAER - PORTPATRICK SECTION

By the summer of 1862, the final section of the company's line, from Stranraer to Portpatrick, was complete and ready for opening. Some seven miles long, it was heavily-graded: for almost the whole of the four miles from Stranraer to the summit point at Colfin, 326 feet above sea-level, the line rose at 1 in 72; the descent to Portpatrick was considerably steeper, most of it at 1 in 57. It was difficult to build. Over the Piltanton Burn, 1¾ miles from Stranraer and close to the village of Lochans a large viaduct was necessary, built of whinstone rubble with arches of brick - thirteen arches, each of 36 feet 9 inches span, with a maximum height of 73 feet. Near this viaduct the driving of cuttings through boulder-clay proved a predictably arduous task. Approaching Portpatrick, the line curved round through heavy rock-cuttings, almost at the cliff's edge; the railway builders established a smithy in the ruins of Dunskey Castle, on its perch high above the waves. So the line continued to its designated terminus on the hillside, opposite Dinvin Mill. Like the rest of the main line, the Stranraer - Portpatrick section was made with a single track, but space for the expected second line was provided.

In September 1860, the directors stated to the half-yearly meeting of shareholders that these works were "well advanced and under excellent management", while Blyth reported that though here, as elsewhere, progress was hindered by bad weather, they had been "carried on with commendable vigour". Messrs. Nelson had had, as yet, barely six months of work on the contract, but after a further six months he was able to say that in spite of "the severe and long-continued storm during winter", more than half the earthworks had been executed; all the piers and abutments of the great viaduct were far advanced, and the arches would be begun very shortly; good progress had been made with the masonry of

## Rails to Portpatrick

the small bridges, and about 2½ miles of permanent way were laid. In May 1861, the directors told Blyth to put up a goods shed "at the High Station" at Portpatrick, and to "execute the Harbour Branch and Station arrangements according to plans submitted, but to delay putting up booking-offices".

There was a setback in July, when two arches of the viaduct fell. Fortunately this occurred late one Saturday night, long after the workmen had left and when there was no one near. By the end of October the viaduct was described as nearly finished, but two weeks later a tragic accident happened. Two youths, aged nineteen and sixteen, were crossing with a cartload of stone when part of the wooden staging gave way. Thrown from a height of over 60 feet, they were both killed, while a third youth, who had been "turning the travelling crane", was badly injured. The staging had evidently been loosened by heavy falls of rain.

Early in December, to the great excitement of the villagers, a locomotive came to Portpatrick, though when they first waited for it they were disappointed, as it sustained a mishap similar to those which befell the engines that had set out previously from Stranraer to Glenluce, and Castle Douglas to Newton Stewart. About two miles from Stranraer the carriage bearing it, pulled by fourteen horses, had sunk into the road, where it had to be left overnight. Next day, after sinking three times in the first 500 yards, it eventually reached "the Port" without further accident. Operations on both days were directed by Mr. Nelson, junior, and Mr. Middleton, his manager. The engine was soon to be seen regularly at work, "dragging four wagons up the incline from the village towards the farm of Portree, where a portion of embankment is yet in an unfinished state". Good progress was also being made with the bridge that was to carry the Harbour Branch over the main road; the iron girders were in position, and it was expected that the permanent rails would be laid by the end of the year, and the dressing and finishing of the stone abutments completed in early spring.

Some time before this, the workmen on the part of the line passing through the Dunskey Estate had been invited to an entertainment at Dunskey House, provided by the proprietors, the Hunter Blairs. About 300 men marched in procession from Portpatrick, to be welcomed at Dunskey House by "Lady and Sir Edward Hunter Blair and friends". Sir Edward complimented them on their good conduct while in the neighbourhood, and hoped they would enjoy the fare provided for them; to which the men responded with cheers. An item is mentioned here that does not occur in accounts of the earlier entertainments at Dunragit - the guests were "afterwards regaled with beer".

This makes pleasant reading, but the last notice we must take of the men who built the Portpatrick Railway is a tragic one. At the summit point of the Portpatrick section, the directors decided to establish a station, Colfin, and here also a by-road to some farms was crossed on the level. Early in July 1862, as one of the last tasks remaining to be done on the line, three labourers were blasting rock, preliminary to fixing a gate at this crossing, when a terrible accident happened.

In the words of the *Free Press*:

"... the fusee - which consisted of straw filled with gunpowder - ignited the charge sooner than was expected, and before the men could get clear, two of them were dangerously injured. Dr. Fleming - we may almost say providentially - happened to pass a few minutes after the accident, while going to visit another patient, and at once proceeded in the most energetic manner to render surgical assistance. After the unfortunate men had been removed into the nearest house, one of them, John Rafferty, belonging to Glenluce, was found to have sustained a fracture of both bones of the left leg, leg and arm being also torn and bruised with the stones and gunpowder. As soon as the fractured bones were adjusted and his injuries otherwise attended to, he was removed on a litter to his lodgings a little distance off. The other man, named William Mars (from the neighbourhood of Newton Stewart), was much more seriously injured, the right eye being completely destroyed and the left so severely damaged as to occasion grave doubts of a complete restoration to sight. His face was also much torn, cut, and bruised, and some of the bones splintered. After the gunpowder had been removed from his eyes, and his other injuries attended to, Dr. Fleming conveyed him to Stranraer to be for a time under surgical treatment. From the latest accounts we are glad to state that the injured men are progressing favourably."

The Board of Trade inspection of the Portpatrick section was on 1st August, and the Stranraer Harbour Branch was inspected on the same day. The public service between Stranraer and Portpatrick began on Thursday, 28th August. The rejoicings of the local people were augmented by the arrival of Lord Dufferin and a large party of visitors from Ireland. Although the P P R had thus completed their line within the time stipulated by their Act, the Government, as we shall see, had not fulfilled their part of the original understanding, and the harbour works at Portpatrick were by no means complete. There could, therefore, be no service to and from the North of Ireland as yet, and the first train service on the Stranraer to Portpatrick section was a very meagre one.

MISHAPS; MOTIVE POWER

During their first few months of operation, the company's services suffered a number of mishaps. None of these proved to be serious as things turned out, but some of them might have been. One which makes rather humorous reading was the stopping of a passenger train bound for Castle Douglas on 3rd June 1861, by Mr. McMichael, farmer, of Dromore - in what way, and for what reason, we are not told. It was agreed not to prosecute him, on condition of his donating 10/- to charity; the money was given to the widow of John Kerr, late porter at Stranraer. Much more sinister was the placing of stones on the rails a little way east of Bladnoch Viaduct on the evening of 16th March, gravely endangering a Stranraer-bound train. £5 reward was offered for information leading to conviction. Two similar incidents occurred, in the same neighbourhood, in June, and the directors got a report from the Chief Constable. In December, the driver of the morning train from Stranraer saw a large piece of wood lying on the rails as they were crossing Luce Viaduct; he had not time to stop, but fortunately the locomotive sent the obstacle "spinning" out of the way. The directors, understandably seriously concerned, offered the then very large reward of £20 for information leading to conviction, and applied for a detective from Glasgow. Though we read nothing about any results of the inquiries, there is also no news of further obstacles being put on the line. When an obstruction is next mentioned, in March 1863, it was one "caused by the neglect of Mr. Drape, station-master, Creetown, in not communicating a written notice which he had received of a special train, and also by the neglect of the gang of platelayers of which Andrew Campbell is foreman in not exhibiting signal flags as required by the company's rules". Drape was to be severely reprimanded and fined two weeks' salary. Campbell was to be fined a pound. Campbell subsequently complained that his fine was excessive, and it was reduced to 10/-, the offence being his first. This makes a welcome touch: Campbell was prepared to appeal to the great men of Galloway who formed the majority of the board of directors, and who would tend to look upon him as a personal servant, against the penalty they had themselves imposed on him; and his appeal was allowed.

In due course the company needed to add to the tiny stock of locomotives they possessed at their time of opening in March 1861. To the three Sharp, Stewart 0-4-2 mixed traffic engines (Nos. 1-3) they expected very soon to add two 2-2-2 passenger engines, also designed by J. E. McConnell, of the L NW, and by the same makers. In the meantime, they had borrowed an engine from the L N W, an 0-6-0 designed by Ramsbottom and just built at Crewe. During the following summer, they decided to buy this engine for £2,750, a condition being that no charge would be made for the time it had been in their possession so far, and it became their No. 5. No. 4 was another 0-4-2 mixed traffic locomotive, "a duplicate of No. 1", ordered from Sharp, Stewart in the spring of 1861 and delivered early the next year. The 2-2-2 passenger locomotives were Nos. 6 and 7; they had arrived by the summer of 1861, though not before Walker, the company's locomotive superintendent, had been sent to Manchester to investigate delay in delivering them. The directors considered getting a tank engine, but in June 1861, decided to defer the matter. A year later, they were considering a report Walker had prepared on bogie engines, and decided to send Sharp, Stewart a tracing "of the new engine suggested by Mr. Walker". A 2-4-0, it was built in 1863, and became the P P R's No. 8. Incidentally, in June of that year the company accepted a tender for the supply of locomotive coal for one year; they were to pay 9/1½d per ton for this, delivered at Castle Douglas, and to receive eighty tons per week.

They added steadily to their rolling-stock, and by the end of 1863 had 17 passenger carriages, 166 goods vehicles, and nine vehicles such as horse-boxes.

## STAFF

In April 1861, a cheery gathering of some thirty officials and employees was held in the King's Arms, Stranraer, "to quaff a bowl of punch to the future prosperity and happiness of the secretary, Mr. Ingram, who had that day entered the happy bonds of wedlock". The following autumn, the company appointed an additional senior officer, making Mr. Cumming Thomson their Inspector of Permanent Way at a salary of £130. Thomson, who was currently employed on the harbour works at Stranraer lived in the town, which may well explain why the directors chose him in preference to Blyth's nominee, Mr. Fleming.

There were, of course, numerous appointments of staff. Porters and station-masters, and also train guards, had a suit of uniform allowed them annually. The tender for uniforms accepted by the directors in March 1863 was as follows:

| | |
|---|---|
| Station-master's suit | £2.5.6 |
| Guard's suit | £2.19.6 |
| Guard's top coat | £1.13.6 |
| Goods guard's suit | £2.1.0 |
| Porter's suit | £1.10.6 |

Ready for the opening of the railway, three porters were appointed at Stranraer: one at Glenluce, one at Kirkcowan, two at Newton Stewart, one at Creetown, and one at New Galloway. The Parton station-master applied for a porter in May, and one was engaged in November. The wages of William Scott, goods porter, Newton Stewart, are given as 15/- per week, and those of David McHaffie at Stranraer were "increased" to the same rate; William Campbell, also at Stranraer, got 13/-. One of the original Stranraer porters, John Kerr, died soon after his appointment, and the directors behaved towards his widow with paternal benevolence. Apart from passing to her McMichael of Dromore's "donation" of 10/-, they made her the considerable gratuity of £20. This was paid into the Savings Bank in her name and also that of Ingram; not more than £5 was to be withdrawn annually, both signatures being necessary.

Much interest attaches to the appointment of station-masters. Most of the company's employees were selected by George Guthrie, factor to the Earl of Stair, or a small committee of directors, of which he was almost always a member. It is likely that several advantages followed from this, with jobs given to local men, proved integrity of character and good previous work records rewarded, and family circumstances of applicants given consideration. A potential serious disadvantage of the procedure, however, in the case of the station-masters, is obvious: that arising from the appointment of men without previous railway experience. It is true that such appointments were not always detrimental[1], and this was best instanced in James Nish, first station-master at Glenluce. Nish had never worked on a railway before. A native of Glenluce, he had been apprenticed to a draper in Stranraer, then had gone to London to gain business experience. When the P P R opened, however, he became the Glenluce station-master. From the beginning of 1863, his salary was £1.1.0 per week, with a rent-free house. The station was no mere country retreat; there was no Wigtownshire Railway and no Girvan line then, so that Glenluce was the railway centre for a wide district, including such places as Portwilliam, Whithorn and New Luce. Nish proved fully competent and very enthusiastic, and soon became a very popular figure in the area. He set up a business as a coal and lime merchant - with the consent of the Railway Company - and in this he prospered. In about 1872, when he would be aged around forty, he retired from railway work to devote himself entirely to business on his own account, but he had earned a high reputation for efficiency, courtesy and helpfulness, which no doubt contributed considerably to his continued success in his later career.

The difficulties found by some of the first station-masters were not, moreover, necessarily due to incompetence. Michael Green, first stationmaster at Crossmichael, resigned before the line was opened. His successor was R. Kirkpatrick, and he was expected to live at the cottage beside the level crossing at Danevale, and take charge of the gate. Perhaps it was this condition that had led to Green's resignation; the crossing, over a by-road, was more than a mile south of the station, and presumably the stationmaster's wife would have to look after the gate. Eventually, in July 1861, a Mrs. McReand was appointed gatekeeper at Danevale. By July 1863, Kirkpatrick had resigned; the directors received a "memorial" from the people of Crossmichael, the contents of which are not recorded. The village got its third station-master in the person of John Gordon. Gordon, who lived at Bridge of Aird, Stranraer, prior to the opening of the railway, had, up till now, been station-master at Palnure, where his wage was 15/- a week; his wage at Crossmichael is not recorded. Robert Armstrong, porter at Kirkcowan, was promoted station-master at Palnure in his place. Armstrong had charge of Palnure for the rest of his working life, until failing health forced his retirement in 1901.

There were, however, several cases where brief tenure of office was undoubtedly owing to unsatisfactory performance. Newton Stewart's first stationmaster, James Kennedy, had previously worked in the post office there. It is certainly surprising to find a man without railway experience appointed to this, one of the principal stations. By May 1861, there was obviously friction between him and the company, and early in the following year Dalrymple, Guthrie, Ingram and Grafton interviewed James Cook, "presently at Auchtermuchty", and appointed him to Newton Stewart, receiving "a note of his removal expenses" and paying his expenses in coming to the interview, 30/-. The newcomer was from Fife, where Sir William Dunbar played so notable a part in the development of the railways. This extract from the Dunfermline Saturday Press illustrates the status that could be held, and the respect and affection that could be earned, by the stationmaster of even a very small town in those days:

"Auchtermuchty. Mr. James Cook, our intelligent and active station-master here for some years, has received an appointment to a better situation on the

# Rails to Portpatrick

Portpatrick Railway at Newton Stewart. He leaves this with the goodwill of all his employers, as well as of the public at large, having always discharged his duties with great fidelity and much courtesy. He was (on Thursday morning) waited onby a deputation of the inhabitants, who presented him with a purse of sovereigns as a testimonial of the esteem in which he has been held here, and of the hearty good wishes with which he is followed to his new sphere of labour."

The directors had thus made sure that they got an able man to replace Kennedy, but Kennedy turns up again in a much humbler capacity, in charge of their tiny outpost at Colfin. His salary at Newton Stewart is not recorded; at Colfin he got 14/- a week and a rent-free house. Here, too, he had his troubles at first, though of a different kind. In early September 1862, his house at Colfin was newly-built, and the plaster was still wet. Rather than sleep in the house, he walked from and to Stranraer. One week-end, someone broke in and made off with his trunk, containing clothes (though fortunately not his best, which were at his friend's house in Stranraer). After this misfortune, however, it seems likely that more tranquil days dawned for him.

At Stranraer, too - the company's other chief station - they had difficulty in getting the right man for the job. Ready for the opening, John Wallace was appointed, at a salary of £80, but by the New Year, 1862, he had been succeeded by Donald Taylor, at the same salary. By June, Taylor had been given notice and was being offered £5 to cover his removal expenses. Grafton, Guthrie and Ingram were to see "Mr. Colvin, clerk, Glasgow and Paisley Joint Station, Glasgow", and if they found him satisfactory, to appoint him to the vacancy. Dunragit's first station-master, David Campbell, also failed to please, Grafton reporting in May 1861, that he had been "under instruction at Stranraer for several weeks, but had made little or no progress in acquiring a knowledge of his duties". The directors decided to give him notice, paying him 8/- per week for the time he had been at Stranraer, on condition that he left Dunragit almost immediately. It seems he did not comply with this condition, as a few weeks later he was appealing to be allowed to stay. The result of his appeal is not mentioned, but the implication appears to be that it was rejected. A year later, J. H. Murdoch was to be instructed at a station and if found satisfactory to be appointed stationmaster at Portpatrick at 18/- per week. In a few weeks, however, David Watson had been appointed, at 19/-. Within six months, Grafton was complaining that Watson "had fallen behind with his books and was otherwise remiss in the discharge of his duties". It seems clear that Watson was subsequently dismissed, as in July 1863 the directors heard letters from Watson himself, and also from Mr. McClew, Dinvin, factor on the Dunskey estate, and a shareholder in the P P R, with a memorial of the people of Portpatrick in his favour. They resolved to "adhere to their former decision". Watson may have been inadequate, but the support he won from the local people, led by McClew, suggests that he had given proof of good intentions.

Dromore was another station which had, at first, only temporary custodians.

## Rails to Portpatrick

In July 1861, Grafton was instructed to "see if Mr. Blythe, telegraph clerk, Gatehouse, will suit for Dromore Station". It seems he did suit - at 16/- a week and a rent-free house - but not for long; in November he was to be informed that "his services will not be any longer required". His successor was John Alexander, a newcomer to the area, with previous railway experience. Alexander soon made a very favourable impression, but his promising career was cut short by a fatal accident on New Year's day, 1863. He had gone to Creetown by the 5.55 p.m. train, spent some time with friends, then set out on foot along the railway for home. The account in the *Free Press* says that "Although he had been joining in the festivities of the day, he was quite able to walk." Next morning he was found badly injured beside the line, near the farm of Greenburn. It was thought that, having recently been very ill, he had become exhausted and collapsed, his injuries being caused by the engine of the evening express from Stranraer striking the back of his head. He died the following evening. He left a widow and children, for whom tragedy was softened somewhat by the kindness of the people of the district, especially the Swainsons, of Goatend Farm, Gatehouse.

Following Alexander's death, Mr. Blacklock, the Parton station-master, was transferred to Dromore, and this brought to Parton a man who was to give the P P R a most remarkable record of service. No one could impute to James Mirrey lack of relevant experience. Born in New Cumnock, Ayrshire, about 1826, son of a farm labourer who became an iron worker, he had gone into the engineer's department of the future G S W when the latter's main line was open only as far south as New Cumnock, then become a porter at Sanquhar station. After his marriage, he emigrated, and spent seven years as a station-master in Canada, first at Bothwell, then at Thamesville, on the Great Western Railway. Concern for the health of his family led to his return to Scotland, and he took a job as porter at Mauchline before getting his appointment as station-master at Parton; his wage at Parton was 17/- a week. Like one of the Stewart kings, he seems to have been resolved not to go on his travels again, and was to stay at Parton for the remainder of his life, well over forty years, during which time he came to be held in very great respect.

BENEFITS OF THE RAILWAY; THE MAIL SERVICE; THE *BRITON*

In the first months of the railway's operation, there were numerous enthusiastic reports of the benefits it was bringing to the region. On the first day of the public service, a merchant in Stranraer urgently needing delivery of some goods telegraphed to London at 3 p.m.; the goods were delivered to him at noon the following day. During the summer of 1861 there were many consignments of cattle, both from Galloway and from Ireland via Stranraer, to places in England, including Newcastle upon Tyne and Norwich, but particularly industrial Lancashire, which was Galloway's chief market; while a completely new departure was the dispatch of cheese from the Glenluce district to England. Referring to passenger traffic, a correspondent at Newton Stewart wrote:

# Rails to Portpatrick

"This station, on the arrival of the up and down trains, which meet here in the afternoon, presents a very interesting and busy appearance. The wonder is where all the parties come from, and how the Galloway people could have tolerated so long the old, slow and easy mail coach, with its limited accommodation."

In the Glenkens district of the Stewartry, the people soon found a notable increase in the number of visitors through the railway, and the buses provided by local hotel owners to connect with New Galloway and Parton stations. Mr. James Ball, of the Bedford Hotel, Princes Street, took a lease of the hotel at Ken Bridge, which was expected to attract many "distinguished" visitors to the area.

One of the greatest benefits the line was expected to bring was a big acceleration of the postal service. This did not come immediately, as no agreement existed between the company and the Post Office. The mail-coach, after operating for over 50 years, ran through Galloway for the last time on Tuesday, 12th March 1861, the day the public service of trains began. Many of the villagers of Glenluce gathered to take their farewell as the coach passed through for Castle Douglas, and no doubt there were similar scenes elsewhere. For some months however, the mail-bags were brought to and from Castle Douglas by gig, while the P P R and the Post Office haggled over the terms of a contract. In April, a petition was exhibited for public signature at all the P P R stations in favour of such a contract; but it was not until mid-October that the railway began to carry the mails from intermediate places, and even so their remuneration had not been settled, T. E. Harrison, the eminent engineer of the English North Eastern Railway, having agreed to arbitrate between the two sides. Still, the change was nonetheless helpful to the local people. At Stranraer, for example, the English mail now arrived by train due at 11.30 a.m., instead of about 5 p.m. as before, and business people could send off replies to their correspondence the same day.

But there was no sign yet of the hoped-for Mail Service to and from Belfast and the North of Ireland. The P P R directors were anxious to establish a daily service of steamers that could carry the mails, as well as the large traffic in goods and passengers that it was hoped to build up. In August 1860, a deputation from the North of Ireland, including Sir Hew Cairns, M.P. for Belfast, had visited Portpatrick and Loch Ryan. They came on the Giraffe, one of Burns' steamers, "a very splendid steamer, though not the fastest on the Clyde", and on the basis of her performance the PPR directors concluded that the passage from Larne to Stranraer could be made in regular service in little more than two hours, and that from Belfast to Stranraer in 3 hours 20 minutes. The Donaghadee to Portpatrick passage might be made in a little over an hour. In June 1862, however, the directors resolved to memorialise the Admiralty about delay in the harbour works at Portpatrick. Nothing of any moment had been done to improve the entrance, and there was no prospect of a steamer on the Portpatrick and Donaghadee station that year. Fears were growing in the district lest the Government should back out of their undertaking, and the hopes that had been raised of an end to the deep economic depression that had settled on Portpatrick since the withdrawal of the Admiralty packet service in 1849, were already receding. A year later, in a Commons Committee on Portpatrick Harbour, chaired by Sir W. Dunbar, Sir Hew Cairns strongly opposed the spending of any more public funds there, and expressed the ominous preference for compensating the railway company for their expenditure on the Stranraer to Portpatrick section rather than going on with the harbour works. The Government, however, professed a determination to honour previous commitments, and Dalrymple was able to tell the next P P R half-yearly meeting that a new grant of money had been made for the harbour and a new assurance given by the Treasury that the route to Donaghadee would be adopted as a mail passage. In their report to the half-yearly meeting following, in March 1864, the directors said that the harbour works had been "prosecuted with increasing energy", but when actually addressing the shareholders Dalrymple showed himself very sceptical on the subject, and, in fact, by November the directors were asking the Board of Trade "the reason of the stoppage of the works at Portpatrick Harbour".

Pending the completion of the Portpatrick works, the company had sounded the Government about the possible carriage of the mails via Stranraer. Though getting no encouragement in this, they were still anxious to develop this route, which in any case they had always intended to be taken by heavy goods traffic. Already, in April 1861, the Albion and Scotia steamers of the Glasgow, Stranraer and Belfast Steamboat Company were maintaining a twice-weekly service to and from Belfast in connection with the trains at Stranraer. There was only one steamer a week during the following winter, but from mid-May, 1862 there were three. In June, the local press reported increasing patronage of the route, but passengers were having to hurry straight from the station to the pier so as to catch the steamer, and it was suggested that a short interval for "breakfast or some other refreshment" would be welcome.

The railway directors, however, were convinced that a daily steamer service was essential if the traffic potential of the route was to be fully developed, and early in 1862 a meeting was held in London with representatives of other companies with a strong interest in the matter - the L N W, G S W, Newcastle & Carlisle, and North British - and a "cordial understanding" reached. It was intended to place a steamer on the passage daily from early summer, but in August the P P R were still trying, unsuccessfully, to induce a shipping firm to provide a boat. The decision was taken to buy a steamer outright, but arrangements could not be completed until a guarantee against financial loss was given by the L N W, Caledonian, P P R, Northern Counties of Ireland, Carrickfergus & Larne, and Castle Douglas Companies. It was at length agreed to establish a regular weekday service from 1st October; the line from Carrickfergus to Larne being far advanced, the steamer would operate to and from Larne, and not Belfast, while the trains would be able to go alongside the boats at both harbours.

Through carriages to and from Carlisle were run on the express train that connected with the steamer at Stranraer; between Dumfries and Stranraer the train called only at Castle Douglas and at Newton Stewart. The steamer was the *Briton*, an iron paddle steamer, newly built for the Glasgow, Stranraer and Belfast Steam Packet Company by Tod & McGregor at their Meadowside yard, and now purchased by directors of the P P R and the Carrickfergus & Larne Company. Her dimensions are given as: length of keel and forerake 175 feet; beam moulded 24 feet; depth moulded 12 feet; tonnage, o.m., 492; h.p. 150, and fitted with patent condensers. "The after-cabin contains accommodation for 116 passengers, and the forecabin for 300, while the quarter-deck is spacious and convenient. There are four life-boats on board, with gearing of every description ready for any emergency." Her commander was Captain George Campbell, aged 34, a native of Garliestown, who had gone to sea at sixteen and become master of the ship on which he began his career; as master of the *Earl of Carrick* he had carried stores to the troops in the Crimea.

The first day of the new service was the stormiest for six months, and the *Briton* lost about 35 minutes on the Channel crossing. Nevertheless, there were the greatest rejoicings at Larne on her arrival, with music playing and small cannon firing. The railway to Carrickfergus was opened that day; as yet there was only a temporary pier at Larne. The advertised time for the Stranraer-Larne passage by the *Briton* was 2 hours 45 minutes, and in December the P P R directors claimed that she had "performed the passage generally with regularity", though on 19th and 20th December there were such tremendous gales as to prevent her sailing at all.

By the New Year, it was clear that the company were likely to make a loss on the first three months' working of the steamer. A landslip on the Carrickfergus to Larne railway, interrupting the Irish traffic for several weeks, had not helped matters. The directors, however, were obviously determined to make the service succeed, and sent a deputation to County Durham to see the West Hartlepool Steam Navigation Company, whose managing director assured them of his company's intention to send Continental traffic for Ireland by the Larne route. The half-yearly meeting of the P P R in March were told that whereas receipts for the six months ending January 1862 had been £7,443.8.11, those for the same period ending January 1863 were £9,612.9.2; traffic by the steamer had been below expectations, but the directors thought it had not yet had a fair trial. Sir W. Dunbar, however, expressed himself strongly in favour of discontinuing the steamer as soon as possible.

A few months later, pressure was coming heavily from the other side of the Channel to abandon the service. George Gray, a director of the Northern Counties Company, wrote in the Belfast News Letter that in addition to a payment of £440 as their proportion of the £3,388 loss incurred in the first six months' working of the steamer, his company's annual working expenses were being increased by £600 to £700 by the need to run two additional trains daily to Carrickfergus. But the P P R continued to do their utmost to keep the service going. The directors admitted that only the expense of the steamer was preventing the company's accounts showing a surplus, but the Irish traffic was increasing - the trade in cattle was heavy, despite very keen competition from the Fleetwood and Morecambe routes - and they were obviously hopeful that if the service were kept up, there was a good prospect of its becoming profitable. The C S W and L N W evidently approved of their attempt to keep the steamer going.

Dalrymple appears to have thought that the Irish companies, too, would have been prepared to go on if a larger vessel had been put on the passage, but the P P R felt unable to join them in providing this, or, alternatively, to buy their shares in the *Briton*. In December 1863, Edward Cotton, manager of the Northern Counties Company, to whom the Carrickfergus & Larne Company were leased, visited Glasgow, where he vainly appealed to the G S W to take the P P R directors' shares in the *Briton* and put her on the passage from Ardrossan to Larne, "or take an equal share in another and more suitable boat" for that passage. It was announced that the steamer would be withdrawn from the Stranraer-Larne service on 31st December. There were brief rumours that the express train might continue; some Belfast business men were said to be forming a company to put a new and more powerful steamer on the Belfast to Stranraer passage, and the express might still run in connection with this. Nothing came of the idea, however, and ship and train alike ran for the last time on New Year's Eve. The *Briton* was sold to the Bristol Steam Navigation Company, and sailed between the Bristol Channel and the South of Ireland for nearly thirty years.

Nevertheless the P P R were soon making arrangements to try to ensure a better chance of success for a new attempt at establishing a cross-channel service, while at the same time they sought to improve their future position and prospects by a close relationship with one of the big main-line companies.

# Rails to Portpatrick

**CHAPTER FOUR**

An Advantageous Alliance

WHEN the P P R's first Act, in 1857, gave the G S W powers to work their line, the G S W was the only railway at Dumfries. Early in 1860, however, a group of local men promoted the Dumfries, Lochmaben and Lockerbie Junction Railway, which, if built, would form a link between the rival systems of the G S W and C R. The C R seem to have been apprehensive from the start lest the creation of this link should damage their interests; the G S W, however, appear to have taken an apathetic attitude at first. They neither aided nor opposed the Bill for the line when it was before the Commons in April 1860, and Sir Andrew Orr, chairman of the G S W, evidently had deep doubts whether the line would ever be built. J. F. Smith, the G S W's secretary at the time, claimed afterwards that he advised the spending of £10,000 or £15,000 to get control of the company promoting it. He pointed out that, Lanarkshire coal being generally superior to that of Ayrshire, if the new line was built people in south-west Scotland would be likely to get their coal supplies from Lanarkshire instead of from Ayrshire as at present, so benefiting the C R at the expense of the G S W. As however, in spite of his initial scepticism Orr saw the building of the Lockerbie line going forward, the importance of the future routing of traffic from and to the P P R line, with its anticipated daily communication with Ireland, came strongly home to him. He turned to Smith for a remedy, and acting on his advice the G S W now secretly bought up shares in the Castle Douglas and Dumfries Company, in order to have complete control over the access to the P P R line. At the same time, the C R were offering to work the Lockerbie line at the remarkably low figure of 30% of total receipts.

The G SW also made sure of their control of the Kirkcudbright Railway, a ten-mile single-track branch from Castle Douglas. In 1860, now that the railway to Castle Douglas was open, there was heard again in the Stewartry the suggestion of transferring the court houses, etc., from Kirkcudbright to Castle Douglas, the latter being more central and more easily accessible, and so making the new town largely created by Sir William Douglas the county seat in place of the ancient burgh by the mouth of the Dee. The people of Kirkcudbright saw that to parry the threat they must have a railway, and they and their sympathisers bestirred themselves to raise capital. Among the sympathisers was Murray Dunlop, of Corsock, M.P. for Greenock, who reached an agreement with Sir A. Orr and other directors of the G S W whereby the G S W would provide half the capital needed if the other half could be raised locally. The offer and challenge were accepted; and in the words of M. McL.Harper "by the energy and ceaseless labours of the magistracy, councillors, inhabitants, and assistance of 'ain born bairns' resident abroad, the object was accomplished". The railway was opened early in 1864, and like the Castle Douglas line was worked from the start by the G S W.

Meanwhile, the G SW had considerably angered and alarmed the C R by coming to an arrangement with the North British Company at their expense. In 1862, the C R lost their monopoly of direct railway communication between Carlisle and Edinburgh when the Waverley route of the N B was completed by the opening of the "Border Union" line from Carlisle to Hawick. The C R had done their best to deny the NB access to Carlisle, but the N B defeated them by leasing the Port Carlisle Railway, with its running powers over the C R at Carlisle. The G S W were soon sending goods traffic originating on their system, and destined for Edinburgh and north thereof, by the new route - using the Gretna-Longtown cut-off - instead of by the C R as previously. Lt.-Col. Salkeld, the C R chairman, subsequently complained that positive instructions were given to every station-master in Ayrshire and on the G SW main line to send unconsigned traffic by the N B instead of the C R wherever possible, and that the G S W issued circulars to customers, canvassing them to send goods by the N B rather than the C R. The C R's anger was the greater in view of an agreement made between them and the G S W in 1853, one provision of which was that each company would encourage and foster the other's traffic as much as possible. They would certainly be unlikely to miss any chance they might get to retaliate against the G S W, and an opportunity very conveniently came their way in the form of the affairs of the P P R at this time.

We saw earlier that towards the close of 1859, when the P P R were in great need of the G S W's further subscription of £40,000, the G SW in effect made this conditional upon their being given the working of the P P R. They subsequently set their price for working the line at 72 % of total receipts. When this ruthless attempt to exploit the P P R's difficulties failed, the G S W withheld the £40,000, using the excuse of the absence of a further contribution from the County Down Company; their representatives ceased to attend P P R board meetings, and they virtually lost interest in the P P R for the best part of four years. Not surprisingly, the opening of the Lockerbie line, under C R management, in September 1863, brought them into contact again; on the one hand, the P P R agreed to a G S W request to send Edinburgh traffic via Gretna, while on the other, the Castle Douglas Company, acting on G S W orders, declined to allow P P R trains "in connection with Lockerbie traffic" to run on their line. The P P R warmly welcomed the arrival of the C R at Dumfries, partly because of the prospects of developing their traffic by the new communication with the C R main line, and partly because of the opportunity which the intensification of G S W and C R rivalry might give them of improving their position generally.

The P P R, whom the G S W's defection had forced to raise a large sum on debenture, now announced their intention of applying to Parliament for additional powers. These reflected the changed situation. Two bills (they became law in July 1864) would empower the P P R firstly to issue £20,000 of new shares in place of 2,000 on which calls had not been paid; to borrow £10,000; to make Working Agreements with the C R or L NW and to run trains over the Castle Douglas line, and over the G SW at Dumfries; secondly to obtain steamers and put them on the passage Portpatrick~ Donaghadee, Stranraer-Donaghadee, Stranraer-Larne, or Stranraer-Belfast, and to raise up to £72,000 for the purpose. In November 1863, Maxwell of Munches, the Castle Douglas Company's chairman, urged a meeting of the G S W and P P R boards with a view to a compromise which would "unite the railways in the south-west of Scotland in that close alliance which nature had so strongly marked out for them". The P P R offered to withdraw their bill dealing with finance, Working Agreements and running powers, if the G SW would now contribute the £40,000, and at first it seemed that Maxwell's efforts were to be rewarded. A meeting of directors of the G S W and P P R did take place at Carlisle on lst December, at which according to the G S W, Sir William Dunbar assured them that the P P R would give them the preference in their negotiations with other companies; and by mid-month the G S W had certainly proposed taking additional shares to the value of £40,000. They still insisted on working the P P R, though their terms were now 45 % of gross receipts.

A further meeting was arranged for the 16th, at Dumfries.

The P P R, however, called off this meeting, and Dunbar was subsequently reported as admitting to the Commons Committee considering their bill that the P P R had treated the G S W with rather "scant courtesy". Having received such shabby treatment from the G SW in the past, and been left by them, as Dunbar said, "in a state of uncertainty and suspicion", the P P R had welcomed a rival offer. According to Dunbar, it was "an accidental interview" between Dalrymple and Salkeld, the C R chairman, that led to an acceptable offer by the latter company, though the C R were insistent that the actual approach had come from the P P R. The P P R directors, to quote Dunbar again, reflected on the adage concerning a bird in the hand and decided to close with the C R offer. The C R were to subscribe £40,000 and "eventually if desired" to work the P P R line at a maximum rate of 43 % of the gross receipts, this rate to diminish as traffic increased; and the L N W were to subscribe £10,000. It seems that the L N W had themselves submitted identical terms for working the P P R, but there is no suggestion of serious competition with the C R, and indeed the fact that the L N W, which had been their consistent supporter, were the allies of the C R may well have been an inducement to the P P R to come to an agreement with the latter. The G S W, in a last bid to prevent the agreement, sent Andrew Galbraith and James Lumsden as plenipotentiaries to the P P R board meeting of 5th January 1864, offering now the same terms as the C R, but in the event they could only protest at the signature of Heads of Agreement between the P P R and the C R. It was now the turn of the G S W to complain of a breach of the agreement of 1853.

It thus appeared that the friendliest relations had come about between the P P R and the C R, with the G S W decisively defeated. But this was by no means the end of the story. The P P R directors stated to the half-yearly meeting of March 1864, that they believed the agreement "would secure the immediate payment of a dividend on this company's stock, while traffic cannot fail largely to increase under the management of so powerful a company as the Caledonian". At a C R shareholders' meeting in April, however, there was some strong criticism, led by the influential Mr. McGavin, who complained of the P P R, in their parliamentary bill, exploiting the rivalry of the C R and G S W, and in an allusion to contemporary European politics declared that he "did not think the Caledonian Company had anything more to do in working the traffic between Castle Douglas and Portpatrick - they had no more right there - than the Austro-Prussian army in Denmark". Lt.-Col. Salkeld, in reply, said he thought the agreement with the P P R would be very profitable, all the traffic obtained having a very long run over the C R line. The G S W had deliberately broken their agreement with the C R by subscribing to the Glasgow Union line, and they had repeatedly refused C R requests for a conference. In decidedly incongruous language, however, he then referred to "an old saying, that the quarrels of lovers were the renewal of love", and appealed for McGavin's help in settling the differences with the G S W.

With or without such help, things moved quickly towards a major reconciliation during the following weeks. The initiative came from the C R. In May, there was correspondence between Dalrymple and Salkeld, arising from a proposition just made to the P P R by the G S W. Whatever the details of this proposition, the C R were doubtless seriously alarmed at the prospect of the very low terms which were likely to have finally to be accepted for working the P P R if the fierce bidding against each other of the two large companies continued. Better to agree to share the prize whose value would otherwise be so gravely impaired by their cut-throat competition. At mid-June the C R proposed to the G S W a joint working of the P P R, to include also the L N W, on the terms offered by the C R a few months before; the C R's subscription of £40,000 was to remain "provided the Portpatrick Company give their consent to this arrangement". Understandably, the idea of their line coming under this joint control did not appeal to the P P R board, who sought to steer the C R back towards their previous agreement; and after further correspondence of Dalrymple and Salkeld, the C R were soon agreeing to work the P P R from the coming August, and guaranteeing an additional subscription of £10,000 by the L N W. There followed, however, a series of meetings in London between representatives of the C R and G S W boards, the outcome of which was nothing less than the arrangement of terms for an amalgamation.

It is doubtless this remarkable development which explains why the C R did not, in fact, begin to work the P P R in August; while the *Kirkcudbrightshire Advertiser* was soon denying a rumour that the working was to have commenced on 1st September, adding that "no definite arrangements have been come to in the matter". By that date, it is true, the sudden, startling prospect of the amalgamation of the rivals had dissolved. A critical meeting had been held on 2nd August, following which the G S W recorded that "it having been found impossible to adjust the details so as to secure the position of this company, the negotiations for amalgamation had been discontinued". Still, the C R were evidently willing that the G S W should work the P P R – "take the Portpatrick" as they expressed it - on condition that the C R should have power to appoint their own carrying agent for traffic from it. This condition, however, the G S W refused to accept.

Following the breakdown of their negotiations with the C R, the G S W submitted detailed terms for a Working Agreement to the P P R board. The latter drew up detailed terms and sent them to the CR. The matter was settled at last during September, when after Dalrymple had reported on continued negotiations with the two big companies the P P R board directed the preparation of an Agreement "on the basis of the terms accepted by the Caledonian Company". This agreement the C R board described themselves as accepting "on G S W terms". We shall see that the terms of the actual Working Agreement were lower than those previously agreed on by the C R and P P R, which the G S W had presumably undercut in their last ditch-effort. Though having lost the long-drawn-out battle, the G S W still persevered to safeguard their interests so far as possible by asking the P P R to make an agreement with them "similar to the agreement with the L & N W Company dated 10th November 1859". In September 1859, when the Lancaster & Carlisle Company were negotiating about a further subscription of £60,000 to the P P R, they had sought to make a condition that the P P R would "contract to send all the traffic for the South arising on or beyond their line by the L & C so far as it forms the nearest and most commodious route". The L & C were being leased to the L N W at the time. An objection to the condition was raised by Sir A. Orr, representing the G S W, and a majority of the P P R board supported him. A deputation was appointed to meet the L & C and L N W boards. It would seem that the L & C's condition was in the event accepted, and that the G S W were now prepared, presumably, to offer some kind of inducement to the P P R in return for a similar concession to them. The P P R sent a copy of their request to the C R, and the matter is not mentioned again.

The Working Agreement came into operation on 1st October 1864. It was approved by an extraordinary general meeting of the C R in November, though not without criticism, George Smith claiming to know that several G S W directors thought they were "quit of a bad job, and the Caledonian was welcome to it". Salkeld was at pains to emphasise how the C R had consistently been guided by pure self-interest throughout; of the P P R's complaints about their high-handed treatment by the G S W, "We might have probably disregarded all that", he said contemptuously, had the G S W treated the C R fairly, but in the circumstances "The opportunity was fortunately given us of taking back as much as they had taken from us." He followed this up with an assurance that should the resolution approving the Working Agreement be negatived, "it would be one of the greatest calamities that could possibly occur to us".

The Agreement was unanimously approved by the P P R shareholders early in December. After explaining the Agreement, the directors added that the L N W had subscribed the additional £10,000; that the directors had been enabled to pay off about £30,000 borrowed on debenture; that sufficient means were now provided to pay off the whole of the company's liabilities, including the expenses of the two recent Acts of Parliament; that the balance of £377 due under the guarantee of the *Briton* was "now finally settled", and that they were confident that a small dividend on the ordinary shares could be declared at the next general meeting.

By the terms of the Working Agreement, the C R were to work the P P R for 21 years, from 1st October 1864 to 1st October 1885. They were to take over plant amounting to £37,235.7.0; at the termination of the Agreement, this was to be handed back to the P P R. Working expenses were chargeable to the P P R on the gross earnings of their line, after deducting cartages, parcels, annuities and passenger duty, as follows:

> When traffic receipts were at or under £10 per mile per week 38 %
> When above £10 and under £11.10.0 per mile per week 36%
> When above £11.10.0 and under £15.10.0 per mile per week 34%
> When above £15.10.0 and under £19.5.0 per mile per week 33%

The C R were to "uphold" the line, and to appoint and pay the staff employed on it. The P P R were to pay their own secretary, their feu duties, rates and taxes, and all parish burdens. The C R were to pay them £300 rent for the workshops at Stranraer. The gross traffic (less passenger duty) was to be accounted for monthly to the P P R by the C R, deducting from it cartages, parcels, annuities (i.e. half the sums payable to the town councils of Stranraer and Wigtown in lieu of toll and dues) and the percentage for working.

Many years later, when the P P R as a separate concern ceased to exist, the Earl of Stair described the Working Agreement as "the best ever put on paper in this country", and paid tribute to Sir William Dunbar as having made it possible by his sound judgment. That the P P R by astute diplomacy secured an excellent bargain, there can be no doubt. The hopes that had been voiced on both sides of large financial gains were not to be realised, however; and given this fact, the thrift, not to say parsimony, of the P P R, and the keen awareness on the part of the C R of the very favourable terms on which the latter were getting their services, the alliance between the two companies was destined to be an uneasy one.

**CHAPTER FIVE**

Slow Progress

WHEN the Lockerbie line was opened, in September 1863, the train times on the P P R were altered accordingly, and there were notable changes in fares on the P P R line. All second class tickets were abolished, except through tickets to stations on other lines; third class returns were introduced, and first class fares reduced. This was hailed in the local press as "a great improvement upon the present arrangement". The practice of attaching a passenger carriage to the goods train from Castle Douglas, which, as we saw earlier, was introduced in late April 1861, seems to have been short-lived; when in March 1864 the secretary of the Kirkcudbright Company suggested this, the P P R declined "because a similar attempt had been made on a former occasion and caused much dissatisfaction among the public". It is not surprising that people should have complained about what must have been a decidedly tedious and bumpy journey. An additional train, however, was run from January 1863 between Portpatrick and Stranraer on Friday mornings for people wanting to go to the market in Stranraer. This was known as "the Portpatrick Market Train", and was run at the request of J McClew, of Dinvin, factor on the Dunskey estate.

Early in 1865, second class fares were restored on the P P R line; from 1st April all the passenger trains on the line were parliamentary, with third class fares at the statutory rate of a penny per mile. From 1st April, too, an additional passenger train was run, making four in each direction, daily except Sundays. The C R were by now working the line, and there had recently been complaints from the G S W that tickets were being issued by the 7.30 a.m. train from Stranraer by the C R to Glasgow, but refused by the G S W route. This in spite of the fact that there was a much better connection for the north with that train by the G S W than by the C R. The P P R directed that passengers asking for tickets via the G S W were to receive them. By April 1865 the C R had come to an agreement with the G S W giving them running powers over the Castle Douglas Company's line, and this was reported as considerably facilitating the movement of through passengers and good north and south. This same year, the G S W (Additional Powers) Act sanctioned the use of Castle Douglas station by the P P R "in perpetuity"; the P P R paid £75 rent per annum to the G S W. The C R, however, were contemplating a separate line of their own to connect Dumfries with the P P R, for in September surveyors were reported working in the countryside between Dumfries and Parton for this purpose.

The dividend that the P P R shareholders had been encouraged to expect was duly announced at the half-yearly meeting in September 1865. This was the first dividend the company had paid since their line opened four-and-a-half years previously, and it was only 1%. The directors praised the C R for the spirit in which they were putting the Working Agreement into effect, pointed out that the dividend was solely from local traffic, and anticipated "a much larger return" when through traffic with Ireland became available. Nevertheless, the very limited receipts encouraged the parsimony of the P P R and, making them extremely wary of incurring any new expenditure, led to serious friction with the working company over suggested improvements to their line.

The improvements comprised passing-places on the P P R line, and houses for station-masters and platelayers. These were recommended in October 1865 by the Perambulating Committee of the C R, who estimated the cost at £2,500, to be paid to the C R by the P P R with 4% interest within five years of the date of expenditure by the C R. At the time the only passing-places on the P P R between Castle Douglas and Stranraer were at New Galloway, Dromore, Creetown, Newton Stewart and Glenluce. The C R wanted loops at Crossmichael, Loch Skerrow, Kirkcowan and Dunragit. The only houses provided for station-masters by the P P R so far were at Crossmichael, Dromore, Palnure, Glenluce and Colfin. The C R proposed also the construction of more sidings at Stranraer.

The P P R claimed that under the Working Agreement they were not liable for expenditure of more capital on additional works. However, "from a desire to co-operate with the Caledonian Company in developing and improving the traffic on the line", they offered to erect the station-masters' and platelayers' houses, and waiting-rooms "and necessary conveniences" at the stations named in the C R report, estimated to cost £1,040, provided the C R constructed at their own expense the other works they were asking for. This offer was made in February 1866. The C R proposed referring the matter to an arbiter, while they drew attention to the serious obstruction of traffic through the absence of a passing loop at Dunragit and requested the P P R's "immediate attention" to this. The P P R's reply was to withdraw their offer, and to postpone consideration of the reference to an arbiter. The C R thereupon told H. Ward, their general superintendent, to slow the trains on the P P R line from 1st May till suitable passing-places were made.

The proposed sanction, however, turned out to be impracticable, Ward indicating that it would greatly disorganise both local and through working; he "begged" the C R directors that the loop at Dunragit be made at once. This was at mid-April. The P P R next refused the reference to arbitration, and took legal advice on their obligations under the Working Agreement. Whatever the details of the advice they received, in June they agreed to the original C R proposal about the various works and payment for them. This they claimed to do from a "desire to act harmoniously with the Caledonian Company"; they were not liable for such expenditure, and their present action must not be held as a precedent.

The passing-places were soon made. The following year, the C R erected a water tank at Loch Skerrow. But there was very little progress at this period with the houses for station-masters and platelayers. The C R submitted plans, only to be told by the P P R that "the accommodation is insufficient". £50 was to be spent on a cottage at New Galloway station to make it suitable for a station-master's house, but that was all. An interesting and surprising item shows up in the negotiations between the P P R and Hannay, of Rusko, the local proprietor, over proposed houses for platelayers at Dromore. Hannay suggested that the railway company should build a small hotel at Dromore. This proposal, however, the P P R declined.

During the latter part of 1868, the P P R were in dispute with their working company over numerous issues. The C R sought in vain to induce the P P R to agree to the line being worked by train staff instead of by telegraph. The P P R were unsuccessful in a bid to persuade the C R to accept changes in the rates for local traffic which the former believed would stimulate this traffic. The P P R protested at the C R's discontinuing the Dumfries-Lockerbie train in connection with the 6.40 p.m. from Stranraer, which had cut off communication with the north by the latter; and they recorded their determination to resist C R proposals for the reduction of the train service on the P P R line itself. The P P R dividend at this time was 1¼%, having fallen from 1½% the previous year. It was decidedly not a happy state of affairs; but the C R were also in a difficult position now, partly due to their involvement in the second attempt to establish regular daily steamer communication with Ireland.

THE STRANRAER-BELFAST PASSAGE

During 1865, Parliament granted another £10,000 towards the works at Portpatrick Harbour, and these were now pressed quickly forward to completion. There was still no sign, however, of the Government restoring the Donaghadee passage as a mail route and so making possible the establishment of a steamboat service. In the meantime, the C R put steamers on the Stranraer-Belfast passage.

This service was provided on the basis of an agreement with the P P R, whereby the latter were to raise £30,000 in purchase-money for two steamers, the money to be repaid to them by the C R when the agreement expired. The C R were to operate the steamers and pay the whole of the working expenses of the service, though aided by an annual contribution of £800 from the P P R. The agreement was to last at least seven years; it was expressed in writings exchanged by the companies and approved by their respective boards, but the formal deed on the subject was never signed by the C R. The service was begun by the paddle steamer *Fannie* on 4th December, 1865, with sailing-times, train connections, and fares from Belfast as shown in Fig. 4. There was no express train to and from Stranraer; the steamer is recorded as taking 3¾ hours on the 52-mile passage.

The *Fannie* had been built by Caird & Company, Greenock, in 1859; at her best she was capable of a speed of 15 knots, and she was a bockade-runner in the American Civil War. Her length was 231 feet, her breadth 26 feet, and her gross tonnage 650; she had simple oscillating engines, with two cylinders. "Her engines", wrote the *Free Press*, "are 250 h.p., which, we understand, can on an emergency be worked up to nearly 1,000. She has two funnels and patent floats. Her accommodation for passenger, cattle and goods traffic is superb. Besides the usual cabins below, she has a deck saloon, elegantly and comfortably fitted up. She has accommodation for 300 cattle, with the advantage of a gangway for the animals to walk to and from the 'tween decks, instead of their requiring to be swung up and down as in most other cattle steamers. A number of horse stalls have also been carefully fitted up on deck". The *Fannie* was subsequently joined on the passage by her sister-ship the *Alice*, built in 1857 and also a successful blockade-runner.

The first results of the new service were distinctly discouraging. The time of year was unfavourable, while the prevalence in some areas of Britain in 1865-6 of a serious cattle disease - the rinderpest, or steppe murrain - interfered with the movement of cattle and led to the entire suspension for a time of the trade between Ireland and Great Britain. In addition, the railway companies had been unable to get acceptable terms from the Post Office for the carriage of mails to and from Ireland.

With the coming of summer, matters improved. From 1st August, the service was accelerated, so that a passenger leaving Euston at 10 a.m. could arrive in Belfast about 2 a.m. next day; many more passengers were carried, there was an increase in goods traffic, and the trade in cattle had recommenced. But for passengers, at least, the service can hardly have been very attractive at the best of times, as witness the complaints of Provost Guthrie of Stranraer at the P P R half-yearly meeting in September 1866. Belfast-London travellers, he said, had to wait two hours in the middle of the night at Lockerbie, and the train through Galloway called at "paltry" stations. How poor this was compared with the service provided by the Holyhead route! He considered the steamers to be slow: their average speed was only 12 knots, whereas those on the Holyhead passage did 17 or 18, and Burns' steamers from Glasgow and Greenock to Belfast, competing with the railway, did 15. Arrival in Belfast in the small hours was disagreeable; passengers from Holyhead reached Kingstown at 6 or 7 a.m. He thought smaller steamers would do, and one fast one rather than two slow. The C R directors were to bLarne: their selfish policy was concerned only with north-bound traffic, taking very little account of that for the south. Some "uncharitable" people thought the C R were deliberately neglecting the P P R traffic so that they could buy the P P R up on easy terms; Guthrie himself did not believe this, and considered that the C R would respond to suitable pressure. The Earl of Stair (whom we met earlier as Viscount Dalrymple - he had succeeded his father in 1864) replied to the criticism of the connecting train that it was a matter of money - "nothing was so expensive as a fast train" - and an express would be put on if the company got a subsidy for carrying the mails.

# Rails to Portpatrick

During the months that followed, the service had once more to contend with adverse fate in the shape of the projected Fenian rebellion in Ireland, and though this turned out to be a "non-event"- at least partly because of the exceptional severity of the winter - it had the usual effect of unsettled political conditions on trade. In their half-yearly report in March 1867, the P P R directors said that there was "no reason to be discouraged", but at the ensuing meeting Colonel McDouall, of Logan, admitted that the steamers were not successful, claiming that they were too large for the company's purpose. To economise, only one steamer was then on the station. Lord Garlies, heir to the ninth Earl of Galloway, who became a director of the P P R that year in succession to Sir J. McTaggart, described the Stranraer-Belfast passage as "an entire failure". Efforts were made to meet some of the criticisms of the service: in the autumn of 1867 the *Alice*'s sailing times were changed; she now left Belfast at 9.30 a.m. and returned at 9 p.m. There can, however, be no doubt that the C R were very anxious to abandon the service at the first opportunity, despite their agreement with the P P R about a seven year minimum period, and they did not have to wait long for their chance.

On the morning of 24th January 1868, the *Alice* made the crossing from Belfast only with great difficulty, battling through a tremendous storm, and though by a feat of seamanship her commander, Captain Barker, got her into Loch Ryan, he had to lay to off Cairnryan for about two hours, while a badly damaged paddle-float was cut off, before she could come up to Stranraer pier. Mr. Blackwood, the P P R locomotive superintendent, put men on board to carry out repairs, but it was not until 8 p.m. next day that the *Alice* could sail again for Belfast. For a few days more she made the passage, but after 30th January the service was suspended. The Board of Trade certificate for the *Fannie* had been allowed to expire, and the C R now made the damage to the *Alice* an excuse to discontinue the passage. The P P R board in their March report stated that there was an obligation to maintain the service, and repairs to the *Alice* were going well, but the C R had no intention of carrying on. The passage was abandoned, and the two steamers were sold to the London & South Western Railway for their Southampton-St. Malo service. The *Alice* survived to 1898, the *Fannie* to 1890.

The P P R warmly resented the withdrawal of the steamers, and for a time relations between them and the C R were emphatically bad. They made several unsuccessful bids to recover the two annual payments of £800 they had made to the C R under their agreement which, they had understood, was to hold for at least seven years. Though their dividend showed only a marginal improvement - to 1½% - while the steamers were running the P P R line had benefited by £2,000 per annum, so they were not losers. The C R certainly were. According to Sir William Dunbar, the C R had given up the steamers owing to pressure from the shareholders, who claimed that the agreement with the P P R was illegal. Sir Andrew Agnew, while complaining of the "perfect apathy" of the C R about the Irish traffic, which alone could make the line remunerative, admitted that they had difficulties with their shareholders; the latter were clamouring for economy. The C R were, in fact, going through a crisis, a shareholders' investigation committee being appointed in 1868.

Under the influence of the investigation committee the C R board sought better relations with the G S W, and in the spring of 1868 meetings took place of senior officers of both with a view to the settlement of various matters in dispute between the two companies. The P P R traffic was among the subjects discussed, and in June the C R approved a suggestion arising from one of these meetings "that the amount of traffic carried between Dumfries and the west and Carlisle and the south, via Lockerbie by the Caledonian and via Annan by the G S W, be ascertained, and divided in fixed proportions hereafter; the traffic being worked via Annan, thus economising the expenses of the Caledonian". In July, the C R noted the settlement of "sundry disputes" with the G S W. About the same time, the G S W recorded that the arrangement about P P R traffic was to begin on 1st August, and to continue seven years. The traffic between Dumfries station, the P P R line and England was to be divided between the two companies according to the proportions in which it had been carried during the two preceding years, and all to be worked via Annan. The *Glasgow Morning Journal* reported that the G S W were about to take over management of the P P R traffic from the C R, with a hint that they might take over the working of the P P R also. As in 1864, a close alliance between the rivals seemed immediately in view; but now, as then, the prospect was doomed to sudden dissolution. The plan for the P P R traffic was abruptly put aside. Changes on the P P R line were confined to reductions in the service provided by the working company. We saw that the C R introduced a fourth daily passenger train in April 1865; by October 1866, following the construction of the new passing-places, they had provided a second daily goods. As previously noted, in the summer of 1868 they cut off communication to the north by the evening train from Stranraer, by taking off a Dumfries-Lockerbie train; and soon after, in face of vigorous protest from the P P R board, they discontinued one of the four passenger trains on their line. There was clearly a need for this train, for eighteen months later the P P R applied for it to be restored, but the C R instructed James Smithells, their general manager, to "decline with the best grace he can".

PORTPATRICK HARBOUR

Yet another source of serious friction with the C R was the latter's demand of a share in the compensation paid to the P P R by the Government following their abandonment of Portpatrick harbour in 1868. By an Act of that year, the P P R were to receive £20,000 and a loan of the whole of their debenture debt for thirty-five years at 3½%. In demanding a share in the £20,000, the CR claimed that the maintenance of the Donaghadee Passage by the Government had been "the very basis and foundation of the Caledonian Company undertaking to work the Portpatrick line at the low rates specified in the Working Agreement". This claim had doubtless a certain grounding in fact, since the C R were not interested in the P P R except as part of a trunk route to Ireland, partly supported by the Government; but, as the P P R pointed out, it had no legal force. The only payment to which the C R were entitled under the Working Agreement, the P P R continued, was a proportion of the gross traffic receipts; the £20,000 was to replace part of the P P R capital that had been spent on unproductive works, and it could not in any sense be deemed a traffic receipt. It would be applied for the benefit of their shareholders, and the C R would benefit in proportion to the amount of P P R stock they held.

The P P R thus dismissed the C R claim, which served only to exacerbate relations between the two companies; but it is hard not to feel some sympathy for the CR. They were passing through a time of great financial difficulty, which had led to a revolt among the shareholders: the results of their connection with the P P R were so far very disappointing, so that they regretted their agreement to work the line, especially at such low rates. Their loss on the Stranraer-Belfast steamers had been, to quote Lord Garlies, "a great tax upon the pockets of the Caledonian shareholders"; and there was the recent reluctance of the P P R to co-operate in the carrying out of necessary improvements on their line. At the same time, the Government's decision over Portpatrick harbour was a very great setback to the P P R, for which the payments offered were very inadequate compensation. They had spent some £75,000 on the costly Stranraer-Portpatrick section of their line, with the clear understanding that the Government would maintain Portpatrick harbour, and reinstate the short sea passage of twenty-one miles to Donaghadee as a Royal Mail route. There were continual delays in the completion of the harbour works, then no sooner were they finished - at a total expense of about half-a-million sterling since 1821 - than the Government announced that the harbour was unsuitable for a Mail Service, and refused to maintain it. Let us see how this came about.

The Board of Trade had in recent years taken over control of harbours from the Admiralty, and in 1866 they sent an engineer to inspect Portpatrick, who submitted an extremely unfavourable report. He claimed that the entrance was silting up. McDouall, of Logan, told a subsequent P P R half-yearly meeting that there was no sand to cause this, but debris from the new dock had been washed round and had partly blocked the harbour entrance; it was the fault of the engineer in charge of the works. A second criticism by the Board of Trade engineer, not to be explained away, was the difficulty of entering and leaving the harbour in "dark and stormy weather". The Board of Trade expressed their views about the future maintenance of the harbour at the national expense in strong terms. In a communication to the Treasury in November 1866 they wrote that they "trust they may no longer be the instruments of wasting public money in carrying out an undertaking that was originally vicious and which can never be, in their opinion, of any public service".

In the negotiations which followed, the Earl of Stair emphasised that the

P P R could not possibly undertake the maintenance of the harbour; the Government had always made it clear that the steamboat service for passengers and mails must be established by a private company, without any aid from the Government apart from a fair price for carrying the mails, and even if it should be the only means of getting the mails sent by the short sea passage, it was out of the question for the P P R to maintain the harbour in addition to the financial involvement they would have to accept in the provision of a service of steamboats. Lord Garlies, a very enthusiastic advocate of the short sea passage, visiting Belfast in the summer of 1867, was disappointed to find that the Chamber of Commerce there had totally rejected the route. The Board of Trade considered Portpatrick to be unsuitable for use during the hours of darkness, and while some influential men in Belfast would accept a day passage rather than have none at all, it seems that the majority of business men there insisted on a night passage, failing which they were prepared to forego the route altogether.

All this was very discouraging, but the P P R were unwilling to acquiesce in the situation. The Treasury now officially admitted the claims of the County Down Company and the P P R for compensation due to the abandonment of the short sea passage, but the P P R suggested to them that Sir Luke Smithett, of Dover, be employed to inspect Portpatrick harbour and report on its suitability as a mail packet station. Sir Luke had had fifty years' experience in the packet service, and had been many years in command of a steamer on the Portpatrick-Donaghadee passage. In November, however, Ward Hunt, Secretary to the Treasury, told them that in the Treasury's opinion it would not be in the public interest to give a subsidy for carrying the mails via Portpatrick, and that they were prepared to pay the P P R £25,000, with the gift of Portpatrick harbour. The P P R, rightly describing this as a "crisis", now took upon themselves to invite Sir Luke to make the inspection, which he did almost immediately.

Smithett's report was in the hands of the P P R by the end of the year, and, as they had obviously expected, it warmly upheld their views about Portpatrick. They seem to have had great confidence in its efficacy to change the Government's mind; copies were at once dispatched to the Earl of Derby as Prime Minister and Ward Hunt at the Treasury, while Ingram wrote to the County Down Company that the P P R were ready to join them in putting steamboats on the Portpatrick passage "in the anticipated prospect of the Government reversing their late decision in consequence of the report of Sir Luke Smithett". The Irish company, however, preferred to wait on events. Their scepticism proved fully justified. In their report to the half-yearly meeting in March 1868, the directors of the P P R informed the shareholders that in spite of Smithett's "most favourable" report the Government would not sanction the use of Portpatrick as a mail packet station. Instead, they had approved the acceleration - at considerable expense - of the Mail Service between Dublin and Belfast, in connection with the express service from England via Holyhead. The improvement in the postal service to the North of Ireland thereby made fell far short of what the Portpatrick route would give, while it failed altogether to provide the better postal communication between Belfast and the important manufacturing towns of Northern England that the Portpatrick route was intended to supply. The establishment of the short sea passage as a convenient route for passengers, one of the chief objects of the original Treasury minute of August 1856, had been completely ignored.

At the meeting, the Earl of Stair made it clear that he believed the P P R must at last admit defeat: "We must all acknowledge," he said, "the melancholy fact that the Government have now finally given up Portpatrick harbour". Referring to the proferred compensation, he commented that since in addition to the £75,000 spent on what he now significantly described as the "branch line to Portpatrick", the P P R had sustained loss through the absence of mail and passenger traffic with Ireland, this was "scarcely a boon to the company". The directors were seeking more adequate compensation. Lord Garlies said that recently he had been using all his influence and doing all he could in favour of the short sea passage, but he must endorse the remarks of Lord Stair. In his view, there were three reasons for failure, the most important being the opposition of the Belfast business men to a day passage, while another was the great prejudice existing generally against Portpatrick as a harbour, and a third the storm damage at Portpatrick during the severe winter the previous year, which he thought had certainly influenced the Government.

By the autumn, after long negotiations, Stair was able to announce better terms of compensation. The Government would pay the P P R £20,000 and make them a loan of their entire debenture debt of £153,000, for 35 years at 3½%.. The board recommended acceptance on the principle of half a loaf being better than no bread, but it would be difficult indeed to disagree with Stair's concluding comment, that "We have been far from well treated by the Government".

This was not quite the end of the sorry story. The Fenian disturbances had drawn widespread attention in Britain to problems in Ireland; the General Election of November 1868 had brought the Liberals into office with the strongest Government the country had had for many years, while their leader, Gladstone (with grave implications for the future of his party), saw the pacification of Ireland as his personal mission. Lord Garlies, who in the election had been returned to Parliament as Member for Wigtownshire ousting his fellow-director of the P P R, Sir Andrew Agnew, thought there might now again be a chance to persuade the Government to maintain Portpatrick harbour. Himself a Conservative, he said of Ireland that "The improvement of that country (whatever our opinions as to the mode) we all agree to be the question of the hour." Pressure from Ireland, he thought, might yet induce the Government to maintain Portpatrick harbour. It was the only thing that could do this; but there was support now in Ireland for the development of the short sea passage as originally intended. Mr. Johnston, M.P. for Belfast, was to move for a Select Committee of the Commons to inquire into promoting the short sea passage and maintaining Portpatrick harbour in a satisfactory state. Lord Garlies deserves credit for his enthusiasm and persistence, but it was a forlorn hope. He may appropriately be permitted the last word on this subject, and it is emphatic. Addressing the half-yearly meeting in March 1870, he said, "The time has now gone by for us to say anything more about Portpatrick harbour, and the short sea route to Ireland that way. That is doomed."

THE SHORT SEA STEAM PACKET COMPANY

During the final stages of the attempt to persuade Government to honour their commitment in connection with Portpatrick harbour an attempt was made by a private company to establish a daily steamer service on the short sea passage. This was the Donaghadee & Portpatrick Short Sea Steam Packet Company, formed in the spring of 1868, with a capital of £10,000 in £5 shares, by twelve business and professional men of Donaghadee and Belfast and John McClew of Dinvin, Portpatrick, factor to Sir Edward Hunter Blair, of Dunskey. Early in June, having met a deputation from them, the C R authorised through bookings between Portpatrick and principal stations in Scotland and England, in connection with their proposed steamer, and in the afternoon of Saturday, 11th July, the steamer, the *Dolphin*, duly arrived at Portpatrick.

The *Dolphin*, an iron paddle steamer, had length of keel 170 feet, breadth of beam 21 feet, gross tonnage 240; engines simple, one cylinder. She was built by R. Napier, of Govan, in 1844. On her arrival at Portpatrick with a party of excursionists from Donaghadee, after a passage of slightly less than two hours, she had a hearty welcome, and Sir E. Hunter Blair, Provost Guthrie of Stranraer, and numerous Scots and Irish gentlemen met in her cabin and drank to her success on the passage. She began her daily sailings on Monday, 13th. County Down trains left Belfast at 7.45 a.m. and 1.40 p.m.; the steamer sailed from Donaghadee at 9 a.m. and 3.15 p.m., and through trains left Portpatrick at 1.10p.m. and 6.15p.m. In the other direction, through trains reached Portpatrick at 11.50 a.m. and 5.5 p.m.; the steamer sailed at 12.25 p.m. and 6.40 p.m., and the Belfast trains left Donaghadee at 4.25 p.m. and 8.50 p.m. The times at Belfast and Donaghadee were Irish time, between which and Greenwich time there was twenty minutes difference. Passengers had to make their own way from the "High Station" in Portpatrick to the harbour, about half a mile. The passage cost 3/- cabin and 1/6 steerage for the single journey, and return tickets were available for 4/- cabin and 2/- steerage. Each morning a special train met the steamer at Portpatrick to take excursionists to Castle Kennedy. The new service was well patronised, the number of passengers carried daily approaching 100 and sometimes exceeding it. On Saturday, 25th July, 203 passengers made the crossing, while those concerned were pleased and, no doubt, relieved to see that on Tuesday, 28th, a day of boisterous weather, the steamer had no difficulty in entering and leaving Portpatrick harbour. Following the withdrawal of the *Alice* in January the Glasgow & Stranraer Steamship Company had provided a fortnightly sailing between Stranraer and Belfast; when the summer came they had increased this to a weekly service, but from early August it was reduced to fortnightly again, doubtless owing to the Short Sea Company's service.

Also, in early August, the CR put on an additional train between Stranraer and Portpatrick daily in connection with the *Dolphin*. Leaving Stranraer at 11 a.m. to reach Portpatrick at 11.20, and Portpatrick at 12 noon arriving at Stranraer at 12.20, it is called in the time-table the "Steamboat Train". On Thursdays during August, the *Dolphin* made a third crossing, "weather permitting and casualties excepted", leaving Portpatrick at 7 a.m. so that excursionists could catch the 8.50 train from Donaghadee to Belfast. They could have about four hours in Belfast, or seven hours in Donaghadee if they chose to stay there, before returning from Donaghadee with the 3.15 p.m. sailing. The "Short Sea Company" were certainly doing their best to make their service known and well used, but they were pressing their elderly little steamer hard. A failure of the service, which occurred this month, illustrates alike one of the *Dolphin*'s deficiencies and the difficulties presented by such small harbours as Portpatrick and Donaghadee even in the summer season.

A correspondent described in the *Free Press* how some visitors had spent, involuntarily, a week-end in Donaghadee through being unable to make the passage back to Portpatrick on the Saturday afternoon. There was a heavy sea, which evidently produced indecision as to whether to start for Scotland or not. Matters having been resolved in the affirmative, in the attempt to swing the ship "to allow her to steam straight through the narrow channel which forms the entrance to the harbour", one of her lines broke. The passengers learned, "from the crew and others not in command", that they were not to go across, and had to find such lodgings as they could in Donaghadee until Monday morning. The company, the letter concluded, should see that their "splendid paddle steamer" had at least a supply of stouter lines on board.

In September the passage is advertised to be made by the "splendid paddle steamer *Dolphin* or other suitable vessel". This may reflect the negotiations which had been taking place since July between the "Short Sea Company" and the P P R. The latter had agreed to make an interest-free loan of up to £5,000 towards the cost of a new steamer built expressly for the service and capable of making the passage in 1½ hours at most. A further condition was that, before the contract for building the steamer was signed, satisfactory arrangements should be made with the Government for the maintenance of Portpatrick and Donaghadee harbours in a condition suitable for the service. Garlies, Col. McDouall of Logan, and Ingram were to represent the P P R on the board of the "Short Sea Company", whose other directors were W. R. Anketell, J.P; Hugh Creighton, Little Clandeboy; Daniel Delacherois, J.P., Donaghadee; John McClew, J.P., Dinvin; J. M. Pirrie, M.D., Belfast; and William Valentine, banker, Belfast. Garlies told the P P R half-yearly meeting that he hoped none of the shareholders would begrudge the loan of £5,000, as he had no doubt the increase in traffic over the line would amply reimburse them; of the *Dolphin*, however, he said that she was "certainly not so well adapted for the passage as was desirable".

# Rails to Portpatrick

An interesting development took place on Friday, 11th September, when the C R began running passenger trains on the Harbour Branch at Portpatrick. Advertisements of the service carried a note, "The train now comes alongside the steamer at Portpatrick". In curving round beneath the cliff-tops and out along the hillside above the village to reach the "High Station" the track changed direction from west to north. As a result, at the station it faced away from the harbour, access to the harbour branch being gained by a back-shunt and only a few vehicles could be transferred to or from the branch at a time. The gradient of 1 in 35, of course, prohibited anything more than light loads in any case. Henry Ward, the C R's general superintendent, suggested that they ask the P P R to provide passenger accommodation at the harbour. The C R replied that the P P R were to construct passenger sheds if they thought proper to do so; the likelihood is that the P P R did not so think.

From Monday, 21st September, the steamer made only one sailing daily, leaving Donaghadee on the arrival of the 7.40 a.m. train from Belfast, which was timed to reach Donaghadee at 8.48, and Portpatrick, on the arrival of the 5.5 p.m. through train. There was a considerable increase in fares, the single journey now costing 5/- cabin and 2/6 steerage, while monthly returns were 6/6 cabin and 3/6 steerage. Despite the lateness of the season, excursion parties were still hoped for, and special trains would be run for them. After a few weeks, however, the service was suspended, following some accident to the *Dolphin*.

At the P P R half-yearly meeting in March 1869, Lord Garlies regretted the over-haste of the "Short Sea Company" to start their service, which had led them to put an unsuitable boat on the passage, but admitted that in some three months of operation it had carried 8,000 passengers. He reported that the "Short Sea Company" were contemplating selling the *Dolphin* and providing a completely suitable vessel. He himself knew of such a vessel, and anticipated the agreement of the various companies concerned to buy it, if the Government would consent to maintain Portpatrick Harbour. On 16th April, however, the motion of Mr. Johnston, M.P. for Belfast, for a Select Committee of the Commons to inquire into the promotion of the short sea passage and the maintenance of Portpatrick harbour, was lost, and with it the last faint chance of getting the essential Government co-operation in the re-establishment of the passage. The "Short Sea Company" resembled the P P R in their refusal to give up easily. Having auctioned the *Dolphin* for £1,700 in the summer of 1869, they reported a loss on operations to date of £2,551.19.0, but resolved to approach the P P R and County Down Company again with a view to reopening the passage under their joint management the following spring. But there could no longer be any question of this: the "Short Sea Company" had reluctantly to retire; and the subsequent attempts to reopen the passage, in 1871, 1873 and 1891, were brief ventures by others. In 1873, the Government officially abandoned Portpatrick harbour, and thereafter the massive outer works were swiftly devastated by the tremendous storms to which the coast is subject.

# Rails to Portpatrick

RE-ESTABLISHMENT OF THE STRANRAER - LARNE PASSAGE

On the same occasion, in March 1869, when he expressed to the PPR shareholders his final hopes regarding the Portpatrick passage, Garlies had added that "If the Government abandoned the harbour, the Portpatrick board would consider it useless to persevere in their endeavours to establish the passage, and would use all the means in their power towards the promotion of another sea-service to some port in Ireland from Stranraer." Needless to say, the Belfast & Northern Counties Company had continued to press the claims of the Stranraer-Larne passage, and towards the end of 1868 it had been rumoured that a movement was on foot for the reopening of this passage through the co-operation of the Northern Counties Company with one of the Scottish railway companies.

Experience with the *Briton* and with the Stranraer-Belfast service had revealed to the interested companies the wide seasonal variations in passenger traffic, the advantage to them by the increased traffic that the steamer brought to their lines, and the disadvantage by the difficulty of making the steamer pay for itself. Following the collapse of remaining hopes for Portpatrick, negotiations took place towards putting on a Stranraer-Larne steamer, and to overcome the difficulty just mentioned it was proposed that the various companies should make rebates to the steamer in respect of traffic for and from it passing over their lines, and should agree on through rates and division of traffic receipts between themselves and the steamer with a view to enabling the steamer's expenses to be paid out of its proportion of receipts. If agreement could be reached, the Irish companies were prepared to find half the necessary capital for providing a steamer.

It was not until the summer of 1870 that an agreement could be concluded. The first negotiations broke down owing to the opposition of the L N W. As Stair told the P P R half-yearly meeting in April 1870, there were "so many conflicting interests involved"; the L N W were concerned in the services from Fleetwood and Greenock to Belfast; nevertheless, he had strong hopes that they would eventually come into an agreement - after all, they had a "large stake in our undertaking". Garlies, too, referred to the great difficulties involved in negotiating over the Stranraer-Larne passage, with "so many different interests at work", and some of the negotiating companies demanding "very minute information". At the end of July, the P P R were seeking the support of the C R for limiting the rebate for steamer traffic to £8,600 a year instead of £7,500 as wished by the LNW, but agreement was reached at last during the next week or two, the parties being the P P R, C R, L N W, Northern Counties and Carrickfergus & Larne Companies. The negotiations must have been tedious, strenuous and, at times, exasperating, and the problem of reconciling the numerous interests that came jarringly together in the affairs of the railways of Galloway and the short sea passage was, inevitably, to recur constantly in years to come.

On the Irish side of the Channel a powerful influence on behalf of the revival of the service was that of James Chaine, of Ballycraigy, who had bought

# Rails to Portpatrick

Larne harbour during the 1860s and through whose vigour and perseverance Larne rose to its position as one of the leading provincial ports of Ireland. It was due to his efforts, also, that the 3-ft. gauge railway was built which, from 1877 to 1932, connected Larne with the Northern Counties Company's main line from Belfast to Derry at Ballymena; the "Steamer Express" which ran regularly over this line during these years, covering the twenty-five miles in an hour, was the fastest 3-ft. gauge train in Ireland. Chaine who was M.P. for County Antrim from 1874 to 1885, had a very attractive personality, good-natured, humorous, hospitable, and charitable in the full sense of the word. When he died in 1885, aged forty-three, he was buried in his yachtsman's outfit on the hillside above Larne harbour, in an upright position and looking out to sea. The 90-ft. round tower of granite at the entrance to the harbour was built two years later, by public subscription; "the contributions", so read the tablet over the door, "of every class in this mixed community, irrespective of creed or party, all cordially united in esteem and affection for the memory of the late James Chaine".

The P P R were to pay £10,000 out of the £20,000 Government compensation for the abandonment of Portpatrick as their half of the capital for a steamer; "gentlemen on the other side of the Channel" would find the remainder. The railway companies, according to Lord Stair, had agreed to a one-third rebate, for five years, on all traffic passing over their lines in connection with the steamer. He hoped a new vessel for the passage would be ready the following spring (1871). A second-hand steamer had been considered, but none suitable for the passage could be found. He hoped that when the steamer was put on, the P P R would be able to put forward a claim for better arrangements for carrying the mails on their line.

Stair's first hope was not fulfilled, as by the following March the order for the steamer had yet to be placed, though good progress had been made in arranging the new train service with the C R. Chartering a steamer in the meantime had been considered, but none of the vessels offered had proved suitable. The Earl had better luck, however, in his second aspiration, for after years of intermittent negotiation, in which the P P R, the C R and the Post Office continually found themselves at loggerheads with one another - it was a favourite contention of the Post Office that insufficient letters came through Galloway to justify any increased expenditure - the Post Office now agreed to a payment of £980 per annum in addition to the £520 previously paid, so that additional trains might be run to improve the local Mail Service. fn return for a further annual payment of £174, the P P R and C R agreed to include a sorting carriage in the new trains. These trains restored the regular weekday passenger service on the P P R line to four in each direction. The down train left Castle Douglas at 6.45 a.m., having connected there with the Limited Mail, and was due at Stranraer at 8.50. The bags made up in the travelling post office could be sent off into the countryside immediately on arrival at the stations, and the mail for the whole district between the two towns delivered three hours earlier than formerly. The up mail left Stranraer at 2.30 p.m., to reach Castle Douglas at 4.50. The new arrangements came into force on 1st May 1871. Of the total allowance of £1,674 made by the Post Office for the Mail Service, £674 went to the P P R, and the remainder to the C R to help to cover the working expenses of the P P R; the Post Office also paid 10d. per day mileage for their van between Dumfries and Castle Douglas, which went to the G S W, while by a piece of exquisite cheese-paring the L N W paid 5% interest on one-third of the value of the additional plant needed for working the new trains. The agreement with the Post Office, after so much futile bargaining previously, was, according to the *Galloway Gazette*, mainly due to the influence and efforts of Lord Garlies.

At the half-yearly meeting in March 1871, Stair spoke cheerfully of the prospects of the Larne passage, but this time his remarks met with strong opposition from a shareholder who protested against the spending of a farthing of money on the route. The critic was the Rev. Charles McCaig, an elderly man now living at Lochgilphead but a native of Portpatrick and obviously very warmly attached to the district. He and Robert Campbell, of Craichmore, also proposed a reduction of £200 in the £400 salary paid to Ingram as secretary, and asked how much pay the train guards received. Ingram replied that they had nothing to do with what the C R paid their guards. Stair spoke warmly of Ingram's services, and only McCaig and Campbell voted for their motion to reduce his salary. At the September meeting, however, McCaig returned vigorously to the attack on the subject of wages. The C R men in Glasgow, he said, had been holding a meeting about this, and though he was against trades unions and strikes, he thought they were right to complain. Recalling that the late George Guthrie, factor to the Earl of Stair, had been the means of getting most of the men on the P P R line their "places", he thought the P P R directors should use their influence on the men's behalf now. He claimed that their wages were lower than those of "skilled labourers and artisans", and in a subsequent letter to the *Free Press* said he had learned that the drainers working on the farms near Stranraer could make more than the railway workers were getting.

A year later, McCaig proposed even greater severities against Ingram, but once again his motion - that the secretary's salary be reduced to £150 - was supported only by Campbell. The Earl of Stair declared the meeting closed, but McCaig - aided no doubt by his years and his cloth - successfully insisted on being heard on the subject of wages, specifically mentioning the station-masters this time, and obtained from Stair an assurance that the P P R board would take the matter up with the C R. McCaig thereupon expressed himself perfectly satisfied, and went on to reaffirm his opposition to unions and strikes -"if he had been in Parliament he would have put them down with a firm hand, along with all injurious conduct on the part of the few. They were the greatest despotisms, these unions". In some ensuing correspondence in the press, however, he described Ingram's duties as "light and easy", while Campbell claimed that some of the shareholders at the meeting agreed with them about Ingram's salary, but were "overawed by the

# Rails to Portpatrick

presence of so many of our county magnates". He alleged that lack of talent for business in the said magnates was harming the P P R, and urged the shareholders to "try to introduce a little more of the business element into the directorate, and thus ensure that economy which is so essential to raise the Portpatrick Railway Company from its present struggling condition".

Campbell's concern for economy seems to have centred almost wholly on getting a reduction in Ingram's salary, while his strictures on the local aristocracy were certainly unfair to such men as Stair, Sir William Dunbar and Garlies, who gave abundantly, and always gratuitously, of their time and energy in the railway and other affairs of their native province, of which they were still very much looked upon by the local people as the natural guardians and leaders; and who, furthermore, could scarcely be justly accused of lack of business acumen. Ingram, too, though doubtless now receiving a large salary for only moderate exertions, was obviously a very competent and conscientious servant of the P P R throughout his career as secretary. In the company's early period he must have been invaluable and, as Stair once remarked, he did all their legal business, the professional fees for which would have exceeded everything paid to him. Still, we shall see that before long, though in changed circumstances, a big reduction was, in fact, made in the secretary's salary; while we must concede to Campbell the point that the presence of the great men of the province was probably unlikely to stimulate the exercise of freedom of speech at the shareholders' meetings.

As for McCaig's worthy appeal on behalf of the employees, it would not be surprising, however regrettable, in view of the social and economic ideas of the times, the low profitability of the P P R, and the difficulties of the C R as the working company, if the P P R board proved lukewarm, or worse, in their response. There is, however a welcome bit of evidence that they were less unsympathetic than might otherwise seem to be the case. At their meeting on 30th September 1872, just before the half-yearly meeting when McCaig made his second speech on the men's behalf, they had received a petition from the guards for an increase of wages, and recommended it to the "favourable consideration" of the C R.

By a baneful coincidence, there happened within a matter of days of this meeting a tragic accident which graphically emphasised the justice of the guards' claim. In the dead hours of night, a little goods train, consisting of three empty cattle trucks, six loaded coal wagons and a brake-van, was making its way from Castle Douglas to Stranraer and was near the Castle of Park, a little beyond Glenluce, when the cattle trucks came off the rails, to be followed by the brake-van, which was rapidly reduced to a "shattered wreck". The guard, William McCormick, was killed. A native of Kirkcowan, he was "an intelligent man, about thirty-five years of age, and much respected by his fellow-workmen". It was Sunday morning. Wrote the *Free Press* that week:

"A painful circumstance in connection with his case, and which we mention without comment, is the fact that he had been on duty from nine o'clock on Friday night to the time of the accident. That he had not been asleep in the van is proved by the time-book found in his pocket bearing the entry of passing Glenluce at 2.12."

Among senior personnel there was a notable development in 1871, when William Grafton, traffic manager or district superintendent, left to become superintendent of distribution of wagon plant for the C R. Grafton had expected to leave towards the end of 1865; the reason is not recorded, and anyway he did not go. Early in 1871, however, the C R decided to promote him, offering him £350 a year "to begin with" in his new post. Grafton had obviously given the utmost satisfaction at Stranraer, and the P P R strove hard to keep him. Ingram wrote to Smithells, the C R general manager, about "the absolute necessity" of leaving him at Stranraer, and the Earl of Stair wrote to Colonel Salkeld, the C R chairman, to the same effect. The C R insisted and Grafton went, to be replaced by Mr. Powell. Powell was certainly in a most unenviable position, and probably found his stay at Stranraer a very trying time. After little more than a year, the P P R were complaining that he was unable to do justice to the traffic and were urging the return of Grafton, or at least the replacement of Powell by "someone more fitted". In November 1872 the C R agreed to remove him, and to send Grafton back again. The latter's salary was to be £300, implying a large reduction compared with what he was getting in his present post. In December the C R approved "an arrangement with Mr. Grafton" but did not record the details. He was certainly back at Stranraer early in the New Year.

By this time the promised daily steamer had been operating between Stranraer and Larne for several months. The delay in 1871 may well have been partly due to the difficulty of raising money on the Irish side of the Channel. In August the Carrickfergus & Larne Company complained of, "very great difficulties" in finding the necessary £10,000, which on the Scottish side, they said, could be found by the mere passing of a resolution. However, they added that the difficulties had now been overcome. The P P R and the two Irish companies formed the Larne & Stranraer Steamboat Company, and in the autumn the contract for a new steamer, to be built specially for the service, was placed with Tod & McGregor, of Partick, for £18,500. It was decided to name her *Princess Louise*, after the daughter of Queen Victoria whose marriage to the Marquis of Lorn was the "Wedding of the Year" in 1871.

The Launch took place on 6th May 1872, and the ship reached Stranraer on 25th June. A large crowd cheered the approach of the long-awaited newcomer, and as she touched the wharf in the dusk of the summer evening she was "boarded at all points". The *Princess Louise* was a two-funnelled paddle steamer, length 211 feet, breadth 24 feet, depth 13 feet, registered tonnage 260, gross tonnage 500. She had steeple engines, nominal h.p. 200, with two cylinders. She had ample accommodation for up to 500 passengers. The railway companies realised, of course, the great importance to the success of the route of encouraging passenger traffic, particularly business men. Steerage passengers were provided with good cover, and the saloon accommodation on the new boat was luxurious. Her bow, stern and paddle-boxes were decorated with heraldic insignia and enlarged medallion portraits of the Marquis and Marchioness of Lorn.

The *Princess Louise*'s commander was Captain George Campbell, who had commanded the *Briton* on the Larne passage in 1862-4. Campbell had captained two vessels on the Irish Sea in the mid-1860s, during the short-lived attempt of the North British Railway Company to establish a steamboat service between Dublin and Silloth; after which he had served on the "Laird Line", as it became known later, between Londonderry and the Clyde. He returned now to Stranraer, and was to spend the long remainder of his career on the Larne passage, with the highest credit. He had chosen his deck officers and crew, with one exception, from Stranraer men; the engineers and firemen were local people, too.

The *Louise* began her regular week-day sailings on 1st July. She made the crossing at the same times of day as the *Briton* had done - to Larne in the late morning, and to Stranraer in the early evening. An express train met her at Stranraer. Her speed, however, did not come up to the specification in the contract, and the matter had to be referred to Tod & McGregor, who made some alterations. On her return to the station at the end of the year she gave great satisfaction, making the passage in indifferent weather in a little over 2½ hours, "the late train" for Carlisle and the South, connecting with her at Stranraer, was "starting very punctually".

This makes an appropriate note on which to move to our next chapter, which deals with a happier period in the P P R's history.

**CHAPTER SIX**

Better Times

THE mid-Victorian period saw an amazing expansion of British commerce, accompanying and following the gradual adoption by successive governments of a policy of almost completely free trade. The remarkable growth of industry also enabled agriculture to flourish as never before. Railway development both helped to make possible, and was itself encouraged by, this prosperity, which reached its peak in the years 1869-74. Galloway might, relatively speaking, be distant from the established main centres and chief paths of trade, but, especially since the renewal of daily communication with Ireland took place in these years of unprecedented well-being, it would be surprising if national economic progress did not find some reflection in the fortunes of the P P R.

In fact, the company's dividend did begin to look more respectable during this time, improving from 2%. in September 1872, just after the *Louise* had started her daily sailings, to 3½%. eighteen months later. There were difficulties at first, such as the need to increase the steamer's speed, while until an extension was made to the quay at Larne (finished by March 1873) she could not carry a full cargo of goods. Advertising the route cost the P P R £100 for the year ending 30th June 1873, though they did not pay until three years later, after "explanations" from the C R. Towards the end of 1873, the *Louise* had to go to the Clyde for overhaul. The "Laird Line" paddle steamer Garland replaced her on the Larne passage, returning to Glasgow the Saturday before Christmas. Over 100 people had a free trip aboard her from Stranraer to the Clyde. The next day Captain Campbell and his crew brought the *Louise* back to Stranraer. The weather was very bad, but she ran the measured mile at 14 knots and reached Stranraer in about seven hours from Greenock. In June 1874, the P P R, after long discussion, lent the Steamboat Company £1,500 as accounts were overdue, creditors were pressing and "there is no funds to pay". That summer, however, a great increase of traffic was reported on the short sea passage, which was being taken "taken advantage of by all classes", and Captain Campbell gave the *Free Press* a detailed statement (Fig. 6).

At the half-yearly meeting in March 1875, the Earl of Stair was able to report agreement with the Post Office for carrying the mails between Northern England, South and South-west Scotland, and the North of Ireland, by the short sea passage. This long-sought-for arrangement was concluded on terms scarcely favourable to the P P R – 2/6 for every 100 letters carried - but Stair, while describing this as "a trifle", said the board had accepted "on the principle that small fish are better than none", reminding us of his comment on the Govenment's offer of compensation for the abandonment of Portpatrick harbour, that half a loaf was better than no bread. The mails were carried by the Stranraer-Larne route from 1st February.

This development strengthened the various companies concerned in the intention they had already been forming of buying a second steamer. As things were, they had to charter a steamer when the *Louise* was laid up for repairs and Board of Trade inspections, and this was expensive, while in addition the Garland had dismayed her charterers by her ravenous coal consumption. Moreover, it was planned to fit the *Louise* with new boilers, in which case she would be laid up for some time. The P P R offered the Steamboat Company an interest-free loan of the £10,000 remaining of the Government compensation for abandoning Portpatrick harbour, and suggested to the C R an improvement in the terms of the Working Agreement in return for their and the L N W's grant of a rebate, reduced now to 20% of the gross receipts for traffic to and from the steamers carried over their lines.

The loan of the £10,000 to the Steamboat Company was authorised by a special meeting following the half-yearly meeting in March 1875. Stair informed the shareholders that the Northern Counties and Carrickfergus & Larne Companies had given "a material guarantee" of their intention to subscribe the same amount. Appreciation of the improvement in the P P R's affairs was expressed by James Hosack, a Liverpool business man, interested in the Lancaster & Carlisle Railway, and also owner of the property of Ellerslie, Kirkcudbright, who generously, though possibly somewhat ebulliently, described the line as "a great success". The shareholders, he said, were much indebted to Stair and the gentlemen associated with him, who ought now to have some remuneration. Stair replied that they should wait until the dividend rose a little higher. At present, this remained stationary, at 3½%. By now the great period of mid-Victorian prosperity was over, to be succeeded by a time of deep depression, but it was a while before the effects of this were seen in the company's revenue. As the Larne passage became established, traffic of all kinds grew steadily, and in September 1876 the directors were able to declare a dividend of 4%, the highest the company had yet paid; a year later this was improved to 4¼%, despite generally depressed trade. The directors continued to give their services gratuitously.

The new steamer, the *Princess Beatrice*, was built at Belfast by Harland & Wolff, and launched at Queen's Island on 4th November 1875. Mr. Harland, remarking that she was the first mail steamer built in Ireland, expressed the hope that there would soon be two sailings on weekdays and one each Sunday. They were not such Sabbatarians on the Irish side, he said, as to object to a trip to Scotland on Sunday to see their friends. In the Scotland of those days, however, there could be no such liberal interpretation of the fourth commandment, and David Guthrie, who as we shall see presently was chairman of the Girvan & Portpatrick Junction Railway, replied that he meant, "if he was spared", to have two vessels in the service "every lawful day", but on the other side they had strict ideas about the Sabbath, and "if there was to be a steamer on the Sabbath it must come from the Irish side". W. R.

Anketell, of the County Down Railway, intervened with the obliging information that, if desired, his company would be happy to allow a Sunday boat to run from Donaghadee to Stranraer.

The *Beatrice* made her trial trip on 3rd February 1876. She was a paddle steamer, very similar in dimensions to the *Louise*: length 235 feet, breadth 24 feet, depth 13 feet, registered tonnage 257, gross tonnage 550, engines double diagonal simple, n.h.p. 200. She had one funnel. The *Louise* was now laid up, her crew, under Campbell's command, manning the new vessel, which over the next few weeks made the passage in an average time of 2 hours 35 minutes. The C R and L NW having agreed to a 20% rebate, the P P R authorised a modification of the Working Agreement whereby in future the C R were not to get less than 36%. of gross receipts. The P P R regarded this as a very good arrangement, as it was already seldom that the C R got less than 36% anyway, and the rebate which was granted in exchange was essential if the steamer was to continue. Explaining these matters to the shareholders' meeting in March, Stair summed up the state of P P R affairs as "altogether satisfactory".

THE SERVICE (1); STAFF

In face of such good progress, it may well surprise us at first to find that there were numerous people in Galloway who felt unable to share Stair's satisfaction. But the explanation is not far to seek. It lay in a problem that was to recur constantly in future years, never to be fully resolved; that of reconciling the needs of the through traffic to and from Ireland with those of local traffic, within the limits of practical possibilities in a commercial concern.

The companies were obviously anxious to provide a good service of express trains to connect with the steamer. There was a difficulty in September 1872, when the G S W were evidently delaying the P P R express at Dumfries; this was to await the arrival of a G S W train from Carlisle, which the C R absolutely refused to allow to leave Carlisle before their own train witch provided the connection via Lockerbie with the P P R express. A year later the P P R were complaining to the C R about "want of sufficient locomotive power"; no details are given. On the whole, however, the express service seems to have gone well; in August 1874 it was reported that with heavy tourist traffic the trains were very regular, and the *Louise* was "seldom kept waiting a minute beyond her time".

No sooner, however, had the Larne passage been reopened and the new through service begun than there were strong and bitter complaints about the inadequacy of the service for local traffic. "There can be no doubt", ran an editorial in the *Free Press*, "the present arrangement of the trains, however answerable for the thro' traffic, is not at all suitable to this locality. A change immediately is imperative". The Dumfries Courier wrote of "astounding complaints" from Galloway about the new service - "at Dalbeattie communication to and from Wigtownshire is all but entirely cut off"; the feud of the C R and the G S W was suspected as the real cause. It was not the only cause, but it doubtless contributed, and this ill-feeling was to be bad for Galloway for many years to come.

As time passed and no improvement was made in the local service, some people provided for themselves as they had had to do before the railway came, and rode or drove a horse; parties were reported "mustering up" and hiring conveyances to go by road. This last was specially likely to be the resource of people visiting markets. In the autumn of 1875 the P P R, after consulting the C R, refused a request from farmers in the Dromore district for the morning express to call on Fridays to pick up for Newton Stewart Market (the expresses called regularly at Creetown, but this was "to water the iron horse", as a contemporary put it). A little later, however, moves being made towards providing regular road transport from Glenluce for people wanting to visit Stranraer Market, the companies proved more responsive, and the Glenluce market train, which had been one of the casualties of the revised service, was restored.

In November 1873 the *Galloway Gazette* had reported that passenger trains commonly ran late, twenty minutes being quoted as typical, and continued:

"We may remark here that at Newton Stewart station all the officials are overworked - there are too few hands for the work that has to be done; and the consequence is that it is no uncommon thing for the porters to be on duty eighteen hours at a stretch . . ."

A recent accident had revealed that a pointsman at the station had been on duty only six weeks:

"He knew next to nothing of the work; and it is significant if not alarming that the man who has succeeded him is said to be even less experienced."

An item published at about this same time indicates a means by which some of the station-masters supplemented their small incomes. In a list of the agents who sold the *Free Press* newspaper, and took in subscriptions and advertisements, in December 1873, appear the names of Mr. Kennedy, station-master at Colfin; the Duragit station-master; Mr McKenzie, station-master, Kirkcowan; and Mr. Richardson, station-master at Portpatrick. In a decided change of emphasis and locality, we learn from the unlikely source of the Valparaiso Mail of the tragic fate of Mr. Donaldson, a former employee of the P P R who, after living for some time at Castle Douglas, had emigrated and found work as an engine-driver in Chile. In January 1875 he was killed by a stone as his engine was passing Limache station on the Valparaiso & Santiago Railway. "This is not the only case", commented the paper, "in which the drivers have been thrown at by the miscreants who live in the wretched hovels along some parts of the line. The murderer is still at large, and no attempt seems yet to have been made to arrest him. Donaldson's wife and family live in this country". The story prompts reflections on the economic and moral progress of the intervening time.

The sombre mood induced by this event is intensified as the space of a few months brings us to a sad milestone in the history of the P P R, with the death at age 48 of Alexander Ingram. Ingram was born at Echt, near Aberdeen, where his father was minister, and came to Stranraer about 1848 to join his brother, who was a solicitor, legal and political agent to the Earl of Stair, and editor of the Earl's newspaper, the *Wigtownshire Free Press*. His brother left the district after three or four years, but Ingram carried on the business, though soon giving up the editorship of the paper. He obviously had the Earl's full confidence, and was the natural choice for secretary when the P P R was started. A very public-spirited man, he became the leading citizen of his adopted town: he was agent for the Clydesdale Bank, Clerk to the Peace, and a Clerk to the Circuit Court of Justiciary; he took a prominent part in carrying out various schemes of town improvement, and was associated particularly with the building of the new Court House; a member of the Parochial Board, he became a magistrate and chairman of the School Board, and for the last five years of his life he served as provost. But long before his early death he was frequently ill; the hard physical and mental effort and heavy responsibility entailed by his many duties overstrained him, and in the words of the *Free Press* "seem to have worn his health away". He wanted to stand down as provost in 1874, and agreed to serve a fifth term only after much persuasion and a public dinner in his honour. As his health worsened, however, he refused his friends' appeals to rest, and not until the late spring of 1875 did he leave the comparative austerity of Galloway to seek some betterment at a famous spa amid the genial luxuriance of rural Worcestershire; but now even there no betterment was possible, and Provost Ingram died at Malvern on 15th June.

Some 700 people attended the funeral in Stranraer. The cortege passed to the cemetery to the accompaniment of the solemn toll of the town hall bells, and all the shops and other places of business closed for 1½ hours. Ingram left a widow and two boys.

He was one of those men who bid fair to make themselves indispensable to those they serve, and whose full worth is sometimes realized only after they have laid down their tasks. His successor as secretary of the P P R was the obvious choice, his partner James McKenzie. At the next half-yearly meeting the Rev. C. McCaig inquired what salary McKenzie would receive. Stair replied that it would be £200, with £50 for office accommodation. This large reduction was very similar to what McCaig himself had vainly proposed in 1871, and he described it as "perfectly satisfactory". He went on to move a vote of hearty thanks to Stair, adding that "had it not been for his activity and energy, in connection with Mr. Ingram, the Portpatrick Company would not have been in the position they were that day". It was kindly and generously said; but it was no more than the truth.

## STRANRAER PIER

Had Ingram lived, it is likely that the dispute which forms the greater part of the next stage of our story would have been avoided. We saw that the East Pier, or Railway Pier, or Steamboat Pier, at Stranraer, where the steamers could berth at any state of the tide, was provided by the Town Council, and that the P P R agreed to pay the Council an annuity of £1,100 in commutation of harbour dues and petty customs. The pier was mainly of wood, but the pier head and the approach from the shore were of stone. Until 1873 passengers by the steamer had to make their own way over the wooden section from and to a platform on the stone approach where the trains stood; in March of this year, however, the P P R sanctioned the use of "the small engine now at Stranraer" to take passenger carriages along the wooden pier. This saved passengers considerable inconvenience, but for some years yet it was a grievance with them that no shelter of any kind was available to them on the pier.

Meanwhile, the matter of repairs to the pier became urgent. It was part of the agreement between the Town Council and the Railway Company that the former would maintain the pier, meeting the expense from the annual payments by the company. In July 1875, the P P R resolved to tell the Council that repairs were needed, but, evidently anticipating difficulty from the start, they added that if these were not done within a reasonable time they would do them themselves, and deduct the cost from their payments to the Council. The Council's reply was to request a larger annuity from the company to enable them to carry out the repairs. The company said the Council were bound by their agreement to maintain the pier; the repairs were necessary immediately to prevent accidents, and if they were not begun in four weeks the P P R would complain to the Board of Trade.

By March 1876, however, nothing had been done, and the P P R took counsel's opinion. In June the Council were denying liability, and the company instructed McKenzie to take the steps recommended by counsel. But the dispute brought home to the P P R the difficulty and potential danger of sharing control of the pier with the impecunious Town Council, and a few months later they had resolved to take over the pier by Act of Parliament. They commissioned James Leslie, C.E., who had had charge of the pier's construction, to report on the cost of putting it into a state of repair so as to last for about fifteen years, and also on that of replacing it with "a permanent structure of iron or otherwise". He was also to prepare a plan and sections for the company's "Pier Bill". In the meantime, they pursued their legal action against the Council.

The Town Council opposed the "Pier Bill" in Parliament, but it passed the Commons in March 1877. By this time the company had abandoned their proceedings in the Court of Session; they subsequently paid the expenses of £57.13.2 which the Town Council had incurred in this action. The bill became law in June, as the Portpatrick Railways Act of 1877. The east pier was vested in the P

P R; they undertook to maintain and improve it; they took over a debt of £20,000 to the Scottish Provident Institution incurred by the Town Council when they began building the pier, and they were to pay the Council a reduced annuity of £500. They might raise £30,000 in additional capital, and borrow a further £10,000. They were to share use of the pier and its facilities with the Girvan & Portpatrick Junction Railway, whose line, after countless delays, was to be opened that autumn, and the Girvan Company were to make them various payments in return: half the annuity to the Town Council; interest, at a rate yet to be settled, on half the cost of acquiring and improving the pier, including the £20,000 debt to the Provident Institution and the expenses of the Act itself; and a proportion, also yet to be fixed, of the cost of maintaining the pier, and of any future extensions and improvements. The pier was to be managed by the Portpatrick & Girvan Joint Committee, with three members from the P P R and three from the Girvan Company. These arrangements obviously left great scope for friction between the two companies, and we shall see that this soon came about.

The P P R borrowed the money for the repairs to the pier from the Exchequer Loan Commissioners. They gave the contract to John Lane, of South Shields, who carried out most of the work by the close of the year. In July, following an inquiry from the C R, they had again authorised the running of trains on the pier "with the light engine", being prepared to assume responsibility in the event of any damage to the pier as a result. At the September ordinary general meeting, Sir William Dunbar complained strongly about the Town Council's opposition in Parliament; it had resulted, he claimed, in the expenditure of £8,000 or £9,000 "in an unnecessary struggle" - most of the money might as well have been cast into Loch Ryan.

Had the Town Council not opposed the bill in Parliament, the company would have been prepared to increase their annuity from £500 to £600; they would have done this even after the decision in the Commons against the Town Council, but the latter had insisted on carrying the fight to the Lords.

The Earl of Stair told the meeting that it was now hoped to provide much better accommodation at the pier for passengers by the steamer. In March 1876, the board had appointed a committee to consider their "strong recommendation that immediate steps be taken to provide shelter" for the passengers. A plan prepared by Mr. Gibson, C.E., was now considered, but it would involve too much expense, and had to be modified. During 1878, however, "an extensive and commodious covered platform" was built on the pier for the benefit of passengers - the original Harbour Station at Stranraer. At the close of 1879, asphalting of the roadway on the pier was reported almost finished, and early the following year a small steam crane was provided. It had a lifting capacity of 30 cwt. at a radius of 28 feet. It was to give strenuous service.

THE GIRVAN LINE AND THE "STRANRAER SECTION"

We read of four projected railways in Galloway in the 1870s, and of these, two were built. One of the latter was the Wigtownshire Railway, of which much in our next chapter. This had been completed by 1877. In the following year a line was proposed which would have continued the W R northward from Newton Steart over thw moors to Barrhill in Ayrshire where the Girvan & Portpatrick Junction Railway, also completed in 1877, had a station. The whole of its length would have lain across very sparsely populated country, and it could have done little more than duplicate the Girvan Company's line into Galloway from Barrhill, so that it is not surprising that it was not built. A second proposal which was not carried out, however, was a line with a stronger claim to existence: this was the Rhins of Galloway Railway.

The Rhins Railway was promoted chiefly by Mark J. Stewart, of Southwick in the Stewartry, who was M.P. for the Stewartry and had acquired the property of Ardwell in the Rhins by his marriage with the heiress of Sir John McTaggart. Stewart was a director of the P P R, and had always strongly supported the Girvan line, the completion of which, in 1877, no doubt encouraged him to bring forward his own scheme. A line of about 13 miles was contemplated in the first instance, beginning at Stranraer and passing by Lochans over flat, highly productive farmland through the parish of Stoneykirk to the eastern shore of the Rhins peninsula at Sandhead. From there it was to run along the coast past Ardwell and Chapel Rossan to a temporary terminus at New England Bay, whence it might be extended to Port Logan, or Drummore, or both.

The route was surveyed by Robert Johnson, C.E., engineer of the W R, who estimated the cost of construction as £60,000. This was to be raised in £10 shares, with power to borrow up to £20,000 more. Mark Stewart was chairman of the Provisional Committee, with James McDouall, of Logan (like Stewart, a director of the P P R), vice-chairman; the Earl of Stair supported the scheme. Hopes were high: in addition to serving the rich agricultural district the line would pass through, there was talk of direct steamer communication with Liverpool from Chapelrossan or Portlogan and, more realistically, of developing Drummore, with its several advantages of situation, as a seaside resort. It was expected that the railway would greatly increase demand for the rich milk of the district in Glasgow, where it might arrive late in the morning, to be served, to quote Stewart, in the "coffee palaces all over the town into which men of business went for a refreshment, generally a glass of milk between two and four o'clock in the afternoon". The Act for the railway was obtained in June 1878. Building the line would commence, it was hoped, in the spring of 1879.

It was a very bad time, however, to try to raise money. Agriculture was depressed; there was a remarkably widespread depression of trade. The chief proprietors of the district rallied to the scheme, but humbler people held back. Matters were made much worse by the failure in October 1878 of the City of Glasgow Bank. This disaster, reminding us of a kind of insecurity familiar enough then though hardly thought of today, made it impossible for many who had promised to take shares to honour their commitment. It was known that others would be unable to meet calls on their shares owing to the state of trade. The directors persevered for some time, but there was no prospect of getting the additional support that they needed and they had reluctantly to acknowledge defeat and obtain an Act authorising the abandonment of their plan in April 1883. This was not, however, the end of schemes for a railway in this part of the Rhins.

The fourth projected line came into existence, it is true, but with great difficulty, and with at least equal difficulty survived the first fifteen years of life; yet by an irony of fate, a century later it was to be Galloway's sole remaining railway. This was the line linking Girvan in Ayrshire with the P P R, the Girvan & Portpatrick Junction Railway.

The Treasury minute of August 1856, on the basis of which the P P R was promoted, had made the provision of Government aid for improving Portpatrick harbour conditional on railways being built to connect "the Port" not only with Dumfries, but also north with Glasgow. In 1856, there was already a line from Glasgow as far as Maybole. This was to be extended to Girvan, and a survey by John Miller, C.E., of the country between Girvan and the P P R, near Dunragit, produced the very remarkable estimate that a railway between those places would cost under £7,000 per mile, while the ruling gradient might be 1 in 200. The inland route followed by this survey was favoured by the Earl of Stair, as opposed to the alternative, a route along the mostly very rugged coast between Girvan and Stranraer; the coastal route had been that intended for the Glasgow & Belfast Union Railway, one of the multitude of abortive schemes promoted in the "mania" year 1845.

The P P R's promoters, however, soon extricated themselves from the commitment to provide a northward link with Glasgow, and when some years later others announced their intention of providing it, the P P R were decidedly unfavourable. Another survey of the inland route had been made, from Girvan by Pinmore and Pinwherry, passing along the hillside high above the village of Barrhill, winding over the extremely desolate moors to New Luce and thence running down to a junction with the P P R at East Challoch, and in 1865 the Girvan & Portpatrick Junction Company obtained their Act. David Guthrie, Provost of Stranraer, was their chairman, and the directors included Sir J. C. D. Hay, Bart., M.P., and Colonel McDouall, of Logan, who were also directors of the P P R. But the P P R gave the new company no support. The next year, it being reported that a survey was being made for a line by the coastal route, Stair called a special meeting of the P P R board, which spoke of "new lines of railway at present uncalled for" and commissioned George Guthrie, the Earl's factor, to see interested parties with a view to preventing either of the proposed lines being built. It was implied that, should his efforts fail, the inland route might be regarded as a lesser evil. It augured ill indeed for the future that the P P R saw the new "Girvan Company" in no better light than this.

# Rails to Portpatrick

It was natural that the P P R, whose early years were proving far from prosperous, should be apprehensive at the prospect of a new railway that would provide a much shorter route to Glasgow and other places than the P P R gave in connection with the G S W and C R at Dumfries. The "Girvan & Portpatrick" planned to complete a route of 100 miles from Stranraer to Glasgow; by Dumfries and the G SW the distance was 156 miles, and by Dumfries and the C R 164½ miles. But for some time - years in fact - it seemed their fears were groundless, as the G & P P could make no progress at all. At the latter's ordinary general meeting in October 1866, Guthrie reported that the directors were "most disheartened" by the apathy of some of the local landowners and farmers, which in some cases was due to a preference for the coastal route. In April 1867, the P P R declined the appeal of a G & P P deputation for support. An approach the following year to the G S W, who owned the line from Glasgow to Ayr and worked the Ayr-Maybole and Maybole-Girvan lines, had a similar reception.. At the October ordinary general meeting the G & P P board had to report that at present they did not see much prospect of carrying out the undertaking.

Matters improved, however, with the great upsurge of prosperity around 1870, and at the end of July 1871 it was reported that the building of the G & P P line would begin at once, the works being expected to take less than two years. At the next ordinary general meeting of the P P R, Stair extended a welcome to the new line, though this was probably no more than a courteous acceptance of the inevitable. The forecast which he echoed, of the early completion of the line, proved very inaccurate, and meantime a dispute arose between the G & P P and the P P R.

It had always been contemplated that G & P P traffic would pass over the P P R between the junction at East Challoch and Stranraer. When late in 1871 the G & P P proposed obtaining running powers, the P P R set up a committee to negotiate with them and the C R. At the same time, however, lest no agreement could be reached, the G & P P surveyed a route for a line of their own to Stranraer. This ran parallel with the P P R, on the north side, to within three-quarters of a mile of Stranraer Station, ending at a terminus in St. John Street. Branches were to connect with the P P R west of Culhorn Avenue and with the P P R Harbour Branch. During the winter the companies failed to agree on terms for use of the P P R line. Stair said that the second line to Stranraer was unnecessary; the P P R could accommodate all traffic, doubling their own line if need be. They had offered the Girvan Company "not only fair but liberal terms", and would oppose their present bill in Parliament. His comments provoked the strong dissent of David Guthrie, who was himself a member of the P P R board.

The G & P P's bill, which became law in August 1872, gave them running powers over the P P R from East Challoch to Stranraer and the Stranraer Harbour Branch; these stretches of line were named "the Stranraer Section" and came to be separately managed. While the bill was before Parliament the two companies came to terms, and the proposed extension of the Girvan line to Stranraer was abandoned. But we shall see that this was rather the beginning than the end of troubles over the Stranraer Section.

The G & P P encountered serious financial and other difficulties during the next few years. In September 1875, a tremendous storm destroyed several of the newly-erected works. When the G & P P suggested to the P P R the transfer of Dunragit Station to the meeting of the two lines, which became known as Challoch Junction, and the appointment, under their Act of 1872, of a joint committee to arrange the traffic on the Stranraer Section, the P P R replied that the proposals were premature. The death of Ingram in June was most unfortunate for the G & P P. David Guthrie had been his closest friend, and if Ingram had lived, it is certain that his influence would have been freely used in the attempt to create good relations between the two companies. Next year the P P R deferred indefinitely consideration of Guthrie's proposal for a second daily steamer service, and were evasive over his requests for additions to Stranraer Station and for doubling the track between Challoch Junction and Dunragit. Through great perseverance, the G & P P line was now nearing completion, but the ill-feeling between the boards of the two companies increased. Early in 1877 the resignation of Mark J. Stewart from the P P R was reported; Stair was to try to dissuade him. Stewart had always been a protagonist of the G & P P. In March came the resignation of Guthrie himself.

Now the Girvan line was finished: a hard road, heavily graded and curved, its thirty-one miles having cost well over half a million sterling. The Joint Committee was established at last, the P P R appointing the Earl of Galloway and Dougald Maclaurin, of Fernhill, Portpatrick, and leaving the C R to nominate the third member allowed them. Guthrie attended the P P R board meeting on 28th July; it was announced that the new line was about to be opened, and the meeting agreed to Guthrie's request to be allowed to bring traffic into Stranraer station. On 31st, however, a special meeting of Stranraer Town Council approved a petition to the Railway Commissioners in favour of immediate access by the Girvan Company to the station. The P P R were willing for the company's trains to run over their line, but the C R claimed the accommodation at the station was inadequate. The townspeople generally had signed a petition to the same effect. Guthrie told a G & P P meeting in Glasgow that a Working Agreement with the G S W had been completed, and the works at Stranraer station - chiefly sidings and signals - were progressing rapidly, but added that the C R had delayed these works until the last possible moment.

It was intended to open the line for goods on 27th August and for passengers on 1st September. On 16th August, Major-General Hutchinson, the Board of Trade inspector, had said that he saw no objection on grounds of safety to trains of both lines coming into Stranraer, but the C R maintained their objection, and when on 25th the G S W sent two engines down to be ready to start the goods traffic, they were not allowed to pass Challoch Junction. On 6th September, the P P R instructed

McKenzie to ask the C R when the extra works would be ready. On 19th, the Girvan line was opened for passengers as far as New Luce, buses running to and from Stranraer to connect with the trains. Hutchinson made his inspection of the finished works at Stranraer on 27th, and the official opening of the G & P P was on 1st October.

Guthrie used the occasion to deplore "miserable and petty opposition" by the C R and P P R. The C R, he said, had kept the G & P P out of Stranraer because they wanted the whole of the late summer traffic - "the most important part of the year" - to themselves. Now the G & P P would still not be able to get through to Stranraer for some days, and this time it was the fault of the P P R: "some miserable squabble between them and the Caledonian Company about some letter". He was angry with Stair for calling the G& PP "a rival line", and went on to assert that all the way the G & P P had had little local support, but a good deal of local opposition. A lot of the stock had been taken up in Glasgow and Edinburgh and in London, Manchester, Whitehaven and other English towns.

Within a few weeks of the Girvan line opening, the C R's Mr. Ward was proposing reductions in fares on the PPR in view of the lower fares now available between Glasgow and Dunragit, Castle Kennedy and Stranraer via Girvan. The P P R declined, but they were well aware of the quantity of traffic that the much shorter new route was taking from their line. Stair described it as "a great amount". The C R were disturbed, not only because of their interest in the P P R but also as the G S W were in control of the new route. But the G & P P's troubles were far from being over when the trains began running over their line. There is a strong hint of this in the difficulties that arose in connection with providing more new works on the Stranraer Section. Apart from the sidings and signalling already mentioned, block telegraph had been installed on the Section; then, with the increase in traffic, came requests for a passing-place at Castle Kennedy. These led to some farcical manoeuvres. First, the P P R utterly refused; soon after, they agreed to immediate action; then they countermanded their consent because the G & P P would not contribute to the cost; next they threatened to approach the Board of Trade over the matter; then they ordered the work to proceed provided the G S W paid half the cost; more than three years later, and five since the original request had been made, they were still arguing with the G S W about payment, while the loop-line was not in fact made for many years more. There was a similar dispute over further additions to Dunragit station, which were ordered and then deferred because the G & P P refused to pay part of the cost. This subject was complicated by the total destruction by fire of the wooden buildings at Dunragit at the end of 1879. The P P R doubtless showed merely their normal parsimony in these matters; the tight-fistedness of the G & P P, however, was due to serious financial straits.

The fact was that, though the completion of their line had been widely looked forward to as a major improvement in communications in south-west Scotland - which it undoubtedly was - it could not attract the volume of traffic necessary for it to pay its way, especially in view of the very high cost of construction and the unfavourable operation of the Working Agreement with the G S W. In addition to difficulties which sprang from the depression of agriculture and trade, a serious disadvantage was the alternative facilities offered by the steamers from the Clyde along the coast and to the North of Ireland, with their very competitive rates. So the grave difficulties of the G & P P continued, and swiftly approached a crisis. By the summer of 1879, at the request of creditors, the Court of Session had put the company in the hands of a judicial factor. When he took over, their lack of funds had involved them in deep contention with the P P R over the Stranraer Section.

The P P R had already had a prolonged argument with the C R over maintenance of the section. When it was over, Stair dismissed it as an "unfortunate misunderstanding", but it had been taken to both the Railway Commissioners and the Court of Session, no less a person than Richard Moon had offered his services as mediator, and it makes, in fact, a vivid illustration of the chronic mistrust between the two companies. It was settled at a conference in London, one of the conditions being that henceforth the C R would nominate all three of the members previously allowed the P P R on the J C. Then the dispute with the G & P P arose. Their 1872 Act had given this company running powers over the part of the P P R called the Stranraer Section, and also over the line from Stranraer to Portpatrick and the Harbour Branch at Portpatrick, which was named the Portpatrick Section, though the latter was never used by the Girvan Company. The provisions about payment were these:

The G & P P were to pay the P P R a yearly sum, amounting to the interest on half the cost of the purchase of land for and the original construction of the Section. The cost and the rate of interest were to be as agreed between the two companies. Failing agreement they were to be decided by arbitration. In fixing the yearly sum, the state and condition of the Section when the G & P P began to use it were to be taken into consideration.

The two companies were to pay for maintenance of the railway and the stations and works in proportion to the use they had of them. The state and condition they were in when the G & P P began to use them were to be taken into consideration.

If, as a result of increased traffic, it became necessary to enlarge any of the stations, the two companies were to pay the cost in proportions to be agreed between them, or, failing agreement, to be settled by arbitration.

In March 1878, at the instance of the G & P P, the fixing of half the cost of construction of the Stranraer Section was sent to arbitration. The sole arbiter was to be the distinguished engineer, Thomas Bouch. He was to decide the payments due to the P P R in respect of the G & P P's user of Stranraer pier also. A long delay ensued. In March 1880, Stair told the ordinary general meeting of his company that the board were expecting "the final award from Sir Thomas Bouch" daily, but as he said, "No doubt his mind has been much occupied with various matters, particularly the dreadful disaster at the Tay Bridge." Sir Thomas gave his award on 11th June. It covered all the items payable by the G & P P for user of the Stranraer Section under the 1872 Act. Its terms were as follows:

The total cost of land for and the original construction of the Section, regard being had to its condition when the G & P P began to use it on 5th October 1877, was £59,740.17.8. The G & P P should pay the P P R a yearly sum of £1,344.3.4¾, equal to interest at the rate of 4½% per annum on £29,870.8.10 - half the above-mentioned total cost.

The two companies should pay the expense of maintaining the section in the proportions of three-fifths by the PPR and two-fifths by the G&PP

The total cost of station enlargements necessitated by the coming of the Girvan Company was £11,509.4.5½. Each company should pay half - £5,754.12.2¾.

As regards user of Stranraer pier, under the P P R Act of 1877:

The G & P P should pay the P P R £250 yearly, as half the annuity of £500 due from the P P R to Stranraer Town Council.

The cost of acquiring and improving the pier, including the £20,000 debt to the Scottish Provident Institution which the P P R had taken over from the Town Council, was £34,293.17.10. The G & P P should pay the P P R a yearly sum of £771.12.3, equal to interest at the rate of 4½%. per annum on £17,146.18.11 - half this cost.

The two companies should pay the expense of maintaining the pier in the proportions of two-thirds by the P P R and one-third by the G & P P.

The cost of extensions and improvements to the pier, due to increase of traffic or other causes, was £1,235.8.9½. Each company should pay half - £617.14.4¾.

Months went by, and no payment of any kind was forthcoming from the impecunious G & P P. In May 1881, the P P R began an action against them in the Court of Session; by this time they owed the P P R over £10,000. As a result of this action, in February 1882 the G & P P were interdicted from running over the P P R line. With characteristic determination, the Girvan Company kept up a service of a kind by running trains to and from New Luce, but, noble as it was, this alone would not get them out of their difficulties, and that year they introduced three bills in Parliament. The purpose of these was to authorise the sale of the G & P P; to incorporate a new company, the "Stranraer & Girvan", and enable them to buy the G & P P ; and to enable the G & P P to raise more money. The P P R considered that parts of all three bills were prejudicial to their interests and opposed them, jointly with the CR. In the outcome the bills were amalgamated as the G & P P Junction Railway (Arrangement) Act of 1882. The P P R were well-satisfied with this result, which maintained the efrect of the interdict they had obtained in the Court of Session and gave their claim against the G & P P priority over those of other creditors, whereas the original bills would, in their judgment, have set both these matters aside. The Act gave the G & P P power to borrow £30,000 (the G S W had agreed to contribute £20,000 of this), and with it the company intended to pay what they owed the P P R and to buy plant and rolling stock with a view to working their line themselves.

Nothing had been paid the P P R by March 1883, when they declined the G & P P's offer of a mortgage on account of their claim. Thereafter, however, things rapidly improved; a new Working Agreement with the G S W was negotiated in May, and on 1st August the interdict was lifted and the through service to and from Stranraer resumed. In September, the P P R board reported to the shareholders that the Girvan Company had made payment of the sums due, a total of over £12,000. The Girvan Company's directors took charge again, and a brighter prospect gleamed briefly for the ill-fated concern.

NEWTON STEWART STATION

An important development on the P P R during this period was the improvement of Newton Stewart station in connection with the opening of the first stage of the Wigtownshire Railway in March-April 1875. There had always been a passing-place here, with up and down platforms, and a loop line which ran well behind the up platform. Passengers had to cross the main line to get from one platform to another. The W R made a junction with the P P R west of the station. Its coming led to several changes.

In June 1874, "considering that they will derive certain advantages from the Wigtownshire traffic", the P P R agreed to share equally with the W R expenditure not exceeding £4,000 on works at the station. They would lay out all the money required if the W R paid 5% interest on their half. The arrangement was conditional on the C R accepting the new facilities in lieu of any charge to the W R for working expenses or station maintenance. One of the first changes, in October, was the abandonment of the Harbour Branch at Portpatrick and the lifting of the rails, to be used in new sidings at Newton Stewart.

During the following months the back of the up platform was built up, and a new loop put in to serve the additional platform so created, which was to be used by W R passenger trains. The original loop beyond this was lengthened about eighty yards and its use restricted to goods trains, while a new cross-over for up passenger trains approaching the station was put in, below the junction with the W R. These two changes gave more room for goods trains shunting, reducing the risk of collisions by making it hardly ever necessary for them to go on to the main line.

Two signal boxes were erected. There was the west box, north of the junction with the W R; it had twenty-three levers, including four spare, in its interlocking frame, and there were two electric repeaters, one connected with the telegraph room at the station and notifying the signalman when trains bound for Newton Stewart left Kirkcowan or Creetown, while the other was for the distant on the W R line. At the other end of the station was the east box which was not built until some months after the opening of the W R. In July 1875 the P P R authorised Grafton to "take and use at Dromore station the old hand signal taken down at Newton Stewart". Changes to the station buildings included a new waiting room, a veranda on the down platform, a new "passenger shed" on the up platform, where the old veranda had been demolished, and a goods office. In 1878, we read of arrangements for premises at the station for selling "newspapers, refreshments and books".

As there were no through booking facilities to and from the W R, all passengers, except those using only the down P P R trains, had to cross the P P R main line, so it is not surprising that there were soon requests for a bridge. The tale of the footbridge at Newton Stewart station is one of decidedly long-drawn-out preliminaries, punctuated by spells of contention, familiar in the provision of new works on the P P R. At the end of 1877, they agreed to the bridge, the expense to be shared by the W R; the latter offered to pay half, and in March 1878, a plan was submitted. The proposed structure spanned the main line, and also extended over the loops and sidings, leading to the public road a little beyond. The Earl of Stair moved that the P P R pay half the cost of the part over the main line, but not of the rest. The Earl of Galloway, who was chairman of the W R, moved that the plan be adopted as a whole. Galloway's motion got no seconder, and that of Stair was carried. Then nothing was done at all, until at the close of 1879, Grafton raised the matter again and the P P R repeated that they would build a bridge over the main line if the W R would share the cost. Again nothing can have been done, for in March 1880 the P P R had received petitions from the Town Council and people of Newton Stewart. They now quickly obtained plans and estimates, and resolved to build the bridge, the W R paying them 5% per annum interest on half the cost. It is not clear whether or not the sidings were bridged as well as the main line.

In 1883, Grafton approached the P P R about a turn-table for engines at Newton Stewart. The P P R replied that if this was necessary for the proper working of the line, it was for the C R to supply it. It was not supplied; and we shall meet the subject again.

HOUSES AND TRACK

The movement towards providing houses for station-masters and platelayers, which in the last chapter we saw get under way, only to come to a stand in 1868, made leisurely progress again from 1872. The Creetown station-master applied for a house. He probably lived in the village, a hilly three-quarters of a mile from his station. The P P R asked the C R at what stations they were willing that the P P R should build houses, the C R paying interest on the expenditure in lieu of the rent allowances that they made to the station-masters at present. For some time nothing happened; then after a new initiative by Grafton, the P P R agreed to accept 4% per annum interest from the C R on the necessary outlay for houses for station-masters at Newton Stewart, Creetown, Parton and Kirkcowan, and platelayers' cottages at Dromore and New Galloway. Plans were prepared, taking the station-master's house at New Galloway as a model, and tenders received. It was now summer 1875, but at last the work went forward: such progress, however, was too good to be true and the contractor absconded, causing a further delay. The houses and cottages were finished during 1876.

During these years, the state of the permanent way also called for attention. In 1871, the P P R refused to contribute to the cost of relaying the track with heavier rails, but the C R recorded their decision to renew it with 75lb. rails. In 1874, the P P R refused also to contribute to the cost of fish-jointing their line, which the C R now proposed to do for the first time. It is clear, however, that there was cause for concern about the condition of the line. The P P R received a letter about the state of the permanent way from B. C. Nicholson, a prominent shareholder, who was later to succeed David Guthrie on the board. They sent the letter to the C R, who obtained a report on the permanent way from Mr. Woodhouse, of the L NW, and ordered another from their own Mr. Graham. Early in 1875, Graham was instructed to discharge some permanent way inspectors on the P P R, and the C R reported receiving a memorial from "James Ross, late superintendent of works" and an anonymous letter from "a shareholder". The C R expressed a wish to relay the P P R with steel rails and tried twice to induce the P P R to share the expense of steel rails and fish-jointing. Both attempts failed, and for the time being some re-laying was done with iron rails. Steel rails were, in fact, soon used however, and the fish-jointing went ahead, while in 1878 creosoted sleepers were being supplied. Obviously a full-scale programme of track renewal was in hand, and this was still in progress when the P P R ceased to exist as a separate concern in 1885.

THE SERVICE (II)

From the peak of 4¼% in September 1877, the company's dividend declined steadily until, in the black year of commercial depression 1879, it stood at only 2¼%. Recovering with the recovery of trade, it reached 4¼% once more in the prosperous year 1883, diminishing to 3¼% in 1885.

Many people in Galloway continued to believe that, in their quest for commercial viability, the P P R and C R concentrated on the needs of the through traffic and provided only a restricted, inadequate local service. They had good reason for this belief. In the autumn of 1877, when the P P R paid their highest dividend, "A Regular Traveller" complained in the *Free Press* about the "jog-trot system" that local passengers had to accept. The down express in the mornings called regularly at New Galloway, Creetown and Newton Stewart, the up express in the evenings at Newton Stewart and Creetown. There were three slow trains in each direction. The early morning mail train to Stranraer had been withdrawn - leading to a lengthy dispute between P P R and C R over disposal of the £1,000 subsidy paid to the latter under the agreement of 1871 - and the first local train of the day did not reach Stranraer until 11.25 a.m. This was, to quote "A Regular

Traveller", "much too late for many people who have market business of many kinds to attend to", and to make matters worse the last slow train of the day to Castle Douglas left Stranraer as early as 2.50p.m. A passenger carriage was attached to the goods leaving Creetown at noon and timed to reach Stranraer at 2.25. Timings at the intermediate stations were uncertain, and "A Regular Traveller" gave a recent example of this train taking over four hours on its journey to Stranraer. It was, in any case, of little use to people wanting to return the same day, whose only means of getting back, unless they were going to Newton Stewart or Creetown and could wait for the express, was the passenger carriage on the 4.25 goods to Creetown, timed to take nearly three hours. In 1881, in agreeing to a three months' trial of alterations in the service proposed by the C R, the P P R insisted on a market train being run from Creetown to Stranraer. The chief feature of the alterations - commencing 1st June - was an additional down stopping train, leaving Castle Douglas at 12.5p.m. and reaching Stranraer at 2.20. The evening goods, with third-class passenger carriage attached, now left Stranraer at 4.45p.m. to reach Castle Douglas at 9.25; from 1st November it went only to Creetown. The last up stopping train continued to leave Stranraer early in the dayat 2.45p.m. - while the regular calls of the express in the evenings were now Dunragit and Newton Stewart.

In 1877, there were two passenger trains daily from Stranraer to Portpatrick and a passenger carriage was attached to the 8.50a.m. goods, timed to reach Portpatrick at 9.15; three passenger trains daily made the return journey.

Turning to the through service, the performance of the two steamers was improved by alterations made in 1878 in the case of the *Louise* and in 1883 in that of the *Beatrice*. The *Louise* was fitted with new boilers, increasing her nominal horse-power from 200 to 347, while the *Beatrice* was given new boilers and new engines, her nominal horse-power being raised from 200 to 325. The *Beatrice* had been engined by her builders, Harland & Wolff, but her new engines were supplied by D. Rowan & Co., of Glasgow. The subject of a second daily sailing came up occasionally; in 1878 the Steamboat Company suggested a double service daily from July to September. Nothing was done as yet, but there was strong support for the idea on the Irish side of the Channel.

In June 1880, there was mention of a sleeping car on the express trains, presumably an example of the early West Coast Joint Stock, with communal saloons and the berths arranged longitudinally. The West Coast Conference had decreed that up to 4p.m. each day the berths on the up express should be at the disposal of Edward Cotton, manager of the Steamboat Company, in Belfast.

The P P R gave this only their temporary acquiescence; the matter is not referred to again.

"A Regular Traveller" said in his complaint to the *Free Press* that Grafton was quite willing, on notice, to stop the express at minor stations to pick up or set down cross-Channel passengers. There must have been times when, as a result of this, the train was not much of an express. In October 1878, the PPR were considering "facilitating" the up express, being concerned at its missing the Dumfries and Carlisle connections. A year later, however, we meet James Hosack again, complaining at the ordinary general meeting that the up express now called regularly at Dunragit. He had been on the train one night recently and only one passenger had got out at Dunragit; he thought it too bad to stop a train for one person. Criticism of the express service reached a peak when in May 1882, Mr. Stewart, the Steamboat Company's secretary, wrote in very strong terms to McKenzie.

An accelerated service and a reduction in fares, he said, were essential in view of the great improvement about to be made in the Fleetwood - Belfast service of the L N W and Lancashire & Yorkshire Companies. The service between Carlisle and Stranraer was far too dilatory; with the present London-Carlisle trains, through passengers ought to be in Belfast much sooner, and unless this was provided for his directors feared the collapse of the Larne route. Complaints were many and loud. Now that an alternative route to the south was available, annoyance at being taken round via Lockerbie was leading many regular patrons to change at Dumfries and go on by the Midland route, or to stop using the Larne route altogether. Many business men in Belfast strongly favoured the Larne route for the Mail Service, but there was general agreement among them that the present train service in Scotland ruled out the use of the route for the London mails. Cotton followed up Stewart's complaints with a letter to James Thompson, the CR general manager, in which he proposed this revised timetable:

| CARLISLE TO BELFAST | | G.M.T. | BELFAST to CARLISLE | | Irish Time |
|---|---|---|---|---|---|
| Carlisle | dep. | 5.15 a.m.* | Belfast | dep. | 4.30 p.m. |
| Castle Douglas | arr. | 6.45 a.m. | Larne | dep. | 5.20 p.m. |
| Stranraer | arr. | 8.15 a.m. | | | |
| | | | | | G.M.T. |
| Stranraer | dep. | 8.20 a.m. | Stranraer | arr. | 8.25 p.m. |
| | | Irish Time | Stranraer | dep. | 9.00 p.m. |
| Larne | arr. | 10.35 a.m. | Castle Douglas | arr. | 10.30 p.m. |
| Larne | dep. | 10.45 a.m. | Carlisle | arr. | 12.5 a.m. |
| Belfast | arr. | 11.30 a.m. | | | |

* After arrival of L N W and Midland trains.

Cotton made it clear that he was assuming the provision by the G S W of a special service between Carlisle and Castle Douglas via Annan. "I am not aware", he said, "whether you can work out this time-table via Lockerbie".

# Rails to Portpatrick

On the subject of fares, Cotton gave the following comparison of the charges by the Fleetwood and Greenore routes and by the Larne route:

| BELFAST TO LONDON | Single | | | Return | | |
|---|---|---|---|---|---|---|
|  | 1 | 2 | 3 | 1 | 2 | 3 |
| Via Fleetwood or Greenore | 45/- | 35/- | 21/- | 75/- | 58/6 | 35/6 |
| Via Larne | 58/6 | 45/- | 27/6 | 100/- | 75/- | 55/- |

He went on to quote the fares from London to Dumfries:

| Single | | | Return | | |
|---|---|---|---|---|---|
| 1 | 2 | 3 | 1 | 2 | 3 |
| 46/- | 36/2 | 26/11½ | 90/2 | 70/10 | 53/- |

He continued:

"If you make the return fares about the same as Dumfries, there would only be a temptation for passengers going beyond Dumfries to take Belfast tickets; and I believe such an arrangement could be made to check the tickets on board the steamers, so that you could be in a great measure protected from paying us for passengers we do not carry. I think the 1 and 2 single fares could be higher than Dumfries."

In his reply, Thompson was adamant that the Lockerbie route must be kept; he offered, however, this accelerated service, which, he said, was the best possible, to commence 1st July:

| | | | | | | |
|---|---|---|---|---|---|---|
| London (Euston) | dep. | 9.00 p.m. | Belfast (Irish time) | dep. | 4.15 p.m. |
| Carlisle | arr. | 5.00 a.m. | Larne (Irish time) | arr | 5.5 p.m. |
| | dep. | 5.15 a.m. | Stranraer Harbour | arr. | 8.15 p.m. |
| Lockerbie | arr. | 5.48 a.m. | | dep. | 8.40 p.m. |
| | dep. | 5.55 a.m. | Castle Douglas | arr. | 10.14 p.m. |
| Dumfries | arr. | 6.25 a.m. | | dep. | 10.17 p.m. |
| | dep. | 6.30 a.m. | Dumfries | arr. | 10.52 p.m. |
| Castle Douglas | arr. | 7.5 a.m. | | dep. | 10.57 p.m. |
| | dep. | 7.10 a.m. | Lockerbie | arr. | 11.25 p.m. |
| Stranraer Harbour | arr. | 8.55 a.m. | | dep. | 11.32 p.m. |
| | dep. | 9.5 a.m. | Carlisle | arr. | 12.8 a.m. |
| Larne (Irish time) | arr. | 11.25 a.m. | | dep. | 12.15 a.m. |
| Belfast (Irish time) | arr. | 12.15 p.m. | London (Euston) | arr. | 8.0 a.m. |

The C R would have no objection to fares being "somewhat reduced", and Thompson invited Cotton to consult the other interested parties and inform him what reduction would be acceptable to them. The P P R gave their approval to the faster service, though with a hint that they could have wished a greater acceleration; and they made a condition that the slow train now leaving Dumfries at 9.30a.m. be altered to depart at 11.15. They were willing to concur in any reduction of fares acceptable to the other companies concerned.

In the outcome, the only change in the express service taking effect from Ist July was the departure from Belfast at 4.15 p.m. instead of 4.00 - and by the end of the year it was back to 4.00 again. The matter of fares is not referred to again. At ordinary general meetings in 1882-3 Hosack again criticised the through service, urging the need for closer relations with the Midland Company to develop the alternative route to the south. He mentioned passengers from the south arriving at Dumfries by G S W train having to wait 11 hours to continue their journey into Galloway, complained about the inconvenience of being taken round by Lockerbie by the C R, and argued also that through passengers for north-east England were inconvenienced by having to stay overnight in Carlisle because there was no train to take them on to Newcastle. This, he claimed, was hindering the development of an important branch of the P P R's passenger traffic. Stair replied that the North Eastern Company had been applied to, but had declined to put on a connecting Carlisle to Newcastle train. He played down the inconvenience of the Lockerbie route, and wlcomed Sir William Wallace, Bart., of Lochryan's account of how one night recently the up boat train from Stranraer had been two hours later in starting and had missed the connection at Carlisle, but a special express had been put on to take the passengers "all the way to London". This, said Stair, showed "the anxiety of the Caledonian Company to meet the requirements of the route".

Stair's comment was doubtless true; but the solicitude of the C R and L N W was probably due partly also to their consciousness that they no longer held a monopoly of railway transport between Glasgow, Carlisle and London. The competition of the Fleetwood route from London to Belfast, too, was formidable - even taking fully into account the important advantage of the Stranraer-Larne route in the shortness of the sea crossing - and the alarm of the Steamboat Company at the impending acceleration of the service via Fleetwood is very understandable. Though their proposed reduction of return fares is one indication of their alarm, the fact that the Belfast fares via Larne were already so little above the Dumfries fares shows the vigour of the competition for the traffic across the narrow seas. It is likely, however, that the Steamboat Company's attitude reflected also the influence of the G S W-Midland alliance. That alliance was very close; the companies had come near amalgamation in 1872, and they were soon to have the same chairman. By now their alternative Glasgow-London service was established, and their competition with the West Coast route made it inevitable that they should seek a larger share in the traffic by the short sea passage. They had already, of course, a foothold at Stranraer, through the G & P P.

The Lockerbie route between Dumfries and Carlisle was indisputably devious and time-consuming; nevertheless, the Steamboat Company's emphasis on the route's share of Larne for the "dilatory" Scottish train service is noteworthy. Cotton's statement, when referring in his letter to Thompson to "a special service" via Annan, that he had "every reason to think the G & S W Co. would agree to work such a service", is significant; as also is Thompson's exaggerated language in reply, "The proposal to practically close our own route via Lockerbie we cannot for a moment entertain". Both parties showed a lively awareness that large conflicting interests were involved.

The C R and L N W had hitherto resisted attempted encroachment by the rival alliance so far as possible. An application for through bookings by the P P R and short sea passage and the Midland route had been made in 1876, when the M R's line from Carlisle opened, but they were not granted until 1880. There were no through carriages, and connections at Dumfries with Galloway trains could be very poor. It was certain, however, that there would be public demand for better facilities. The G S W had the direct route to Carlisle via Annan; the M R route to London served numerous important places not directly accessible by the L N W, and though the journey to the capital itself was slower than by the West Coast route the M R were renowned for their attention to passenger comfort. Hosack, connected with the Lancaster & Carlisle and apparently likely therefore to favour the L N W cause, expressed to the P P R meeting in September 1882 his regret that the P P R did not have stronger links with the M R and do more to develop the alternative route to London. "In regard to a new lease", he added, "I think we must look something towards the Midland Co.".

He was hinting, obviously, at the fact that the P P R's Working Agreement with the C R would soon have run its course: a fact which naturally considerably increased the interest taken by the two great Anglo-Scottish alliances in the future of the P P R and the short sea passage. The manner in which this aspect of their rivalry was ultimately resolved could hardly have been foreseen; few would have conceived it possible. We shall see presently how this highly unlikely solution came about. First, however, we must trace the story of the Wigtownshire Railway.

# Rails to Portpatrick

SECTION TWO

# THE WIGTOWNSHIRE RAILWAY

**CHAPTER SEVEN**

"Wheatley's Railway"

THE extension of railway communication into the Machars (i.e. plains) of Wigtownshire," wrote M. McL. Harper, "has, by developing the "resources of this rich agricultural district, tended greatly to its prosperity and proved a great boon to the inhabitants". This notable development had begun earlier, by means of steamers plying between the little ports of the Machars - or Lower Wigtownshire as it is also known - and various destinations, the great cities of Glasgow and Liverpool in particular. Since long before this, the greater part of traffic to and from the district had gone by sea, and the inhabitants of the ports had very strong seafaring traditions. The steamship, in conjunction with the rapid growth of industry and industrial populations elsewhere and the spread of railways in those areas, made possible a big expansion of this sea-going trade. The best-known, and best-loved, steamboat in the district was the *Countess of Galloway*, the property of local owners, the Galloway Steam Navigation Company, and successor to an earlier boat of the same name that began sailing to and from Liverpool in 1835. A report in the *Free Press* in September 1875 gives a forceful impression of the impact which this service had made on farming in the region:

"Formerly, the rearing of stock for stall-feeding purposes was either altogether unknown, or was only in its infancy, and the present writer can very well remember the time when the entire fat stock of his own immediate locality consisted of a solitary pig, in addition, it might be, to an unhealthy or superannuated cow. But the neighbourhood (of the Isle of Whithorn) stands pre-eminent, even in Wigtownshire, for the number and quality of fat stock reared, and forwarded by steamer to the English markets."

In April of the same year the paper had reported an arrival of the *Countess* at Garliestown:

"... from Liverpool with one of the heaviest cargoes she has landed here for years past - manures, feeding stuffs and merchants' goods - and bringing also several passengers. She left on her return to Liverpool with 72 head of cattle, 200 sheep, 20 pigs, and upwards of 1,200 gallons of Bladnoch whisky for Australia, and a number of passengers. She was to call at the Isle (of Whithorn) to complete her cargo".

In the year ending 30th June 1875, the steamer earned a total of £6,932.17.3, in respect of passengers, livestock and goods; while the less frequent Glasgow steamer earned up to £2,500 per annum about this time. In 1873 the tonnage of the steamboats cleared at Wigtown for Wigtown, Garliestown and the Isle totalled 12,818. The introduction of a railway in the Machars would radically change all this; but the success of the steamers, and the benefits they had given the area, made the people the more aware of the even greater advantages that a railway would bring. It is not surprising, therefore, that when the P P R line was built, demands arose for a line to serve the Lower District of the Shire, by-passed by the P P R as it hurried to the west coast.

In February 1862, Lord Dalrymple, the P P R chairman, with George Guthrie, Ingram, and Blyth, engineer of the P P R, visited the country between Newton Stewart and Sorbie to see if the P P R could support the local proprietors in building a railway there. Sir William Dunbar was warmly interested, but unable to be present because of his Parliamentary duties. At the next P P R half-yearly meeting, Dalrymple expressed the hope that the line would be built, from Newton Stewart to Wigtown and Whithorn, saying that it would run through some of the richest parts of the county and would also prove an important feeder to the P P R.

A meeting took place at Wigtown in January 1863, when Blyth estimated the cost of the line from Newton Stewart as £20,000 to Wigtown, £60,000 to Sorbie and £85,000 to Whithorn. Dalrymple and Dunbar spoke strongly in favour of the line, while R. Vans Agnew, of Barnbarroch, expressed the rash conviction that "the undertaking would pay extremely well". Wigtown Town Council were willing to contribute £2,000. A different note was struck by Stair H. Stewart, of Physgill, the county convener, who had been one of the promoters of the P P R. He was influenced by the fact that the P P R had not yet paid; he thought the time inopportune for the new line, and counselled delay. He agreed, however, to join the provisional committee now set up, which included also the Earl of Galloway, Dalrymple, Dunbar and Vans Agnew. Later in the year a survey of the proposed route was made by Thomas Bouch. The matter then drops from our view, to reappear during the period of unexampled prosperity around 1870.

On the 8th September 1871, there was a public meeting at Newton Stewart, chaired by Lord Garlies, son and heir to the Earl of Galloway and M.P. for the county, and including the Earl of Stair, Colonel McDouall of Logan, and R. H. Johnston Stewart of Physgill among the other local notables present. A large committee was appointed, and met on 16th to discuss the route to be taken by what was described in the official minutes as the "Machars Railway". Garlies moved in favour of a line from Newton Stewart running to the west of the Barrhill, thence to Wigtown and passing to the east of the town. The Town Council had advocated this route when offering their £2,000 in 1863. Beyond Wigtown, Garlies suggested a route by Kirkinner, thence east of North Balfern farmhouse to Sorbie; from here the line would run to within three-quarters of a mile of Garliestown and then by Broughton Skeog to Whithorn.

# Rails to Portpatrick

This resolution, however, was opposed by Sir W. Dunbar. Back in 1862, a scheme had been mentioned for a line into the Machars that would branch from the PPR at Kirkcowan, and miss the county town of Wigtown altogether, but the P P R directors were reported as considering this "out of the question". A similar suggestion at the meeting in 1863, by a resident of Portwilliam, had been greeted with strong disapproval. Now, however, Dunbar moved for a route from Kirkcowan, south by Whauphill to Sorbie, Garliestown and Whithorn. Wigtown, he proposed, should be served by a separate branch, either from Newton Stewart station or from Nether Barr, on the P P R about one-and-a-quarter miles south, whichever would be cheaper. "The scheme propounded (in Garlies' resolution)", he claimed, "was not such as would serve the best interests of the public, least of all reconcile the private interests within the county". It was very important to provide direct communication with Glasgow and Ayrshire: in thinking of this in terms of a route via Kirkcowan, Dunbar was clearly anticipating the carrying out of the G & P P scheme. He went on: If the Portpatrick line had been constructed with a spur to Wigtown - as undoubtedly would have been the case if they had had money to accomplish it, inasmuch as it is the county town - he did not hesitate to say the general feeling would have been in favour of carrying a line from Kirkcowan by Culmalzie and Whauphill to Sorbie, and thence to Whithorn.

Lord Stair disagreed with him: he could not see it would pay to send a branch line to Wigtown, or to take a railway through a barren and uncultivated country, rather than through a cultivated one.

Dunbar's motion was heavily defeated, but he then moved an amendment to Garlies' resolution: the line was to go by Wigtown, but on leaving Kirkinner was to continue to Sorbie, not by North Balfern but by Whauphill "as surveyed by Mr. Bouch in 1863". This was unanimously agreed to. Sub-committees were appointed for each parish in the district to collect subscriptions and report to the next meeting.

Dunbar returned to battle over the route of the line at a second public meeting held in Newton Stewart on 6th October, when he proposed that it run to the west of Wigtown, about a mile west of Kirkinner, and so to Whauphill. Not surprisingly, he was again gravely defeated. A new committee was appointed, and entrusted with the promotion of a bill in Parliament. Garlies was chairman, having been proposed by Vans Agnew, and Vans Agnew vice-chairman, having been proposed by Garlies; the interim secretary was Will McClure, a Wigtown solicitor and law and political agent to the Earl of Galloway. J. H. Tolme, London, was engaged as consulting engineer. At its first meeting, the committee unanimously agreed to adopt the name "The Wigtownshire Railway Company."

From the first the committee showed an intense concern for economy. Tolme informed them that by reducing his estimate for stations and taking land for only a single line the total cost would not be more than £90,000; they "impressed upon him the importance of keeping down the cost as much as possible". Their bill provided for a capital of £96,000 in £10 shares. When £60,000 had been raised, they might borrow £20,000, and when the whole sum had been subscribed they might borrow £12,000 more. The bill authorised construction of a tramway, using the public roads and with locomotives forbidden, from their line near Garliestown to the harbour there. This provoked objections from the Burgh Council of Wigtown, who could hardly be expected to favour this proposed link with a harbour so superior to their own. The committee soothed them with the assurance that the tramway, which had been recommended by Bouch in 1863, was included in the bill solely to avoid the expense of a separate application at some future time, the powers sought being merely permissive. The Garliestown Harbour Committee, however, offered a subscription of £400 on condition that the tramway was made "to and along" the harbour. None of the subscription would be paid until the decision was taken to build the tramway.

The Bill became law on the 18th July 1872. The first meeting of directors of the new company was on 27th September. They were Lord Garlies (chairman), R. H. Johnston Stewart of Physgill (vice-chairman), the Earl of Stair, R. Vans Agnew, M.P., J. Palmer Palmer, James McLean and James Drew. McClure was confirmed in office as secretary, at a salary of £150 per annum. McLean, a solicitor and banker at Wigtown, and Drew, a Whithorn solicitor and Chamberlain to the Earl of Galloway, were very active members of the board throughout the company's existence. In their report to the company's first ordinary general meeting, the, board stated that there had been no opposition from the proprietors, tenants or occupiers of land; as yet, however, less than half the capital had been subscribed, mostly by "parties locally interested", and the directors, in urging the shareholders to co-operate further, assured them that they were "confident that if the whole capital were subscribed the line could be so speedily and economically constructed as to be certain to prove remunerative".

By April 1873, the board were in a position to let the contract for construction of the line from Newton Stewart as far as the neighbourhood of Sorbie, over 13 miles. The contractor was John Granger, of Aberdeen. The word 'Machars', meaning 'plains', can be misleading as a description of Lower Wigtownshire, much of which is undulating ground as a glance at the gradient diagram of the W R (Fig. 7) will suggest, with some rich agricultural land certainly, but some stony, barren places, too. However, the only major obstacle on Granger's contract was the River Bladnoch, south of Wigtown. Between Newton Stewart and Wigtown the going was straightforward. Granger broke ground about 20th August at Barbuchany, near Newton Stewart station. Near Mains of Penninghame, and on the Moss of Cree, near Carsegowan, he was soon reported to be making vigorous progress. In January a start was made with laying the permanent way, and by July 1874, except for Wigtown station and the junction at Newton Stewart, previously described, the Newton Stewart to Wigtown section was ready for inspection.

The siting of Wigtown station had caused some debate. The W R's resident engineer, Robert Johnson, had first suggested the Geddesland, at the north end of the town, as placing the station farther south, and near the port, threatened to involve the expense of making the necessary works in a rock cutting. Investigation revealed, however, that there was much less rock than he had feared, and a comparison of costs indicated that the station be built at Maitland, "in close proximity to the port and more accessible to Bladenoch and the country around". He had measured the ground from the Market Cross to the site at Maitland - 946 yards. The difference of level between the station platform and the Cross would be 93 feet, giving an average inclination of approach to the town of 1 in 30. From the Cross to the Geddesland site was 682 yards. The difference of level would be 97 feet, and the average inclination of approach to the town 1 in 21. After considering Johnson's report and viewing the ground themselves, the directors gave their unanimous approval to the Maitland site. In their hurry to open the section, they ordered temporary buildings of timber with slated roofs, but soon after this they authorised the erection of permanent buildings of stone. They had hoped to set traffic moving by 1st September, but serious difficulties arose in their attempts to make arrangements for the working of their line.

The obvious direction for them to turn for this purpose was towards the C R, and they had lost no time in doing so, obtaining from the C R in reply, in September 1871, the assurance that they would be prepared to work the W R so long as they worked the P P R also, and that they would do it at cost price. Naturally, the C R were extremely wary of incurring financial loss through the W R after their decidedly unprofitable experience of the P P R, while the W R had even more cause for parsimony than the P P R. It is hardly surprising, therefore, that lengthy negotiations followed this superficially promising beginning. The W R thought that cost price might prove more than it was advisable for them to undertake to pay for the working of their line, and they sought therefore to limit their commitment to certain agreed percentages of the gross receipts. At first, in April 1873, it seemed that the C R were prepared to accept these terms, though with strong misgivings. Their general manager, Smithells, assured Galloway (Lord Garlies had at this time just succeeded his father as Earl) that his directors "desire that the railway should be made". Negotiations continued for some months, however, about the sliding-scale of percentages of their gross receipts that the W R wanted. In November the W R were accepting the latest C R terms, but in February 1874 they were declaring the C R terms "objectionable" and asking Galloway and Ingram to seek a revision. Stair had retired from the W R board the previous year, nominating Ingram his successor. Ingram, though life was ebbing, shouldered the additional task, and there is abundant evidence in the records of the value placed by the W R on his experience and judgment.

In July, the W R announced their acceptance of the terms which had appeared so nearly agreed to in April 1873, though protesting at the illiberality of the C R. They had almost decided to work their line themselves; but, wrote McClure to Smithells:

"The disadvantage of such a course would be the risk of maintaining such an amicable relationship with your board as they would desire, and which should be for the interest as well of the greater as of the lesser company."

The C R were to work the line at cost price during the remainder of their Working Agreement with the P P R, provided the W R did not have to pay more than the agreed percentages of the gross traffic receipts. The upper limitt of the scale was to be 80% when the gross traffic receipts were less than £5 per mile per week. and the lower limit 50% when the gross traffic receipts were between £50 and £60 per mile per week -although the actual cost to the C R might be more.

Next, McClure was urging Smithells to send a draft agreement for the W R to consider, with a view to opening their line to Wigtown not later than 1st September. He added that the Board of Trade had agreed that turntables might be dispensed with at Newton Stewart and Wigtown if the traffic was worked by a tank engine, and inquired whether, should the W R approve the draft agreement, the C R would be prepared to work the line with a tank engine. A few days later, he said the W R proposed working the line with a tank engine only until the line was completed, when they would provide turntables at the termini (i.e., of course, Newton Stewart and Whithorn) unless they were dispensed with unconditionally by the Board of Trade. To J. H. Tolme, McClure wrote that the C R would not bind themselves to work the line with a tank engine at all times; evidently they wanted to be free to use "an ordinary engine and tender" if the tank locomotive broke down, or was otherwise unavailable. The Board of Trade agreed to this, and now - the end of August - McClure wrote to Smithells with a very urgent request for the draft agreement. But a new difficulty had arisen.

On 15th August, McClure wrote to Smithells that the W R would require a stipulation in the Working Agreement making the C R responsible for all loss or damage "occasioned by defects or insufficiency of plant furnished by you or through the negligence, carelessness, culpability or want of skill in your servants". The W R would be responsible for any loss or damage "occasioned by accidents arising from any other cause". "My board", he went on, "feel confident that yours will see the reasonableness of the above limitation as your board will have the selection and control of the servants and plant". To this Smithells sent a reply which, so McClure wrote to Drew on 19th, "leaves us no hope of any concessions from the Caledonian Company as to liability for accidents".

McClure wrote again to Smithells on 26th:

"I have today submitted to my directors your letter of the 18th and, as they are very desirous the working of this line should be commenced as early as possible, they desire me to say they are disposed to give up the limitation of liability stipulated for in my letter of 15th and to consent to your company working this line upon the principle of cost price as defined in your letter of the 11th instant. Now that the limitation of liability proposed by them is to be waived, my directors, of course, understand a clause will be inserted in the agreement under which your company will be bound on a well-founded complaint by this company or their officers to remove any inefficient or objectionable servant and to remedy any defect or insufficiency in the plant supplied by your company for the working of this line."

To such a clause, however, the C R would not consent, and the W R had to accept from them a draft agreement leaving it out. On 16th September, McClure wrote to Smithells:

"The proposed heads of agreement are in most of their stipulations so onerous for this company and several of them are of so unusual a character - as, for instance, the condition that we shall be responsible (though deprived of all control) for the consequences of accidents arising from the default of the servants or plant of the working company - that my directors have deemed it incumbent upon them carefully and seriously to consider the course which it will be their duty to pursue.

"The conclusion at which they have arrived, with much regret, is that they cannot, with a reasonable regard to the interest of their constituents, accept your terms.

"My directors are now of opinion that your board do not think it will be in any way to the advantage of your company to come under an agreement to work the Wigtownshire line, and that they have therefore no alternative but to look elsewhere for the means of working it - a course of proceeding to which they presume your company can have no objection."

The C R replied, McClure informed Drew on 24th, "in the terms anticipated". Such was the ignominious end to the story of the W R's protracted attempt to induce the C R to work their little line. They now applied to the C R for their consent to Grafton, traffic superintendent on the P P R, giving his services to the W R as their traffic manager also. They proposed a salary of £60 per annum. "Our line is a short one and the amount of immediate expected traffic not large." The C R consented, but the matter was by no means settled without friction; the W R naturally wanted to pay Grafton his salary direct, but the C R insisted that it be paid through them, and got their way. Grafton's appointment took effect from 1st January 1875. In view of the arrangements that were eventually made for working the W R, his task would never be a demanding one, and at the end of 1878 his salary was reduced to £40, "now that the duties are so much lighter".

It now seemed that the W R would have to be prepared to work their line themselves, and they contemplated opening it with only two trains each way daily. Towards the end of 1874 they resolved to buy plant: one or two tank engines, six passenger carriages, one "goods break", and ten goods wagons. They consulted several leading traffic managers and locomotive superintendents, all of whom evidently counselled them to buy new engines and carriages. Among the experts so consulted was Alex. Walker, former locomotive superintendent on the P P R and now with the Cambrian Railways; he specially recommended Beyer, Peacock engines. Walker obviously did a good deal for the W R at this stage, for they subsequently voted him £21 "for trouble and outlay inspecting and advising board as to purchase of rolling stock". Despite the advice received, with their characteristic financial stringency the W R sought to hire engines, getting no offers, however; they were willing to consider "a reasonable offer" of all the plant at a fixed rent.

Meanwhile, the line was being extended, south from Wigtown to Sorbie. In June 1873, in a letter to H. B. Dewar, W S, Edinburgh, McClure had outlined the advantages the railway would bring to the Barnbarroch Estate, the property of R. Vans Agnew, one of the company's directors, which the extension to Sorbie would serve:

"I think you noted in reference to Barnbarroch Estate in Kirkinner Parish that the tenants at present cart most of their coal, lime and artificial manures from Wigtown harbour, and ship most of their grain and other produce there, and that it is a distance to none of them of less than three and to most of them of four to six miles. On the Wigtownshire line these tenants will mostly, if not all of them, have a station within two miles of their steading, and will, in consequence, be able to work their farms with fewer horses and at less expense otherwise, an advantage the proprietor will share in the shape of increased rental at the expiration of current leases."

The River Bladnoch was crossed by a low-level lattice-girder viaduct, with two 69 feet spans and a centre pier of whinstone. Considerable extra expense was caused by the need to erect cofferdams so as to get in the foundations at 15 feet below the river, with a steam pump to keep them dry, and additional masonry. Just beyond the viaduct was Bladnoch siding, provided at the request of the shareholders of the district, who claimed to have been promised it when Sir William Dunbar advocated that the railway pass to the west of Wigtown. The signalling here, as at the station built later at Garliestown village, was by Tweedy & Company, of Carlisle; elsewhere on the W R it was by Saxby & Farmer.

In December 1874, a special meeting authorised the company, under their Act, to borrow up to £20,000. The whole of this had been raised, at 4½%, by the end of March. Among the mortgagees was George Linton, capitalist station-master of New Galloway, who lent £100. The company's borrowing powers could now be used because a new contribution of £7,000 by the Earl of Galloway brought their share capital to a total of over £60,000. People blamed others, wrote McClure to Galloway this month, "for the railway not reaching Whithorn at this time, but all I have heard speak on the subject acknowledge your lordship has done your part most handsomely". The £7,000 was for the farther extension of the line to Garliestown. On the 22nd December, Granger began operations on this section, at Low Blair and Inch.

Among the visitors to the district at the New Year came a distinguished railwayman who, during the next few years, was to make himself not only well-known, but regarded with great esteem and affection, in this area, where as yet he was a total stranger. This visitor was Thomas Wheatley, a Yorkshireman who had become locomotive superintendent of the North British Railway in the 1860s and done very good work in that capacity. He had recently, however, been ejected on account of his misappropriations. He had replied to the W R's advertisement for plant, surprising them, however, with the suggestion that he might not only supply plant, but work the line for them on terms to be arranged. McClure invited him to come to see him and Johnson, the resident engineer, and subsequently wrote to Galloway, "I am glad to say that he, though a stranger in this district, has formed a good opinion as to the line and prospective traffic."Wheatley expressed hopes of opening to Wigtown on 1st February, and two influential voices, those of Drew and Ingram, were raised in his behalf. His formal offer to the W R board was dated from his home, near Glasgow, on 7th January, 1875. He was willing to supply plant and materials and to work and maintain the railway for five years from its date of opening, for 65% of the gross receipts:

"No doubt, for some time after the opening of the railway the traffic will be light, and the expenses, so far as I am concerned, very heavy, and I am sure you will consider my offer quite reasonable when you take all this into consideration ... I have every confidence that should I take the matter in hand, with the attention and energy I give to it, you would have every satisfaction and good pecuniary results therefrom."

The W R directors could not, of course, ignore Wheatley's ejection by the NB: that ejection, however, had been reluctant, and the N B board had no wish to obstruct Wheatley in his new venture, so that the W R were soon well enough satisfied with his credentials to invite him and his son, W. T. Wheatley, to a meeting at Newton Stewart on 21st January, where good progress was made towards a formal agreement. Such an agreement, on the basis Wheatley had proposed in his offer of 7th January, for five years from 31st July, was sealed on 22nd March. By that date, the line as far as Wigtown was already open for goods.

On the 20th February, McClure wrote urgently to Wheatley in Glasgow:

"Mr. McClelland, of Bladnoch distillery, is about to order his stock of coals, and if assured by Tuesday first that the first of them could get over our rails he would, instead of bringing them by sea, give us the benefit by ordering them to be forwarded by rail at the rate of 20 or 30 tons per week until his stock be made up."

On the 25th he wrote to James Gordon, seedsman, Castle Douglas:

"The lessee of our railway telegraphs 'an engine will leave Glasgow early on Monday morning and we shall contrive if possible to commence on Tuesday morning'. For goods traffic."

# Rails to Portpatrick

Tuesday would be 2nd March. Meanwhile, Granger undertook to have a water tank in operation at Wigtown; the C R, by referring to the incomplete state of the alterations at Newton Stewart, roused suspicions of "throwing further obstacles in the way of our opening"; and Wheatley arrived in Newton Stewart, taking up residence at the Crown Hotel.

On Monday, March lst, there duly followed the promised locomotive, under its own steam, from Glasgow, with driver David Stirling and fireman James Pirie, who were to work on the W R. Bought by Wheatley from the N B, it was a 2-2-2 well tank engine, with 5 feet 6 inch driving-wheels, built at the N B's St. Margaret's works in 1856. Painted W R green, it became the company's locomotive No. 1. Next day, leaving Newton Stewart at 12.10 p.m., it hauled to Wigtown a C R carriage in which rode McClure, Granger, Johnson and Wheatley, making an inspection of the line. Twenty-five stoppages were made over the seven miles, and time taken to lock the gates at the level crossings. The tiny train reached Wigtown station at 1.30 p.m., welcomed by a large crowd of cheering spectators. Its return to Newton Stewart was accomplished in under 20 minutes. The line was opened to goods traffic on Wednesday, March 3rd.

Preparations for the opening to passengers were now pressed forward. Some second-hand four-wheeled carriages were obtained. Fares were decided at 1½d. per mile (with no odd half-pennies) third class, except by the Parliamentary trains, and 2d. per mile first class.; while return tickets "for the following the day of issue" were to be available by all trains at 1d. per mile third class and 2d. per mile first class. Third class season tickets were introduced at 10 guineas per annum and 5 guineas for six months. The opening took place on 7th April. The service was of four trains in each direction every weekday, one being a goods with a third class passenger carriage attached. There now arrived engine No. 2 of the WR: this was an 0-4-2 pannier tank bought by Wheatley from the N B; it had been built by R. & W. Hawthorn as a tender engine in 1848 and rebuilt by the N B in 1870.

On 9th April, McClure wrote to Wheatley:

"I am instructed by my board to say that they are satisfied with engine No. 1 and with the coaching stock placed by you upon the line, but that they must express their dissatisfaction with engine No. 2 in so far that while it might suit you for the working it is not such an engine as the directors could undertake to take over at the termination of the Working Agreement in terms of clause 18. I have no doubt you will see the reasonableness of this objection to engine No. 2, and if you wish to retain it for the working you will please send me a holograph letter stating that notwithstanding this engine may be in use upon the railway at the termination of the agreement, the company shall not be bound by clause 18 to take it over at valuation.

"My directors, while expressing their present satisfaction with engine No. 1 and the carriages, and proposing the above middle course as to engine No. 2, reserve intact their right under clause 18 to object hereafter to any of the rolling stock which they may discover to be defective or insufficient."

About two miles north of Wigtown the railway crossed on the level the road leading to the farm of Carslae. Mr. McClelland, of nearby Glenturk, asked the company to build a house for a gatekeeper beside the crossing. They replied that for the time being they would pay "a small sum, say £1 or so, annually" to the cottar in the nearest house to the crossing "for attending to open the gates for parties going to Carslae on business". In May it was decided to build wooden platforms at Causewayend and Mains (of Penninghame), where the 10.20 a.m. and 4.20 p.m. trains would call on Fridays - Newton Stewart market day. In June it was agreed that the first and the last up and down trains would call daily. The fares to and from Newton Stewart and Wigtown were to be 6d. single and 9d. return, third class. A goods siding was authorised at Causewayend, and also a water tank. The latter cost the W R £111, and was the result of a dispute with the P P R over the use of the supply at Newton Stewart.

At mid-May the district received a visit from the C R's Mr. Smithells. Though his stay was very brief, he assured McClure that he had much enjoyed it, and that he "had no idea Wigtown was such a pretty little place". McClure was pleased to be able to show him that over 170 passengers had been booked at Wigtown station that morning. The traffic reached a notable peak on 25th June, the day of Newton Stewart horse fair, when "Mr. Wheatley found his own seven carriages insufficient, and had to borrow three third classes from the Portpatrick Company".

Meanwhile, construction south of Wigtown was going forward. In March, Johnson reported that progress to Sorbie was very good; Bladnoch viaduct was completed, and a start was about to be made with the station buildings at Kirkinner, Whauphill and Sorbie. About half the permanent way was laid. On the extension to Garliestown, the works were light, and progressing well. Some additional expense was incurred in excavating the sites for the station yards, owing to the high proportion of rock. The station buildings, called temporary, were to be "of the most economical description": "Outside lining and sleepers spruce, corner posts larch, lining on outside walls and ceilings of ladies' waiting-room and booking-office white pine, and stuffed with sawdust, and all other timber foreign, no floor in shed." Garliestown station, on a slope looking towards the extensive policies of the Earl of Galloway, was to be of stone. In September, when it was still under construction, a contributor to the *Free Press* commented: "We observed the buildings have the appearance of being the neatest, most comfortable, and most expensive station on the line, considering its proximity of Galloway House *cela va sans dire*."

The line was opened to Garliestown on 2nd August. A new type of train staff was now introduced on the W R, designed, according to the *Free Press*, by Wheatley, on the original suggestion of Mr. Stewart, the Newton Stewart station-master. On the 20th June of the previous year, 1874, there had been a serious collision on the then single line west of Dalbeattie between a ballast train which had been pushed by its locomotive from Dumfries, had obtained at Dalbeattie the staff for the section to Castle Douglas and which at the time of the accident was returning from the ballast-pit to Dalbeattie, and a west-bound goods which it should have crossed at Dalbeattie but which had instead been allowed to continue into the section, with a ticket issued from a book that had not been in the box at all. The driver of the ballast train and the fireman of the goods died as a result of the collision. The new staff used on the W R was designed to prevent the kind of abuse of staff-and-ticket working that had produced these tragic consequences. It was described as "more in the form of a small case with a locked compartment at each end in which the tickets for each direction are kept. When it is gone the tickets are away also, and risk of accident is much lessened. It has a handle to be carried by".

The W R agreed to a payment of £175 per annum for conveyance of the mails between Newton Stewart and Garliestown and the intermediate stations "by all the company's passenger trains or such of them as the P M G may select". In April, McClure had written to Galloway, then at his London residence, on this subject, in terms which throw interesting light on the hard bargaining between the Post Office and railway companies over mail contracts, as well as on the hitherto existing Mail Service in the region and the improvement the railway was to make possible:

"Mr. Scot, of the G.P.O., Edinburgh, who visited the district, expressed his opinion our offer was much more than the Post Office paid for the present service between Newton Stewart and Whithorn. Our offer, however, should not be contrasted with this expense alone. Had we the mails, not only the present gig from Newton Stewart by Garliestown to Whithorn, but also the gig from Kirkinner to Portwilliam and the mail runner from Garliestown to Sorbie and the Second Service by the coaches from Newton Stewart to Whithorn would be dispensed with and the public very differently accommodated. The Post Office will say they will be charged for carrying the mails to Whithorn from Garliestown and from Whauphill to Portwilliam, and for runners to meet the bags at each station. As omnibuses will be running to each train carrying mails, this expense will be little. The letter deliver (er) will, in cases such as Wigtown, meet the trains, and in the other cases we know the 'bus drivers will carry the bags to the Post Office for a trifle. Your lordship will be told the Post Office get the mails from Newton Stewart to Whithorn carried by gig for £120 per annum, and that we ask 16/- per day, that is £250-8/- per annum for carrying by train. The gig only gives one service. We give the Post Office the opportunity of giving three each way. Besides, the Post Office could not, now that trains are running, get anyone to carry the mails for £120. It is well known that mail gig contractors always looked to local parcel traffic to pay their drivers' wages and profit. The train will take away the chance of parcel traffic and the result will be that the Post Office have to pay as much for a single mail-gig service as we are asking for a train service as often as the Post Office choose to send mails."

The W R's new terminal at Garliestown was about a mile from the harbour. The proximity of the railway led to increased trade at the harbour, and this emphasized the inconvenience of having to cart goods to and from the station. Two examples at mid-September were a cargo of 200 tons of deals for the Messrs. Callander's sawmills at Minnigaff, landed at the harbour and having to be carted to the station, and wheat for the Whitehaven market which arrived at the station from West Barr, Newton Stewart, and had to be taken in carts to the harbour. The need for communication by rail between station and harbour was pressing; the tramway authorised by the Company's Act would obviously not be an adequate link, so a branch line of railway was projected. This was the future Garliestown Branch of the W R, but the word "Tramway" had taken firm root, and was used to refer to the branch for many years to come, not only among the local people but also in the official records, far on into the days of the Joint Committee.

A list of subscribers to "the Tramway" in January 1876, exclusive of the Earl of Galloway, contains twenty-two names, mostly with two or three shares to their credit. The Garliestown Harbour Committee had taken sixty-three shares. The new line was ready by March. Slightly over a mile long, it followed a very winding course and had one or two steep pitches. The Board of Trade inspection took place on March 29th, when "A heavy engine was brought specially for the purpose of testing the skew bridge over the burn at the West Lodge entrance to Galloway House park." A declaration under the common seal of the company about this time states that the branch will be worked on the principle of one engine in steam. A second such declaration gives directions for observance of the Locomotives Act of 1865 at the level crossing over the public road from Garliestown to Sorbie and Whithorn, adjoining the skew bridge just referred to:

"All trains on the said branch will stop some yards short of the gates which close the railway at the said level crossing, and the gatekeeper will then open the gates, and precede the train, displaying a red flag. The gatekeeper will also close and lock both gates after the train has passed."

East of this level crossing was the new station, a wooden one, to serve the village of Garliestown, and beyond it the track continued to the harbour. The branch was opened on 3rd April. There were four through passenger trains every weekday, to and from Newton Stewart. A report in the *Free Press* tells us that on 3rd May "a much greater number of passengers than usual" arrived on the *Countess of Galloway* in time for the first train of the day to the Upper District, and adds that by means of "the tramway" goods could now be transferred straight from the ships in the harbour to the waiting trucks, and taken from the quay direct by rail towards their destinations.

# Rails to Portpatrick

In the space of a year, the W R had acquired two Garliestown stations, the "original" one and the "new" one. For a time, they appear in the records under a variety of names. In February 1876, "Garliestown Passenger Station" appears for the "original" one; in March "Garliestown Upper" and "Garliestown New"; in a return to the Assessor of Railways and Canals this year, "Garliestown Junction" and "Garliestown Village". In February 1877, the board directed that "the original Garliestown station at the junction" be called Millisle in future, to distinguish it from "the new station at Garliestown". The term "Millisle Junction" occurs in July 1877. In their return to the Assessor of Railways and Canals this year, the company use the names "Millisle" and "Garliestown", and so the matter rested.

The company decided to convert the buildings at the future Millisle station into dwelling-houses for railway workers "in the event of its being found a fair rent can be got for them". The buildings were, in fact, made into two cottages for engine drivers and their families. In 1880 they were occupied by David Stirling and James Pirie, the rent paid by Stirling the previous year being £5.10.0.

In May 1876, Wheatley acquired the engines which became W R Nos. 3 and 4. They were "Addison" and "Gardner" of the L N W & L & Y Joint Committee. "Addison" was an 0-4-2 tender engine with 5 feet driving-wheels, built by Sharp, Stewart in 1860, while "Gardner" was originally an 0-4-2 saddle-tank, built by Beyer, Peacock in 1856, but was converted by Wheatley into an 0-4-2 tender engine, with an old four-wheeled tender from the L & Y.

At the beginning of the year, Wheatley had proposed a reduction of the first class fares, from the original 2d. to 1½d. per mile. We are probably correct to infer from this that patronage of the first class accommodation had been disappointing. The W R board consulted Grafton, and the outcome was the reduction of all first class fares to 1½d., fractions of 1d. to count as 1d., from 1st February. There was no provision in the fare-tables, however, for the use made of the company's line a short time after by Edward Carroll, cattledealer, of Wigtown, who while inebriated drove a horse and gig after nightfall along the railway from Garliestown to Whauphill, four-and-a-quarter miles. On his arrival at Whauphill after this remarkable journey, timed at exactly 8.37 p.m. by the station-master, Daniel McDowall, who must have been more than startled, Carroll was asked by the latter where he had come from. Carroll thereupon notified him that he came from "h - - l", and furthermore that he was returning thither. McDowall rejoined that if he had been ten minutes later he would probably have been there by that time; he referred to the fact that "the down train" was due in ten minutes. When the train arrived and the driver, David Stirling, found out what had been happening, he was furious, and on getting back to Wigtown stormed away to complain, first to Wheatley and then to the Provost. By the time the matter came to court, however, he had cooled off, and proved a reluctant witness against Carroll. Sheriff Rhind, having described Carroll as "an active and useful business man in the country", fined him £10 for driving the horse and gig along the railway "to the imminent danger of the lieges or passengers".

## Rails to Portpatrick

The company were, of course, anxious to complete their line and reach Whithorn, but they had difficulty in raising funds. It was a problem for them to pay for the extension as far as Sorbie. An approach to the C R for help got a very cold reception. In February 1876, however, Galloway told the board that if each of them would add one-fifth to the number of shares he held already, he himself would take up the whole of the company's share capital of £96,000 that remained unissued. The response was favourable, and the company were thereby enabled also to exercise their powers under their 1872 Act and borrow up to £12,000. £25,000 of new capital was needed to complete the line to Whithorn. Johnston Stewart of Physgill came forward with an offer to take another £10,000 in shares, provided others subscribed the remainder of this new capital by 1st June. Drew and McClure thereupon began a vigorous personal canvass of local people, and correspondence with "non-residents" who might be sympathetic and forthcoming, and the results were very satisfactory. On 1st June the board accepted Granger's tender for the Garliestown to Whithorn section, with a view to opening not later than 1st July next year.

In September 1876, the W R resolved to seek a new Act of Parliament. Its provisions would be partly retrospective. The abandonment of their tramway, and the construction of their branch, to Garliestown harbour would be sanctioned, as would the crossing on the level of the public road at Broughton Skeog, on the Whithorn section, and the building of a station there. The company would be empowered to raise a further £24,000 in shares, and to borrow £8,000. They might make Working Agreements with the C R, P P R, G S W, L N W or Midland Companies. Only over this last item was there any difficulty; the L N W objected to the inclusion of the G S W and the M R, and the M R objected to the inclusion of the M R. The L N W's attitude annoyed the W R. "Through the Caledonian Company", complained McClure, "we have since the opening of our line sent all our English traffic, by no means inconsiderable, over the L N W without any consideration from them". Galloway was given full powers to deal with the situation, and following his personal intervention the opposition of the L N W was withdrawn. The M R were left out of the bill, on their own insistence. The bill became law on 28th June, 1877.

Progress with the building of the Whithorn section was slow at first, or so thought Wheatley, who complained about the matter to the board. In the later stages, delay was caused by heavy rains. The board successfully requested Board of Trade permission to dispense with turntables at Newton Stewart and Whithorn, on their undertaking to continue to work the passenger traffic with tank engines only, as they were now doing. In April 1877, Wheatley bought another tank engine, W R engine No. 5. It came from the N B and was a 2-2-2 well tank, built at St. Margaret's in 1856 and very similar indeed to No. 1. A declaration under the common seal of the W R announced that from the opening of the Whithorn section, the whole line would be worked by train staff combined with absolute block telegraph. The year before, the board had authorised provision of "a special wire with new instruments along the line, for working on the block telegraph system". The board accepted the offer from the Post Office of £250 per annum for the carriage of mails between Newton Stewart and Whithorn and intermediate stations by all passenger trains. They said they should have a larger payment; the sum they were, in fact, getting, was what they had asked earlier, when their line was open only as far as Garliestown. Meanwhile, in the *Galloway Gazette* of 10th February, "O.B." had celebrated the completion of the new section by anticipation in by no means unworthy verse.

### A WHITHORN RAILWAY RHYME

Ye mind, some sixty simmers back,
When half oar toun was roof'd wi' thack,
Oor street, a steep and rugged track -
Oh, how unlike a Railway!

Wi' slated hooses strong and neat,
We noo hae got a spacious street,
Whaur folk can walk wi' slippered feet -
But still it's no' the Railway.

Oor new clock lichted shows the 'oor,
The parish kirk has got a toor,
An', better still, up to our door
Has come the Wigtown Railway.

Lord Galloway, gude worthy man,
The enterprise at first did plan,
An' great an' sma' pit to their han'
To help to mak' the Railway.

A while it stood at Sorbie Mill,
For want a' cash to mount the hill -
But Johnston Stewart, wi' richt gudewill,
Has brocht us up the Railway.

We'll a', on this eventfu' day,
Aside oor toils an' troubles lay,
An' them that canna sing can say
Some speech about the Railway.

Oor Provost at the laigh toun en'
Will, nae doot, ask his Lordship ben,
Wi' ither patriotic men,
Wha helped to get the Railway.

# Rails to Portpatrick

The best a' wine, nae doot, they'll hae,
An' best a' biscuits frae Macrae -
Enough to tak' an' some to lae -
In honour a' the Railway.

The Wigtown Provost, he'll be there;
We hope he'll get han'some share –
He said oor toun had nocht to spare,
T'inaugurate the Railway.

An' a' the lieges up the street
In every public hoose will meet,
Till some will scarce can keep their feet -
To pledge the Wigtown Railway.

An' at the very far'est en',
An' doun the Raw an' up the Pen',
In biggest hoose and sma'est den –
They'll talk aboot the Railway.

Even veesitors, wi' ready clink,
Will naethin' get to buy but drink;
Oor merchants winna speak or think
On ocht except the Railway.

Bonfires we'll hae on every hill,
Wi' barreis fu' o' Wigtown yill,
An' stronger drink frae Bladnoch still -
Sent doun along the Railway.

Teetotallers, whate'er they think
Aboot the use a' stronger drink,
Will quaff caud water till they blink –
Rejoicing ower the Railway.

What gudes we noo may hae to spare,
Be't kintra growth or merchant ware,
Is sure to find a sale somewhere -
Thanks to the Wigtown Railway.

What gudes we want, be't coarse or fine,
At price accordin' to its kin',
We'll get by Scotch or English line,
An' doun the Wigtown Railway.

# Rails to Portpatrick

> Oor lawless loons that tak' delicht,
> To curse an' sweer, and rage an' fecht,
> May get to Wigtown jail that nicht -
> To patronise the Railway.
>
> Oor laigh toun en' has long escapit
> The birch an' broom; 'tis seldom scrapit;
> But we'll hae't clean an' better shapit -
> When leadin' to a Railway.
>
> Noo fill us up nae scrimpit sip,
> But fill your glasses to the lip -
> Three hearty cheers -"Hurrah! hip! hip!
> Hurrah! hurrah! the Railway."

(Laigh - low or lower; ben - come inside; lac - leave; the Raw-King's Road, Whithorn, cf. "Route du Roi", the road by which royal pilgrims came to the shrine of St. Ninian at Whithorn Priory; the Pen' - The Pend, the entrance to the Priory, a passage between two houses with rooms above, still to be seen today; clink - money; blink - glance brightly; kintra - country.)

Major-General Hutchinson carried out the Government inspection of the Whithorn section on 7th July. He rode on the footplate of a C R locomotive, accompanied by Grafton, Blackwood, the P P R's locomotive superintendent, Johnson, Granger and McClure. The locomotive with its tender was said to weigh over 40 tons. The inspection, which lasted over two hours, was witnessed by Galloway, the burgh officials of Whithorn and other gentlemen, who had their own special train. A huge crowd awaited the engines and train at Whithorn, and as they arrived a flute band played a cheery tune; while "by young and old, to whom the iron horse was a novelty, it was examined with great interest".

At the luncheon in the town hall which followed, Galloway remarked that he thought the railway system in Wigtownshire would not be complete until a line was open from Whauphill to Portwilliam. There was talk of such a line, and he was sorry Sir Herbert Maxwell was not present to tell them whether there was any prospect of progress with it at that time. Sir Herbert had just succeeded his father, Sir William Maxwell, who had not cared for railways. Sir Herbert became closely connected with them, but perhaps he did not welcome the idea of a railway passing near his mansion at Monreith; perhaps as the owner of the harbour of Portwilliam he feared the effect of railway competition on the sea-going trade; perhaps he was influenced by respect for his father's wishes: however this may be, what Galloway had seen as the finishing-touch to the railway pattern of the Shire was never put, and traffic for Portwilliam continued to use the station at Whauphill, six miles inland.

## Rails to Portpatrick

A weekday service of four passenger trains each way continued with seven each way on what now became the connecting service between Millisle and Garliestown. There was an up goods train in the mornings, and a down goods in the afternoons. Through passengers to and from Garliestown had to change at Millisle, where a new exchange platform, called in the W R records "Millisle Centre Platform", was built and furnished with a wooden "umbrella" shelter. Passengers starting or finishing their journey at Millisle had to walk along the line between the "old" platform and the new one. The station that had seemed to be intended for Broughton Skeog was not built, but a goods siding and, early in 1878, a passenger platform "similar to that at Causewayend" were provided, beside the level crossing over the public road to Sorbie. There was another level crossing near Chapel Outon, close to the Whithorn terminus, and both crossings gave McClure cause for anxiety during the first weeks of operation. On July 13th he wrote thus to Wheatley:

"I enclose a copy of another complaint from Mr Clanahan, Outon. Surely it would be better to place a lad at the crossing until the house is occupied than run the risk of accident or litigation. Please attend to this."

On July 18th, while on holiday at Buxton, he wrote again, strongly remonstrating with Wheatley over his "having had the Broughton Skeog level crossing gates shut across the road on Friday last and no person in charge". He continued:

"Mr. Johnson will push on the building of the lodge. Meantime the company hold you responsible for the safe and proper working of this crossing, and surely it is your interest to avoid all risks and for your own protection to place a proper person at once in charge of these gates."

To Johnson, McClure wrote that he was "much astonished" at the complaints, adding, "This cannot be allowed to be repeated."

In March 1878 the board agreed to Wheatley's request to let the level crossing cottages at Carslae near Wigtown, Inch near Sorbie (sometimes called Old Tower, after the ruin nearby), and Broughton Skeog to him, the rent for each cottage being £5 per annum. Wheatley was to take bond from the occupants of the cottages to attend carefully to the gates. The cottages at Carslae and Old Tower had been provided by Galloway the previous year, and he had leased them to the W R for nineteen years at a charge of 5 % per annum on the outlay, the land being given free. In 1880, Outon is included with the places mentioned above in a list of names of crossings where the cottages were let to Wheatley, and it is stated that the occupants lived rent free in return for looking after the gates. The crossing near Mains of Penninghame is not mentioned.

## Rails to Portpatrick

Stone station buildings were provided at Whithorn, the money to pay for them being lent by Johnston Stewart, who agreed to interest at not more than 4%. The station-master applied for a house to be erected on waste ground at the station, and for some of the ground to be used for potato-planting. The board refused the house, but would allow the potato-planting "in the same manner as had been done at other stations".

At Wigtown the station buildings were also of stone, but there was even there only a single platform, as at all the W R stations (though we ought probably to except the exchange platform at Millisle, with its two faces). There was, as at the other stations, a goods shed, and additionally a wooden carriage shed, provided at Wheatley's request in 1876 and extended in 1882, and a workshop. Towards the end of 1876, Wheatley made a modest request for a wooden workshop, but the board, influenced, no doubt, by the risk of fire, agreed to give him one of stone and slate. Here the rebuilding of some of the W R locomotives would take place, so remarkable a feature of Wheatley's rule at Wigtown, especially considering his very limited resources. We saw that on its arrival in 1876, No. 4 was rebuilt as an 0-4-0 tender engine. It was not successful as such, and seems to have been very little used. About the end of 1882, Wheatley restored it as far as possible to its original condition and, as an 0-4-2 saddle tank again, it gave good service. In 1883, No. 1 was rebuilt as a 2-4-0 well tank, and fitted with a large cab. Towards the end of 1877 an iron engine shed was provided, the tender accepted being that of Messrs. Main, Clydesdale Ironworks, Glasgow, whose price was £147.10.0; particulars of the proposed new building, so the W R records state, were "sent us by our man working at Mr. Drew's roof". There was also a passing-place at Wigtown.

At Kirkinner the station was of wood. There was a passing-place here originally, but in 1884 W. T. Wheatley got the board's permission to remove it. Whauphill station was of wood, and there was a passing-place. The station buildings at Sorbie were of wood until 11th June 1880, when they were burnt down, following which they were rebuilt of stone. At Millisle there was the exchange platform with its umbrella-type shelter, and beyond it the original Garliestown station and a passing-place. There was an engine shed at Millisle, though this was the former goods shed, and not until early in 1881 did the board formally authorise its conversion for this purpose. We have seen, however, that engine drivers were living in the original station buildings in 1879 and 1880, and this would not have been the case if engines had not been stabled nearby. At Whithorn there were the stone-built terminus buildings, with a runround loop.

There were signal-boxes at Wigtown, Millisle, and possibly Whithorn. Elsewhere there were open ground-frames. The duties of signalmen were carried out by the station-masters and porters. Four porters were employed, probably at Wigtown, Whithorn, Garliestown (in view of the harbour traffic) and Whauphill (in view of the Portwilliam and district traffic).

# Rails to Portpatrick

There were facilities for watering engines at various points on the line, but the only really dependable sources were at Causewayend, where the W R had provided their own supply after their disagreement with the P P R over use of the supply at Newton Stewart, and, from 1882, if not earlier, Newton Stewart, the W R having in that year consented to pay the P P R £12 per annum for such supply as they might need. There was water available at Broughton Skeog - from a well, which the W R deepened. The sources other than the two main ones, however, were subject to total failure in the event of drought. At such a time, June 1884, McClure, in a letter to Drew, thus describes the result of interruption of the supply at Sorbie by a Mr. White, presumably the owner of the water:

"Mr. White today cut off the water supply to Sorbie, and the tank is almost empty. Some of the engines cannot take as much water at Newton Stewart or Causewayend as will bring them back. If Mr. White would only halve the water with Mr. Wheatley for a few days until Whithorn supply can be used the difficulty could be met."

Drew's influence was to be brought to bear:

"I understand you will be passing on Saturday. Perhaps if you would ask Mr. White to meet you at the station you could induce him to share fairly with the company."

By the end of 1885 the water tank at Wigtown was disused, and that at Whithorn was very dilapidated.

A genial informality was clearly always a strong characteristic of the service provided on the W R. Soon after its opening to Garliestown, Harper described it as "...one of those pleasant, unhurried, single-rail lines, where the same engines and carriages go backward and forward so many times a day, and the train moves along at such a loitering pace among the trim little stations that we have plenty of time to note and admire the scenery".

The enginemen and guards would become well known, not only to the regular passengers by the trains, but to all the people who lived and worked near the line. Though there is no hint of this in the official records, one or two accounts from other sources suggest that the informality of the service reached extremes. Thus a correspondent in a newspaper named simply as the Chronicle, quoted in the *Free Press* in May 1904, and writing of the ealiest days, when the line was open only to Wigtown, tells us that "The engine-driver and guard, by mutual arrangement, halted the train whenever they saw a likely passenger." Once, he continues, they saw "frantic waving from a somewhat ragged individual in a field", and obligingly stopped, only to find that the gesticulations emanated from a "tattie bogle" (Anglice, scarecrow). According to another reminiscence, that of the Rev. Dr.

Gillespie in *Humours of Scottish Life*, a property qualification had been introduced by the time the line was open to Whithorn: ". . . if a landlord, large farmer, or any other person of consequence appeared at any point along the line, and held up his hat, the train was stopped to pick him up". The author relates how one day a farmer who stopped the train explained that he was paying his workpeople that day, and needed change of a pound note; he got his change, and farmer and train went their respective ways.

On a different note, we find in the summer of 1879 complaints by the W R to the P P R and G & P P about connections between the latter two companies' trains at Dunragit being missed "by a few minutes each way forenoon and afternoon". Surprising at first acquaintance, this unbusiness-like state of affairs was probably a result of the hostility between the two companies. The W R explained how it was bad for the two companies and for the W R. Passengers from and to the south-west part of the Lower District were driving to Dunragit and New Luce stations instead of taking train from Whauphill to Newton Stewart and thence by the P P R to Dunragit, and vice versa. Passengers from the Newton Stewart district were driving to Barrhill. Many commercial travellers who would have gone home by train on Saturday evenings to Glasgow and other places, returning on Monday mornings, were prevented from doing so. The W R requested the retiming of the other companies' services so that there were at least two reliable connections daily each way at Dunragit. It was obviously in the interests of the P P R and G & P P to comply, and the necessary adjustments were made.

About two years later, there is evidence that some of the W R trains may have been missing connections at Newton Stewart. Writing to Drew under the heading of "Irregularity of Trains", McClure infers that the up trains were late owing to their being delayed in starting out from Newton Stewart on the down run to Whithorn, though there is a suggestion too that progress in the up direction might sometimes have been unduly dilatory:

"If the Newton Stewart officials would only make a point of starting our trains at time - advertised time - except when the main line trains are not in, a great point would be gained and Mr Wheatley would then have no excuse for the up trains being late. By starting punctually from Whithorn and Garliestown he has sufficient time, even supposing he has live stock to lift, to reach Newton Stewart at his advertised time."

The leisurely progress of the W R trains certainly prevented a disaster on a day in September 1880, when one of them, steaming along near Sorbie, collided with a number of jagged stones "as large as an ordinary sized turnip" which had been laid on the track. The engine jolted, but stayed on the rails. There had been several instances lately of stones being put on the line, but this time the culprit was found - a girl, aged 14, belonging to the neighbourhood. It was said on her behalf in court that there was "an entire absence of ill-intention on her part".

# Rails to Portpatrick

Sheriff Rhind, "after a few suitable remarks on the very dangerous and highly reprehensible act the girl had been guilty of" sent her to prison for 20 days.

Unfortunately, there was one case in which the informality and easy pace of the little rural line had less happy results. McClure shall recount it. In a letter to the Board of Trade dated 8th July, 1885, he says:

"I regret to have to report that about 9 o'clock last night, while our 7.50 passenger train from Newton Stewart to Whithorn was running between Millisle station and Whithorn, the fireman (Robert Armstrong) fell from the engine. The driver did not observe him fall, and so far as I can learn no person did. As soon as the driver missed him, he stopped his train, and ran back. Armstrong was found on the side of the line in an unconscious state, and much cut and bruised about the head and face. He was put into the train, taken to Whithorn and had his wounds dressed. He now lies at Whithorn in a precarious condition."

To Drew next day McClure gives further details:

"The enclosed shows one of the firemen had a bad fall from his engine on Tuesday night. He is thought a little better this morning, though still unconscious. It appears the driver and fireman were looking from opposite sides of the engine at a hare that was running between the metals, and it is likely Armstrong overbalanced himself or missed his hold of the rail."

The story closes on a pleasanter note than might well have been expected, for six weeks later the hardy fireman is reported to be recovered from his injuries and back again at work.

From 30th September 1880, third class fares were charged at the Parliamentary rate by all W R trains. Although the company's rate for third class return tickets was only 1d. per mile, they had been charged passenger duty on these tickets because they were available by trains on which the third class single fare was above the Parliamentary rate. They were now getting rid of passenger duty on all except first class tickets, and they hoped to benefit both by the saving of duty and by an increase in the number of passengers carried. "It will not be necessary", McClure told Wheatley, "that each train stops at Mains (of Penninghame) and Causewayend, but your time bill will, I expect, have to contain a notice that passengers will be set down or lifted at those places on notice to the guard". It seems that, during the summer of 1883, if not before, reduced Saturday fares were in operation, at single fare for the double journey. This was abandoned the following year in favour of an idea of W. T. Wheatley's, details of which are not given. At the same time, his proposal to allow season tickets at two-thirds the standard rate to boys aged 14 to 17 going to school in Newton Stewart was approved by the board.

# Rails to Portpatrick

During these years, there was a good deal of concern about the state of the permanent way. The line had not been open throughout for two full years when anxiety over this began. W. T. Wheatley subsequently stated that not only were prices high when the W R was built, but the rails proved to be of poor material. Apart from this, Johnson, as resident engineer, thought that not enough surfacemen were employed to take proper care of the line. They were insufficient, he claimed, to maintain the permanent way and attend properly to the drainage of the cuttings - "on good drainage depends the life of sleepers". There were at present (March 1879) four gangs: Newton Stewart - Causewayend (two men); Causewayend - Bladnoch Bridge (two); Bladnoch Bridge - Barwhanny Private Road (near Whauphill) (two); and Barwhanny - Whithorn plus the Garliestown Branch ("the Branch") (four). It certainly seems a severe minimum, and Johnson urged the employment of five gangs, each of three men: "Without this", he warned, "the line will go gradually down".

Six months later, Johnson included in his report the following criticisms:

"Sleepers. These show an increase of decay and I strongly urge on the lessee the necessity of keeping the ballast clear and free from weeds, dock leaves and moss.

"Nothing is more injurious to sleepers than a strong growth of vegetable matter amongst them, and the existence of such indicates a scarcity of hands employed on the surface work.

"It is further desirable to clean and trim the slopes, cutting grass and weeds, and to thoroughly clear the side drains.

"The lessee will probably find it desirable to reopen the Kirkinner ballast pit to supply the other portions of the line.

"The distant signal and electric repeater at Newton Stewart are not working, and 1 assume that the battery wants recharging. This is a simple matter and should be attended to in as much as the Board of Trade inspector laid great stress on the company providing a repeater to indicate the correct working of the distant signal which from its position cannot be seen from the cabin.

"The station-masters and porters at the intermediate stations should be ordered by the lessee to pay due attention to the signal apparatus under their charge, keeping the levers clean and reporting any defects or repairs required. The same applies to the condition of the waiting rooms and the water supply to the closets."

These are not trivial criticisms, and the WR could obviously scarcely be said to be operating at a peak of efficiency. There are dangers in informality, as in most things, and it may well be that the informality which is otherwise so attractive a feature of the W R at this period bred an element of casualness, with the inevitable loss of efficiency in consequence. The chief causes, however, of the defects Johnson noted are likely to have been financial stringency and inadequate supervision, the latter, to a great extent, the result of the former. It had been assumed from the start that the W R must practise rigorous economy, and by this year, 1879, when the early hopes of remuneration and modest profit had been disappointed, and the outlook worsened by severe depression in commerce and agriculture, this was naturally felt to be more than ever essential.

In July, Drew approached Mr. Carlyle, permanent way superintendent on the P P R, with a view to his making regular inspections of the permanent way and works of the W R at a fee of 20/- per inspection. The C R objected, however, whereupon McClure inquired of Carlyle if he could "recommend someone, say an active, intelligent foreman platelayer, who would be competent to do the work we want and give us his whole time for a moderate weekly wage". Probably as a result of this, Daniel Brown, inspector with the C R at Carstairs, was offered the post of first inspector of permanent way on the W R. The "moderate weekly wage", however, gave problems of interpretation. The W R offered Brown 25/-, but he wanted 30/- and a three or five years' engagement. The W R would not agree, and the best McClure could suggest meantime was that Brown should consent to an engagement terminable by three months' notice on either side, in which case the board might agree to an advance on the 25/-. Brown was not interested, and the W R advertised for an inspector of permanent way. In November, McClure sent Drew applications received from Joseph Downes, 18 Orchard Street, Carlisle; John Harrison, of Kirknewton, near Midealder; Alex. B. Fraser, 3 Robertson Place, Leith Walk, Edinburgh; F. J. O. Howell, 2 Wolverley Place, Severn Road, Canton, Cardiff; and G. S. Lindsay, Mill Cottage, Blackburn near Bathgate. It seems, however, that none of these was followed up, for in January 1880 the board were arranging with Johnson for him to be responsible for inspection and reports to the end of July. They knew Johnson would be leaving the district soon; but in spite of the unsatisfactory condition of their permanent way they evidently disliked the prospect of engaging a full-time inspector "for a moderate weekly wage".

What Wheatley thought of the same prospect is not recorded, but he can hardly have viewed it with favour; similarly, he cannot have been much pleased at Johnson's criticisms of the way and works, justified though these doubtless were. The subject, however, now became involved with that of the renewal of his Working Agreement, which was due to expire on July 31st.

In March the W R approached the C R and G S W to see if they were willing to offer terms for working their line, but they would scarcely be surprised when both declined. A committee of the directors then conferred with Wheatley and his son, W. T. Wheatley, at Wigtown. Wheatley submitted an estimate of his monthly expenditure on working the W R, which is very interesting in the information it gives us about the staff he employed, the wages he paid them, and his other expenses. This estimate showed a total monthly outlay of £411.8.0 - £4,936.16.0 per annum, exclusive of expenditure on permanent way, fencing materials, and interest on rolling-stock. The traffic receipts for the two years since the full opening of the W R averaged £7,941 per annum: they showed a fall from £4,046 in the half-year to 31st January 1879 to £3,641 in the following half-year. For the half-year to 31st January 1880 they were £3,642. Whenever the receipts fell much below £4,000 per half-year, Wheatley was certain to incur a loss on the working.

The committee told Wheatley they were confident a good recovery would follow, but Wheatley may not have felt able to share this confidence, and in any case he was very worried about the large outlay that was going to be necessary on the permanent way. Johnson said that about seven tons of new rails were urgently called for, along with nearly 2,000 sleepers. On the basis of investigations he had made, he thought it likely that between Newton Stewart and Wigtown one in twelve sleepers was decayed seriously, and between Wigtown and Millisle one in fifteen. There was also the matter of rails which were badly laminated. Wheatley wanted the company to bear part of the cost of the new rails and sleepers. In an attempt at compromise, he offered to work the line for the reduced percentage of 62½, if the W R would provide all the rails and sleepers for renewals. He would pay a fifth of their cost, and accept from the W R half the value of the old material taken out. It is a sign of the very difficult straits that both parties now found themselves in that the W R made considerable efforts to get Wheatley to forgo another ½ %, while Wheatley just as earnestly insisted that this was impossible, for "as you must be aware the last two years I have only realised a bare living".

The W R also wanted Wheatley to agree to take only a fifth of the value of the old material. Wheatley replied by outlining the amount of work that would need to be done in preparing the new materials for use. He had, he said, 201 rails in stock each of which would have to have twenty holes drilled in it; while the new sleepers should all be pickled in boiling tar, "as this would, I am assured, make the life of them almost double". The apparatus for this would be expensive, and there was labour in addition. The terms of the eventual settlement make rather curious reading. Wheatley accepted only a fifth of the value of the old materials; but the W R paid him £5 for each 1,000 holes that he drilled in the rails, and £5 for each 1,000 sleepers that he tarred. He would pay a fifth of the cost of the new rails and sleepers. The W R would allow him 62½ % of the gross traffic receipts. The new Working Agreement was sealed on July 29th; it was to run until July 31st, 1885.

Wheatley did not live to complete his second lease. His health declined, owing to heart trouble, and people who saw him at Wigtown station on the afternoon of March 12th, 1883, noticed that he was looking very poorly. He died at his home, Woodside, Wigtown, at 7.30 next morning, aged 62. His passing was felt as a personal loss by many, as in the few years he had been in the district he had won a place in the deep affections of the local people. Long after his death the W R line was still sometimes spoken of in the area as "Wheatley's Railway". In the tribute penned by McClure, and read by Galloway at their next meeting, the directors of the W R expressed their high regard for him and his services. Wheatley had arranged in his will for his lease to be taken over by his wife and two sons, with one of the latter, W. T. Wheatley, as manager. As McClure wrote to Galloway three days after his death:

"Poor Mr. Wheatley has provided in his settlement for the lease being worked out under his son, so that for the present we will not be pushed for any new working arrangements."

In the same letter McClure explained.

"I send your lordship a report as to our financial position, which I had prepared for the financial committee . . ."

The death of Wheatley had occurred at a critical stage in the company's afrairs.
We saw how the company's receipts had fallen in 1879. At first, the directors had spoken of encouraging revenue and the possibility of a dividend, but increasing depression in trade and agriculture, combined with bad weather - a protracted frost during the winter of 1878-9 and a very wet summer to follow - changed matters greatly. Neither agriculture nor climatic conditions showed the hoped-for recovery. Writing to S. Swarbrick, a barrister, of The Cedars, Tottenharn, towards the end of 1883, McClure said that the company's hopes of increasing their passenger traffic and making a saving of £100 per annum on passenger duty, when they reduced their third class fares to the Parliamentary rate by all trains three years previously, had been disappointed. The agricultural depression and bad weather during the holiday season in both 1879 and 1880 were responsible. Agriculture in the district had not recovered from the depression, and this in turn had seriously affected the company's goods and mineral traffic. The result was a very difficult financial situation.
In September 1882, bearing in mind that £13,100 previously borrowed on mortgage would fall to be repaid the following Whit-Sunday and that the company could not hope to repay this sum unless new funds could be raised meantime, the board had advertised in various papers for loans at 4%. On 22nd March 1883, McClure had to report to them that, the company's security being considered inadequate, not a single new lender had been obtained. He described how, of the total issued share capital of £114,380, £72,020 was held by the present directors and £12,980 by other local landowners, as follows:

# Rails to Portpatrick

| The Present Directors | | Other Local Landowners | |
|---|---|---|---|
| The Chairman | £35,040 | Lord Stair | £7,580 |
| Deputy-Chairman | 24,000 | Sir Herbert Maxwell | 3,000 |
| R. Vans Agnew, Esq. | 5,000 | James Parlane, Esq. | 2,400 |
| Colonel Hathorn | 4,000 | | |
| Lord Borthwick | 2,500 | | --------- |
| | | | £12,980 |
| J. Drew, Esq. | 1,080 | | |
| James McLean, Esq. | 400 | | |
| | ---------- | | |
| | £72,020 | | |

This left in the hands of others only £29,380. McClure went on to explain what he saw as the only way by which the company could extricate themselves from the impending grave situation. Having considered his advice, the directors decided to guarantee personally the payment of interest for the next three years to those of the mortgagees entitled to repayment at Whitsun, who in return for this guarantee would agree to postpone repayment till the end of the three years.

The company's mortgagees were written to with the offer of these terms, and in the event, with only two exceptions, they accepted the terms, or a modification of them. The two exceptions were "expected not to press for payment in the meantime". Thus the proposed solution proved effective, and while the company's circumstances remained very disheartening to those who had put confidence and capital in it, and indeed to all who wished it well, the shadow thrown over its future had been lifted. And at this same time, new prospects were opening. On 19th November 1883, the directors noted "Portpatrick Company's application to Parliament", and henceforward the story of the W R becomes merged in that of the Joint Committee.

## SECTION THREE

# THE PORTPATRICK & WIGTOWNSHIRE JOINT RAILWAYS

## CHAPTER EIGHT

Sale and Transfer

IN the autumn of 1877, when the P P R dividend reached 4¼%, Sir William Dunbar spoke to the shareholders of the "excellent property" they had, which "sooner or later" large railway companies would be eager to buy. It was, evidently, to "the great companies of the south" - the English companies - that he looked for such advances. During the first half of 1882, with the expiry of the Working Agreement with the C R coming into view, the Earl of Stair approached Richard Moon, the chairman of the L NW, regarding the terms on which the L NW and the C R might be willing to acquire the P P R in perpetuity. Whatever Moon's reply may then have been, a year later he was in touch with M. W. Thompson, chairman of the G S W and of the M R, on the same subject; in May 1883, Thompson reported to the G S W board on a meeting of the board of the M R where these communications were discussed, and was authorised to continue them, and to conclude an arrangement whereby the G S W, the M R, the L N W and the C R would jointly take over the P P R. In August, the C R board, having heard correspondence between Thompson and their chairman, J. C. Bolton, M.P., regarding joint acquisition of the P P R, authorised an examination of the P P R line by an M R engineer.

Agreement between the two great rival alliances thus seemed to have been reached comparatively, and surprisingly, easily, and we may regard it as certain that this was to a considerable extent due to the initiative and influence of Moon, mindful as he must have been of the way in which the P P R had played off competing companies against each other some twenty years previously. But the rate of progress was illusory. During November 1883, numerous meetings were held in London of representatives of the four companies, including sometimes those of the P P R also; at that of 9th, arrangements were agreed upon for the notices of the Parliamentary bill that would give effect to the joint acquisition. Three weeks later, however, signs of a rift appeared when the subject of running powers for the C R and L N W over the G S W's Dumfries-Castle Douglas line was discussed. The G S W were willing to continue to the C R the running powers granted them by the Castle Douglas Railway Amalgamation Act of 1865, on the same conditions - payment of a mileage proportion of through rates and fares, after various deductions, including 25% for working expenses, and subject to a minimum - and to grant these same powers to the L N W also, but this was not enough, at any rate for the L NW. Details of the dispute are not recorded, but by December the collapse of the negotiations was regarded as a strong possibility; the petition for the bill, under the seal of the P P R only, was deposited by that company "in the hope that an arrangement may be arrived at". On 18th January 1884, Moon wrote to Stair that the bill must be withdrawn "if the Midland Company do not waive their objection before the end of the present week".

The reference here to "the Midland Company" is probably misleading. Most likely it ought to be plural. Our source of information for this item is the C R minutes, and a little earlier these minutes refer to the G S W and M R together as "the Midland Companies"; it is likely that the objection Stair had in mind had been put forward by the G S W - M R alliance, not by the M R alone. It happens that the M R were in dispute with the C R and L N W at this time over a claim the latter companies were making against the M R in connection with Carlisle Citadel station, which was settled by compromise the following summer, but while this doubtless did not help the negotiations over the P P R, we have the clear statement of M. W. Thompson, in a letter to Moon dated January 23rd, that the differences which led to the collapse of these "relate exclusively to the terms and conditions upon which the Caledonian and L N W Companies are to use that portion of the G S W Railway between Dumfries and Castle Douglas". On January 26th, the G S W heard three letters from Stair to Thompson, and copies of two from Stair to Moon, all written in the attempt to get an agreement on the L N W and C R running powers so as to enable the bill to go forward; they remitted the matter to Thompson. At a P P R board meeting held at the Westminster Palace Hotel on 7th March, it was decided to withdraw the bill, which had already had its first reading, on 18th. This was done, said the P P R, at the request of the four companies. The second reading was postponed meantime, and no further expenses were to be incurred after 18th.

With their report to the shareholders at the ordinary general meeting at Stranraer on March 28th, the P P R directors included some of the correspondence leading up to the withdrawal of the bill. This was published in the *Free Press* also. Thompson's letter to Moon, just quoted, appeared, as did one from Moon to Stair, dated 21st February, in which he deplored the frustration of his strenuous efforts at agreement:

"Having done all in my power to make a friendly arrangement in the interests of the various companies concerned, and having, for the sake of peace hereafter, made considerable sacrifices as regards this company and the Caledonian . . ."

In a third letter, of February 22nd, Stair wrote to Thompson of his keen sense of the P P R having been "let down" by the big companies:

"I cannot help expressing my extreme disappointment that the band of union among the four great companies, so easily effected for the purpose of imposing terms on the Portpatrick Company, should have snapped asunder just when the necessity for fulfilling their engagement to their feeble neighbour became imperative."

# Rails to Portpatrick

A fourth letter printed, from Stair to Moon and dated 7th March, included a claim for the companies to reimburse the P P R with the expenses incurred in promoting the bill which was now about to be abandoned. Stair repeated his question, first asked nearly two years previously, as to the terms on which the L N W and C R would buy the P P R. Failing an agreement with them, he warned, the P P R must seek an alliance with the M R and G S W, or work their own line, preparation for which, in view of the forthcoming expiry of the Working Agreement with the C R, could not be much longer delayed.

The Earl's disappointment must have been intense. He told the ordinary general meeting that the bargain made with the would-be purchasers was "an admirable one" - a dividend of 3½% guaranteed by the two most powerful companies in England and their counterparts in Scotland. He must have been fervently hoping that the P P R would not, in fact, be forced into a position where they had to work their line themselves again; indeed, he told the meeting that the P P R could not stand alone. This statement was disputed by the sanguine James Hosack, who quoted the dividend of 11% guaranteed to shareholders in the L & C on that company's amalgamation with the L N W, and the 10% being paid by the little Maryport & Carlisle Company; recommended a double set of rails for the P P R line to enable the company to "work it themselves at a good profit"; and proposed also a new "branch" to Dumfries, avoiding the G S W line from Castle Douglas, so that the P P R might "make better terms for their through traffic". All these observations may well strike the reader as showing notable lack of informed and careful thought, and most unlikely to be taken seriously by any competent board of directors; yet as regards Hosack's last point, it is a fact that a year later the P P R ordered the payment, through their vice-chairman, of thirty guineas to a Carlisle firm of engineers, Messrs. Ross & Liddelaw, as "a small testimonial in respect of their services (they having declined to accept professional fees) in surveying a line between Parton and Dumfries".

A person finding some consolation in the breakdown of the negotiations was the Rev. A. Urquhart, veteran Free Kirk minister of Portpatrick, who wrote thus to the *Free Press* of 27th March 1884:

"Whilst the failure of negotiations for the sale of our railway must have caused disappointment to many, we have reason to be thankful that we have escaped from the danger of public desecration of the Sabbath, to which we should have been exposed under the wider arrangement which was contemplated. The directors of the Portpatrick Railway Company are entitled to the highest credit, and deserve the gratitude of all Christian men, for the extraordinary firmness of moral principle with which they have upheld the sacredness of the weekly rest. And the continuance of their exclusive management gives hope of their continued faithfulness on that point which has ever carried blessings manifold both spiritual and temporal; whilst the disregard of it has been most remarkably associated with ruin in the history of public works in Galloway, not excluding the harbour at Portpatrick."

Mr. Urquhart's forebodings about the attitude of the big companies toward Sunday observance, though very understandable, were, however, to prove unnecessary.

The course of the negotiations had naturally been watched with great interest, and not a little anxiety, by the Earl of Galloway and the other directors of the W R. Such was the secrecy observed that though Galloway was one of the P P R directors, the W R board did not learn about the negotiations until the notices of the P P R's application to Parliament were published in November 1883. Needless to say, they then moved quickly to protect W R interests, seeking to persuade the large companies to take over their line on the same terms as the P P R. They were very conscious of the drawback imposed by the W R's financial position, and in the attempt to counter this they emphasised ways in which the P P R and the big companies had benefited from the W R, without the W R gaining anything in return. On November 14th, following up a meeting of Galloway and himself with Moon at Euston two days previously, James Drew wrote to Moon stressing this argument. He supported it with information supplied by McClure which illustrates for us the extent to which the W R line had diverted all kinds of traffic in the district it served from sea to land carriage. Pior to the line's opening nearly all the traffic in goods, livestock, parcels and minerals was sea-borne. By putting off the bi-weekly steamers to Liverpool and the bi-monthly and occasional steamer to Glasgow, etc., the W R had brought a large increase in the passenger traffic of the P P R and the four big companies, and had received no rebate in respect of any of this: a reasonable rebate, McClure suggested, would have yielded 1 % on the whole £114,339 share capital of the W R. A 10% rebate on other kinds of traffic would have yielded more than 1%. During the twelve months to 30th June 1875, the year of the W R's opening, the Liverpool steamer's receipts for passengers, livestock and goods totalled £6,932.17.3; those of the Glasgow steamer were between £2,000 and £2,500. In 1873 the tonnage of steamers cleared at Wigtown for the various ports subsequently served by the line was 12,818; in 1882 it was only 4,075. Various savings, McClure claimed, might have been made if the line had been worked as part of a large system, and a large company could probably place the W R's loan capital as debenture stock at about 3½%, giving a further profit of £250 per annum. Drew added:

"It is understood that a rebate to a branch line like the Wigtownshire, bringing and carrying to and for the other companies as it does traffic formerly sea-borne, at a higher rate than even 10%, is not unusual."

On 15th November, McClure wrote to Drew that he was going to Glasgow to see Mr. Wainwright, general manager of the G S W, and would take the opportunity to see James Thompson, the C R's general manager, if Wainwright thought it desirable. The W R board decided to send Galloway, Drew and McClure to the meeting of general managers to be held in London on 29th, with instructions to press the company's claims for acquisition on the same terms as the P P R, but this plan had to be abandoned when they learned that the general managers had no powers to treat with them. By 12th December, however, McClure was telling Drew that he hoped to "hear a favourable report from Lord Galloway of his London mission".

This presumably refers to the P P R board meeting held in London on 14th December, when members heard a report of negotiations between Stair and Dunbar, for the P P R, and Moon for the L N W, C R, M R and G S W, in the course of which Moon had made the offer to buy the P P R for a guaranteed 3½% to the shareholders. The meeting adopted Stair's resolution to recommend acceptance. Galloway, however, dissented. He protested at the publication of notices relating to the sale of the line without the previous concurrence of the board, and said that three conditions ought to have been made. A through service from London to Belfast, faster than by other routes, should be guaranteed, with serious consideration given to a double service each weekday - one leaving London by night, as at present, the other serving Scotland and the North of England by day - and to a single service on Sundays. There should be an assurance that the local service would be "commensurate with the needs of the district". The WR line should be included with the P P R in the sale:

"The line forming the stalk of the letter T, which the two lines form between them - and having in consequence contributed to the Portpatrick (as shown by the Clearing House returns) to an extent of a dividend to the latter of from 1 to 1½% per annum."

On December 29th, McClure wrote to Galloway with a copy of a letter just received from Stair, in which, he commented, "His lordship takes a most erroneous view of the benefits this company have brought to the other companies." Writing to Stair on 19th January 1884, McClure claimed that the increase in P P R dividends since 1873 had been due to a considerable extent to the opening of the WR line. The parcels traffic with the Machars district arose chiefly in London, Liverpool, Manchester, Birmingham and Glasgow, and nine-tenths of it, he claimed, would be sea-borne without the W R line. He would be sorry if Stair, who had been one of the first directors of the W R and had so largely aided in its promotion, should come to view W R interests in any other way than as identical with those of the P P R "or to depreciate its importance as a feeder to that company and through it to the other railway companies interested in the bill now being promoted by the Portpatrick Company".

## Rails to Portpatrick

At a P P R meeting in London on the 6th February, Stair replied to Galloway's protest at the December meeting. They could not seek the guarantee of speed that he suggested for the London-Belfast service, because speed was regulated by the P P R's capacity as a single line "to admit of such extreme speed as is contemplated by Lord Galloway"; and also the requirements of the Post Office, for the Mail Service had to be considered. As for a double service, the need for this depended on the demands of the traffic, which the guaranteeing companies were most unlikely to neglect. It would be, he continued, "absurd, as it was inexpedient, to make the sale of the line conditional upon the establishment of a single service on Sundays". On the subject of the W R, Stair asserted that if the P P R directors had made its inclusion a *sine qua non* of any agreement to pay a fixed dividend on the P P R's capital, they would have very ill understood their duties to their shareholders. The W R had an independent body of directors quite capable of conducting its affairs and looking after its interests, and, he went on:

"The guarantee obtained by the Portpatrick Company, so far from obstructing, has paved the way for a proposal to the guaranteeing companies by the Wigtownshire directors for a sale and transfer of their line on similar terms, or any other terms they think fair and reasonable."

He disputed Galloway's claim as to the value of W R traffic to the P P R, quoting some figures in support of his contention.

So far, Galloway and McClure seem to have had no inkling as to the differences that had arisen among the four big companies and which were soon to result in the collapse of the negotiations. When visiting Glasgow in mid-January, McClure had called on Wainwright in the hope of news, but found him away from home. On 26th, he wrote to W. A. Loch, Parliamentary agent, Westminster, that "this company never contemplated such an agreement between those great rival companies would be possible", and went on to express his forebodings regarding its implications for the W R. The latter had been looking forward to competition between the C R and G S W for their traffic when the C R's Working Agreement with the P P R expired in 1885, but if the P P R's bill passed Parliament there would be no such competition; on the contrary, the four companies might work the P P R traffic to the W R's disadvantage. As a last resort, the W R decided to oppose the bill, but as late as 8th February McClure was telling Galloway that he was still hoping that the companies would grant terms that would make opposition unnecessary. At the London meeting of the P P R board two days previously, however, where Stair gave the answer to Galloway just described, he reported on the course of the negotiations and explained the dispute that had come about. The meeting resolved to let the bill go to a first reading, "so as to afford every opportunity to the guaranteeing companies to reconsider their position before abandoning the bill".

At the next P P R meeting, on March 5th, Galloway answered Stair's criticism of his views, saying, however, that he would confine himself "to very few remarks as the likelihood of the bill proceeding farther seems so doubtful". He claimed that when he had spoken of making the London-Belfast service faster than by other routes, he meant the provision of "a proper train service between London and Castle Douglas via Annan", which in itself would ensure "a more speedy delivery of letters in Belfast than by any other route". Stair's remark about the capacity of the P P R line was irrelevant. The requirements of the Post Office were the very point the P P R board should have insisted on the four companies undertaking to fulfil before permitting any arrangement for the sale and transfer of their line. Reverting to his original point about the local service, he was not inclined to press the need for a guarantee on this, but he doubted whether the bill as drawn gave adequate safeguards on this without a previously signed agreement on the part of the four companies to ensure fulfilment. On the subject of the WR, he remained of the opinion that the P P R should have negotiated for their inclusion, or at least given them the opportunity of being included in the bill. He insisted "most emphatically, from the figures before me, that the chairman's estimate of the Wigtownshire traffic is entirely erroneous, and greatly below the mark of reality".

We have seen that the bill was withdrawn on 18th March. On 15th April, the C R board heard a letter from George Findlay, general manager of the L N W, to their chairman, J. C. Bolton, concerning the W R, and approved the draft of a reply. A few weeks later, McClure thought the negotiations might have started again, or be about to do so; writing to Galloway at his London address of 17 Upper Grosvenor Street, on 30th May, he advised him not to approach any of the four companies about working the W R, but to keep inquiring of their managers "whether negotiations are re-opened and if so what stage they have reached". It seems that Moon got them going again by the proposal that he made to the C R about this time that their two companies should work the P P R jointly, "on the same terms as the present". On 3rd June, the C R board agreed that "in case of need" they would join the L N W in an extension or renewal of the Working Agreement: they were presumably prepared to consent to the existing terms being continued to the P P R; between themselves, the two working companies would arrange terms "in proportion to the receipts accruing to each company from traffic to and from and over the Portpatrick Railway". They would have gone on making heavy losses in working the P P R, but their terms would doubtless have been gladly accepted by the P P R board if all prospect of selling the P P R line at advantageous terms had vanished, and they would have had the compensation of keeping out the G SW and M R. But Moon would certainly hope that news of this scheme would restore, and improve, the chances of an agreement among all four companies, and this result, in fact, swiftly followed. Before the end of May he had met M. W. Thompson and discussed with him the P P R and also the G & P P, whose line gave the G S W access to Stranraer. On the same day that the C R agreed to Moon's proposal about working the P P R, the G S W board approved terms on which Thompson was to communicate with him with a view once again to the joint acquisition of the P P R by the four companies.

Henceforward, though there would be much work to do and numerous difficulties to resolve in what was, after all, a major business exercise, matters went comparatively smoothly. The directors' report to the ordinary general meeting of the P P R in September 1884 said of the proposed sale of the line:

"The board are glad now to state that the differences alluded to are practically settled, and that a new bill, with the same object, will be prosecuted next session, which the directors have reason to expect will pass into law."

There were indications that the W R might be included in the new bill. An inspection of their line by the C R's engineer, George Graham, was intended. McClure wrote thus to him on 2nd September:

"Kindly let me know at what hour you intend to start upon your walk from Newton Stewart station and 1 will know where to find you during the day. I hope you will be favoured with equally fine weather to that which we have had of late".

On 19th, a C R engineer was reported examining Bladnoch bridge, and on 25th a special train carrying a party of C R directors travelled from Newton Stewart to Whithorn and back. On 6th October, McClure wrote to Samuel Swarbrick, a London barrister, who gave the W R very valuable help at this period:

"In the year ended 31st July last, our cost of working and maintenance, with rates, taxes, etc., absorbed 76% of traffic receipts. Had we been worked on the Portpatrick's terms we would have paid a dividend almost equal to theirs."

He lists the W R's rolling stock, etc.. at the same date, 31st July 1884, as follows:

| | |
|---|---|
| 6 engines | 7 /3rd class carriages  1 carriage truck |
| 2 tenders | 3 composite carriages 2 brake thirds |
| 2/ 1st class carriages | 3 horse boxes         31goods wagons |

The other plant comprises:

| | |
|---|---|
| 1 planing machine | 1 drilling machine |
| 1 wheel lathe | 2 stationary boilers |
| 1 vertical engine * | Engine fitters' and blacksmiths' tools |

The furniture of the office and stores at Wigtown

The furniture, ticket cases, dating frames, etc., of seven stations.

(N.B.-*vertical engine-Presumably the tramway engine that the Wheatleys are supposed to have brought from Yorkshire or Lancashire, but which was never used on the W R)

## Rails to Portpatrick

The negotiations over the acquisition by the four companies of the W R at the same time as the P P R took place during October. On 28th, the G S W heard a report on them, and a letter from John Noble, the M R's general manager, to Wainwright, dated 29th, setting out the terms on which it was proposed that the companies should take over the W R; they approved the terms. The leading part in the negotiations seems to have been taken by Noble and the L N W's George Findlay, as it was they who wrote on 4th November to Galloway:

". . . embodying the terms on which they were prepared to recommend the four companies to take over the Wigtownshire Company, viz: To take over all capital and revenue liabilities as from 31st July 1885 and pay 1¾% on the ordinary stock £114,339 -the Wigtownshire Company discharging all revenue liabilities up to 31st July 1885".

The new parliamentary bill came before a meeting of directors of the WR on 17th December. Galloway described how he and Drew had had "sundry meetings" with representatives of the four companies. As he had told the board at a meeting early in November, the companies would not go beyond guaranteeing £1.15.0% to WR shareholders. The bill contained the best terms the deputation could get. It had been prepared for introduction into Parliament at a conference in London the week before, called by Martin and Leslie, parliamentary agents, and which McClure had attended on behalf of the W R. The petition for the bill had been forwarded to London the previous day, 16th, sealed with the common seal of the company. The bill was being promoted by all the companies concerned, and not by the P P R and W R in separate bills as originally intended. Galloway claimed for himself the chief credit for bringing about this change, which, he said, had been achieved "with some difficulty". The meeting approved the bill's principles, and the actions of the deputation.

On 17th February 1885, both the C R and the G S W considered letters from Thos. Dalgleish, S.S.C., Edinburgh, offering the pier and harbour at Isle of Whithorn for sale. The C R declined, but the G S W decided to refer the subject to the four companies, and Wainwright asked McClure for information. Two letters which McClure wrote in reply on 24th February are interesting:

"I am in receipt of your telegram of today. The pier and harbour for sale belonged to the Burgh of Whithorn and was until the opening of our railway the port of Whithorn. It is situated at Isle of Whithorn, a village about three miles south of Whithorn, the terminus of this company's line. Prior to the opening of the railway the harbour had a considerable traffic and was the principal source of the burgh's revenue. Our line being in connection with the harbour of Garliestown, four miles north-east of Whithorn, the bulk of the sea-borne traffic from and to Whithorn and district is now diverted to Garliestown - the railway rate from

Garliestown being less than half the cartage from Isle of Whithorn. The loss of the harbour revenue and some litigations in which the Town Council were engaged have rendered the burgh bankrupt, and the pier and harbour are included in the prospectus advertised by the trustee for sale on Saturday post. I enclose copy advertisement. Until recently a considerable number of hands were engaged at the Isle in shipbuilding. The harbour is a safe and easily accessible one and will have, I should say, 18 to 24 feet of water at high tide. I see from the bankruptcy proceedings a sum of £940 borrowed by the Council from the Loan Commissioners was expended on the harbour a few years ago, and that the rent received by the burgh is this year only £33. Previous to the opening of the railway the rent was £200. It was rumoured some traders and farmers in the neighbourhood were going to club and buy the harbour for their own traffic but unless the trustee's price be a very small one, this project will not be carried out. I have not learned if there is to be an upset price but will try to do so and wire you tomorrow.

"The railway could be easily extended from Whithorn to the Isle, which is a good sea bathing place, and in case the four companies might, in the future, wish to do so, or acquire Garliestown harbour, it might be good policy in them not to let the Isle harbour get into other hands. In the circumstances this harbour, I think, could be purchased for a trifling sum on which its revenue would meantime pay interest."

"Isle harbour. I chanced to meet the Town Clerk of Whithorn this forenoon. He is agent in the burgh sequestration. He told me no upset price as yet fixed - that the matter was under consideration of the trustee. He knew of no likely offerers, except Mr Duff who is the principal trader in the district. Mr. Duff had at one time indicated he would give £420, but the Town Clerk said he, Mr. Duff, would not now make the offer.

"Mr. Drew, who has been to see the harbour lately, thinks £200 would have to be expended upon it soon. We therefore conclude it will not sell at over £300. I wired you accordingly".

The railways never did buy the harbour, however, either at Isle of Whithorn or at Garliestown; and the railway was never continued to "the Isle".

At the ordinary general meeting of the P P R on 27th March, it was resolved to form "a large and representative committee" of shareholders to arrange a presentation to the directors, since they had always given their services gratuitously. A special meeting was then held to approve the Sale and Transfer Bill, nineteen shareholders attending in person and forty-one represented by proxy. The motion proposed by Stair and seconded by Galloway, approving the bill, was carried unanimously. There seems to have been an air of satisfaction and contentment.

Stair remarked that the P P R had wanted to get as much as they could, and the four companies wanted to give as little as possible, but he "thought it was fairly arranged". He discounted danger of neglect of local traffic. Having brought the matter before the representatives of the four companies in London, he had been bidden to make his mind easy, "for when the companies were competing for the traffic they would be sure to get a good service".

A special meeting of W R proprietors (twenty shareholders were present in person, with an unspecified number of proxies, including six directors) held the following day also gave unanimous approval to the bill, which, it was stated, had been introduced into the House of Lords. On 24th April, McClure wrote to Drew that he had just received copies of petitions against it by the Scottish Provident Institution and by Mr. Chaine, M.P. for County Antrim. The Provident Institution were concerned about the £20,000 they had lent Stranraer Town Council and Chaine about Larne harbour, which was his property. McClure refers to these as "additional" petitions, so there must have been another objector, or others. A clause was added to the bill transferring to the four companies and the Joint Committee the liability for the debt to the Provident Institution which the P P R had accepted in 1877. By mid-July the bill had reached the committee stage, the only petitioners against it now being the G & P P. Two new clauses were added at their instance. In a letter to Galloway (addressed to him in his capacity of Colonel of Volunteers, at The Camp, Ayr) dated 27th July, McClure commented:

"I received today the reprint of the bill as amended in the Commons Committee ... There is nothing in the amendments that can prejudicially affect this company, and so far as I can see the two new clauses do not much improve the G & P P. In fact, Mr. Wainwright, in reference to them, said he did not consider they would add £5 to the saleable value of the G & P P."

McClure referred in the same letter to a related subject that was causing the correspondents no little concern at this time - the working of their line after the end of the current month, when Wheatley's lease expired, until the new owners could take effective charge. He had met Wheatley and obtained from him in writing his terms for continuing, but the L N W's Mr. Findlay must approve before they could be accepted. McClure hoped to hear from Findlay next day, 28th but he did not. Time was desperately short and McClure's impatience was understandable. On 29th, however, he was able to write to Galloway as follows; we can sense the deep relief expressed by the last sentence:

"Working of the line for August. Having no reply from Mr. Findlay to my letter forwarding Mr. Wheatley's on Saturday last, I wired Mr. Findlay this afternoon and have now a most satisfactory reply as follows:

"'Your telegram all parties concerned agree to Mr. Wheatley's proposal as to working line during month of August I write'.

"All the difficulties that loomed before us this day week have therefore disappeared and I hope all our anxious days on behalf of the Company are now past."

At a P P R general meeting held on 17th November, James Hosack gave notice that at the forthcoming winding-up meeting of the company he would move the grant of "a certain sum" to the board, and "also a certain sum" to the secretary and auditors, for their services to the company. This idea seems to have caused some controversy with the C R, Richard Moon joining in, doubtless as conciliator. On 22nd December the C R agreed to support his proposal "provided that not less than half the £1,000 be divided amongst the officials". The winding-up meeting of the P P R took place on 30th, and the payment of £500 to the company's officials is recorded. It had presumably been part of Moon's proposal that the "certain sum" should be £1,000; there is no mention in the records of payments to the P P R directors, or of the presentation that a committee of shareholders had been going to arrange. The story of the P P R closes with a dispute with the C R over money; particularly unfortunate, certainly, coming at this stage, but by no means uncharacteristic of relations between the two companies throughout their association. The P P R meeting of 17th November had carried unanimously a motion by Hosack for the board to make a claim against the four companies under clause 5 of the new Act, which dealt with the rights and obligations towards one another in financial matters of the P P R and W R and the Joint 'Committee during the period of transfer, and take counsel's opinion if their claim was not acceded to. This claim would appear to have been for £1,907.10.0, which sum the winding-up meeting empowered Stair and Dunbar to take all necessary steps to recover "from the Joint Committee or the four companies or both, and to divide any sum that may be received among the shareholders". Major Green Thompson, a C R representative on the P P R board, moved an amendment to the latter motion, seeking to add the words "subject to the claim against this sum for the share of the Portpatrick Company in the loss appearing in the steamer's balance sheet", but he did not get a seconder. The C R board, having received a report from Green Thompson, decided to ask the G S W to join them in urging the Joint Committee to apply for an interdict against the P P R. On 19th January 1886, the matter was referred to as having come before the Dean of Faculty: further developments are not recorded.

In contrast with this rather squalid item, it is pleasant to read the tribute which Stair paid to the absent Dunbar at the P P R winding-up meeting. Having acknowledged his major contribution to the making of the Working Agreement with the C R in 1864, Stair went on to say, to the accompaniment of cheers, that "it was also owing to his great tact and knowledge that the negotiations with regard to the sale of the line were brought to a successful issue".

# Rails to Portpatrick

Nothing marred the good humour and goodwill that distinguished the final meetings of the W R, which took place on the appropriate date of New Year's Eve. At the final board meeting, the directors expressed their gratitude to Samuel Swarbrick for his great trouble and valuable services during the negotiations. Swarbrick seems to have given his services gratuitously and had just declined their offer of a piece of plate. They went on to record their warm appreciation of the services given by the Wheatleys:

"Both gentlemen, from the commencement of the lease, devoted themselves assiduously to the accommodation of the public and development of the traffic of the district, and early won for themselves, and to the close retained, the confidence of the directors and the goodwill of the public."

"The announcement of Mr. W. T. Wheatley's removal from the district owing to the transfer of the line will be received with regret by the wide circle, who, during his eleven years residence, must have come to esteem him as the directors do, not only as a railway official, but for his general business abilities, public spirit and private worth, and they will not fail to assure him of their good wishes for his future welfare, usefulness and prosperity."

Hearty thanks were given also to McClure for his work as secretary and gratuitous help in various ways. McClure, who was currently Provost of Wigtown and later to serve for many years as town clerk, had been granted £87.10.0 in addition to his salary for the five months since the Act became law "as his remuneration as law agent, for extra services in connection with the winding up of the company".

The various tributes ring true, and are well above the standard of the merely conventional acknowledgement that sometimes passes on such occasions. At the winding-up meeting which followed this board meeting, Sir Herbert Maxwell, M.P., moved that:

"The shareholders express to the chairman and directors their sense of the discretion and ability with which the company has been managed by them for the last fourteen years and their hearty thanks for their lengthened gratuitous services and the manner in which the company's affairs have been brought so nearly to a conclusion."

Seconded by C. A. Routledge, banker, the motion was agreed to with applause. Galloway, commenting on the long and difficult nature of the negotiations for the sale of the line, illustrated the point with an effective little anecdote. The chairman of one of the big companies, he said, had told him that "it was not easy for a man to hold an umbrella over four people; it was still more difficult in the case of five; and in the case of six it was almost impossible".

## Rails to Portpatrick

The Companies' Bill had passed into law as the Portpatrick and Wigtownshire Railways (Sale and Transfer) Act on 6th August. "Vesting Day" under the Act was the first of that month. A new 3½% stock was to be issued, called "The Portpatrick and Wigtownshire Guaranteed Stock", and totalling £473,790. Holders of P P R stock would receive an amount equal to the nominal value of their holdings in the P P R, but W R shareholders would get only £5 of the new stock in exchange for each £10 share.

The Act gave running powers over the G S W line between Dumfries and Castle Douglas to the C R and the L N W; the terms were the same as those granted to the C R in 1865, except that the mileage proportion payable to the G S W was no longer to be subject to a minimum. On identical terms, the M R also gained running powers over the C R between Carlisle and Gretna Junction, and the L N W over the C R between Carlisle and Dumfries via Lockerbie. All these running powers applied only to traffic "to, from, over or beyond" the systems of the companies to whom they were granted "from, to, over or beyond" the P P R and W R lines: carriage of or "interference with" traffic arising or terminating on the systems of the companies over whose lines the powers were granted was forbidden.

Management of the railways was entrusted to a committee, "the Portpatrick and Wigtownshire Joint Committee", to be made up of two representatives from the boards of each of the four owning companies. Richard Moon and Miles MacInnes were appointed by the L N W, M. W. Thompson and R. A. Allison by the M R, J. C. Bolton and Hugh Brown by the C R, and the Earl of Galloway and Benjamin Nicholson by the G S W. The chairman was to be chosen from the representatives of the four companies in alternation, and was to hold office for one year. Moon was elected the J C's first chairman. He was probably the author of the humorous, and very appropriate, metaphor quoted by Galloway in his anecdote; certainly he shared with Dunbar the accomplishment of the nearly impossible in bringing the six companies to agreement. But his appointment as chairman was most likely simply a gesture in his honour, as in a matter of weeks he had resigned, being succeeded by MacInnes, while his place as a member of the J C was taken by Theodore Hare. MacInnes, Allison and Brown were appointed to the P P & G J C; all the J C, except Moon, were to be directors of the Larne & Stranraer Steamboat Company. John Thomson was the J C's secretary, his salary being £200 per annum. His office was at Carlisle Citadel Station - he was already secretary of the Joint Committee that controlled the station where the committee's meetings were ordinarily to be held.

The P P R and W R were called "the Joint Line" in the Act; they have been described as "The Premier Scottish Joint Line". Let us see how they fared under their new masters.

# Rails to Portpatrick

### CHAPTER NINE

The New Broom

FOR the first months of the Committee's rule, temporary arrangements were made for working the Joint lines. The C R continued to work the P P R line up to the end of October, at cost price. Wheatley worked the W R line until the end of November, for which he was paid £166.13.4. His engines and rolling stock were bought by the J C. They were valued at £5,192.10.0, but Wheatley disputed this and obtained payment of £6,400. He was appointed the J C's locomotive foreman at Stranraer, but left in April 1886 to become general manager of the G & P P.

The general managers and traffic superintendents of the owning companies were instructed to "arrange a joint time-table for goods and passengers and endeavour to arrange for one or both of the Scotch companies to work the trains". The C R and G S W undertook to provide engine power for the P P R line, at a mileage rate, each working certain trains daily. They were to take turns, for periods of two years, in supervising the locomotive working of the W R, maintaining the plant and rolling stock, supervising the permanent way and works, and the telegraphs, of both lines, and taking charge of the J C's law business in Scotland. The C R took the first period. From 1892, the period was extended to three years.

The coming of the J C brought a new traffic manager to Stranraer. At their meeting of 3rd October 1885, it was moved that they advertise for a traffic manager, "excluding any official now or formerly in the service of the four companies". It is significant that the proposer and seconder of this motion were the representatives of the M R and the G S W. The C R and L N W representatives moved the appointment of Grafton. The matter had to be referred to the standing arbitrator, who decided in favour of advertising. From 115 applicants the J C selected William Cunning, of the Belfast & Northern Counties Railway. So, for a second time, and now irrevocably, Grafton was removed from the post which he had filled with consistent diligence and credit. He did not, however, have to leave Stranraer again, as the C R and L N W appointed him their joint traffic agent there - his office was in North Strand Street - and in this capacity he spent the remainder of his working life, at a salary of £200 from each company.

WORKS STATIONS

On 6th and 7th January 1886, officers of the owning companies, accompanied by Cunning and, between Stranraer and Challoch Junction, by Hutchinson, manager of the Stranraer Section, made an inspection of the Joint Lines, and their subsequent report gives us some very interesting information. They made numerous recommendations for improvements several of which concerned the stations. At

Castle Kennedy, the platform was too short for the trains; ashes from Stranraer engine shed were to be laid down "in such a position as to fill up the ground, with a view to the extension of the platform at some future time". At Kirkcowan, though there was a passing-loop, there was a platform on the up side only. It was "extremely desirable" that a platform be provided on the down side, and Cunning was to inquire fully into the working, with a view to this. The down platform at Newton Stewart was too short, causing inconvenience in dealing with the boat train; it was lengthened about 80 feet. At Millisle, where, as we saw previously, passengers had to walk along the line to get to the exchange platform, "some narrow escapes from accident" had occurred; a footpath was now provided, "between the old platform and the new one", passing behind the signal-box, and fenced off from the line, with a planked crossing between the path and the end of the exchange platform. The officers recommended that the accommodation platforms on the W R, where trains had ceased to call since the J C's taking control, should be removed.

Several more improvements to stations took place during the next few years. On the morning of 21st August 1886, as the down boat express was standing at Glenluce station, Robert Thomson, junior clerk at the station, was badly hurt, due to the unlikely event of a passenger stepping on him! The train was too long for the platform, and as Thomson was walking along beside the part of the train projecting beyond the end of the platform, the passenger stepped down on him from one of the carriages, causing him a broken leg. Following this accident, the platforms at Glenluce were extended to a length of 130 yards, which Cunning described as "about the accommodation required for the boat trains". A shelter was then provided on the up platform, though only after some local residents had requested it. A little later, a similar shelter was erected on the up platform at Creetown, again in response to a petition from local people. The previous absence of such shelters is another indication of the strict economy practised in P P R days, and scarcely surprises us; more startling, however, is the description of Newton Stewart platforms in October 1889 as "constructed of clay and gravel, and (they) become very sloppy and dirty in wet weather". Concrete was to be laid down, though only "at such places as the engineer may consider necessary". Third class passengers were also being inconvenienced due to "small articles of goods traffic" being stored in their waiting-room; a new wooden shed was to be provided for these articles. Towards the end of 1891, the people of Newton Stewart district petitioned the J C for "comprehensive improvement and enlargement" of the station; the outcome was the erection of a new waiting-room and veranda on the island platform. Soon after, a refreshment room was opened; it had been let to Mr. T. Absee, of the Queen's Arms Hotel, for £4.10.0 per annum, the J C stipulating that it be run on temperance principles.

Residents of Parton, who petitioned late in 1891 for a shelter on their single platform, met with a negative response. The officers considered that they were "as well provided with shelter as most other small stations on the line", Cunning defining this as "a good general waiting-hall and ladies' waiting-room". The Earl of Stair requested improvement of the accommodation at Castle Kennedy station, with no recorded result. More successful was Mr. Cunninghame, owner of Dunragit House and estate, who was in a position to - and did - bring heavy pressure to bear on the J C. He informed them that he would not continue their lease of the vital ballast pit at Dunragit "unless the much needed improvement of Dunragit station is carried out". It seems that reconstruction of this station, following the fire in 1879, had never been completed. The JC ordered the necessary works to be carried out at once.

On the W R line, the wooden buildings of Whauphill station were burned down on 15th January 1889. A plan was drawn for new buildings of stone, to include a house for the station-master, but the expense was considered too great and a wooden replacement was provided. In the same year, the J C decided to erect a gatehouse for the public crossing at Garliestown. The estimate was £200. The lowest tender received. however, was for £320.2.10. Direct labour, therefore, was employed - "our own men, and take fresh tenders for the plumber, slates and plaster work only". The result was a triumph of thrift: early in 1891 the gatehouse was reported finished, at a total cost of £132.

WATER SUPPLY

Following their inspection in January 1886, the officers made several recommendations on this subject. Most of them concerned the WR line. The tank at Causewayend, and the tank and crane at Wigtown, now disused, should be removed. The tank at Whithorn was very dilapidated, and not high enough for the water to reach the cattle docks and waterclosets at the station; it should be raised three feet. They referred also, however, to difficulties about the water supply at Creetown, and proposed removal of the tanks and cranes there, and the erection of a crane on the down platform at Newton Stewart instead. The subject of water supply on this section of the P P R line was to recur for some years. In October 1885, the J C noted that Mrs. Grant, of Barholm estate, who currently received £10 per annum for the water to Creetown station, would cancel the arrangement unless she received £20. They decided to investigate alternative sources in the district. In March 1886, they authorised provision of a water column and connections at Newton Stewart, stating that these were to replace the facilities at Creetown, which were to be done away with. Three years passed, and then Cunning was complaining of the "very inadequate" water supply "for locomotive and other purposes" at Newton Stewart. He saw the Town Commissioners, who provided the supply, and reported that the pipes were clogged with mineral deposit, but steps would be taken before the summer (of 1890) to have them cleaned out. He urged the J C to improve facilities for storing water at the station, so that surplus water might be retained overnight for use next day. No further action should be taken until the effect of cleaning out the pipes was seen. The position was obviously very unsatisfactory, but there was no improvement for some time - conditions, in fact, got steadily worse.

At Stranraer, the water supply was obtained from a well, with the aid of a pumping-engine. In May 1886, Robert Dundas, engineer in charge of the C R's Southern Division, complained about this supply as "defective". A supply, he claimed, could be obtained from the Town Council for about £36 per annum, and the pumping-engine could then be removed to Whithorn to improve the "very inconvenient" supply there. Early next year, he was supported by Drummond and Smellie, locomotive superintendents of the C R and G S W. The matter was deferred for consideration, Dundas urging "the importance of keeping the well clean from which the water supply is at present drawn". In spite, however, of a further intervention by Drummond, in favour of an agreement with the Town Council "because of inadequate water in dry seasons", the officers decided that the expense was unnecessary, the present arrangement never having failed and being adequate for the purpose.

THE TRACK, AND METHODS OF WORKING

The officers reported in January 1886 that at Stranraer it was the practice for down passenger trains arriving at the station to run past the down platform and then back to the up platform, where the passengers were set down. This piece of informality, which had doubtless been found convenient to both passengers and staff, was to cease, and down trains were to unload at the down platform. They found also that, at stations on the P P R line, "for convenience of working, the plan had been adopted of running the trains to either platform (where there are two) almost indiscriminately". Disapproving of this, they recommended that:

"All stopping trains ought to run to the proper (left side) platform; that trains in both directions running through the station without stopping should pass over the main line unless they have to cross another train, and instructions should be given that in the event of its being necessary to run a train, which usually passed on the main line, through the loop, the signals should be kept against the train until the speed has been sufficiently reduced to enable it to pass through the loop without inconvenience, it being understood that, consistent with the due observance of these instructions, the main line must, as far as practicable, be kept clear for non-stopping trains."

As, however, "the present arrangements have been in force for a considerable time", they were to continue until Cunning had gained enough experience of the line to be able to decide the best way to improve them.

The officers learned that all the signals on the line were lit by candle lamps. They recommended the substitution of petroleum lamps "as new ones become necessary". The J C, however, ordered the change to be made at once.

# Rails to Portpatrick

The officers had found the P P R line, despite its very moderate length, to be worked in a variety of ways. The Stranraer to Portpatrick section was worked by train staff, without ticket; the Stranraer harbour branch by staff and ticket; the Stranraer section, Stranraer to Challoch Junction, by Tyers' block, without staff or ticket; and the Challoch Junction to Castle Douglas section by telegraph, with no block or staff and ticket arrangements. Anxious to impose a uniform system of working on the main line from Stranraer to Castle Douglas, they ordered an investigation of the relative merits and cost of Tyers' ordinary block system with staff and ticket added, and block with electric train tablet. Following this investigation, the J C ordered the introduction of the train tablet system between Challoch Junction and Castle Douglas. The estimated cost was £1,750, compared with only £750 for the combined staff and block, but no change in signals would be necessary, whereas the staff and block system would mean considerable signal changes. Train tablet working was begun from Challoch Junction to Newton Stewart on December 1st, 1886, and from Newton Stewart to Castle Douglas on 1st of the following month. Instruments were placed at Challoch Junction, Glenluce, Kirkcowan, Newton Stewart West Box, Newton Stewart East Box, Creetown, Dromore, Loch Skerrow, New Galloway, Crossmichael and Castle Douglas Junction. The cost of introducing the system on the Stranraer section had been estimated at £570; the conversion was authorised by the P P & G J C on 28th October 1887.

Before long, the J C found themselves plunged into the very expense they had been so anxious to avoid - that of new signalling. Following the Armagh collision in June 1889, the Regulation of Railways Act required the interlocking of signals and points. There was no interlocking at most of the J C's block posts. They had to draw up a plan for "Improvement of stations, proposed alterations of platforms, lines and signalling", according to which the stations were to be taken in this order, with the estimated expenditure shown: (1) Kirkcowan, £930 (it seems the second platform was now to be added); (2) Creetown, £460; (3) Dromore, £685; (4) Glenluce £640; (5) Crossmichael, £685; (6) New Galloway, £580; (7) Loch Skerrow, £620; (8) Parton, £25; (9) Palnure, £25. In April 1891, the officers noted that "the interlocking of points and signals, the provision of double platforms, and other improvements, are now completed and brought into use, except in the case of Loch Skerrow, which is expected to be completed in a few days". The new signal cabin at Loch Skerrow was opened on 6th May.

A year later, there was being tried experimentally at Glenluce station "a new mechanical device for interlocking the tablet slide with the starting signal". It was hoped that this, the invention of Cunning, would overcome the objection made by the Board of Trade, at their inspection of the system, to the absence of such interlocking. Cunning's device was successful, was approved by the Board of Trade and adopted at Glenluce, Kirkcowan, Creetown, Dromore, Loch Skerrow, New Galloway and Crossmichael at a total cost of not more than £3.

While these developments were taking place on the P P R line, a programme of track replacement had been in progress on the W R. In December 1885, Dundas had reported to the J C that:

> "Some portions of the (W R) line being in very bad order he had directed the necessary repairs to be made, and he thinks it desirable that a commencement should be made with relaying the line, and in relaying he proposes to adopt the same class of permanent way as on the Portpatrick line in place of the light, flat-bottomed rails, the work to be proceeded with from year to year in a moderate way until the whole is brought up to the same standard at the Portpatrick."

The JC adopted Dundas' suggestion of 80lb. bull-headed rails as standard for the Joint Lines. Relaying of the W R line, from Newton Stewart to Whithorn, was completed in 1889. There had been a small amount of relaying on the P P R line.

There was a proposal to give Whithorn a turn-table. This was part of a larger plan, suggested by Drummond and Smellie early in 1887. The old 40 feet turn-table at Stranraer was to be transferred to Whithorn; a 50 feet turn-table was to be installed at Stranraer, so that more powerful engines could be turned there; a turn-table was to be installed at Newton Stewart; and a shed for two engines was to be provided at Newton Stewart also. The J C pointed out that the Girvan Company had an interest in the existing turn-table at Stranraer. If it was now inadequate, they should be consulted, and they should bear part of the cost of the change. In June, the officers decided that the provision of a turn-table at Whithorn ought to be postponed; there was no serious inconvenience, especially since the W R line was likely to be worked by tank engines in the future. The new turn-table at Stranraer would cost £670; it should be postponed, for there was no real need of it at present. Neither could they recommend the large outlay implied at Newton Stewart; the W R engine, which now stood overnight at Newton Stewart, would, in future, leave its train there and run light to the shed at Wigtown, only fourteen miles per day of light running being involved. Altogether, the locomotive superintendents' proposals had met a very negative reception, though Stranraer got its larger turn-table in 1892.

A turn-table at Newton Stewart had, of course, been suggested by Grafton in 1883, and in 1889 we find the renewal of another proposal first made in P P R days - that of a passing-place at Castle Kennedy. The officers referred to "serious delays that frequently occur to trains running over the Stranraer section". The J C supported them, but the Ayrshire & Wigtownshire Company, who in 1887 had bought the G & P P for £155,000, objected to provision of the crossing-place and, their objection being upheld on arbitration, the matter had again to be postponed. In November 1891 the J C noted receipt of a letter from Lord Stair in favour of doubling the line between Stranraer and Challoch Junction; this was not done, then or at any future time.

# Rails to Portpatrick

There is a brief but interesting note during these years of an engine turntable at Portpatrick. Early in 1891, the officers recorded that one of its girders was broken, repairs being estimated at £12.

## THE TRAIN SERVICE
### GOODS TRAINS

In April 1887, the J C, considering the charges per train mile made by the C R and G S W for engine power to be unduly high, decided to invite all the four owning companies to tender for the provision of engine power from 1st August. Their invitation was accepted by the C R, the G S W and the L N W. The tenders submitted by the two Scots companies were the same; that of the L NW was slightly lower, and the J C recorded their acceptance of it. For a brief time it seemed that the black locomotives of the great English company would steam through Galloway in place of the familiar blue of the C R and the more recently arrived G S W green; but in September the J C continued the locomotive working to the Scots companies, they having offered slightly more favourable terms. In inviting the tenders, however, the J C gave specifications regarding the class of engine needed on the P P R line, which provide some interesting information. Engines handling goods trains, they stated, should be able to take loads as follows:

|                              | Loaded goods wagons | If assisted by a pilot engine |
|------------------------------|---------------------|-------------------------------|
| Castle Douglas-New Galloway  | 35                  | 48                            |
| New Galloway-Dromore         | 23                  | 35                            |
| Dromore-Glenluce             | 28                  | 42                            |
| Glenluce-Stranraer           | 35                  | 48                            |
| Stranraer-Newton Stewart     | 28                  | 42                            |
| Newton Stewart-Dromore       | 23                  | 39                            |
| Dromore-New Galloway         | 26                  | 30                            |
| New Galloway-Castle Douglas  | 35                  | 50                            |

3 loaded cattle or mineral wagons equal to 4 loaded goods wagons.
3 empty goods or mineral wagons equal to 2 loaded goods wagons.
    Brake van not included in above loads.
    Maximum train 50 vehicles.

In December 1889, there were three goods trains into Stranraer daily, and three out. Shunting averaged ten hours daily, which the officers wanted reduced. A goods left Stranraer at 8.30 a.m. in 1887; in 1890 there was a goods from Castle Douglas to Stranraer Harbour at 8.25 a.m. and Castle Douglas to Stranraer at 2.25 p.m.; in 1893 one left Stranraer at 11 p.m. There was an 11.30 a.m. goods Newton Stewart-Castle Douglas in 1888, returning from Castle Douglas at 5.30p.m., though this may have run on certain days of the week only.

# Rails to Portpatrick

In 1886, the JC gained an estimated total of 3,160 tons in extra goods traffic, following a dispute between the G & P P and the G S W as a result of which the Girvan line was closed for two months and carried only restricted traffic for another four. The P P & W proportion of the through rates for this traffic was estimated as 4/6 per ton. There was an estimated loss of 1,002 tons during the first half of 1887, accounted for by the very low prices of turnips, which had stopped traffic in this commodity altogether for the time being, but in the corresponding half of 1888 receipts for mineral traffic increased by over £180, more coal being sent over the line, and those for livestock showed an increase of more than £860, due to "a largely increased cattle traffic from Ireland". During the second half of the year, the Irish cattle traffic was described as "extremely heavy". As we shall see presently, there were frequent complaints about delay to the evening boat express from Stranraer, owing to the extent of the perishable traffic (e.g. fish, dead fowl) from Ireland.

It is likely that the goods traffic on the W R line was increasing during the late '80s. In February 1887, a C R engine was reported to have been hired to work temporarily on "the Wigtown Branch", and in September it was stated that the P P & W goods engine was too light for the traffic on the W R line in the winter months, so that a C R engine would have to be used. The goods engine referred to was W R No. 3, the Sharp, Stewart 0-4-2, originally of the Fleetwood, Preston & West Riding Junction Railway, and bought by Wheatley from the L N W and L & Y J C in 1876; the only W R engine to be painted black. In March 1889, the officers reported the P P & W guard's van as being too light for the goods train on the W R line. For safety in working, a van had been hired from the G S W, though the J C soon after bought one from the M R. A C R engine is mentioned working on the W R line in December 1889, and two months later Drummond wrote of the old No. 3: "This goods engine No. 3 is quite unfit to do the work it is called upon to perform, and is, in fact, utterly done". Soon after, Drummond and Smellie informed Cunning that "the goods engine (No. 3) was worn out and not worth repairing, and that a Caledonian engine had been sent to replace it".

PASSENGER TRAINS

The time-table agreed on for the Joint Lines by the four owning companies came into force on Ist November 1885. The magnificent M R had already proclaimed their larger presence in Galloway in the following characteristic manner, described in the *Free Press* of 8th October:

"The Midland and Glasgow & South Western Railway Companies are now running the St. Louis Pullman car between Stranraer and London daily. The car is a model of modern art, and through the courtesy of Mr. Baillie, the conductor, we have been enabled to give some idea of it to those of our readers who have not seen one. The car is about 36 feet long, entered by a door in the centre. On either side, as you enter, are two saloons or rooms with a lavatory and cabinet between them. The rooms, which are beautifully carved and finished, are mahogany inlaid with white maple, boxwood and ebony. The two centre rooms are used as saloons, and fitted up with table, seats, mirrors, etc. The two end rooms can be used as private drawing-rooms, and are handsomely furnished. The spring seats are covered with flowered claret plush, and can be converted into beds. There are four sleeping berths in each room, two upper and two lower. The upper ones can be folded up when not in use. Each berth is richly decorated with flowered curtains made of silk and wool, and in each room is a double lamp which gives abundance of light. The whole carriage is heated with hot water pipes from one of Baker's patent American stoves. For ventilation, a neat little window screen is used, and in summer the heated air is carried off by means of a deflector, which can be used at pleasure."

In contrast with this, we read the order issued in March 1886 forbidding the practice, which had evidently obtained in P P R days, of carrying passengers in the guard's vans of goods trains. From July 1886, local second class bookings on the P P R line, which had been abolished in 1863 but restored two years later, finally ceased. Second class bookings between the P P R line and the C R and G S W lines were also discontinued; but through second class bookings from and to the L N W line were available as before. In April 1890, the J C recorded that the only second class bookings carried on the line were those of the L N W, the passengers travelling in L N W carriages. Some 4,000 additional passengers travelled over the P P R line in 1886 in connection with the Highland and Agricultural Society's show at Dundee. The next year, the J C introduced excursion tickets to London, from Stranraer, Newton Stewart and Whithorn, at 50/- first class and 25/- third class by L N W or M R, and 37/6 second class by L N W. There were five excursions; the outward journey had to be made on a specified day in May, June, July, August or September, but the tickets were available for return any time within sixteen days. A similar five excursions to London had been allowed in 1888 "in connection with those from Belfast via Stranraer". Repeated in 1889, they realised £233.12.6, and the J C were happy to revive them the following year. Meanwhile, in 1887, they had agreed to Cunning's suggestion of cheap Saturday to Monday tickets during the summer, available to Castle Kennedy, Stranraer and Portpatrick from local stations more than twelve miles away. These, too, must have been remunerative, for they also were continued in the ensuing years. In 1889, a summer excursion train was started, from Stranraer to Portpatrick and back, on the Wednesday half-holiday. It was anticipated that revenue would considerably exceed the estimated expenses of 14/- for each double journey.

In their specifications in connection with the locomotive working in 1887, the J C laid down that for the boat express trains engines were required "able to take fourteen ordinary vehicles, but the usual load may be about eleven". For other passenger trains they should "be able to take fourteen ordinary vehicles, but the usual load may be about six". They added that one sleeping car or bogie vehicle was to be regarded as equal to two ordinary vehicles. During these years, there were the boat express and three through local trains each way daily, except Sundays. In September 1891, however, there was introduced a new local between Stranraer and Newton Stewart only. It left Newton Stewart at 9.15a.m., after the arrival of the 8.10 from Whithorn, called at all the intermediate stations, and reached Stranraer at 10.5. Leaving Stranraer at 7.55 in the evening, and calling at all intermediate stations, it arrived at Newton Stewart in time for the 9.5 to Whithorn, and also took forward from the intermediate stations passengers wanting to join the up boat express at Newton Stewart. In several respects, therefore, the new train was a notable improvement. It gained among the people of the district the affectionate name of "the Wee Train", and was to chuff to and fro across the shire for many years to come.

The subject of connections with the Girvan line at Dunragit came up again in June 1887, when the J C agreed to a suggestion from W. T. Wheatley, as manager of the Girvan Company that the morning (down) boat express should call at Dunragit. A more surprising check to the progress of the down express, noted in June 1890, was a call at Kirkcowan to leave a horse-box. There were constant complaints about delays to the evening boat train. In December 1887, Cunning said that it was frequently late in leaving Stranraer, due to the steamer being late and more time now being needed to load the Irish perishable traffic on the train. This traffic was obviously increasing. A year later, after complaints from Cotton about the train being late in starting, it was decided to send the perishable traffic, when it was particularly heavy, by a special train, to follow the passenger express. At present the express frequently needed a pilot; under the new arrangement the pilot engine could haul the special train, and the number of coaches on the passenger express would be reduced. Almost immediately subsequent to this, however, the express was reported to be regularly running late, owing to "the slow steamer" being on the passage and the G S W insisting that the train call at Dalbeattie. The Belfast Chamber of Commerce, now very keenly interested in the use of the Larne route for an improved Mail Service, complained of the slowness of the trains between Carlisle and Stranraer. Before the end of 1889, however, Cunning was expressing concern at the large number of special trains that were being run with the Irish perishable traffic, and pointing out that the traffic was unremunerative when the special service was provided. The situation was clearly something of a "vicious circle".

It was once again from the Irish side that most of the pressure for the development and improvement of the route came. Soon after the J C took control, Cotton repeated the appeal he had made in 1882 for fares by Larne to be made competitive with those by Fleetwood. He again returned to the theme in 1890, drawing attention to the much higher fares via Larne, the improvements recently made in the accommodation provided on other routes and the fact that passengers using one of them could return by an alternative route, e.g. outward via Fleetwood and inward via Liverpool. Once more he suggested, as he had done in 1882, that the fares from London to Dumfries should be made applicable to Belfast. The officers agreed to consider this, though they pointed out that already the through fares to Belfast were the same as those to the stations on the Joint Line, and very little higher than those to other stations west of Dumfries. The second summer service by express train and steamer, in demand for many years on the Irish side, was introduced in July 1890, and became a regular feature of the route. Reduced fares came into force in June 1891. They followed Cotton's proposals closely: single fares from London to Belfast, and vice versa, were reduced from 58/6 first class, 45/- second class, and 27/6 third class, to 55/- first class and 42/6 second class, the third class fare staying the same; and return fares from 100/- first class, 75/- second class, and 55/- third class to 92/- first class, 71/- second class, and 50/- third class. The comparatively high fares via Larne were due to the much longer train journey involved; it was now to be hoped that prospective patrons would consider the difference that remained to be reasonable, in view of this fact and of the related advantage of a short sea crossing. Reports were encouraging. In the first four months following the reduction of fares, 581 additional passengers were recorded, the J C's proportion of receipts being £83.13.9. A side-effect of the reduction was that it became cheaper to travel from London to Joint Line stations, also, and the officers noted with satisfaction a total of 104 more such passengers, bringing the J C an increase in revenue of £43.0.9.

No such developments could be expected on the W R line, the J C's "Wigtownshire Branch", where indeed passenger facilities were at first curtailed rather than improved. The closure of the wayside halts obviously inconvenienced some people, for the J C soon got a petition asking for them to be reopened. They declined this, as also a later request for one train each way daily to call at "Broughton Siding". They discussed providing seat cushions in the third class carriages, resolving in the negative. From the beginning of 1888, passengers were allowed to ride on the afternoon goods from Newton Stewart on market day, Friday. Short morning and evening trains introduced to connect with the boat trains, however, were poorly patronised, carrying an average of only three passengers a day, so that they were discontinued in June 1888 after six months' trial. Dissatisfaction with the service provided on the W R line is evidenced by the petition from the Town Council and inhabitants of Whithorn received by the J C in 1891. Details are not recorded.

The J C thus made several improvements in the passenger facilities on their lines, but the regular local service continued inadequate for the needs of the people. The big companies remained primarily interested in the through service, as commercial considerations required them to be. Even the express service gave rise to complaints, impossible to remedy without bringing about new problems. The sheer impossibility of reconciling the claims of the different kinds of traffic on the lines, within the bounds of commercial viability, is a theme which runs the whole length of our story.

Motive power on the W R line called for a good deal of attention. The need for more powerful engines was increasingly felt. In April 1887, the officers recommended the replacement of the existing engines in the near future by tank locomotives, and the J C declared their intention that "eventually that line shall be worked by the same engines and under the same arrangements as the Portpatrick line". We saw how the old goods engine No. 3 had to be replaced, at least in winter, by a C R engine. In the same letter of February 1890 in which he condemned No. 3 as "utterly done", Dugald Drummond described all the old W R locomotives as "too light for the traffic, and becoming very costly in repairs". He urged their replacement by main line engines as quickly as possible, though the best of the old engines might stay to work the Garliestown branch. In April, however, after a conference with Drummond and Smellie, Cunning reported that the old engines were "for the present in a fit state to work the passenger trains".

The disappearance of Wheatley's old, second-hand engines from the scene of which they had been so familiar, useful and genial a part, was hastened by the Armagh collision and the clause of the subsequent Regulation of Railways Act empowering the Board of Trade to insist on the provision of continuous brakes on all trains carrying passengers. This was to come into effect on the Joint Lines in May 1892. Lambie, Drummond's successor as locomotive superintendent with the C R, wrote of the W R line that only the rebuilt Engine No. 1 was at all suitable for fitting with the Westinghouse brake, and only to work trains on the Garliestown branch, though from the state of the boiler and other parts it was likely to do that satisfactorily for several years. "While the carriage stock" he continued, "though old and frail, might run for a short time longer under the present conditions, none of the vehicles are suitable for being fitted with the Westinghouse brake; but the horse-boxes, and possibly one or two of the carriages, might be fitted with brake pipes in order to make them available for working locally, one vehicle at a time on a train, as permitted by the Board of Trade". The officers described engine No. 3 as "for some time laid off work, through being entirely worn out"; it and the tramway engine were to be sold.

The J C, acting on the advice of Lambie and Manson, Smellie's successor on the G S W, decided that of the six W R locomotives, four be sold as scrap, and the others - the rebuilt Nos. 1 and 5 - retained to work the Garliestown branch. Of the original twenty-five carriages, including horse-boxes, three - two brake vans and a brake composite - had been broken up. Three carriages, three brake vans, and one brake composite were now to be withdrawn as worn out. The remainder might continue working for a short time, but none of them was worth fitting with the Westinghouse brake. Three horse-boxes were now fitted with brake pipes, and might be used for local traffic.

As the C R could not provide engines with continuous brake fittings for the W R line by May 1892, the Board of Trade granted an extension of time, and their Order concerning continuous braking took effect on both the Joint Lines in

# Rails to Portpatrick

November. In December the J C noted that of the old W R engines and rolling stock, two engines, nine carriages, three horse-boxes, one carriage truck and thirty wagons remained in use. It had been agreed that replacement rolling stock would come from the C R and G S W, while clearly it was anticipated that motive power would be supplied by the C R. Early in 1893, however, the G S W were supplying engines for all the trains on the W R line, except the Garliestown branch; the J C's own engines, it was noted, were "worn out and withdrawn".

## THE STEAMERS

In 1885, the Steamboat Company made a small profit. This event was, no doubt, all the more welcome for being uncommon, but both the company and the J C were clearly far from satisfied with the service as it was then. The general managers of the companies owning the Joint Lines conferred with Cotton, and it was decided to try to get a deputation from Belfast and the North of Ireland to take up with the Postmaster General the matter of the establishment of a Mail Service by the route. The related subject of the acceleration of the train and steamer service was discussed also, though for the moment no firm decisions were made.

The passage was maintained at this time by the *Louise* and the *Beatrice*. Admiral Dent, marine superintendent with the L N W at Holyhead, described the *Louise* early in 1886 as "in very fair condition ... it may work for many years as it is", but added, "no alteration would make it suitable for an improved service". In December, she was described as "at present in the service, but making bad time". About 300 tons of coal a month were consumed this year, at an average price of about 10/- a ton. The *Beatrice* came in for some high praise following a survey in 1888. Captain Campbell reported that the superintendent engineer and the Government surveyor were very satisfied with the condition of her boilers, and the bearings and brasses of her engines. "The bottom of the vessel", he continued, "is wonderfully clean and free from shell, and its condition is as perfect in other respects as on the day she was launched, and she is altogether a credit to the builders". At their previous ordinary general meeting, however, the Steamboat Company had resolved to ask the railway companies to consider the purchase of a new steamer, "with more speed and better passenger and cattle accommodation than is afforded by the *Beatrice*." Campbell suggested that it should be capable of doing the passage in two hours instead of the present 2¾ hours, and stated what he regarded as suitable dimensions. It was going to be far from easy, however, to raise the necessary capital. The Irish members of the Steamboat board stated that there was no prospect of anything being raised on their side towards the cost. The J C for the present came to no decision about the purchase, while the C R board resolved to "resist as far as expedient".

Meanwhile, the Steamboat Company and the J C had been trying to induce the Government to sanction the erection of a fog-horn at the lighthouse on Corsewall Point, the entrance to Loch Ryan. After several unsuccessful attempts to get this sanction, serious delay was caused to the steamer on the Larne to Stranraer passage on the evening of 22nd September 1888, when Campbell had to anchor off Corsewall all night. Writing to the Steamboat Company of "the great difficulty and danger now experienced", Campbell suggested the provision of fog-horns like that of the *Beatrice* at Corsewall and at Skermaghan Point on Islandmagee, at the entrance to Larne Lough. £1 a year retainer might be paid to a man to work the horn in fogs at the times the boat would be passing, with a few shillings for each occasion his services were required. The extra man at Corsewall lighthouse was willing to make himself available, and a man living close to Skermaghan could be got. The whole cost of the idea would not be more than £10 a year. The Steamboat Company authorised Campbell to carry it out.

Soon after, however, a deputation, consisting of Galloway, Miles MacInnes and Findlay (general manager of the L N W) met Hicks Beach, President of the Board of Trade, in a renewed attempt to get consent to the erection of the fog signal at Corsewall lighthouse. When Hicks Beach replied that the expense could not be incurred owing to the state of the Mercantile Marine Fund (a fund set up to provide lights and other benefits to seafarers, and financed from various sources, principally light dues), the deputation suggested the firing of a gun during foggy weather "as at the South Stack lighthouse near the entrance to Holyhead harbour". This, of course, would be intended to warn all shipping, and not only the company's steamer. But by May 1889, the Board of Trade had sanctioned expenditure on the siren signal, which was duly installed a year later. It was "worked by oil engines, with four blasts in quick succession every three minutes, high-low, high-low".

When the Steamboat Company first contemplated acquiring a new vessel, they had very much in mind the establishment of a second daily service, to begin in time for the Glasgow Exhibition of 1888. Though the matter of the new steamer had to be deferred, the company still hoped to operate a double service using their existing steamers. They appointed a sub-committee to organise this, and Campbell was reported to be getting the *Louise* ready to start the service on 1st June. In May, however, came a proposal by Mr. Burns that if the double service were abandoned, he would make return tickets by the Belfast-Glasgow service via Larne available for return, within seven days, by his Glasgow-Belfast steamers. The sub-committee at first favoured acceptance; there are several signs that they were very apprehensive of possible financial loss by the new service. Burns then had a meeting with the G S W board, and succeeded in persuading them to accept his offer instead of supporting the new service. Cotton was instructed to seek the views of Mr. Findlay of the L N W and Mr. Noble of the M R. Findlay was in favour of the double service; there was no reply from Noble. After long discussion, the sub-committee agreed to go ahead with the double service, from 1st June.

Immediately, however, they were confronted with the refusal of the G S W to run trains in connection with the Second Service. They held another long discussion, in the course of which their attitude hardened. They deplored the G S

W's action "on the pressure of Messrs. Burns", and saw it as an unfortunate precedent. They were "now of opinion that no effort should be spared to carry out the decision of the board as to this Second Service". Cotton was sent to Glasgow, to see M. W. Thompson, general manager of the G S W and the M R. But this meeting showed that their determination, for the present at any rate, was in vain. The G S W absolutely refused co-operation. Very regretfully, the Steamboat Company acquiesced in abandonment of the scheme, noting that the original suggestion for it had come from the G S W chairman, which made that company's sudden change of view the more deplorable. Cotton was to negotiate with Burns about implementing the latter's proposal.

The provision of a new steamer - and, incidentally, of a Second Service during part of the year - was brought to the fore again by the suggestion from the Post Office, in March 1889, that they might seek a reduced payment for the carriage of letters by the Larne route. This forced the Steamboat Company to consider with urgency the establishment of a faster service, and at the same time roused once more hopes of agreement with the Government for a larger service of mails. H. McNeile, the company's chairman, spoke of the *Louise* as now totally unfit as a reserve boat. Running from 28th January to 9th February after the *Beatrice* had broken down, she had proved so slow that it had been almost impossible to keep up the connections. Since the *Beatrice* was built, improved vessels had been put on all the other routes. Messrs. Burns had just provided a very fast new steamer for their Ardrossan route. It was agreed that the delegates of the English and Scottish railway companies would bring the matter before their boards, and get the capital for a new steamer sanctioned.

As part of the ensuing financial arrangements, the Steamboat Company was wound up. The independent shareholders, all on the Irish side, were bought out at 12/6 in the £. Provision was made for paying off the loans made by the P P R and the Carrickfergus & Larne and Belfast & Northern Counties Companies. By 1893, the Steamboat Company had been replaced by the Larne & Stranraer Steamship Joint Committee, with a capital of £100,498.3.8, £19,747.0.11 from each of the Scottish and English companies and £21,510.0.0 from the Belfast Company. Four of its six members represented the P P & W Joint Committee, the others the Belfast Company. In practice, profit or loss made in working the steamers was divided among the contributing companies in proportion to their interest in the traffic. Cotton continued as the conimittee's manager, and Cunning was their agent at Stranraer. Their secretary was John Thomson, secretary to the P P & W J C.

Of nine tenders submitted for building the new steamer, that of W. Denny & Bros., Dumbarton, was accepted. The contract was entered into by the P P & W J C. Of the contract price of £46,500, as much as possible - a total of over £20,000 - was paid out of money received from the Steamboat Company in repayment of the loans to them from the P P R and the Irish railway companies, while the remainder of the price was shared by the four English and Scottish companies. Among several improvements made at Larne was a 70 feet extension to the North Pier to accommodate the new steamer, and McNeile, of the Steamboat Company, spoke of the great need of better provision for. the comfort and convenience of passengers at both Larne and Stranraer. Following an inspection of the pier and station at Stranraer Harbour, the officers described the station as "totally inadequate for the proper conduct of the growing traffic" and drew attention to the "considerable expense from time to time in patching up the wooden part of the pier". They called the J C's attention to the urgent need for improvements.

In December 1889, the J C received a report by Dundas and Adam, engineers, proposing two schemes, one to cost £11,560 and the other £20,000, for improving Stranraer pier. The report was brought before the P P & G J C, but the J C and the Ayrshire & Wigtownshire Company could not agree, so the matter went to arbitration. The arbitrator's award, given in August 1890, ordered the adoption of the smaller scheme. The J C, however, now strongly favoured the larger scheme, and by the end of the year were conferring with John Blair, W.S., owner of the A & W, on the subject. Blair, however, had recently acquired the A & W as a speculative investment, his chief concern being to sell it at a profit, and not until this aim had been achieved could any agreement over the pier be reached. He at length found a purchaser in the G S W, who bought the A & W for £235,000. The G S W took over management of the A & W line on 1st February 1892, and later that month they and the J C decided to carry out the larger scheme of improvement. The G S W's contribution would be only £5,780 - half the cost of the smaller scheme ordered by the arbitrator in 1890. The larger scheme involved doing away with the wooden part of the pier and making it solid throughout.

The new steamer was launched at Dumbarton on 23rd January 1890; she was named *Princess Victoria.* She was a steel paddle steamer, length 281 feet, breadth 36 feet, and depth 13 feet; she grossed 1,100 tons. Her engines were compound, with 2 diagonal cylinders, nominal h.p. 624. The contract had specified a guaranteed speed of 18 knots in regular work, with a coal consumption of 2¾ tons. She went on her trial trip on 22nd April.

"Over a distance about equal to that between Stranraer and Larne and against an unfavourable wind the vessel maintained a mean speed of 19¾ knots, equal to about 22¾ miles per hour. The engines made 47 revolutions to the minute, with 110lb. pressure at the engines and 115 lb. at the boilers. There was 100 tons dead weight on board, and the draught did not exceed that specified, viz. 9 feet."

On 24th April, a large party boarded the *Victoria* for a pleasure trip. At the dinner which followed, P. Deniny, junior, paid tribute to the great interest shown, and valuable advice given, by Captain Campbell throughout the ship's construction. Expressing his belief that it was through the efforts of the Irish companies that the ship had been built, Denny went on to urge them to persuade the Scottish companies to provide faster train services to Stranraer. Mr. Wolff, of Harland & Wolff, claimed that his firm had had the offer to build the *Victoria* but could not accept owing to other work.

The *Victoria* reached Stranraer about 1p.m. next day. Before she passed Cairnryan, hundreds of people were already lining the foreshore to witness her arrival. Opinions about her varied. Some spectators were disappointed at the appearance of the new vessel, built for speed on lines conspicuously different from those of the *Louise* and *Beatrice*. A more generally favourable reaction would certainly have come about had the onlookers been able to see the interior of the ship. She proved to need about 135 tons of coal a week on the passage, the price being 12/- a ton, delivered on the pier at Stranraer. In June, the *Louise* was sold to Mr. Lowther, of Belfast, for £2,200. She subsequently had a useful career as Islay (III) of the MacBrayne fleet until she was wrecked on Sheep Island, Port Ellen, in 1902.

So far, the attempt to introduce a second daily service had resulted only in a clear illustration of the conflicting interests involved in the provision of the steamer service, and of the train services through Galloway, but feeling on the Irish side of the Channel in favour of the Second Service was now stronger than ever, and Cotton lost no time in applying to the J C for their co-operation in the matter. He pointed out that the *Victoria* took a total of only about four hours daily to maintain the single service, and submitted a draft time-table of trains in connection with a Second Service, whereby a departure from Belfast at 9.30 a.m. would give arrivals at Glasgow at 4 p.m., Edinburgh at 5.50, Carlisle at 3.43, Newcastle at 6.35, Liverpool at 7.45, Manchester at 7.25 and London at 11. In the down direction, passengers leaving Newcastle, Carlisle, Edinburgh and Glasgow in the morning would reach Belfast at 3.45 p.m. The officers were not enthusiastic, thinking the additional trains would not be justified by the traffic. Cotton managed, however, to persuade them to give the new service a trial, and it began on 14th July. A new "Paddy" train ran between Stranraer and Carlisle and Stranraer and Glasgow, becoming known in each case as the "Midday Paddy". In August, the officers noted that the service was "fairly well supported, and daily improving", and it was continued to the end of September. During the period the Second Service operated, there were 191 additional passengers by the "old" service compared with the previous year, and the new service carried a total of 10,216. The "Midday Paddy" on the P P& W line carried an average of 35½ "Irish" passengers on each single journey; the hitherto sceptical officers seemed satisfied. The double service was revived the following summer, and each succeeding summer until 1914.

THE MAIL SERVICE

In 1886, the J C secured considerably improved terms from the Post Office for carrying the local mails. By an agreement taking effect from 1st July, they received another £1,000 per annum for this service, making £2,924 in all. The Post Office gained the right to send mail-bags by any train on the P P R and W R lines, and the times of certain trains might not be altered without the Postmaster General's consent.

The most important development of this period, however, in connection with the Mail Service was the improved service with the North of Ireland. As with the improvement of the steamer service, the initiative and pressure to bring this about came from Ireland. In June 1890, Captain McCalmont, M.P., led a deputation to the J C on the subject, and a report was drawn up, including a draft time-table. As when the new steamer was proposed, the great question was where the money was to come from. The report estimated the extra cost of the improved service as £25,000 per annum at least.

But feeling on the matter in the North of Ireland was running very high. At a meeting in Belfast on 16th December, business men of that city and the leading provincial towns complained of "serious inconvenience and loss" through the defects of the postal service via Holyhead, which they claimed had been "accentuated by many grave irregularities". Over the past eight years they had made several unsuccessful attempts to get a supplementary service via Larne, but they were determined to renew their efforts.

In June 1891, the J C suggested to the Post Office an annual payment of £16,500 for an improved service, including the sums already paid in respect of the local mails and of letters sent by the steamer. The Government, in reply, proposed to adopt the Larne route for a supplementary Mail Service, paying £13,500 in addition to the existing payment of £2,924 for the P P & W lines. The J C accepted these terms, and new time-tables for the accelerated Mail Service came into operation on 1st September. Of the £13,500, £8,000 was to go to the Steamboat Company, £3,050 to the Belfast & Northern Counties Company, £2,000 to the J C and £450 to the G S W. At Larne, the long-hoped-for development was the signal for great rejoicing, with highly excited celebrations on the quays and a banquet, where credit was enthusiastically given to the part played by the late James Chaine in making possible this happy outcome of many years of endeavour.

Thus, the first years of the J C's rule were a period of notable progress. It is true that by no means all the improvements were made on their initiative, or that of their officers, and that some would not have been made at all, at any rate at this time, without strong pressure from elsewhere. Certainly, however, no such progress as was achieved during these years could have been expected had the impecunious WR remained in control south of Newton Stewart, or the parsimonious P P R continued their disputes with the resentful C R over the responsibility for making and paying for improvements on their line. It is true also that the J C maintained a keen concern for economy that occasionally calls to mind strong recollections of their predecessors. But this was very understandable, in view of the heavy outgoings they had continually to meet, which included paying off the considerable debts they had inherited from the P P R and W R, and finding the dividend guaranteed to the former shareholders. By April 1888, a total of £98,202 in mortgage bonds had been paid off, while at the end of that year each of the four owning companies was called on to pay £504.1.8 to make up the amount of public works loans just paid off, and, additionally, £900 to meet the J C's bank overdraft. In the half year ending 31$^{st}$ July 1889, working expenses on the Joint Lines came to 111.78% of total traffic receipts; in the same period of the previous year they had reached 99.11 %. In April 1890, payment of the dividend had overdrawn the bank £14,911.8.7, and there are numerous references in the records for the next three years to payments by the owning companies for loans paid off and towards the guaranteed dividend.

The final payments by the companies in connection with the public works loans were not made until 1913, and meanwhile the limited profitability of the Joint Lines and the losses made by the steamers continued. We shall not be surprised, therefore, to find the pattern established during these early years, of a genuine spirit of improvement combined with a strict regard for economy, maintained throughout the J C's period of rule.

**CHAPTER TEN**

The Trains, 1892-1914

DURING much of this period, various improvements to the railway pier at Stranraer were being made. Following the agreement on the subject between the J C and the GSW early in 1892, the reconstruction got off to a conspicuously long-drawn-out start. There was a fierce dispute with Stranraer Town Council. The J C wanted full control and right of management of the pier and, furthermore, on the ground of the expense to them of deepening the harbour and improving the pier to develop the traffic, from which the town benefited, they demanded their release from the obligation, under the Act of 1877, to pay the Town Council an annuity of £500. This last was a particularly serious matter for the Council, for in 1878 they had borrowed £8,000, to be repaid over thirty years, with the annuity as security. The J C brought unscrupulous pressure to bear, threatening to build a new pier at Cairn Ryan and thereby divert the Irish traffic from Stranraer altogether. Dundas was reported inspecting the ground at Claddie House Point, site of the proposed pier, and between it and Castle Kennedy, with a view to a connecting line of railway. This drastic proposal, with its disastrous implications for the town's future, naturally caused great indignation in Stranraer, but it was not one on which the J C could embark lightly, and by the close of the year 1892 they had come to terms with the Town Council. They gained the full control of the pier that they had been seeking, but the payment of the £500 to the Council was to continue. The agreement was given statutory authority in a bill the L N W were passing through Parliament at the time.

Several months then elapsed before plans were approved for widening and lengthening the pier, and making it solid throughout. Not until the end of 1894 did the J C approve the plan showing the proposed new lines, platforms and station buildings on the pier. Morrison & Mason, of Glasgow, were given the contract for the work on the pier; that for the buildings was given to J. & G. Findlay, Glasgow. The latter contract was not awarded until the middle of 1896. By October of the next year, however, the engineers were able to report that the pier works were completed, and the station buildings almost so. There were four lines of rails between the platforms, with a bay line on the west side. The station buildings were on the west side, adjoining the steamer berth, and there was a footbridge to connect the platforms. A refreshment room was provided, with the stipulation that only temperance refreshments must be sold. Pier and buildings were gas lit. The J C would have preferred electricity - the steamers were electrically lighted - but they considered the necessary outlay too great. The signal-box on the pier was built about August 1897, and the new signals came into use in November. The little

173

steam crane provided in 1878 having become much worn by constant use, a new one was now obtained, considerably more powerful - its lifting capacity being five tons at a radius of 35 feet. The total cost of enlarging and improving the pier was £59,443.17.11, of which the G S W paid £5,780, under the 1892 agreement, and the J C the remainder. There were several further developments between 1898 and 1914. The J C showed an indulgent attitude towards those townspeople who wished to continue what seems to have been an established practice, and use the east pier as a bathing station. To quote a correspondent in the local press in July 1892:

"I believe the railway authorities some time ago gave permission to the Town Council to run a plank platform along the sea side of the embankment. If this platform were provided, and a small shelter erected where bathers could dress and undress, it would be a great boon. Might I also suggest to the young men bathing at the embankment that some addition to the costume of the ancient Britons would not be objectionable, particularly at the time the trains are passing."

In 1899 the J C granted the Town Council's application for leave to build a ledge for bathers on this side of the pier, 500 yards in length. They also agreed to their request for a wicket-gate to give access to the bathing-ledge from Cairnryan Road, near the over-bridge. There is a reference to a bookstall at the Harbour Station in 1902. The next year, they decided on a further extension of the pier itself. This was of wood, and was to be erected along the west side of the pier, at the steamers' usual berth, and along the end "as far as the north-east corner". It was in connection with the purchase of the turbine steamer *Princess Maud*, and was accompanied by a good deal of dredging of Loch Ryan in the vicinity of the pier. The cost of the dredging was £9,123.3.0; that of the pier extension, carried out by Morrison & Mason at £156.10.8 below contract price, £14,699.4.6. In 1905 the J C noted a total expenditure on Stranraer pier since they took it over in 1885 of £83,266.5.5 By 1913, the pier had thus acquired an appearance in many respects similar to that of the recent times; but in that year an addition was made which must have been a very conspicuous and familiar feature in its day, yet which has now vanished. To deal more efficiently with the very large cattle traffic from Ireland, the J C ordered the construction of a landing place and lairage - "six cattle sheds, slaughter-house, offices, etc., gangways and fencing". Messrs. Meikle, Newton Steam Joinery Works, Ayr, did the work, the total cost being £4,096.6.0. The lairage was opened in September.

THE MAIL SERVICE

The mail express service that the pier chiefly served was the subject of recurrent strong complaints by the General Post Office and others. It was alleged to be slow and, even so, unpunctual. In 1893 the Post Office protested that from early July to mid-September the down mail was an average of 14 minutes late leaving Carlisle and 14 minutes late leaving Castle Douglas, while it was an average of 91 minutes late in reaching Stranraer Harbour. In November 1899 the General Post Office reported constant complaints of late arrival of mails at various towns in the North of Ireland. The previous month there had been an average lateness of 56 minutes at Belfast, and at Derry the position was even worse. They warned that they might withhold payment if the railway companies did not perform their part of the contract. The L N W claimed to be taking steps to improve the working of their train from Euston, whose late arrival at Carlisle seems to have been the principal source of the trouble, but they added that its unpunctuality was due chiefly to time lost at the stations by Post Office staff. It was agreed to ask the Belfast & Northern Counties Company to hold connecting trains at Larne when the mail steamer was late, as was evidently already the practice at Stranraer.

To improve the service on the Joint Line, the officers contemplated introducing mechanical tablet-exchanging apparatus. This would permit speeds of 15 miles per hour instead of 10 through the crossing loops. A draft of a revised time-table for the down mail was submitted, conditional on the apparatus being installed. This draft was prepared by Fred. W. Hutchinson, who had succeeded Cunning as the J C's traffic manager in 1895. Hutchinson had been with the P P R from their earliest years, being appointed a clerk in their audit-office at Stranraer in 1861. In 1864 he was moved to the traffic manager's office, and in 1871 he became station-master at Stranraer, a post he held for twenty years, until his appointment as manager of the Stranraer Section. Then came Cunning's resignation, to return to Ireland as traffic manager of the Midland & Great Northern Joint Railways, and the J C decided to end the separate management of the Stranraer Section and appoint Hutchinson in his stead. His starting salary was £250. The J C had parted with Cunning with great regret, but Hutchinson was to be a worthy successor. He now corresponded with W. Melville, the G S W's engineer, and their locomotive superintendent, James Manson, about the practicability of the increased speeds which the provision of the new apparatus would allow.

In his letter to Melville, Hutchinson made a significant comment on the state of the J C's permanent way at this time:

"I assume there can be no objection from a permanent way point of view to the inclusive speed of one of our express trains being increased from 36 to 40 miles per hour. The road, I take it, is as good as can be found anywhere, and it has, I think, been greatly improved in recent years.

Melville replied:

"There can be no objection at all to the express trains running at the inclusive speed which you refer to, of course keeping in view the reduction of speed stipulated".

He had already agreed to the proposed increase of speed through the loop-lines. Manson had proffered a sceptical conunent on this topic:

"I do not know that this alteration will have any appreciable effect on the time of the trains, as I am inclined to think that in many cases the 10 mile limit was not rigidly adhered to."

Manson was probably more in touch with the actual practice of the enginemen than were the officers when they spoke of "the present loss of time in stopping at the crossing places or passing through at very low speed in order to give up and receive the train tablet".

The J C authorised the accelerated service in February 1901; it was to begin on 1st July. The new apparatus, the invention of Manson himself - "Manson's travelling tablet-catcher"- was installed meantime. A comparison of the timings shows clearly that not an earlier, but a punctual, arrival at Belfast was the object of the exercise, most of the time gained by the acceleration of the Carlisle-Stranraer train being used to allow for possible late arrival at Carlisle of the train from Euston.

|  | Previous | New |
|---|---|---|
| Carlisle | arr. 2.48 a.m. | 2.48 a.m. |
| Carlisle | dep. 2.58 a.m. | 3.10 a.m. |
| Stranraer | arr. 5.51 a.m. | 5.47 a.m. |
| Belfast | arr. 8.40 a.m. | 8.35 a.m. |

Not only the J C, but the G S W also were at some additional expense in order to provide the revised service, for the G S W had to run an additional train from Carlisle to Castle Douglas. The Post Office subsidy, therefore, was reallocated, £1,000 being taken from the Steamship Committee's proportion and shared equally between the G S W and the J C.

It was not very long, however, before the General Post Office were again making bitter complaints about the down mail. These culminated in their letter dated 4th March, 1904. There was, they said, loss of time on all stages of the journey: in the departure from Carlisle; on the journey to Stranraer; in the dispatch of the steamer from Stranraer; on the sea voyage, and in the dispatch of the Belfast train from Larne. During January and February an average loss of time of 30 minutes a day had occurred on the journey from Carlisle to Belfast. Better business, it would seem, was the cause of all this inefficiency. The weight of the mail train, the officers explained, had increased from 14 vehicles, 165 tons, when the schedule was agreed, to 19 vehicles, 228 tons, at the present time. Double-heading was now usual between Carlisle and Stranraer, but there were delays due to marshalling at Carlisle and the transfer of mails and other things to the steamer at Stranraer. The train would, in future, be run in duplicate from Carlisle to Stranraer. As for timekeeping on the sea-passage, a new turbine steamer would be put on the service in June.

The duplication of the train between Carlisle and Stranraer prevented the delays complained of at Stranraer harbour, and from the silence of the records we infer that for the rest of this period the Mail Service in the down direction was more efficient. But the duplication caused further expense to the G S W, who worked the trains, and there was fierce haggling over reimbursing them. According to the resultant masterpiece, 6d. per mile was to be paid to the G S W for the "duplicate train" between Carlisle and Castle Douglas: one-third of this by the L N W, one-third by the M R, and one-third by the G S W themselves, but one-third of the latter proportion would be paid by the C R. The J C would pay the G S W 10d. per mile for the journey from Castle Douglas to Stranraer. In 1910, the J C showed great concern about the extent of duplication of the down mail. It was directed to be run in one portion only from 1st February, except in special cases. The officers noted with disapproval that twelve such cases had occurred by 1st April, and ordered that the mail should cease to carry horses for Ireland. It nevertheless ran in two portions eight times during April, seven times in May and ten times in June. It did so regularly in the months of July, August and September. It was essential, Hutchinson was told, to limit the train to one engine load in winter; he must scrutinise the loading daily, and draw the attention of the "parent companies" to any case where extra vehicles were run, contrary to the relevant marshalling circular. The subject does not recur, so presumably the officers were satisfied with the result.

Complaints from the Post Office about the up mail first occur in September 1899, when they quoted instances of its being more than forty minutes late in reaching Carlisle and claimed that it was "constantly failing to effect a junction" with the up day mail there. They added a warning about withholding the contract payments. The officers gave the causes as being late starts from Larne, owing chiefly to the transfer of perishables from the Londonderry mail train to the steamer, which would be investigated; loss of time on the Channel passage, due to "variable circumstances"; the transfer from steamer to train at Stranraer, where Hutchinson was very often in personal attendance and would continue to do his utmost to see there was no avoidable delay; the short station platform at Newton Stewart; collecting tickets at Castle Douglas, which the G S W would discontinue, and occasional extra stops at Dalbeattie and at Annan, which also the G S W would discontinue.

Soon after this, the Belfast Chamber of Commerce, who had been so anxious for the adoption of the Larne route for mails, were saying that since a recent improvement in the service via Kingstown, it was "of very little use" for London letters. They informed the Post Office that unless the service was accelerated they might acquiesce in its being abandoned. The General Post Office informed the J C of these views, called attention to the small number of letters being sent by the Larne route, and suggested an improvement in the service, without which, they said, the subsidy would be difficult to justify.

The officers thereupon proposed a faster up mail, which would be limited to passenger carriages and postal vehicles. The perishables traffic, fish, dead fowl, yeast, etc., had so increased of late years that already a separate "fish train" ran almost daily to cater for it. This was, in future, to run regularly as a booked train, leaving Stranraer at 9.50 p.m. and reaching Carlisle at 1.30 a.m. The J C agreed, and in February 1900 authorised the retiming of the up Mail Service to give a 30 minute acceleration, leaving Belfast at 5.30 instead of 5 p.m., and arriving at Carlisle at 11.47, the same time as before.

As in the case of the down mail, the revised service was introduced 1st July, 1901.

The service seems to have been well patronised during the next few years. In November 1903 the 9.8 p.m. mail from Stranraer was noted as frequently needing two engines, in an effort to prevent which expense railway parcels were to be held back for the 9.42 fish train. The officers, however, found the mail's timekeeping unsatisfactory, and decided that tablet exchanging apparatus should now be provided at the crossing-places for the up trains also, estimating the cost at £30. Meanwhile, the mail was to be double-headed every night. Time was again being lost at Stranraer Harbour. Hutchinson must see that the time allowed there was not exceeded, even if some of the parcels and parcel post traffic had to be left behind. The tablet apparatus came into use on the 14th March 1904, and the pilot engine was withdrawn. The permitted speed through the crossing-loops was now 20 instead of 15 miles per hour, except at Newton Stewart and New Galloway.

But the cross-Channel trade was nothing if not keenly competitive, and in six months the Post Office were in touch with the J C again, drawing their attention now to the recent improvement of the service via Greenore, as a result of which mails for London could leave Belfast 11 hours later than via Larne. The J C gave a negative reply to the inquiry whether they had any similar improvement in mind, but the General Post Office pressed their point. Referring once more to the alleged disproportion between the amount of correspondence going via Larne and the cost to them of the service, the Postmaster General finally, on March 28th 1905, proposed a dispatch from Belfast at least one hour later than at present, and hinted at the reduction of the subsidy.

The J C took this hint very seriously. Retiming of the up mail, making the required concession, "to retain the present mail subsidy", was agreed to in May, and the service which continued for the rest of this period - evidently without serious complaint - introduced. It was a big operation, involving much rearrangement of connections. The fish train had also to be retimed. Already this train had sometimes had to be run in duplicate, and it was expected that this would be necessary more often in the future. It was feared that some of the fish traffic might be lost, owing to the later arrival times at some towns in England through the revised service, but it was not until after 1908 that late arrivals began to cause serious complaint, the reason then being the continuing steady increase in the perishables traffic, which in 1901-08 amounted to an average of seven tons, and in

1909-15 to an average of ten tons, nightly. The later running of the mail and fish trains did, however, mean increased expenditure on wages, due to staff having to be kept on duty longer. This was expected to be £157 per annum at Stranraer and £146 per annum at Newton Stewart. The Steamship Committee were likely to have to spend £400 per annum on additional staff.

Other measures were taken by the J C during these years to improve the movement of their trains. Early in 1904, Palnure became a crossing-place. A loop here had been discussed in 1891, but rejected on account both of expense and also of delay to express trains having to slow to exchange tablets. With the increase of traffic, however, and the introduction of the tablet-exchanging apparatus, by 1903 the officers were considering passing places not only here but also at Parton and at Cairntop, between Kirkcowan and Glenluce. Believing the sections on the P P R line to be too long, they favoured all three, but gave Palnure priority in view of the urgency of relieving congestion at Newton Stewart. So the Palnure crossing was provided, at a cost of £1,700. Cairntop and Parton never became crossing-places.

There were several developments at Newton Stewart. By 1895, trains were being seriously delayed here by the chronic shortage of water. The J C got their supply from the town commissioners, but this supply was inadequate for the needs of the town itself, so that the quantity of water available to the J C was diminishing all the time, a situation that threatened to become very serious. Melville and Hutchinson investigated, and found that by tapping a source on the P P R line at Benfield, about two miles west of Newton Stewart station, the J C might have a good supply of gravitation water at all times; even in severe drought, 18,000 gallons per day had been gauged. Moreover, the water came partly from mossy land, and would be good for boilers. They suggested the building of a tank to hold from 100,000 to 200,000 gallons at the "fountain-head", and laying a pipe to convey the water to Newton Stewart station. The J C authorised the use of this supply, the estimated cost being £600. It came into operation in March 1896, and was reported as "abundant". And when all necessary expenses were allowed for, it was obviously going to be very much cheaper than the supply from the commissioners. In 1912 the J C augmented the supply from Benfield with water from the adjoining Mertonhall estate, paying £10 per annum to the proprietor.

At the same time, the inadequate siding accommodation at Newton Stewart caused frequent delays. New sidings were built, but the Board of Trade, in sanctioning their use the following year, described the signalling at the station as old-fashioned and recommended its replacement, adding that the platforms ought to be lengthened. The J C deferred the expensive item of resignalling until 1901, when the engineer reported that the west box needed renewing and they decided to carry out the whole operation. The resignalling was complete by early 1904 at a total cost of £2,577.2.1. Block telegraph working was established between cast and west boxes at Newton Stewart in 1908. The improvement of the platforms was also protracted. About the time of the Board of Trade report, the station-master, Robert

Mirrey, had complained to the officers about trains being delayed because the main line platforms were too short, but nothing was done and we saw how the platforms were stated to be one of the reasons for the up mail losing time three years later. When the resignalling was decided upon, the officers were divided over the lengthening of the platforms owing to the estimated cost - £250 - and the J C referred the subject to their general managers. Following their reply, the extension of the up and down platforms was at last ordered, in September 1901; not until April 1904, however, was the work reported done. The march of progress on the P P & W could indeed be subject to the handicapper, but the hearts of J C and officers must have rejoiced that the total cost of this particular operation was a mere £133.18.1.

The refreshment room opened at the station, with the stipulation that it should be run on temperance principles, comes into our story again now, for it had not been long in use when a petition was submitted from inhabitants, commercial travellers "and others" in favour of the sale of "ordinary spirituous refreshments". This the J C declined, but very soon the tenant was giving notice, alleging that on temperance principles the room was was not a paying proposition. Advertisements having failed to attract a single offer for the tenancy, the officers recommended that a license be applied for, but in December 1893 the J C directed that the room continue another year on temperance principles, and so it did continue, through that year and the years that followed. By 1909, the J C were thinking of adding a tea room. Miss Law, who had been the tenant since the end of 1894, having given notice, they invited offers for the tenancy of the room, both as it was and with a tea-room added. They accepted the offer of Andrew Kay, baker and confectioner, £5 per annum for the room as it was. In 1913, however, having received complaints about the room, they ordered the tea-room to be provided, the tenant agreeing to pay £10 in rent "from the day the room is ready for use".

THE "SUMMER SERVICE"; HOLIDAYS; EXCURSIONS

The "Daylight Service" in summer to and from Ireland by steamer and express train was well patronised. In 1894 a small increase in the number of passengers was reported compared with the previous year, and the next few years showed conspicuous progress:

| Date | Train | Average passengers per day | | | Estimated value per train mile |
|---|---|---|---|---|---|
| | | 1 | 3 | Total | |
| 1894 | 12.30 p.m. ex SH | 6½ | 45¾ | 52¼ | |
| | 6.29 p.m. ex CD | 7½ | 49 | 56½ | 2/4½ |
| 1895 | 12.30 p.m. ex SH | 7 | 48½ | 55½ | |
| | 6.29 p.m. ex CD | 8½ | 55½ | 64 | 2/7 |
| 1896 | 12.30 p.m. ex SH | 7 | 51¾ | 58¾ | |
| | 6.34 p.m. ex CD | 8 | 64 | 72 | 2/10 |

## Rails to Portpatrick

| 1898 | 12.30 p.m. ex SH | 6 | 55 | 61 | |
|---|---|---|---|---|---|
| | 6.36 p.m. ex CD | 8½ | 68½ | 77 | 3/- |
| 1899 | 12.30 p.m. ex SH | 7¾ | 70¼ | 78 | |
| | 6.36 p.m. ex CD | 9 | 83¾ | 92¾ | 3/8¼ |

Full statistics are not given for 1897, but the estimated value per train mile was 2/9. The numbers quoted were of through passengers, to and from Ireland. The express would sometimes by arrangement make stops not shown in the timetable to pick up or set down through passengers. At his retirement Hutchinson expressed his "grief" at not having always been able to oblige people in this respect.

A great improvement in the connections with the summer service provided at Carlisle by the N E R had been made in 1893, and by 1900 the officers were noting a very conspicuous increase in passenger traffic between north-east England and Ireland. Until 1912 the Second Service ran each weekday from June to September. In 1896 the Steamship Committee and the G S W urged that it be kept up all the year - the G S W no doubt hoping to attract some additional traffic to the Girvan line - but when in 1904 the service was extended over the first fortnight in October the patrons were few, and even this limited experiment was not repeated. In 1912 it was decided to run the Second Service on Saturdays only during June. This was done again the two following years, but it being thought that for some years the service between Carlisle and Belfast on summer Saturdays had been inadequate, in 1914 the "Auxiliary Service" was introduced, to run each Saturday in June, July and August. An express left Dumfries at 1.40 p.m., due at Newton Stewart at 3.1 and Stranraer Harbour at 3.42; the steamer was due at Larne at 5.36 and the train arrival at Belfast was 7.15. Connections with this service were given by morning trains from England, and also by the 12.30 p.m. train from Glasgow via Girvan.

Thanks to the growth of railways, the custom among the middle classes of spending summer holidays away from home was now well established, and the very greatly improved political and social conditions in Ireland during most of this period produced a rapid rise in the country's popularity as a holiday resort for people from many parts of Britain. The J C and their officers showed considerable initiative and energy in the attempt to attract more of this traffic to their route, and also to make south-west Scotland better known to potential holiday visitors on both sides of the Channel. In the latter task they got valuable assistance from the novels with a Galloway setting by the Rev. S. R. Crockett, who was born at Little Duchrae, near New Galloway station, in 1859. The J C themselves made a literary contribution in the form of a guide-book, *Tours in Galloway*, first published in 1898. Its well-informed and attractively-written text was a "labour of love" on the part of their traffic inspector, William McConchie, a native of Kirkcowan; Hutchinson was editor. Over 8,000 copies were distributed that summer, at a net cost to the J C of £14.15.8; the following year the total was 11,000 and the net cost £20, but by

# Rails to Portpatrick

1901 a surplus of revenue from advertisements over expenses of £22 was anticipated, and McConchie received a gratuity of £10 "in view of services rendered". The book was published each year until 1915.

The guides gave details of many special facilities for visitors from Britain to travel via Stranraer and Larne to Ireland. Among them were cheap tickets to Belfast and Portrush for the Giant's Causeway; a circular tour from London, Birmingham, Liverpool and Manchester to Belfast, returning via Greenore and Holyhead; circular tours via Londonderry, Coleraine, Portrush, the Giant's Causeway and the Antrim Coast; and tours to the Lakes of Killarney, to Connemara, to Dublin and to the Isle of Man. In the reverse direction there were bookings to the English Lakes and to London; to Newton Stewart, and thence by horse charabanc to Glentrool, Murray's Monument and Gatehouse; season tickets allowing unlimited travel over eight days between Portpatrick, Whithorn and New Galloway; and a circular tour through Wigtownshire from Douglas, Isle of Man. Summer holiday traffic to and from the Isle of Man via Garliestown was heavy, and prompted the J C to spend over £100 on lengthening the station platform in 1897. The now extremely popular pastime of cycling was catered for, with reduced fares for cyclist visitors to Galloway and descriptions of suggested runs. One of the province's most enthusiastic cyclists, incidentally, was Fred. Hutchinson.

Provision was made also for the golfer, both visiting and resident. When the Wigtownshire Golf Course, near Glenluce, was opened in 1894, patrons were allowed to travel at pleasure party rates, and a golfers' platform was built at Challoch Junction, whence there was access by road to the course. In 1899 the 3.40 p.m. train from Stranraer stopped here each Wednesday and Saturday, April to August inclusive, and the down train passing about 7.10 p.m. called to pick up the golfers for their return journey. This was described as a yearly arrangement. Another favourite resort of golfers, then as now, was Portpatrick, and in 1904 the J C agreed to run an additional train in each direction between Stranraer and Portpatrick on Wednesdays and Saturdays during the winter for their convenience. On five Saturdays during October, however, the trains carried a total of only 135 passengers from Stranraer and 77 from Portpatrick, and after a conference with the Golf Club the proposed Wednesday train was abandoned, and the Saturday train discontinued, "having regard to the early nightfall".

The service on the Portpatrick "Branch" was the subject of recurrent complaint. Though the purpose for which the railway was brought to Portpatrick had not been fulfilled, railway communication had nevertheless brought great benefits, enabling it to develop as a seaside holiday and health resort. The improved appearance of the village reflected the increase of prosperity, modern amenities being introduced and smart new buildings replacing others that were old and often shabby, though doubtless also often picturesque. During the early 1900s Portpatrick was the scene of great activity at all seasons, the railway carried a

# Rails to Portpatrick

remarkably heavy traffic in goods and the resources of the little station and its staff were exerted to the utmost. The great hotel was building on the cliff to the north; on completion it was to resemble from the outside the mansion of a Scottish nobleman, while it had, wrote Harper, "internal furnishings so extensive and luxurious that one has a feeling that the North British Station Hotel has been transported from "Auld Reekie" to this airy home of the gull and the seamew". At the opening ceremony at the end of May 1905, the Earl of Glasgow, father of Lady Orr-Ewing, the owner of the hotel, offered some outspoken criticism of the railway companies. If they did not do more for Portpatrick than they were now doing, he said, the hotel would possibly be shut up. To loud applause, he added that if Portpatrick was to go ahead and be successful, a much better railway service was absolutely necessary. Speaking for the companies, W. G. Belford replied that they had "doubled" the station, and the train service was about to be doubled also.

The station accommodation had been extended during the previous winter. The "doubling" presumably refers to the lengthening of the single platform, which was lengthened again in 1907 - hence the path of the abandoned Harbour Branch passed under the extended end of the platform. As for the train service, in place of the former regular service of three trains each way daily, from 1st June, 1905 - the day the hotel opened to the public - to the end of September there were to be six, from Stranraer at 7 and 9.30a.m. and 12.10, 3.45, 5.42 and 7.45 p.m., and from Portpatrick at 8.45 and 10.55 a.m. and 3.0, 5.0, 6.15 and 8.20 p.m. It was a notable improvement, though by 1914 the summer service had been reduced again to four trains each way, not counting the early morning departure from Portpatrick, to connect with the mail steamer . That year, however, McConchie, who had just been appointed traffic manager on the P P & W in succession to Hutchinson, suggested to the officers some extra trains on Wednesdays and Saturdays, from Stranraer to Portpatrick and Castle Kennedy, "for the development of the half-holiday traffic and to encourage summer visitors in holiday residence in the district to travel about by railway rather than by road". He mentioned the many day excursionists from Belfast who came to Stranraer by the steamer due at 12.33 p.m. His suggestion was approved, and the new facility advertised as follows:

PORTPATRICK, STRANRAER AND CASTLE KENNEDY
Special train services and half-holiday excursions on Wednesdays and Saturdays in July and August.

|  |  | p.m. | p.m. |  |  | p.m. |
|---|---|---|---|---|---|---|
| Castle Kennedy | dep. | 2.30 | | Portpatrick | dep. | 2.0 |
| Stranraer | arr. | 2.35 | | Stranraer | arr. | 2.18 |
| Stranraer | dep. | 1.15 | | Stranraer | dep. | 2.20 |
| Portpatrick | arr. | 1.32 | | Castle Kennedy | arr. | 2.25 |

183

# Rails to Portpatrick

Cheap Return Fares:

|  | Third Class | First Class |
|---|---|---|
| *Stranraer to Portpatrick | 6d. | 1/- |
| Stranraer to Castle Kennedy | 5d. | 10d. |
| *Portpatrick to Stranraer | 6d. | 1/- |
| *Portpatrick to Castle Kennedy | 9d. | 1/6 |

*Valid for return on day of issue only.

These facilities are designed to enable busy people to make the most of the half-holidays.

WORKS; THE LOCAL PASSENGER SERVICE

Among the works on the P P R main line during this period not previously mentioned was the erection in 1900 of a footbridge at Dunragit, at a cost of £215. This seems to have been the result of someone complaining to the Board of Trade about the absence of such a facility. In 1912, a Praed petrol gas plant was installed at Dunragit, to light the station in place of the existing paraffin lamps. The cost for the whole premises, including the signal cabin and station-master's house, was estimated at only about £8, but as if feeling a need to record some justification for the expenditure, the officers noted that "Dunragit is the junction with the Girvan line". The passing place which the J C had sought in vain to have installed at Castle Kennedy in 1889 had been provided in 1895, but requests from Stranraer Town Council in 1904, and the Earl of Stair the following year, to double the track between Challoch Junction and Stranraer were declined, the J C commenting that "with the present single line working the average loss of time is not more than a fraction of a minute per train, and a rough estimate of the cost of doubling the line is £15,000".

Glenluce viaduct was strengthened in 1907, after the discovery of loosening of the stonework, at a cost of about £350. "Extensive" repairs carried out at Big Fleet three years previously had been expected to cost twice as much. In 1896 the Creetown station-master and a local doctor asked the J C to build a footbridge at the station, in view of "the difficulty experienced by aged persons in crossing the line". Their request was refused, but two years later the up platform was lengthened "to accommodate ten carriages". The water supply for locomotives on the down platform at Creetown, which the J C in 1886 had decided to dispense with, was renewed in 1907, a wooden water tank capable of holding 3,000 gallons being provided. In 1912 the J C agreed to increase their annual payment to Miss Grant of Barholm for the Creetown water from £10 to £15, this being considered "not too much for engines, water closets and houses". A water crane had been erected at Parton in 1892, and the level of the tank there raised in 1894. The improvements in the water supply at these two stations were made in response to continual complaints of delay to down passenger trains. This will be a suitable time to look at the regular service of stopping trains on the P P R main line.

Throughout this period, continuing the usual practice in the past, there were three slow trains daily, running the length of the main line in each direction. They were unevenly spaced. From Stranraer there were two morning departures, and the last slow train of the day, apart from the "Wee Train" to Newton Stewart, left before 4 p.m. The earliest down train from Castle Douglas left well after 9 a.m. There was a long gap until the next. at about 3.30 p.m., while the third ran during the evening, the time varying according to the season.

It is hardly surprising that the J C received numerous complaints about the service, including a series of petitions over the years from various local authorities, the most notable coming from the County Council and Burgh Councils of Wigtownshire in 1904. The complaints centred on the inadequacy of the local service, particularly the absence of trains during the middle of the day, the unpunctuality of some of the trains, and unsatisfactory connections at Dumfries and Lockerbie for the north and south. The J C made only one or two small concessions in reply to the complaints, and at the opening of the Portpatrick Hotel, James Drew, the former W R director, now county convenor, was very critical of the service provided in the Shire, claiming that the companies could fill their trains very much better by giving more encouragement to local travellers. Hutchinson replied, however, with praise for the companies and the implication that the difficulties in the way of improvements were insurmountable. He said:

"From time to time the companies had spent a very great deal of money on the line, for which they had received a very small return. Nevertheless, they were at all times willing to give a proper service. Unfortunately, the population of the district was very sparse. He had repeatedly tried to rearrange the service, but found this an impossibility owing to the large number of connections which had to be met. The change would only have made bad worse".

It is clear that the basic difficulty was the same as in the past: to reconcile the needs of the local with those of through traffic. A vivid illustration of this, and of Hutchinson's sincerity and perseverance in trying to get the best possible service for the people of Galloway, is provided by the story of the evening train from Dumfries to Stranraer.

In the "winter" months this train left Dumfries about 6 p.m., a time that suited the people of the province. From the end of 1903 the G S W withdrew in winter their 4.45 p.m. from Carlisle, which gave a connection with the L N W, but the C R came to the rescue, providing a connection via Lockerbie by means of a slip carriage attached to their 4 p.m. express from Carlisle. In summer - June to September - however, the departure time from Dumfries was changed to about 7.30 or 8 p.m. This was to suit the altered times of the owning companies' main-line expresses, but it was a very inconvenient time indeed for the local traffic. The inconvenience was sometimes aggravated by unpunctuality. In March 1902,

Hutchinson was complaining to the officers that during the previous summer the train, due to leave Dumfries at 7.25 p.m., had, on a daily average, left 29 minutes late, to reach Stranraer an average of 46 minutes late. A year later the summer departure from Dumfries was fixed at 8 p.m. The people of Creetown petitioned for the winter timing to be retained all the year, but this was rejected as connections at Dumfries from north and south would be severed. Hutchinson asked for the departure to be brought forward to 7.35, but this too was refused, as it would sever the C R's connection from Edinburgh via Lockerbie, which was to give a later arrival at Dumfries this year. In 1905 he urged that the 6.5 departure be tried experimentally during the summer; it would be "infinitely more suitable" for the Joint Line, and prevent many complaints. Last year, he pointed out, the 8 p.m. train had carried a daily average of only sixteen local passengers between Crossmichael and Newton Stewart, while between Newton Stewart and Stranraer the daily average was three. But his proposal would mean no connection at Dumfries with the C R's 4.15 from Edinburgh and the G S W's 5.30 from Glasgow, and the two companies vetoed it. Hutchinson tried again in 1906, repeating that the later summer timing caused many complaints, and warning the officers that it was leading people to make their journeys by road transport.

    His continual appeals met with no success, but Hutchinson was persistent, and in 1907 he returned to battle with a new set of weapons. He had "pressing applications" to send milk and other perishable traffic from the W R line to England overnight. This traffic could be picked up at Newton Stewart by the evening train from Dumfries, which should reach Stranraer Harbour in time to transfer it to the 10.3 and 10.37 express trains there. This would necessitate a considerably earlier departure from Dumfries than 8 p.m. The L N W and the M R now supported Hutchinson, but the C R and G S W maintained their objection to their evening connections being severed and the 8 p.m. departure continued. To cater for the perishable traffic from the W R, the 10.37 fish train from Stranraer Harbour was to call at Newton Stewart. In 1908, the English companies again gave Hutchinson their support, while the Scots companies remained immovable. In 1909, it was agreed to continue the 6p.m. departure during June, the "Southern companies" saying that the late timing meant a long wait at Dumfries for passengers from their systems, but the C R were alarmed for their Edinburgh connection, and the 8p.m. departure returned for the rest of the summer. This same timing applied in the summer of 1913, and this year the train was seriously delayed, owing to having to pass the up mail and fish trains on its way to Stranraer. Hutchinson availed himself of this as another argument for an earlier timing, and the English companies joined him in favouring a 6.50 departure from Dumfries for the summer of 1914, but 7.30 was the earliest the C R and G S W would tolerate, so the train was to leave Dumfries at 7.30 and Castle Douglas at 8.5, to reach Stranraer Harbour at 9.50.

    To be delayed by crossing the mail and the fish trains, the evening train in 1913 must already have been running late, and this may well have been due to waiting for late connections at Dumfries. In 1907, the 3.30 p.m. down train from Castle Douglas was repeatedly delayed from this cause; the four companies promised to do their utmost to improve the time-keeping of their connections, while Hutchinson added that completion of the water tank at Creetown would also improve matters as the train would no longer have to make extra stops for water at Loch Skerrow. Perhaps the inadequacy of the water supply was at least partly to blame for the unpunctuality of the 8.30 a.m. down train from Dumfries in the summer of 1904, which on a daily average left Castle Douglas four minutes late and reached Stranraer fourteen minutes late: it missed the connection with the Girvan line at Dunragit on thirty-two occasions.

Yet another factor that demanded consideration in arranging the service on the Joint Lines was the claims of the Post Office. This is clearly shown by the controversy over the 3.40 p.m. from Stranraer in 1893-4. In December 1893, Cunning complained to the officers that owing to the G S W altering their main-line train, the connection at Dumfries for Glasgow with the 3.40 from Stranraer had been severed, and through passengers who had previously arrived in Glasgow at 8.50 could not now arrive until midnight. He subsequently received a petition from the people of the P P & W district, asking for an earlier departure from Stranraer. As things were, the P P & W train was due to reach Dumfries at 6.37 p.m., and the G S W's Glasgow express to depart at 6.28. But under the J C's contract with the Post Office, the 3.40 could not be altered without their consent, and this had been withheld. Cunning tried again, "pointing out the importance and urgency of the alteration requested". Meanwhile, however, the G S W again retimed their train, so that the 3.40 from Stranraer would need to run an hour earlier. Not surprisingly, the Post Office would not agree to this, while in any case it was intolerable, from the point of view of the local traffic, that the last stopping train of the day to Castle Douglas and Dumfries should leave Stranraer before three in the afternoon.

Hutchinson had, of course, pointed out a very serious difficulty in the way of providing a service that local passengers could regard as adequate when he referred to the small population of the P P & W district. In 1898, following petitions about the local service, the J C agreed to try starting the "Wee Train" from Creetown in the mornings, and extending it there in the evenings, for the summer. But the experiment was not continued, or repeated. In Hutchinson, however, the people of Galloway had a railway officer who could be relied on to do his best for them, despite the very adverse circumstances, and a further illustration of this is his attempt in 1906 to get a better service between Castle Douglas and Newton Stewart. Telling the officers that complaints were very numerous about there being no earlier train from Castle Douglas to Newton Stewart, and no later train the other way, he submitted the modest proposal of an additional train on one day of the week only, and a draft time-table. As there was no locomotive for the purpose at Castle Douglas, working the new train by locomotive, even for one day, would be unremunerative. Hutchinson therefore suggested the use of a steam motor, which could work the "Wee Train" daily, and his proposed new service as a once weekly extension of this. Far from needing to fear a loss on the new service, he informed his audience they could look forward to a saving in working the "Wee Train". But the officers gave his imaginative suggestion a cool reception. They expressed doubts about the "long stretch of main line" - 53 miles - over which the proposed service would run, and asked for fuller particulars concerning the anticipated saving in working the "Wee Train". The subject is not mentioned again.

Although they had the "Wee Train" in addition to the other stopping trains, many people obviously found the local service between Newton Stewart and Stranraer still inadequate, as instanced by strong complaints voiced at the ceremony held in May 1904, to mark the forthcoming retiral of Sir Herbert Maxwell as M.P. for Wigtownshire. By this time, the J C were running a market train each Friday between May and October from Newton Stewart to Stranraer, leaving at 3.35 p.m. In 1907, they agreed to continue it during the coming winter, at the request of James Craig Limited, livestock auctioneers, of Ayr, subject to Messrs. Craig's guarantee of £3.3.0 per journey. The train did not run during the winter of 1908-9, however, and though it was restored for the May-October period following, the officers recorded their intention of trying "to get an increase in the subsidy of 10/- per train paid by Messrs. Craig Limited". Perhaps the train had been subsidised by Messrs. Craig all along. But they did not increase their subsidy in 1909, and the next year they advised the J C that they would withdraw it altogether. The train, therefore, was not restored for the summer of 1910, and did not run again.

The J C were thus decidedly ungenerous in the provision they made for their local traffic. Given their necessary regard for commercial considerations, this was inevitably so. As in the days before they acquired ownership of the P P & W, the big companies were bound to be primarily interested in the through traffic with their own systems. In the case of the Portpatrick "Branch", which would never have been built had it been known that it must depend on local and holiday traffic only, we shall not be surprised to find the companies providing a service as a particularly grudging concession. They must greatly have regretted the expense of introducing the electric train staff between Stranraer and Portpatrick in 1894-5, in place of the former method of working by train staff without ticket, the change being necessitated by "difficulty with the signalling arrangements at the west end of Stranraer station". There is a reference to an engine shed at Portpatrick in 1905, but it was disused, and the J C let it to Mr. Marshall, the factor of Dunskey, for storing building materials. During most of the year the passenger service was very restricted, with only three daily trains each way, and in 1901, on Marshall's representing to them that the regular 9 a.m. train from Portpatrick was too early for people wanting to travel to Stranraer market on Fridays, the J C agreed to try an additional departure at 11a.m. Between 1st June and 5th November the new market train carried an average of twenty-three passengers each Friday, and the J C were sufficiently impressed with this modest total to continue the train. From 1905, as we have seen, the summer service on the branch was improved, and the market train was not needed then, but it ran each year from October to May. In 1904, the officers considered getting a steam motor for the line:

"A motor conveyance can be run at a cost not exceeding 7d. per mile and one should be ordered for this branch with seating accommodation for about 50 passengers - third class only - divided into two compartments, non-smoking and smoking, with a locker for luggage, and capable of hauling two trailers."

The matter was deferred, as the L N W and M R did not like the idea, and it does not recur. Some years later, however, some people in the district were wondering if the solution to its public transport problem might lie in another kind of motor. In March 1911, Portpatrick Parish Council told the J C that "unless they put on a Friday train at about 4p.m. from Stranraer to Portpatrick they would approach the Stranraer & Drummore Motor Omnibus Company Limited, with a view of establishing a road motor service between the towns named". The J C declined, noting that in October-May, 1910-11, the existing market train, 10.30 a.m. from Stranraer and 11 a.m. from Portpatrick, was used by an average total of four on its outward and seventeen on its inward journey. Whether the Parish Council carried out their threat we do not know; if they did, it had no immediate result. People's dissatisfaction with the existing service, however, and the very limited patronage given to better facilities when the J C provided them, point clearly to the need that was now being felt for an alternative means of public transport better fitted than was the railway to cater for districts such as this. That need, of course, the motor bus was to fill.

The W R "Branch" was a more lively enterprise. In 1901 the traffic was sufficient for there to be complaints about delay under the existing staff - and ticket method of working, and Hutchinson suggested introducing the electric tablet, the estimated cost being £485. The officers were unfavourable at first, but after receiving a statement of delays during March 1902, which the electric tablet would have prevented, and learning that some signals needed renewal and a saving of £150 in the cost of this would be made if tablet working were adopted, they changed their minds, and the system was brought into operation on the W R in March 1903. Tablet instruments were at Newton Stewart West Box, Wigtown, Whauphill, Millisle and Whithorn. The total cost, plus that of the new signalling, was £755.8.9.

There was more resignalling in 1907-8, when the original boxes at Wigtown and Millisle were replaced and boxes provided instead of the open ground frames at Whauphill and Whithorn. The cost of this, together with some resignalling at Portpatrick also, totalled £2,213.3.6. Reconstruction at Millisle also included provision for the first time of direct access from the main line to the Garliestown branch, previously reached only by a reversing siding, and the removal of the exchange platform (the passenger service on this branch having been withdrawn in 1903) and erection of a new platform on the crossing-loop, opposite the station buildings.

The engine shed at Wigtown had been taken down in 1894. This followed the building of a shed at Newton Stewart. The G S W had complained that their two engines stationed at Newton Stewart had to stand at night "in the end of the horse-box siding, within a few feet of the main line", and revived Dnimrnond and Smellie's request for a shed and turntable. The turntable was not provided, but a shed was, though rigorous economy was practised, the building erected being of wood. Two locomotives were stabled there, one for the W R line, the other for the "Wee Train". The Wigtown shed had been getting dilapidated, and it was now demolished. The new water supply at Newton Stewart in 1896 meant that in future W R engines could always be watered there, except in extreme drought. It was most convenient to water them there, though there was "a good supply for the pumping" at Sorbie and Whithorn, which they had had to use during the times of shortage at Newton Stewart before the new supply was provided. Of the three engines needed to work the W R line, one was stabled at Newton Stewart and the others at Millisle. In 1904 the officers showed concern at the eight miles per day of light engine running from and to Millisle shed owing to there being no shed at Whithorn; they considered building a shed at Whithorn, but decided against when they learned that it was likely to cost £500.

The C R and G S W supplied locomotives for the W R during their alternate three year periods of supervision. The engine-men, however, were permanent. In September 1894, the J C noted that the charge for locomotive working on the line was 6/- an hour, including wages, stores, etc.; they added that this did not apply to the Garliestown branch. The latter was worked by Wheatley's rebuilt Nos. 1 and 5. In April 1892, the J C had decided to sell Nos. 2, 3, 4 and 6 for scrap. 2 and 6 are not mentioned in the records again. 3 and 4 were reported sold for scrap in June 1894, as was the tramway engine, the scrap value of all three being £211.16.6. The tramway engine, however, was not scrapped, but survived for several years in a decidedly curious capacity. W. T. Wheatley had resigned as general manager of the A & W in 1891 and bought the George Hotel in Stranraer; there he took the tramway engine, using it to drive machinery which chopped fodder for the posthorses. 1 and 5 continued on the Garliestown branch, but towards the end of 1902 the decision was taken to close the branch to passengers from 1st March following, and in January 1903, J. F. McIntosh, the C R's locomotive superintendent, said that the two little engines were worn out and should be broken up. In June, the J C ordered them to be sold for scrap.

Apart from accelerations, the passenger service on the W R line continued very similar to what it had been originally, with the same number of trains running at much the same times of day. From June 1896 a fifth down train was added, leaving Newton Stewart soon after 6 a.m. for Whithorn. This followed complaints from the Post Office that the previous 7 a.m. departure, a mixed train not reaching

Whithorn until 8.20, arrived there too late, and was furthermore frequently unpunctual. They claimed that a service by road would do as well as this, and would cost them less. So the new early train was introduced, and the mixed train retimed between 8 and 9 a.m.

The closure to passengers of the Garliestown branch was the culmination of several years of uncertainty about the service. In 1894, Cunning drew the officers' attention to the "heavy expense incurred in working the Garliestown branch, and the small traffic upon it". Had their advice been followed, Garliestown would have had a horse tramway service, as contemplated in early W R days. Goods traffic would have been catered for by a daily trip of the W R line goods engine to Garliestown and back. They estimated the total yearly traffic receipts of the branch at £300, while the cost of locomotive working was £457. The cost of working by horses was estimated at £211 per annum. The J C did not act on their recommendations, however, and the first positive step recorded towards reducing expenses on the branch was the withdrawal of two down and three up trains daily, from 1st August 1901. In April 1902, the J C referred the service to the officers' consideration. The G S W, C R and M R representatives recommended closing the branch to ordinary passenger trains. The engines working the W R goods trains could carry on the goods service as part of their daily work; the "cost of running and maintaining the present Garliestown branch engines, both for goods and passenger purposes", would be saved. The L N W representative did not agree. A few weeks later, however, the officers unanimously recommended the total withdrawal of the passenger service, and in December 1902 the J C ordered accordingly. The trains ceased at the end of February 1903, and in their place John Hannah, of Garliestown, ran buses to and from Millisle station, with the aid of a subsidy of £30 per annum from the J C. The subsidy was halved in 1908, so presumably the bus service was adequately patronised.

These changes on the Garliestown branch roused a good deal of complaint from the public, and in any case the service on the W R line was, like that on the P P R line, the subject of recurrent complaint by local government bodies. What was more, between 1896 and 1903 a vigorous individual complainant, Richard Bulman, of Culderry, near Garliestown, corresponded on numerous occasions not only with the J C but also with the Board of Trade about defects that he saw in the W R line service. As with the P P R line, the J C made only a few minor concessions to their critics. In 1898 they ran experimentally, during July, August and September, a Friday market train from Newton Stewart to Whithorn, leaving at 2.30 p.m. The experiment resulted in this train becoming a feature of the regular service, but when in 1904 the County Council and the Wigtownshire burghs asked for a midday train in the other direction, they were refused. The lack of trains at midday was a major source of complaint about the W R line, as it was about the P P R. Not until 1914 was this deficiency remedied officially, for two days of the week only: on Wednesdays and Fridays a train was to leave Whithorn for Newton Stewart at

12.25 p.m.; on Wednesdays it was to return from Newton Stewart at 1.30, white the established 2.30 departure on Fridays was to continue. The Wednesday trains were withdrawn after August 1914, but the Friday trains survived. It is good to know, however, that by a piece of informality reminiscent of the W R in its earliest years, a once-weekly midday service from Whithorn had in practice for some time been provided. In seeking the officers' approval for the Wednesday and Friday service just described, which was his suggestion, McConchie said of the proposed 12.25 from Whithorn:

"This train actually runs every Friday to serve Newton Stewart market, but it is only shown in the public time-table as from Newton Stewart to Whithorn. In the other direction it is regarded as 'empty', though the local people, who have got to know about it, turn up and are conveyed."

GOODS, ETC.

We saw how the perishable traffic from Ireland greatly increased between 1901 and 1915. Other goods traffic from Ireland showed an impressive increase also, from an average of 15 tons nightly in 1901 to 30 tons in 1915, while the latter figure would have been much more were it not for very limited crane power at Stranraer. The total of perishables and other goods combined in 1901 was 6,913 tons; in 1912 it was 10,654 tons; and in 1915 it was 12,828 tons. The trade in Irish cattle also continued very brisk during this time, though the very ample accommodation for cattle on the *Victoria* and the *May* - about 700 head - turned out in practice to be excessive, as from February 1898 to February 1899 more than 400 head were carried on only eight occasions and more than 500 on only three. "On a large number of dates the numbers ranged between 200 and 290."

Cattle were regularly dispatched by train from Galloway itself, too. Though the depression that settled on British agriculture in the mid-1870s was relieved only by the First World War, pastoral farming suffered less than did arable, and thanks to the progressive policy of the Earls of Stair and other landowners, and the vigorous co-operation of farmers and all who worked on the land, farming in Galloway was relatively prosperous. Stock rearing continued to do well, and beef cattle remained a notable export from the province. Game of various kinds continued important, as did vegetables, especially new potatoes. Progressive agricultural policies, however, in this region meant chiefly the encouragement of dairy-farming; more and more Ayrshire cattle were introduced, and milk and related products came to hold a major place among the commodities sent out of the district daily to many different destinations. Numerous creameries were established in Wigtownshire. "At Stranraer", said the J C's tourist guide in 1899, "are the main premises of the Wigtownshire Creamery Company, whose fresh and dainty products of butter, cream, cheese and sterilised milk find a ready market everywhere". There were then other creameries, at Colfin (Wigtownshire Creamery Company), Dunragit

# Illustrations 2

The end of the line, courtesy of Mr Beeching!

## List of Illustrations
## The end of the line, courtesy of Mr Beeching!

(1) 57375 crossing Garlieston Burn bridge.
(2) Rail Tour Special, 1963.
(3) Last train shunting at Garlieston Harbour.
(4) 78026 moves to shunt for the last time at Garlieston.
(5) The last day. 78026 and guard's van.
(6) View of Sorbie Station.
(7) Alex Muir explodes his last detonators.
(8) The end for the Bladnoch Viaduct.
(9) Posing with the driver of the last train from Wigtown.
(10) The Finale. The pick-up train arrives for dismantling the line.
(11) The lifting train on the Bladnoch Bridge.
(12) Cutting up the Bladnoch Bridge.
(13) Preparing rails for cutting, Carslae.
(14) Cutting rails at Carslae.
(15) Unbolting rails at Carslae.
(16) Lifting train en-route to Newton Stewart.
(17) Lifting train at the Clints of Dromore.
(18) Lifting train crossing the Fleet Viaduct near Gatehouse Station.
(19) Wigtown Station at the time of closure.
(20) The mid-week wednesday train at Wigtown Station before closure.

(1) 57375 and Rail-tour crossing the Garlieston burn bridge at Millisle. (Dr. Brewster)

(2) Caledonian Railway 0-6-0 57375 approaching Millisle from Whithorn, hauling a Railtour special in 1963 - the last passenger train to traverse the line. (Dr. Brewster)

(3) Last train shunting at Garlieston Harbour.
(Dr. Brewster)

(4) Guard with coupling hook at the ready stands at the gated crossing between the old Garlieston Station platform and the harbour. Meanwhile 78026 moves for the last time to shunt the two sidings extending under Wyllie's Mill on the quay.
(Dr. Brewster)

(5) No wagons for Whithorn on the last day! 78026 with guards-van crosses Garlieston-Sorbie road bridge after leaving Millisle.
(Dr. Brewster)

(6) View of Sorbie Station from road bridge at time of closure. A new tank or boiler for the creamery lies on the station platform. The Creamery had its own platform on the other side of the single line which was too narrow for the tank.  (Dr. Brewster)

(7) Alex. Muir, linesman, watches his remaining detonators explode as the last train leaves Whauphill.
(Dr. Brewster)

(8) Crane preparing to lift remaining section of Bladnoch viaduct.
(Dr. Brewster)

(9) With David Gladstone in the cab, James Allan and William McGowan pose with guard as last train prepares to leave Wigtown Station.
(Dr. Brewster)

(10) Pick-up train crossing the Bladnoch Bridge on Saturday 13th October, 1964, eight days after the official closure - the FINALE.
(Dr. Brewster)

(11) Lifting train on Bladnoch bridge. Wheeled air compressor trailer visible in rear wagon with air pipes trailing out to power tools.
(Dr. Brewster)

(12) Cutting up Bladnoch viaduct.
(Dr. Brewster)

(13) Wigtown line near Carslae. Measuring and chalking rail cutting points some 200yards ahead of the train visible in the background.
(Dr. Brewster)

(14) Cutting rails near Carslae, Wigtown
(Dr. Brewster)

(15) Two men unscrew chair bolts, near Carslae, on the Wigtown line. Third man knocks out rail chocks.
(Dr. Brewster)

(16) Crossing the tidal Palnure Burn at speed. A diesel loco heads a lifting train of empty four wheel trucks en-route to the Newton Stewart yard.
(Dr. Brewster)

(17) Diesel hauled track lifting train of empties passes distant signal before Gatehouse of Fleet, below the Clints of Dromore.
(Dr. Brewster)

(18) Diesel hauled lifting train of empty flats crosses the Fleet Viaduct near Gatehouse of Fleet Station.
(Dr. Brewster)

(19) Wigtown Station and yard from the south at the time of closure. Note the male and female monkey puzzle trees on the left.
(Dr. Brewster)

(20) The mid-week Wednesday service standing at the platform at Wigtown Station. (Derek Cross)

# Rails to Portpatrick

(United Creameries Company), Sorbie (United Creameries Company) and Bladnoch, near Wigtown (Scottish Co-operative Wholesale Society, new in 1898), while the Scottish Co-operative Wholesale Society established a creamery at Whithorn, too, in 1902. All these premises brought good business to the railways, on which they depended for the regular and speedy transit of their products. Incidentally, we know from the long list in the tourist guide that many "farmers and others supplied butter, eggs, fruit, etc., by passenger train direct to the consumer".

Fish came in large quantities from the North of Ireland and from numerous ports on the coasts of Galloway, especially Stranraer, which from about 1907 was a base for steam trawlers, the boats unloading their catches at the railway pier. We discovered earlier in this chapter the growing importance of the perishable traffic from the district served by the W R line, to distant destinations, at the same period. In 1894, rather than be at the expense of providing staff locking frames, the J C had contemplated closing the goods sidings at Bladnoch and Broughton Skeog. They relented in the case of Bladnoch on finding that its traffic for the year ending 30th June totalled 580 tons, but Broughton Skeog's had been only 119 tons, so they ordered its closure and the lifting of the rails. The W R line's goods traffic was to become much more impressive during the following twenty years.

The carriage of coal into the province, including the supply for the Stranraer-Larne steamers, was an important source of revenue to the J C. In the outgoing direction, though Galloway is deficient in minerals and freestone, the dispatch of granite from the Bagbie quarries, near Creetown, proved a valuable item for some years. In the early 1890's about 700 tons annually passed over the P P R line, mainly for places on the C R and G S W. In 1893, the J C found this traffic slipping away. There was no crane at Creetown station capable of lifting the great blocks of stone; manual loading was breaking the wagon bottoms, and the delays involved were driving business away to the sea transport available from the quay near the quarries. The J C ordered an eight-ton crane, estimated to cost £190. This seems to have resolved the difficulty, and in 1902 the quarrymasters, the Carsluith Granite Company, were trying to persuade the J C to build a line to the quarries; the J C declined, but the careful consideration they gave to the request shows the value they placed on this traffic.

In 1892 the Board of Trade authorised one mixed train daily each way between Portpatrick and Stranraer, and Stranraer and Castle Douglas, and two each way between Wigtown and Whithorn, and Newton Stewart and Wigtown, and on the Garliestown branch. About this time, the goods trains seem to have been under-powered. In September 1893, Cunning drew the officers' attention to the "light class of engines supplied", pointing out that if the working companies would provide heavier engines, like those in general use on their own lines, the J C would save a good deal of expense on pilot engines. The subject was referred to the locomotive superintendents, but the result is not recorded. Nine months later it was stated that a pilot engine was now rarely sent from Newton Stewart to

Creetown to assist the 5.30 p.m. goods from Stranraer up Creetown Bank. Wagons left over by this train could usually be worked forward by the 11 p.m. goods from Stranraer. On the whole, this suggests that no improvement in motive power had taken place so far.

On 2nd May 1896, the 11 p.m. goods train encountered an obstacle on the line near Glenluce. Two metal chairs had been fixed to the rails. The train was not derailed, though the engine was slightly damaged. £5 reward was offered for information, but none was forthcoming. On 16th November 1904, in the same neighbourhood, a large stone was found on the line, having evidently been placed there during the night, and struck by a train. These incidents recall similar ones in the early days of the P P R.

## THE P P R JUBILEE

Happier events of those early days were recalled for readers of the *Wigtownshire Free Press* in March 1911 by the long illustrated article that it published to commemorate the railway's golden jubilee. The article included also some interesting comparisons:

"The total traffic revenue in 1863 amounted to £19,514, and the expenditure to £13,556, while in 1910 the revenue (including, of course, the Wigtown Railway, which was not constructed until much later), exceeded £60,000, notwithstanding the very considerable reduction that has taken place in the rates for the carriage of various kinds of merchandise . . .

"In 1861 the carriage of game to Glasgow by passenger train was 5s. per cwt. It is now 2s. per cwt. Ninepence was demanded for carrying a parcel one pound in weight to London. Today the charge for a parcel weighing one or two pounds is fourpence. The rate for fresh fish from Portpatrick and Stranraer by passenger train was 2½d. per stone of 14 lb., or 1s. 8d. per cwt. Newton Stewart fishmongers now pay only 10d. per cwt. . . .

"Before the opening of the Wigtown branch, passengers were booked through from Stranraer, etc., to the county town, the connection being given with the stage coaches, '*Victoria*' and '*Hero*', which started from Newton Stewart station. First class fare and inside of coach from Stranraer to Wigtown was 5s.; second class and inside of coach, 3s. 6d.; third class and outside of coach, 2s. 6d. To Whithorn the fares were 6s. 6d., 5s., and 3s. 6d., respectively. The present day fares to these places are much the same, but the accommodation is now greatly superior, and the time occupied on the journey is, of course, much less. The excursion fares are, however, now largely reduced . . .

"In 1862, passengers by the 7.30a.m. train from Stranraer did not reach Carlisle until 12.30, and they were over nine hours longer in arriving in London. Nowadays the time occupied on the journey is less by about four hours."

# Rails to Portpatrick

PROJECTED NEW LINES

In September 1893, a deputation, Mr. Forbes of Callendar and of Earlstoun, near Dalry, Mr. Spalding, of Holme, Mr. Young, of Garroch, Mr. Cunninghame Graham, of Dalarran, and Mr. Gillespie, solicitor, Castle Douglas, waited on the J C to seek their support for a revival of the Glenkens Railway scheme. The J C obtained plans and reports from their officers, and found that the proposed line, of 7½ miles from New Galloway station to Dalry, was likely to cost £50,000. Traffic receipts were expected to total £3,000 a year, and working expenses £2,200 a year. As, however, a reduction of £500 was anticipated in the receipts at New Galloway station, a balance of only £300 would be left towards paying interest on the capital borrowed. The J C accordingly declined to build the line, or contribute towards its building, but said they would be willing to work it, if constructed by others, "at a reasonable rate".

The next mention of a proposed railway in the Glenkens was in connection with a considerably longer line. The Light Railways Act passed in 1896, and a scheme was prepared for a light railway to link the P P & W at New Galloway with the G S W at Dalmellington. Early in 1898 the Light Railways Syndicate in London (a corporation formed with a registered capital of £10,000 to obtain powers to build and work light railways, and find the capital for their construction) sought the assent of the J C to a junction at or near New Galloway station. The J C deferred consideration until they received fuller information, and the records do not refer to the matter again.

There is a passing mention in 1905 of a projected light railway to connect the P P & W at Dromore with the town of Gatehouse. The chief proposal, however, of a light railway to serve a part of Galloway was a revival in 1898 of the Rhins scheme of twenty years previously. The initiative in this seems to have been taken chiefly by Hugh Mayberry who, from humble beginnings in the village of Drummore in the Rhins, had risen to a prominent position in the business life of Glasgow, as a land and property agent. Drummore was to be linked with the P P & W at Whiteleys between Stranraer and Colfin, and also near Dunragit. The promoters' estimate of the cost of their lines was £97,384.1.6. They sought running powers over the P P & W between Challoch Junction and Whiteleys, and proposed terms on which they invited the J C to work their lines. The J C's reaction to the scheme was cool and cautious in the extreme. They opposed the request for running powers and also the formation of junctions with their line. They rejected the proposed terms for a Working Agreement. They refused further discussion of the scheme until they had the fullest possible information about it. A little later, they relented so far as to assent to the formation of a junction at Whiteleys, where, however, traffic would have to be interchanged, as they refused running powers to Stranraer.

In May 1899, the Light Railways Commissioners, the Earl of Jersey and Colonel Boughey, came to Stranraer to hear the promoters' application for an Order under the 1896 Act. Much of the evidence was decidedly unfavourable. Several of the landowners were strongly opposed to the scheme, notably the Earl of Stair, who pointed out that it was not clear how the capital was to be raised, and claimed that the dairy farms along the proposed route of the line would be damaged by its cutting across them. Details were given of the existing traffic in passengers, parcels and goods by road between Stranraer and Drummore, the implication being that a railway could not pay. Adam Henry, Ardwell, contractor for the mail coach, said that without the mail contract it would not be worth while running the coach. Peter McGeoch, cattle-dealer, Stranraer, told how he purchased cattle and sheep in all parts of Wigtownshire, and brought them by road. He would never think of putting cattle into a train for four or five miles. Dealers walked cattle from as far as Castle Douglas and even Carlisle. George Watson, agent to Messrs. Little, of Glasgow, who ran a twice-weekly steamer to Glasgow from Stranraer, said the farmers about Colfin and Portpatrick preferred carting their produce to Stranraer to using the railway, and Mr. Agnew, Mark, near Castle Kennedy, annually passed Castle Kennedy station with many tons of carrots, carting them to the steamer. The steamer traffic was increasing; it carried about 800 tons a month. It frequently carried goods for Drummore, Stoneykirk and Castle Kennedy. He did not think his customers would use the proposed railway. W. T. Wheatley, now owner of the George Hotel in Stranraer and a very active burgh councillor, spoke in favour of the railway, but County Councillor James Drew, vice-convenor of the County, former director of the WR, was against it.

  The commissioners refused to recommend the Order. Lord Jersey said they needed "a very strong case", and in view of the whole evidence, and the opposition of the landowners on fourteen out of the nineteen miles of the proposed route, they could not make a recommendation in favour.

  There was, nevertheless, clearly a real need for better transport in the Rhins. This was not quite the last to be heard of a railway there, while the J C were to be the pioneers of the district's motor bus services.

## MOTORS

  During the early years of the new century, motor cars were an increasingly familiar sight on the main roads of Galloway, and motors came to figure prominently in the local news. Motor buses made an early appearance in the province. The J C's own "trail-blazing" on the Stranraer-Drummore route in 1907-8 must have separate treatment, but we may notice now several enterprises of the years immediately following. In 1912, a motor char-a-banc was begun between Dalmellington and Dalry; the fares were 3/6 single and 6/- return, and the service was operated by James Macdonald, of the Eglinton Hotel in Dalmellington, who advertised cars and char-a-bancs for hire. This service, running from 1st June to 30th September only, through the magnificent scenery of the Glenkens, in connection with G S W trains at Dalmellington, and obviously intended mainly for summer visitors, was in no way a competitor with the railways. In 1913 and 1914 it was extended from Dalry to New Galloway town. There had, however, already been motor bus ventures made in direct competition with the train services. In April 1910 Hutchinson warned the officers that during the previous two months, a bus company in Stranraer had run services on several occasions between Stranraer and Newton Stewart, Wigtown and other places; while on 13th November following, a motor bus started between New Galloway town and Dumfries via Castle Douglas, in competition with the trains and the horse-drawn bus linking New Galloway town with the station. The following April, Hutchinson reported a "small decrease" in the passenger bookings from New Galloway, Parton, and Crossmichael stations to Castle Douglas and Dumfries. It was the merest tip of the shadow of drastic things to come. As yet, motors were expensive and unreliable, and it is not, therefore, surprising that when James Campbell, proprietor since 1903 of the horse-drawn buses running between Gatehouse station (formerly Dromore - the change of name took place on 1st January, 1912) and town, approached the J C in March 1912 for financial help towards replacing them with a motor, the J C should have declined. But it was a sign of the rapid advance of the motor as a "status symbol" and well-to-do man's plaything that when the P P & W's veteran traffic manager laid aside his duties, his friends and well-wishers in Galloway should choose to mark their appreciation of his services and affection for his person by the gift of a motor car.

HUTCHINSON'S RETIREMENT

Fred. W. Hutchinson retired at the end of 1913. He was 71, and had completed 57 years of railway service, having started with the C R in 1856, moving to the infant P P R in 1861. He had been traffic manager for the P P & W for 18 years. His salary, originally £250, had been increased to £450 by 1904. Two years later the J C, wanting to simplify administration and make economies, retired John Thomson, their secretary since the J C's inception, at short notice, and made Hutchinson secretary as well as manager. They increased his salary by £100, which included £25 for taking over the secretaryship of the Steamship Committee, another of Thomson's duties. When they learned of his wish to retire, they awarded him an allowance of £300 per annum.

The principal officers of the four owning companies made their parting tributes to Hutchinson in the splendour of the St. Pancras Hotel, in September 1913. His Galloway friends honoured him early next year in the humbler, but no doubt at least equally welcome, surroundings of the King's Arms in Stranraer. Presenting him with the car - of which, unfortunately, no details are available - Provost Young referred to his recreations of gardening and cycling. Hutchinson, he said, was "very fond of a spin on his bicycle, his failing being to go rather far, forgetting that he was not so young as he used to be and thereby suffering to that extent".

The Provost went on to say how local people had hoped for a more up-to-date station in a more convenient part of Stranraer, but that Hutchinson had been unable to gratify their wish through the impossibility of getting all the owning companies to consent. Hutchinson himself, who must indeed not seldom in his career have felt in the position of a man who had to try to serve four masters, mentioned his persistent, though futile, efforts to get goods rates reduced, and claimed to have "pressed his views so strongly as to earn the displeasure of some of the allied companies". He expressed "grief" at not always having been able to oblige people who applied to him to arrange for the summer boat expresses to stop at their local stations, and concluded his very modest little speech with a warm acknowledgement of the benefit he had derived from his early training under the P P R's William Grafton.

So Hutchinson relinquished his long and distinguished command; but he was to continue to be a familiar figure in the district for many years, living until 1932. His successor in office was William McConchie, whom we met as author of the J C's tourist guide. McConchie was then 51. He had begun his career with the P P R as a telegraphist at Kirkcowan, his native village, in 1877, and served as station-master at Dromore and Wigtown before his appointment as the P P & W's traffic inspector in 1888. His salary as manager was to be £450; £150 of this, however, was to be remuneration from the Steamship Committee for continuing to act as their traffic manager, a post he had held since 1905. It is to the story of the steamers that we now turn.

**CHAPTER ELEVEN**

The Steamers, 1892-1914

IN February 1892, there was launched at Dumbarton a new steamer which Messrs. Denny had built for the Stranraer-Larne service. She was the *Princess May*, a sister-ship to the *Victoria*. Her dimensions were the same and, like the *Victoria*, she grossed 1,100 tons and had compound engines with two cylinders; her nominal horse power was 650. She ran her trials on 4th May.

"Over a distance of 28 miles she made an average speed of 20.02 knots, equal to about 23 miles an hour. The engines made 47½ revolutions a minute with 111 lb. pressure at the engine and 116 lb. at the boilers. The draught will be seven inches more than that of the *Victoria*. Making allowance for the higher wind and rougher sea in the one case than in the other, the performance of both vessels is about equal."

The *Free Press* stated her guaranteed speed as 19 knots - one knot more than that of the *Victoria* - and described her as "developing an easy speed of fully 20 knots" between the Cloch and Cumbraes. Peter Denny, Junior, referring to the *Victoria* doing the passage in 1 hour 50 minutes, expressed the hope that the *May* would do it in 1 hour 45 minutes.

The new steamer reached Stranraer on Thursday, May Sth. "Her appearance", wrote the *Free Press*, "is exactly like that of the *Victoria*, from which steamer she is scarcely distinguishable". She took up the Mail Service four days later.

"She left Stranraer in beautiful weather, with bunting flying, but was unable to make her best speed down Lochryan owing to the low water. After getting into deep water the vessel behaved splendidly, and gave the greatest satisfaction to all on board. Speed had to be slackened for a short time owing to the heating of one of the funnels, but despite this the voyage from pier to pier was accomplished in 1 hour 58 minutes. A great number of persons had assembled on Larne pier to witness the arrival of the new steamer, and she was received by a salvo of guns and cheering, which was replied to on board. The vessel was photographed by a Scotch firm as she approached the pier."

The happy occasion was further improved by its being made the opportunity for over 200 regular passengers by the route to make a presentation to Captain George Campbell, who had commanded the *Briton* in 1862-4, returned to the route

# Rails to Portpatrick

when it was re-established in 1872, and was now in command of the *May*. Meeting in the Olderfleet Hotel in Larne harbour, the grateful patrons paid warm tribute to Campbell's consistent efficiency and courtesy. The *May*'s return voyage to Stranraer in the evening was accomplished in 1 hour 57 minutes.

The newcomer had a few early troubles. Her paddle floats proved defective, being too weak. Dennys strengthened them, and soon after, those of the *Victoria* also. Early in 1893, it was reported that her sponson houses had been "several times stove in by the sea". Dennys were to put them in a secure condition at their own cost. In the autumn, a crack was discovered in a paddle arm of the *May*, and cracks in "no fewer than three" paddle arms of the *Victoria*. Dennys were notified of "these serious and unexpected failures". During the *May*'s first months in the service it had been found that she burnt a good deal more coal than the *Victoria*. In an attempt to combat this, retarders were fitted to her tubes, and by the end of 1896 these were reported as successful, making a saving of about nine tons of coal per week, with more regular steaming. The Steamship Committee agreed to Campbell's recommendation that they be fitted to the *Victoria* also.

Economy was very much a watchword with the Steamship Committee, as behoved them considering the financial loss that the service continually incurred. In 1898 they decided that the following staff should be attached to the *Victoria* or the *May* when either steamer was laid up in port:

|  | Per week |  | Per week |
|---|---|---|---|
| 1 Chief Engineer | £3.3.0 | 1 Fireman | £1.0.0 |
| 1 Second Engineer | £2.5.0 | 2 Shipkeepers at 20/- | £1.0.0 |
| 1 Fireman | £1.5.0 | 1 Woman | £0.9.0 |

With this staff, they expected to keep the ships "in such repair that not much would require to be done to them on the occasions of the annual surveys". The next year, they had the painting and overhaul of the *Beatrice* done at Stranraer, and came to an agreement with the C R and G S W that in future as many repairs as possible to all the steamers would be done at the railway workshops there. In 1903, there is a note of the appointment of a boilermaker, his wage to be about 38/- and accommodation for him to be found in the railway workshops.

The *Beatrice* was now the S C's reserve boat. There are occasional references to her being in service, as, for example, in June 1896 when she kept up the Mail Service for two days after an air-pump lever had broken on the *May*, and a year later when a serious defect was discovered in the main crank of the *Victoria* as she was on the point of returning from overhaul at Dumbarton, and the *Beatrice* had to run the Second Service in her stead for nine days. After the latter occasion, the S C received a letter from the Belfast & Northern Counties Company. No doubt this was a complaint about the *Beatrice*'s want of speed. The old steamer's lack of speed and her limited accommodation for passengers and livestock made her unsuitable for the service now, and the S C were already considering selling her and getting another vessel, though for various reasons they did not come to a decision for some years ye..

In 1898, Campbell retired. At the age of 70 he might well have felt that the time had come to lay aside his exacting duties as chief captain, but he had given such general pleasure and satisfaction during his long connection with the service that he must have been sadly missed. The S C made him a yearly allowance of £150 during their pleasure, with the rather extensive condition that "during the continuance of the pension he is to render any service to the Committee which they may require him to perform". Campbell died at his home, Seabank House, Stranraer, in August 1900. The *Kirkcudbrightshire Advertiser* wrote of him:

"He was a skilful officer, careful and attentive, beloved by the men who served under him, and during his long career he never met with a mishap at sea."

The unenviable position of successor to Campbell fell to Captain J. P. Cumming, of Stranraer, whom the S C selected from sixteen applicants. His salary was to be £400. The S C's Captain McCracken, who, like Campbell, had been in the service from the beginning and was in command of the mail steamer at the latter's retirement, was too old to hope for the succession, and they directed that he was to receive "£5 a week wages whether acting as captain or first mate". He died in October 1899; the S C granted his widow a gratuity of £200.

Though a vital section of a trunk route, the steamer service was not in itself a paying undertaking, and from 1896 to 1903 the annual loss ranged between extremes of £55.17.9 and £1,412.9.10. The Second Service run during the summer, however, always paid. The profit in 1895 was £604, in 1896 £422, in 1898 £569, in 1899 £820.10.0, in 1900 £410.6.9, in 1901 £1,426.13.2, in 1902 £1,203 and in 1903 £1,202.11.2. The last figure, contrasted with the overall loss for 1903 of over £1,400, provides a good illustration of the very wide seasonal fluctuations of the traffic. The relatively low profit made in 1900 was attributed by the S C to the price of coal. The lowest tender submitted to them in the late summer of that year quoted a price of 19/3 a ton, while in January 1901 the same tenderer quoted 15/- a ton, and in May, 13/6.

In a new attempt to improve all-year-round patronage of the route, the S C and the railway companies agreed on revised fares between Belfast and London, to begin on 1st June 1898. The ordinary fares in each direction fixed seven years previously were reduced:

|  | 1891 | | 1898 | |
| --- | --- | --- | --- | --- |
|  | First class | Third class | First class | Third class |
| Single journey | 55/- | 27/6 | 50/- | 27/- |
| Return journey | 92/- | 50/- | 90/6 | 50/- |

# Rails to Portpatrick

Much more drastic reductions were offered, for a 12-month trial period in the form of 16-day return tickets, available only from Belfast to London:

|  | First class and Saloon | Third class and Saloon | Third class and Steerage |
|---|---|---|---|
| Return fares (valid for 16 days) | 75/- | 42/6 | 35/6 |

These tickets were continued for a time after the trial period, but they were withdrawn after April 1902, so presumably they were only a very limited success. In 1898, the Great Northern (of England) Company applied for through bookings from King's Cross to Belfast via Newcastle, Carlisle and Stranraer, but were refused - the L N W and M R can scarcely have favoured this proposal.

The S C had deferred decisions about running a double service all the year, and the related subject of building another steamer, until they saw the results of the revised fares. They now agreed, however, to provide some sleeping accommodation on the steamers, an idea they had rejected when previously put to them in 1892 and 1897. The railway companies thought it would be to the advantage of the route, enabling people arriving at Stranraer by train in the evening and who wanted to sail with the early morning mail steamer to sleep on board, instead of going to an hotel. Probably the estimated cost of conversion - £1,000 for each vessel - had deterred the S C in the past, but they now obtained and accepted a tender from Dennys to provide sleeping accommodation for twelve people on the *Victoria* and on the *May* for £300 for each ship. The work was to be done at Stranraer. In April 1899, the S C noted that since the previous November an average of about five berths had been used per night, the charge for each berth being 2/6. During the five months ending 31st March, £62.15.0 had been paid for a total of 502 berths, yielding the S C a profit of £19.5.0.

From the mid-'90s onward, there are regular references to summer excursions being run by the steamers. In 1894, the *Victoria* ran excursions from Stranraer to the Isle of Man, and the following year half-day excursions were begun, on Saturdays in July and August, from Stranraer along the Ayrshire coast and from Larne along the coast of Antrim. The Ayrshire coast excursions included trips round Ailsa Craig, raising an average of £16.17.4 per trip. This soon became established as a favourite excursion, both with the local people and with visitors. On 25th September 1897, the *May* was on this excursion when one of her paddle-wheels broke down; she had to be taken to Dumbarton for repairs which cost £1,180.8.5. This mishap alarmed the J C's officers, who, concerned about fulfilling the obligation regarding the Mail Service, advised the J C to stop the use of the steamers on excursions. The J C disagreed, however, so the excursions must have been profitable activities.

The passage had been maintained since its inception with a very high standard of safety, especially considering the extremely stormy conditions to which the crossing is subject. There are only very occasional references in the records to accidents. On 20th and 22nd November 1895, the *May* grounded in Stranraer harbour, owing to the exceptionally low water, her departure being delayed 20 minutes on the first occasion and 30 minutes on the second; dredging was carried out to prevent a recurrence. In January 1898, the *May* had to be taken out of service for three days following a collision outside Larne harbour. The *Victoria* was being overhauled, so the passage had to be maintained by the *Beatrice*, with the result that the departure from Stranraer of the mail and fish trains was delayed about 50 minutes each night. Later that year the Board of Trade surveyor condemned both the *May*'s paddle-shafts, which had to be renewed, and storm injectors were fitted. The S C noted that the *Victoria*'s paddle-shafts had failed the previous year, and that her recent overhaul had cost £2,448.8.7, including about £1,500 for new paddle shafts.

The *Victoria* was coming from Larne one evening in November 1900 when she collided with the St. Mirren, of Dublin, which was lying at anchor off Cairnryan. The *Victoria* was slightly damaged, and damage to the St. Mirren was estimated at £250. A year later, Stranraer pier was damaged by the motion of the *Victoria* and *Beatrice* lying alongside it in a heavy gale. So terrific was the wind that night that the *May* could not attempt the passage from Larne, remaining there until nine next morning. The *Victoria* and *Beatrice* had to go to Harland & Wolff for three weeks for repair.

We saw earlier how the persistence of the J C secured the establishment of a fog signal at Corsewall Point in 1890. It was probably at their instigation that, as Campbell reported early in 1897, the Irish Lights Commissioners "decided to exhibit a powerful light from the Chaine Monument to guide our steamers clear of Hunters Rock on approaching and leaving Larne harbour". During the next few years there were lengthy negotiations over their application for a light at Milleur Point, the rocky headland at the north-east corner of the Rhins Peninsula. The Northern Lights Commissioners agreed that a gas-lighted bell buoy might be maintained at Government expense, if the S C paid about £500 to provide the buoy. After vain efforts to get the commissioners to pay first the whole and then half of this sum, the S C eventually consented to these terms, and the buoy was fixed in position in January 1900. Instead of being placed near Milleur Point, however, it was put in the middle of the Loch, and more controversy followed. The S C added a complaint that the bell was not loud enough. Then the light went out for four days at the end of January 1901. Cumming was authorised to sign a petition for the transfer of the buoy to a better position. In June 1901, the buoy obligingly drifted from its position, preparing the way for a happy ending to the story as the commissioners subsequently removed it to a place in the loch close to the Point.

# Rails to Portpatrick

About the same time, the S C were trying to persuade the Irish Lights Commissioners to install a fog signal on Barr Point, at the entrance to Larne harbour. In June 1899, Cumming drew the S C's attention to the danger involved in entering the harbour during fog, giving a graphic impression of the disadvantages of the existing precautions:

"The present practice is that a boat with sound rockets and fog horn, all provided at our expense, goes out in thick weather when the steamer is expected, to warn it off the rocks, but this is very unsatisfactory. On the 10th instant the rocket exploded prematurely, blowing a hole in the bottom of the boat and injuring the two men who were in it."

Correspondence with the commissioners followed. A bell was provided, and later a gun, to be superseded in its turn by a siren, the gun available for use in emergencies.

With the *Victoria* or the *May*, or both of them, in service the J C could claim in their public notices to make the Stranraer to Larne passage in two hours, with only 80 minutes on the open sea. The S C were keenly aware, however, of the shortcomings of the *Beatrice* as a reserve boat (her speed in service was 14 knots) and that these were the more important now that their faster steamers were no longer new. In June 1901, therefore, they asked Captain W. H. Binney, marine superintendent with the L N W at Holyhead, to examine the *Victoria* and *May*, report on their condition and say how long they could maintain the service "in as efficient a state as at present", and report also on what type of steamer would be most suitable for the service in the event of their deciding to build a new one.

Binney submitted his report in December. He found the two steamers in good condition generally, but their boilers would need increasing attention, and in three years the question of reboilering them would arise. Having mentioned the *Beatrice*'s inadequacies of speed and accommodation, he went on to point out that the lack of a fully efficient reserve boat meant that the two faster steamers did not get the time and attention necessary to keep them in the best possible condition, a deficiency that would prove increasingly serious as they got older. He strongly recommended the provision of a new steamer, of the twin-screw type. This type of vessel, he explained, was much less liable to breakdown than a paddle-steamer; it was much handier in entering and leaving harbour, and when in port it lay more safely and snugly alongside the quay and was therefore more convenient for working cargo. As for the objection that screw steamers caused too much vibration to be suitable for passenger services, this no longer applied, as vibration had been practically eliminated through the introduction of balanced engines.

He foresaw, however, two difficulties for screw steamers near and alongside Stranraer pier. The ground alongside the pier was irregular; the paddle steamers' paddle-boxes and sponsons kept their hulls about 15 feet from the side of the pier, but a screw steamer would lie alongside the pier wall and the "inequalities" of the bottom would damage her hull. The G S W's Mr. Melville had told him that the ground was fairly soft, but it would not be safe to dredge close in to the pier, as it might disturb the foundations; the twinscrew steamer would have a slightly larger draught than the paddle steamers. Binney therefore recommended dredging the loch for a width of about 70 feet outside the proposed extension of the pier, and for about 800 feet northwards into the loch from the end of the pier, to a depth of not less than 13 feet at low water spring tides. He estimated the cost of this dredging as £3,800. He added that at Larne there was plenty of water, and all that might need to be done there was a slight lengthening of the pier, in pile work.

Binney went on to discuss the dimensions, guaranteed speed, accommodation, lay-out and other matters relating to his proposed new steamer. The S C paid him an honorarium of 150 guineas, but showed themselves in no hurry to act on any of his advice. No. doubt it was the heavy capital expenditure involved that deterred them. In April 1903, however, they at last decided to invite tenders. The intention of the M R to open their new Heysham to Belfast route soon may have influenced them to some extent, but most likely their hand was forced by the necessity only a few weeks previously to send the *May* urgently to Dumbarton for immediate repairs - her cylinders and structure under her boilers had been found in very bad order. This must have made them very conscious indeed of their lack of a suitable reserve boat. In July, they accepted Messrs. Denny's tender for a triple-screw steamer with a guaranteed speed of 20 knots. To ensure this speed, the ship was to have two double-ended and one single-ended boilers. Her propellers were to be driven by steam turbines, this invention of the great Tyneside engineer, the Hon. C. A. Parsons, having proved its worth in marine propulsion during the previous two years. The total cost would be £66,000, and the vessel was to be completed within ten months.

The new steamer, launched on 20th February 1904, was named the *Princess Maud*. Her dimensions, very much as had been suggested by Binney, were length 301 feet, breadth 40 feet and depth 16 feet; her gross tonnage was 1,700. Messrs. Denny built her boilers, which supplied steam to three turbines from the Parsons Marine Steam Turbine Company of Wallsend. One of the latter was a high-pressure turbine, which drove the ship's big central propeller, while the others were low-pressure, driving her two smaller screws. The *Maud* ran her official trial trip on 27th April, when she achieved a mean speed over the measured mile of 20.7 knots. There came a startling development when the Board of Trade refused her a passenger certificate, claiming that her condensers were not strong enough, but Messrs. Denny appealed and a court of inquiry found in their favour.

On the morning of 28th May, a Saturday, the *Maud* left the Tail of the Bank for Stranraer, and that evening and the following day Captain Cumming allowed people who were interested to see over her, an opportunity of which hundreds took advantage. She took up the Mail Service on Wednesday, lst June. An early report by Cumming read:

"So far the steamer is doing well, and can make the passage from pier to pier in about ten minutes less than the paddle boats. The consumption of coal is somewhat greater, but the experience has been too short to speak with certainty about this."

A subsequent report based on the *Maud*'s performance on the Mail Service up to the end of July, continues:

"With a strong beam wind and high sea the ship behaved well and proved herself to be a good sea boat, making the passage pier to pier in 1 hour 52 minutes.
"The coaling, by crane and hopper, has been found to be a great improvement over the old method by barrows; noise and dust are reduced to a minimum, and there is no waste. The work could not be done in double the time by barrows and with the same number of hands. The ship appears to be popular with passengers, as they express themselves highly satisfied with the general arrangement and accommodation. This is specially the case with third class passengers who have been provided with good shelter on deck".

The *Maud* had five additional crew compared with the *May*, giving her a total company of thirty-nine. Cumming quoted figures for the new ship's coal consumption:

        Coal consumed 11/6-25/6    420 tons - 35 tons per day.
        Coal consumed 25/6-23/7    786 tons - 32 tons 16 cwt. per day.

These compared with an average daily consumption by the *May*, on the Second Service during July, of 25 tons 2 cwt. The coaling at Stranraer that Cumming referred to was done in the early hours of the morning, and the noise created must sometimes have been sufficiently disturbing to townspeople, however familiar it had become. Experience soon showed that it was impossible to load the *Maud* in the time available by hand labour, as with her predecessors, so the steam crane at the pier was called to the rescue, evidently with very favourable results. The S C paid the J C 2d. a ton for its use.

The extension of the pier and dredging of Loch Ryan that the coming of the *Maud* had made necessary were completed during the summer. The dredging cost £9,123.3.0 - very much more than expected. Binney had estimated £3,800, while Melville had evidently thought at first that the cost could be kept down to £1,500. The J C recorded their regret that Melville had failed to take new soundings of the loch, leading him to form a very inaccurate estimate of the amount of dredging that would be needed.

During the early part of 1905, Captain Cumming became ill, and the S C gave him leave of absence and a gift of £25. When he returned to duty in the summer, revised tirnings were introduced for the Mail Service, and this necessitated the rearrangement of his duties and those of other senior officers, as the later departure of the mail steamer from Belfast would increase the time he was on duty as sailing captain, and make it impossible for him to continue as both sailing captain and shore captain, as he had previously been. He remained in full charge of the officers and crews in the service, in addition to his shore duty, which included superintendence of the overhaul of the steamers when this was done locally. But he was relieved of his duties as sailing captain, Captain N. McNeill being appointed acting captain all year round, while Mate W. McCalmont was to act as captain of one of the steamers when the Second Service was running.

In this year William McConchie became the S C's traffic manager. Always very keen to encourage holiday traffic, in his new post his enthusiasm found early, but hardly favourable, recognition from his superiors when he was summoned to a meeting of the J C's officers to hear their comments on the withdrawal of the *Maud* from the Mail Service to take excursionists to Ireland, while one of the paddle-boats was left to carry the mail train passengers. The officers minuted that the "Steamboat Manager" was to "keep in view that it was not considered advisable that the turbine steamer should be withdrawn from the Mail Service". The fact that their specific reference was not to the mails, but to the passengers, as having to go by paddle-boat is significant, showing their keen concern to uphold the prestige of the route for passenger traffic.

In 1908 McConchie stated that day excursions from Belfast to Stranraer had yielded the S C an average revenue of £524 for each of the previous six years; coast cruises from Stranraer and from Larne had left a net profit of £258 for the 1907 season. He was arguing against a proposal by the M R that the Second Service should be rearranged so that in future the passage could be worked by one steamer instead of two. The representatives of the other railway companies thought the idea impracticable, for various reasons, but McConchie's strongest contention against it was that the retiming it would necessitate would virtually put a stop to the excursions and cruises.

The Second Service continued decidedly profitable, though it seems to have reached a peak in this respect about 1906 and then to have considerably declined. All the figures, however, are much higher than those we noticed earlier for the 1890s:

| 1904 | £1,662 |
| 1905 | £1,827.2.0 |
| 1906 | £2,079.2.7 |
| 1909 | £1,450.16.1 |
| 1910 | £1,476.4.0 |

Figures are recorded for the average number of passengers carried daily by the steamer on the Second Service in 1909:

|  | June | July | August | September |
|---|---|---|---|---|
| From Ireland | 74 | 162 | 221 | 90 |
| To Ireland | 84 | 196 | 220 | 84 |

The sleeping accommodation on the steamers seems to have been well patronised, a total of 1,512 berths being taken up in the year ending 30th September 1907, compared with 1,175 in that ending 30th September 1900. But the losses annually made by the steamers were also higher now than in previous years:

| 1904 | £1,479.12.11 | 1905 | £2,186.19.11 |
|---|---|---|---|
| 1906 | £1,619.19.9 | 1908 | £1,955.6.10 |
| 1909 | £1,972.8.2 | 1910 | £1,087.13.6 |

Two tragedies occurred at the stage in the history of the steamers to which we have now come. The first was in 1908, when, on the 8th October, the body of J. A. Coleman was found floating in Loch Ryan near Low Craichmore, about two miles north of Stranraer. Coleman, aged 58 at the time of his death, had been about seven years in the S C's service, first as chief steward and then as storekeeper, in charge of all the catering on the steamers, and chief steward on the Second Service. The S C found "the books and all the business of the catering department in a state of chaos", and that Coleman had been in deep financial trouble, to such an extent that "he could neither eat nor sleep for many days and nights before he died". Both to the S C and at the fatal accidents inquiry held at Stranraer in November, Captain Cumming spoke strongly in Coleman's favour as a man of very upright character. He related how he had known of his serious financial difficulties for at least five years, and his evidence and that of other witnesses forms a very sad tale. The jury found that the unfortunate man had died by drowning at the east pier on the morning of 6th October, there being insufficient evidence to show how he got into the water.

The second tragic happening took place the following year. On the 6th August, the *Maud*, commanded by Captain McNeill, left Stranraer on the 6 a.m. Mail Service as usual. It was a foggy morning. About 1¾ miles north of the pier, the *SS Pirate,* of Glasgow, was anchored in the fairway. The *Pirate* was well known in the district. The property of the Argyll & Wigtownshire Steamship Company, she had maintained a bi-weekly service between Glasgow and Stranraer via Campbeltown for sixteen years. Mr. and Mrs. Young McDowel, of Glenluce, were passengers on her this voyage, bound for Ayr. Mrs. McDowel was recovering from an illness. Mr. McDowel called to his wife to come up on deck to see the mail steamer pass by. She did so, and saw the *Maud* come looming out of the fog and make straight for the *Pirate,* which sank as a result of the subsequent collision. Passengers and crew were saved, but Mrs. McDowel died soon after. The S C received demands in respect of goods on board the Pirate damaged by immersion. Repairs to the *Maud* carried out by Denny cost £384.5.0, and a settlement was reached with the owners of the *Pirate* for £2,637.1.7. A long contest ensued over Mr. McDowel's claim re his deceased wife, last noticed in the S C's records in April 1912 as being then before the Court of Session. The collision had by that time cost the S C a total of £4,068.9.8. For Captain McNeill the consequences of the accident were scarcely less tragic than for Mr. and Mrs. McDowel. With effect from May 1910, the S C terminated his services. Captain McCalmont was appointed in his stead, at the same salary of £260.

Despite Cumming's report of the excellent reception given to the *Maud* by passengers on her first taking up the service, it is clear that as she became established on the passage there were numerous complaints about vibration being serious enough to interfere with comfort. In the autumn of 1907, the S C, obviously genuinely concerned at the complaints, referred the subject to Messrs. Denny, who made a number of recommendations, some of which, though not all, the S C acted upon. At the end of December, Cumming wrote to Hutchinson that the replacement of a defective propeller had made a great improvement. He thought that the propeller had been responsible for most of the trouble and that there was now no ground for serious complaint, while a small amount of vibration was inevitable:

"From the fact that vibration was felt when the turbines were running disconnected, and nothing having been done as proposed to improve their balance, I fail to see how we could expect anything more than to bring matters back to their normal condition. It may be that with our light draught nothing more can be done in this ship to make things better, and even were this so I am of opinion that passengers have little reason to complain, as no turbine-driven ship of high speed is, to my knowledge, quite free from a tremor of some sort".

The S C had carried out a suggestion by Dennys that more pillaring be provided in certain parts of the ship, in an attempt to improve matters locally. On 23rd January 1908, Mr. Jackson, representing Messrs. Denny, crossed to Larne with Cumming and Hutchinson to test the results of this. His report was very favourable:

"The steamer is now very free from vibration and compares favourably with any of the cross channel turbine steamers. In my opinion she will remain so as long as the propellers are in good condition.

"My attention was drawn to a small amount of tremor on two of the tables in the smoking room. This room is situated immediately over the dynamo and turbine room, and while the dynamo is working there will always be a little. It is much less, however, since an additional pillar was fitted."

## Rails to Portpatrick

The S C now had three steamers, the *Maud*, the *Victoria* and the *May*. Following their acquisition of the *Maud* in 1904, they had sold the *Beatrice* to Dennys for £1,600 to be broken up. Latterly it was usually in respect of her shortcomings that she figured in our story, but before she was left behind in the march of time and progress she had given as distinguished service as any of the steamers that have worked on the passage. Now the *Victoria* and the *May* were ageing, and in the case of the *Victoria* the matter of reboilering, of which Captain Binney had warned some years ago, had become urgent. In October 1909, Cumming told the S C that the necessary renewals and repairs would cost between £12,000 and £14,000. Rather than face this expense, the S C decided to dispose of her, and the *Victoria* left Stranraer for the last time on the morning of 23rd February 1910, in tow of the tug *Oceana*, having been sold to the Shipbreaking Company Limited, London, for £3,300. The comment of the *Free Press*, that "the fitting in of new boilers would have made her almost as good as new", no doubt overstated the case, but it was a very natural expression of regret at what must have been regarded as the decidedly premature loss of a familiar and welcome sight.

Thus the S C were left with only two vessels, and at a meeting in March 1910 the J C's officers agreed to reduce the period of the Second Service of trains and steamers that summer by about four weeks; it was to run from 13th June to 17th September. Once again they considered running both the sea services with one ship, but the previous objections still held good, including that about the serious effect the necessary retimings were likely to have on excursion bookings from Ireland, since visitors would have so much less time to spend at Stranraer. It was therefore decided to operate the Mail Service with the *Maud* and the Second Service with the *May*, while the TS *Duchess of Argyll*, of the Caledonian Steam Packet Company, was to be chartered as a reserve boat. The charter was to extend from lst April to 15th October; the retaining fee was £100, but necessary alterations to the *Duchess of Argyll* cost the S C £424.15.5, and in the event of her going into actual service there would be a charge of £50 per day. This arrangement was renewed, on the same terms, in 1911. That year the Second Service again did not start till mid-June, but it continued to the end of September.

The *Duchess of Argyll* was, in fact, needed for actual service in 1911. This came about as a result of a spectacular accident involving the *Maud* and Larne pier. The *Maud* was going into the harbour - evidently too fast - on the morning of June 9th when she collided with the pier, running about twelve feet into the wooden jetty. Following this incident, the steamers went astern into Larne and went ahead into Stranraer, an extra five minutes being allowed for going astern out of Stranraer and into Larne. The *Maud* was out of service for a week, her place being taken by the *May*. As the Second Service began on June 12th, it was run for the first few days by the *Duchess of Argyll*.

By this time, the S C were completing the arrangements for ordering a new steamer. The withdrawal of the *Victoria* had given the *May* by far her busiest year since the arrival of the *Maud* six years previously. In October 1910, Cumming warned the S C that about £10,000 would have to be spent on the *May* very soon - probably for new boilers - if she was to be kept fit for regular service, and suggested that instead they build a new ship, and spend only £4,000 or £5,000 on the *May* as a reserve. In April 1911, he reported that she had, in fact, been held in reserve since 10th October, and gave details of her service since 1902:

| | | |
|---|---|---|
| 1902 | 208 days and steamed 14,888 nautical miles. |
| 1903 | 152 days and steamed 10,488 nautical miles. |
| 1904 | 174 days and steamed 11,945 nautical miles. |
| 1905 | 94 days and steamed 6,616 nautical miles. |
| 1906 | 115 days and steamed 7,980 nautical miles. |
| 1907 | 117 days and steamed 8,642 nautical miles. |
| 1908 | 99 days and steamed 7,220 nautical miles. |
| 1909 | 109 days and steamed 7,805 nautical miles. |
| 1910 | 138 days and steamed 10,484 nautical miles. |

The S C had already invited tenders for a new steamer similar to the *Maud*. They had also considered renewed complaints about discomfort to passengers on the sea crossing. From another reference a little later it is clear that the subject of complaint was again vibration in the *Maud*. Further measures to lessen this had evidently been taken, but no details are recorded. The S C noted, however, that "as regards the new steamer under construction, the matter of increased comfort to the passengers is receiving special attention".

The new ship, a second Princess *Victoria*, was built by Messrs. Denny. She was launched on 22nd February 1912, and completed by April. Her dimensions and gross tonnage were the same as those of the *Maud* and like the *Maud*, she was a triple-screw steamer with three sets of Parsons' turbines. The *Victoria*'s turbines (built by Dennys) were supplied with steam, however, by water-tube boilers, built partly by Dennys and partly by Babcock & Wilcox. After the launching, Peter Denny, chairman of the firm, thus described the advantages of the boilers, referring to two steamers built in 1911 for the South Eastern & Chatham Railway Company:

"These, for cross-channel work, had first been installed on board the *Engadine* and *Riviera*. With them steam was able to be raised in a very much shorter space of time. They did not require to keep banked fires, and the quantity of water was infinitesimal, thus saving weight carried. They could also carry a spare boiler, and this, on the Chatham boats, had resulted in the boilers remaining spotless after six or nine months' service".

In the new vessel, he said, the builders had fitted all the improvements that could be thought of, and he expressed appreciation of the help given by Commander Holland, the L N W's marine superintendent, who had put the whole of his experience on the cross-channel service at Messrs. Dennys disposal. The SC subsequently paid Commander Holland an honorarium of £105.

The *Victoria* ran her trials on 16th and 17th April. Commander Holland reported that the various tests had been satisfactorily carried out, and a speed of 20.979 knots attained with an air pressure of 4/10. He gave the results of a three hours' endurance trial:

|  |  |
|---|---|
| Steam Pressure | 162lb. |
| Vacuum | 28½ lb. |
| Air Pressure | 6/10 |
| Revolutions: |  |
| Port | 652 |
| Centre | 531 |
| Starboard | 648 |
| Speed | 20.4 knots |

The *Victoria* went to Stranraer on April 20th, and took up the Mail Service on 29th.

In 1913, to meet new Board of Trade requirements consequent on the loss of the Titanic, an additional lifeboat had to be provided on the *May* and the *Victoria* and two cutters on each ship had to be converted to lifeboats; "additional buoyant deck seats" were also supplied. The following year, new regulations considerably reduced the number of passengers the steamers could carry:

|  | Old Maxima | | | New Maxima | | |
|---|---|---|---|---|---|---|
|  | Passengers | Crew | Total | Passengers | Crew | Total |
| *May* | 964 | 36 | 1,000 | 664 | 36 | 700 |
| *Maud* | 1,455 | 39 | 1,494 | 1,081 | 39 | 1,120 |
| *Victoria* | 1,426 | 39 | 1,465 | 1,081 | 39 | 1,120 |

Special certificates were issued, however, enabling larger numbers to be carried on a daylight passage between 20th March and 30th September:

|  | Passengers | Crew | Total |
|---|---|---|---|
| *May* | 839 | 36 | 875 |
| *Maud* | 1,361 | 39 | 1,400 |
| *Victoria* | 1,361 | 39 | 1,400 |

The *May* was now only occasionally in service. In 1912, she steamed only 504 nautical miles, and in 1913, 425. In 1913, the *Maud* steamed 15,169 nautical miles, being in service on 203½ days. No figures are given for the *Victoria*.

# Rails to Portpatrick

After their acquisition of the new *Victoria* the S C did not restore the Second Service for the full period operated previous to 1910. In 1912, 1913 and 1914, while it ran each weekday, July to September inclusive, it operated on Saturdays only in June. In 1914 the Auxiliary Service was introduced, to run on Saturdays from 30th May (Whit) to the end of August, providing a third crossing to Larne and so to Belfast, with connecting trains at Stranraer, including a new express from Dumfries. The Second Service did very well in 1911, showing a profit of £1,821.13.9, but less so in the two following years, when the figures were £797 and £902. The decline may well have reflected the deteriorating political situation in Ireland.

The figures would be affected also, however, by the higher price of coal. The S C obtained their coal for the summer of 1911 from the Killochan Coal Company at 11/6 a ton, delivered in wagons at Stranraer pier. There then began a period of great unrest among the miners throughout Britain, and the S C established a 'bing' at Stranraer, storing coal against the possibility of a shortage. For the year commencing June 1912, they bought Waldie's Hirstrigg Steam Navigation coal, at 16/- a ton delivered at Stranraer. In the summer of 1913 the same coal cost them 18/- a ton, and supplies were curtailed by labour troubles. They turned to the Killochan Coal Company again, whose price now was 14/9 a ton, delivered at Stranraer. In July 1914, serious labour troubles threatened, in the coalfields as elsewhere, and the S C increased their 'bing' from 829 to 1,580 tons. The latter figure was about one-eighth of the steamers' total consumption in a full year of operation, including the Second Service.

For many years - since, in fact, the *Beatrice* came on the passage in 1875 - a supply of fresh water for the steamers, obtained from a stream near Stranraer, had been kept at the pier. In 1899, the S C were paying £20 per annum for it to the J C. There were now, however, complaints that it was inadequate, and in 1901 an additional supply was provided, at a total cost of £689.5.2. The works involved "raising the tank 5 feet and making it equal to an additional 18,000 gallons, and putting in the necessary new pump and boiler, also new suction pipes from the burn". The S C agreed to pay another £20 per annum, and half the wages of "the man attending to the tank". About the same time, a separate supply of drinking and cooking water was laid on, being obtained from Stranraer Town Council at a charge of 1/- per thousand gallons. In 1913 this, too, was complained of as deficient; the matter was to be remedied by the provision of a larger pipe, the S C undertaking to pay the J C £2 a year more for this supply, making £4 per annum in all.

About 1907 a tank to contain petrol was erected at the pier. This was at the request of the owners of motor cars coming over in the steamers from Larne. At the launching of the second *Victoria*, Peter Denny remarked that he understood 1,000 cars had been carried by the steamers during 1911. We may well see this, in retrospect, as a mere tiny beginning, but no doubt it was an impressive statistic at the time. In 1914 the J C's tourist guide included the following information:

# Rails to Portpatrick

CONVEYANCE OF MOTOR CARS AND CYCLES

Motor cars will be conveyed between Stranraer and Larne by any steamer, if alongside an hour before sailing time.

RATES AND CHARGES.

The Owner's Risk rates for the conveyance of motor cars and motor cycles between Stranraer and Larne, including all charges for harbour dues, cranage, etc., are:

MOTOR CARS AND CYCLE CARS

    Not exceeding 10 cwt., 25/- each.
    Over 10 cwt. and not exceeding 25 cwt., 35/- each.
    Over 25 cwt., 35/-, plus 1/- for each cwt. or part thereof above 25 cwt.
        Company's Ordinary Rates. 25% additional.

|  | Accompanied by Passenger | Unaccompanied by Passenger |
|---|---|---|
| Motor bicycles, each | 3/- O.R. | 4/6 O.R., 5/9 C.R. |
| Motor tricycles, each | 6/- O.R. | 7/6 O.R., 10/- C.R. |
| Motor cycles with fore carriages, side carriages or trailers, each | 6/- O.R. | 10/6 O.R., 14/9 C.R. |

Supply of petrol may be purchased on the quay at Larne or Stranraer on arrival from the other side. Car and cycle tanks must be emptied before shipment.
O.R. - Owner's Risk rate.         C.R.- Company's Ordinary rate.

Excursions by the steamers seem to have reached a peak of popularity in the first half of the very fine summer of 1914. There were trips to Ireland, in conjunction with the Belfast & Northern Counties Company, by any steamer each weekday from 30th May:

|  | Saloon and First Class | Saloon and Third Class | Steerage and Third Class |
|---|---|---|---|
| To Larne | 4/- |  | 2/6 |
| To Belfast | 5/- |  | 3/6 |
| To Portrush | 10/- | 6/6 | 5/- |
| To Londonderry | 12/- | 7/6 | 6/- |

This excursion has a particularly attractive sound:

Round Rathlin, the famous Antrim Coast trip, on Monday, 13th July, by mail steamer from Stranraer harbour at 6 a.m., joining the *Princess Victoria* at Larne harbour at 12.15 p.m., for a cruise along the picturesque Antrim Coast and round the romantic Rathlin Island, getting back to Larne harbour at 4.15 p.m., and to Stranraer harbour at 9.48 p.m. Reduced fares: 5/- Saloon, 3/6 Steerage.

Though rivalled perhaps by this:

"Panoramic" Cruise on County Down Coast. On Thursday 30th July, the *Princess Maud* will leave Stranraer railway pier at 1p.m. for a cruise along the picturesque shores of Bangor Bay (the Rothesay of Ireland), Belfast Lough, Whitehead, Blackhead, and the romantic Gobbins Cliffs, arriving at Larne harbour at 3.45 p.m. (Irish time).

The ship will return from Larne immediately, and be due at Stranraer harbour at 6.30 p.m. Stranraer excursionists may, if they wish, go ashore and remain for the mail steamer at 7.15 p.m.

Cheap excursion fares:

From Stranraer - 2/6 Steerage; 4/- Saloon.
From Portpatrick - 3/- Third Class and Steerage; 4/6 Third Class and Saloon.

Connection from Portpatrick by special train at 12.40 p.m., returning from Stranraer harbour 7.40 p.m., or town station 7.45 p.m.
Stranraer town band will accompany this excursion.

Between these longer trips, a familiar and well-loved short excursion had been announced:

"Round Ailsa Craig, the old favourite trip, on Tuesday, 21st July, by the *Princess Maud*, from Stranraer railway pier at 2 p.m., back about 5 p.m., in time for trains to Portpatrick, Glenluce, Girvan, etc. Fare One shilling."

In the event, however, the large number of people who turned up for this excursion were disappointed, as the *Maud* was, for some reason, delayed in getting to Stranraer until it was too late to set out. But McConchie, who was continuing as manager of the steamers after his recent succession to Hutchinson as traffic manager of the P P & W, always had the welfare of excursionists very much at heart, and he did his best to make things up to these dissatisfied customers by arranging another trip of the same kind for the following Friday.

During the previous month, the *May* came out of her semi-retirement to run several times on excursions from Stranraer. She went on evening cruises to Larne on Saturdays, 13th and 20th June, leaving the railway pier at 7.35 and returning at midnight; the fare was 2/-. On the evening of Wednesday, 17th, she sailed to Ailsa

Craig and the Ayrshire coast, the fare being again 2/-. Patrons were able to combine the pleasures of a cruise in perfect weather with those of a musical evening:

> "The weather was all that could be desired, and during the cruise excellent musical selections were rendered by Stranraer Town Band, under the conductorship of Mr. Sisson, and the Glee and Madrigal Choir, under the conductorship of Mr. Hill, which were highly appreciated. The sail throughout was much enjoyed, and the steamer arrived back shortly after 10 p.m."

This brief extract from the local press gives us, surely, one of the pleasantest items in our story. It provides a very happy picture of one aspect of leisure in the province in those days; a delightful way of spending a particularly delightful late spring evening.

But the British climate is renowned for its variety..............

## CHAPTER TWELVE

### Wind and Snow

IN December 1894, a few days before Christmas, Galloway was struck by a remarkably fierce gale. Beginning from the west in the evening of Friday, 21st, it blew with increasing force, veering to north-west, and reaching its peak the following morning. With the incoming tide, the sea overflowed on to the roads that passed close to the shore at Stranraer and ran along them "like a mill-race", almost waist-deep. It would have been surprising indeed if so furious a storm did not interrupt communications, and in fact both sea and land services were considerably affected.

The 6 a.m. sailing to Larne on Saturday, the 22nd, was cancelled, and as the *Victoria*, which was operating the Mail Service, stayed at her berth at Stranraer throughout the day, there was no evening sailing from Larne either. This may well have been the first time the Stranraer-Larne service was completely suspended since its establishment in 1872. When the storm was at its height the position of the *Victoria*, and also of the *May*, which was being overhauled at this time and was moored at the east side of the pier, was very precarious indeed. As the tide rose there seemed every likelihood of them being carried away. Desperate efforts were needed in the attempt to save them, the men taking part being themselves in great danger, drenched by the raging waters of the Loch and with difficulty keeping their feet amid the constant furious buffetings of the gale. Every available hawser was brought to the scene and made fast, but so tremendous was the strain on them that they seemed likely to part at any moment.

The *Victoria* was kept safely at her berth. The *May*, however, was more vulnerable. The pier was being lengthened, and she was moored outside the new timber piles that marked the limits of the extension; the concrete walls had yet to be built. At about 7 a.m. the snapping of her stern ropes caused her to swing out from the pier. Her other ropes could not hold her for long, and in such a storm it was out of the question to fix another in time. Soon her fore ropes broke also, and she drifted towards the beach with the tide. Before the *May* touched bottom, however, her bow turned very nearly into the wind; and the beach on which she struck was sandy. The retreating waves left her stranded, but erect on her keel and almost undamaged. Harland & Wolff were called in to refloat her, which they achieved on 11th January.

In the case of the *Beatrice*, too, danger threatened long, but she survived the tempest unharmed. Being the reserve boat, she was moored out in the Loch. She dragged her anchors and was carried about a mile eastward, but then her anchors held fast and she rode the storm out safely.

Several train services on that day were seriously delayed. One train, the

# Rails to Portpatrick

8.30 a.m. from Stranraer to Portpatrick, seemed to be in as great and imminent danger as the steamers. As it approached the high viaduct near Lochans, the gale, funnelled by the valley of the Piltanton Burn, was so tremendous that the train appears to have stopped while the wisdom of going on was debated. No doubt, the Tay Bridge disaster of fifteen years before was prominent in the mind of everyone concerned. The passengers freely admitted that they were afraid to cross, and said they would rather get out if the attempt was to be made to take the train over. The driver and guard fully shared their anxiety. The decision was therefore taken to return to Stranraer, and retreating from the storm-ridden valley, the engine propelled its little train back down the line to the safety of the town.

This was the most dramatic impact made on the train service by the storm, but it had some spectacular effects elsewhere in the region too. There were serious delays on the Girvan line. On the P P & W main line, conditions varied. The up trains, being able to "run before the wind", seem not to have been much affected, the only notable change being that, there being no steamer connections from Larne, the 8.50 p.m. mail express from Stranraer left from the town station instead of the pier. It took the local mails and the Post Office van - "the Galloway sorting tender" - and "lifted the usual mails by the way". Down trains, however, were badly delayed, the worst difficulties being encountered by the 3.32 a.m. mail express from Carlisle, which had to battle its way through Galloway with the storm at its height.

The express was divided into two portions, the first carrying a large number of passengers and some mails, the second mails only. The first portion reached Stranraer at 8.13 a.m. The guard described how its two engines had had a hard struggle to climb the steep gradients in face of the tearing wind, specially furiously felt at the viaducts of Wee and Big Fleet, and how 24 minutes were needed to take in water at Newton Stewart, where he himself became air-borne. At several places the tablets had blown away, causing more delays. The second portion of the mail arrived in Stranraer at 10.13 a.m.; it had been delayed over an hour at New Galloway owing to the signal cabin being blown across the line.

The Saturday sailing of the steamer being cancelled, passengers for Ireland had to spend a day and night at Stranraer. Some found accommodation in the town, but many stayed overnight at the station. The next day saw a remarkable, and probably unique, occasion for those days - a Sunday passage to Larne. The storm having subsided, the *Victoria* sailed at 9 a.m. with about 200 passengers. She returned in the evening about 8.40 "with passengers, parcel post hampers, and a few cattle". A special express train from Dumfries and Carlisle met her at Stranraer Harbour – a Sunday train through Galloway!

All three of the down stopping trains on the P P & W main line on the Saturday were badly delayed. The 8.45 a.m. from Dumfries reached Stranraer nearly 80 minutes behind time. The 2.35 p.m. from Dumfries arrived 45 minutes late; it continued through to Portpatrick, another remarkable event of this extraordinary week-end. The 7.25 p.m. from Dumfries did not get to Stranraer till 10.54 - an hour late, but exceptionally heavy traffic from the south had made it 44 minutes behind time in leaving Dumfries.

"THE BIG SNA'"

The notable thing about the storm just described was the exceptional fury of the gale, although very strong winds are, of course, far from uncommon on the west and south-west coasts of Scotland. Much more unusual, in itself, in the relatively mild climate of Galloway, was the snowstorm that broke over the region only a few weeks later, to be remembered for years to come as "the Big Sna'". The snowfall began on 6th February 1895, a Wednesday, and continued until the afternoon of the next day. For once, snow was at its worst in the south-west part of Scotland, and its effect on communications was greatly aggravated by a terrific east-south-east gale which accompanied and followed it.

So great was the storm at sea that the *May*, on the 6 p.m. passage from Larne on the Wednesday, did not reach Stranraer till noon next day. As the hours passed, the fear mounted in the minds of people in the town lest some fatal mishap had befallen her. Great was their relief, therefore, when the sound of her fog horn at length announced her safe approach to harbour. The voyage had surely tested the skill and experience of her commander. Captain Campbell said he had never known such a blizzard. They could see nothing from the deck, and the furious wind drove the fine, frosty snow very painfully in the faces of the crew. As the gathering snow froze on deck, they could move about only with the aid of ropes fixed from one point to another. The ship became sheeted in ice as the spray flung up against her froze on her sides.

There was neither sight nor sound of any other vessel as the *May* forged her way through the stormy darkness. Drawing near the Scottish coast, not the faintest glimmer of Corsewall Light could be made out; but the foghorn - installed a few years earlier through the persistence of the J C – could be heard, and it enabled Campbell to sail his ship safely into Loch Ryan. He took her, at half speed, a distance which he knew should bring her roughly opposite the Galloway Burn, on the west side of the Loch, and here a lead was cast and when the ground began to shelve the ship anchored. Campbell had decided to stay here rather than try to sail up the Loch with nothing whatever by which to direct his course. When later the snow thinned somewhat, he tried to press on, but only prompt action on his part saved the *May* from running on the rocks. It was a narrow escape, and Campbell thought it best to stop again, near a little steamer which had been passed at anchor, presumably opposite Cairnryan. So they waited till the blizzard lessened late on the Thursday morning, when the *May* steamed safely to Stranraer, a happy outcome to a perilous voyage.

For two days the normal cross-channel sailings were cancelled, as the snowstorm had closed the railways leading to Stranraer. Passengers and mails from the south were taken to Ayr, and Campbell sailed there with the *May*, bringing passengers, mails and a large supply of newspapers to Stranraer on Friday evening. The run to Larne was resumed next day, but the railways were still blocked.

The effect of the storm on railway communications in Galloway was by far the worst the province had yet experienced. The W R line was completely blocked from Wednesday, 6th, to Monday, 11th February; mails got through from Newton Stewart as far as Whauphill on the Monday, but not until the following day was the line clear to Whithorn. There were no trains to or from Portpatrick from Wednesday morning until Tuesday morning; the snow gathered thick in the deep cuttings on this line, making its clearance a long and heavy task. On the P P & W main line the last train to get through to Stranraer on Wednesday was the 2.35 p.m. from Dumfries. The 7.25 p.m. from Dumfries, and in the other direction the 3.40 p.m. from Stranraer, both became snow-bound en route.

The 2.35 from Dumfries reached Stranraer only with great difficulty. Three times it was brought to a stop by snow filling up the locomotive's firebox, and the train did not get to Stranraer until 7.40 p.m., instead of the normal 5.30, most of the delay being west of Newton Stewart. The 7.25 from Dumfries nearly became stuck in the snow at Castle Douglas, but it pressed on into the wilds, and by 10 p.m. - the time it was due at Stranraer - had managed to struggle up to Loch Skerrow. It had only two passengers, both bound for Newton Stewart. Earlier that day, the people at Loch Skerrow had looked out from their little cottages at the sullen moors and the scowling sky, and seen the sheep come down from the hills and go scurrying across the ice to take refuge on the tiny islands in the loch with their sheltering trees. By the time the train arrived snow had been falling heavily for hours, and further progress was out of the question. Conditions at the desolate outpost were extraordinarily bad. The guard, Edward Kerr, told afterwards how it took him an hour to battle his way to the engine to see driver Edward ("Ned") Cogie and fireman J. Mangle; the two passengers were not reached till 3 a.m. All went to the platelayers' cottages, where the people did everything possible for them, but their stocks of food were hopelessly inadequate to the unexpected siege. Very fortunately the train carried some foodstuffs, and permission was obtained to raid these to supply the emergency, but even so by Saturday the marooned residents and their involuntary guests were almost without food.

The greatest adventures, however, were experienced by those involved with the 3.40p.m. from Stranraer. Four curlers from Castle Douglas, disappointed of a match at Glenluce by the weather, decided to return home by this train, and joined it at the station, not much behind its normal time of 4.4 p.m., though snow was falling very heavily. A snow-plough had gone along the line earlier that afternoon, bound for Castle Douglas. The outlook from the train windows was gloomy in the extreme, but at first the going seemed safe enough. Beyond Kirkcowan, however, the passengers could feel the carriages lifting on the snow, which naturally roused some very serious apprehensions as to their prospects of further progress. They reached Newton Stewart, and here they had to wait to cross the 2.35 from Dumfries, which was running half-an-hour late. The railway staff were for a time uncertain as to whether their train should go on, but they eventually decided that it should. One of the curlers, who subsequently told the story to a representative of the *Kirkcudbrightshire Advertiser*, had the impression that those in charge at Newton Stewart were mainly concerned just to get the train off their hands, whatever happened thereafter. However this may have been, the sequel showed the decision to have been extremely unfortunate, to say the least.

Having left Newton Stewart, the train ran safely down to the Cree, made the Palnure stop, and climbed most of the way up Creetown Bank. Conditions had become extremely bad, however, and near Creetown distant signal it came to a dead stand, having stuck fast in the snow. Finding that they were close to the station, the passengers were not unduly concerned at first, thinking that if a long delay were to ensue, at least they were within easy distance of food and shelter. But this was to prove a grossly optimistic view of the situation.

Soon after the train came to a stand, an incident occurred which, while doubtless sufficiently annoying to those involved, and not without tragic possibilities, had its comic aspects too. A woman passenger, thinking the train had reached the station, calmly stepped out of her compartment, and forthwith sank below her waist in the snow. One of the curlers went to her aid, the first service he was able to render her being to rescue her ticket, umbrella and bag. His attempt to pull her out of the snow was complicated by her having got a foot entangled in the buried signal wires. Meanwhile, the train had backed a short distance so that the engine could get a run at the snow block, and "the two outside passengers" found themselves nearly opposite the tender. The snow was sweeping over them in great waves, and they could scarcely be seen. The locomotive took its run at the drift, managing, however, to get only a little way farther. The "outside passengers" then succeeded in making themselves heard, and the lady was helped into a compartment; a man left his own seat and worked his way along the foot-board of the carriage to open the door of this compartment for her. The lady seems to have been quite composed during her adventure. The curler remarked that when they met in the village two days later, "this typical woman" was lamenting the loss in the incident of one of her gloves.

After waiting about an hour in the stranded train, the curler determined to try to reach the station, "so near and yet so far". A commercial traveller set out with him, but so terrific was the storm that the traveller soon had to give up, and the curler had to help him back to the train. The fireman, however, who had previously got to the station, now returned to the engine for the tablet, and the curler accompanied him back to the station. They found that four other passengers, out of the total of twenty-eight on the train, had fought their way there ahead of them. At 10 p.m. the railway officials told them they would not be delayed very long, as the snow-plough that had run to Castle Douglas during the afternoon would be coming back. Faith in the plough, however, was to prove misplaced.

# Rails to Portpatrick

Thomas Nicholson, the Creetown station-master, described how, despite many strenuous efforts, the men with the plough could make no headway at all against the drift; the snow swept in on them faster than they could clear it. The curler said that it was nearly 2 a.m. when the snow-plough got to the scene, and the engine's water supply being exhausted, it was practically useless for want of steam. There was plenty of water at Creetown, but at first, he alleged, the officials in charge would not use any, "in case they should have to pay for it".

According to Nicholson - of whom the representative of the *Kirkcudbrightshire Advertiser* who interviewed him wrote that there was "no more genial, courteous, or obliging official in the service" - the engine and plough were in action during the early hours of the morning (Thursday, February 7th), but about three o'clock the men reluctantly gave up the unequal struggle and came up to the station on the engine. William McConchie, traffic inspector, was with Nicholson at the station, and they now decided that no time should be lost in trying to bring up as many as possible of the numerous passengers still, in effect, imprisoned in the train. They therefore sent the men back on the engine, and with great difficulty the men reached the snowbound carriages, but only a very few of the passengers would venture away from the relative safety of the train.

The curler was free with his praise of all the railwaymen present, speaking of their "most heroic endeavours" to combat the snow, which lay very deep and still continued. Regarding another matter which had become very pressing by the early morning of Thursday - getting some refreshments for the passengers, and for the railwaymen themselves - his account, however, was less favourable, and conflicted with that given by Nicholson.

Nicholson related how early in the morning some of the surfacemen struggled the mile to the village, and returned with bread, tea, coffee, condensed milk and other provisions. The return journey, uphill, must have been particularly difficult, with the snow lying so deep and the blinding storm still raging. Some of the passengers had asked for whisky, but the Barholm Arms Hotel would not supply it. This roused bitter feelings among the passengers, said Nicholson, but otherwise they were completely uncomplaining. McConchie had remarked to him how pleased he was to find the people so cheerful and contented. One of the passengers said how much better treated he was now compared with a short time previously, when he had been involved in a snow block near Blair Atholl on the Highland Railway. On that occasion nothing had been done to supply the passengers with refreshments, "although the block occurred within a mile of the residence of the chairman of the line". Another passenger, who had been a steward on an Atlantic liner, was very pleasant and useful, "and cooked tea and coffee for all hands".

The picture that the curler painted of this aspect of events is much less happy. "We have", he commented, "very little to say to the credit of the officials in charge for the manner in which they tried to cater for the hungry passengers". He describes volunteers getting down to the village with an order for bread and cheese and one bottle of whisky for all the people at the station. They were refused the whisky "because they were not armed with an official order from the railway company". Breakfast was eaten at about 7 a.m., an unattractive meal - "dry bread, a small piece of rank cheese, and a very small drop of semi-cold coffee, sipped out of an old cocoa canister in which nails had been kept". Bread and cheese were taken to the passengers who had spent the night in the train.

Whichever of these versions is nearer the truth, the railway workers themselves were unlikely to be in any better state than the passengers. With, that is, two exceptions. Two surfacemen completely disappeared after going to the back of the stranded train to look for a coupling chain. There was naturally great alarm for their safety, and some other workmen spent some time digging about for them in the snow at the rear of the train, without result. Then all the workmen at the station went to the scene and renewed the search. Some were apathetic, however, as though they had suspicions as to the true location of the missing men. These suspicions were proved justified a little later when the two men returned as suddenly as they had gone. Being well acquainted with the district, they had made for a nearby farm, and had there breakfasted on ham and eggs, prepared in an outsize frying pan. Needless to say, their initiative did not meet with the approval of their superiors and workmates, and supervision of them was thenceforward close.

It was now determined to rescue the passengers still in the train at all costs. It being well over twelve hours since the train stuck in the drift, we can appreciate the curler's statement that "their mood and condition may be better imagined than described". The carriages, he said, were almost covered with snow. With great difficulty, the rescue was accomplished. The two women brought from the train, and several of the men, were very exhausted when they got to the station platform. Life was made considerably more tolerable, however, for the occupants of the ladies' waiting-room through the kindness of a lady from the Creetown district, who had intended to join the train at the station, and who now did everything possible for the other women detained there. One of the women was in poor health, and became quite ill, whereupon Nicholson decided to take her to his house. The distance involved was only 200 yards, but conditions being so bad, the lady was put on the engine with the snow-plough, which ran along the line until it was opposite the house, whence she was carried inside.

Meanwhile, some of the male passengers had gone down to the village, but a considerable number stayed at the station. Some of the latter, especially those who were commercial travellers, wanted to be taken on their way with the engine and plough when they started out again for Castle Douglas, and were aggrieved when permission was refused. The event, however, showed that they were fortunate that this was so, as shortly after leaving the station the plough stuck in a snow-drift at Rory's Cutting, about half-way between Creetown and Dromore, and it took the workmen a good while to dig themselves out.

## Rails to Portpatrick

Back at the station, supplying the needs of the inner man was again an urgent matter. Nicholson said of the passengers who remained there that "we cooked what was available, and made them as comfortable as we could". "The officials", stated the curler, "seemed to consider this (providing refreshment) was no part of their duty". A messenger was sent to the village, and returned with a basket of sandwiches, but the curlers being "powerless to perform miracles", they took one sandwich each themselves, the rest being shared out "among the starving crowd". Later on Thursday, the storm became less furious, and most of the passengers went down to the village and the more comfortable quarters there. The railway workers, however, the curler remarked, had no such good fortune, and he cited the case of one of them who was able to sleep in the village on Thursday night, but had to spend all day Friday, and all the following night, at the station. He could not get a bed on Friday night, and there was very little food or refreshment to be had at the station.

The passengers who had gone into Creetown stayed at various houses or at the Barholm Arms Hotel. The curler had warm praise for Mr. Rae, landlord of the hotel, for his vigorous efforts to make his guests comfortable. "Still", he said, "it was a dreary time". And so much was this the case for one of the unwilling guests that on the Friday evening he made an attempt at suicide, by cutting his throat. The attempt was discovered in time, however, and he got medical attention and was fully expected to recover from his wound.

The same evening, the stranded passengers were warned to be at the station at 9 a.m. next day (Saturday, February 9th). Thinking, no doubt, that their long and very trying delay must surely now be at an end, they went, only to find yet another frustrating experience ahead of them, as no train was available, and they had to hang about until four o'clock in the afternoon before they could at long last get on their way.

Meanwhile, the snow-plough was coming back from Castle Douglas, and at Loch Skerrow it picked up the driver, fireman, guard and two passengers of the train marooned there since Wednesday evening. The engine of that train was coupled on, also, and the plough continued its journey through the wilderness propelled by three locomotives. They were several times brought to a halt, as they encountered numerous very big snow-drifts, but the plough at work made a fine sight, flaking the snow sometimes up to 50 feet into the air, while the view of the surrounding hills after the great storm was extremely impressive. It seems likely that all three engines went with the plough to Newton Stewart, whence the engine that had been coupled on at Loch Skerrow returned to Creetown. Certainly, this engine was used to take the passengers at Creetown on their journey east, as the engine that had brought them from Stranraer was disabled - a fact which may explain why they had been unable to leave Creetown that morning. They travelled, however, in the same carriages in which some of them had spent such a terrible night.

# Rails to Portpatrick

The driver and fireman of the disabled engine stayed with it at Creetown, and the driver, fireman and guard of the train stranded at Loch Skerrow took over the train going east. It was still intensely cold, and as the locomotive had to go tender-first, driver Cogie and fireman Mangle wrapped shawls round their heads to get what protection they could on their journey over the wildest part of the line. Guard Edward Kerr told of a depth of snow by the line side of 21 feet at Wedge Rock, between Dromore and Loch Skerrow, while at Wee Fleet the telegraph wires were completely buried. The four curlers got back to Castle Douglas about 5.30 p.m., three days late. Long distance passengers reached Dumfries in time to catch the London train. Guard Kerr, who had left Stranraer on Wednesday at 10 a.m., returned there at 11.35 a.m. on Monday.

It had been hoped to clear the whole of the main line during the course of Saturday, but the tale of adventure and misadventure was not yet complete. As the snow-plough was working between Newton Stewart and Kirkcowan in the early evening, both engines were thrown on their sides, and the men on them flung into about nine feet of snow, putting them in considerable danger of their lives. A crane and a squad of workmen had to be telegraphed for from Kilmarnock and Hurlford; they reached the scene at 10 a.m. on Sunday. A long-drawn-out struggle followed, one of the engines being put back on the rails at four o'clock that afternoon, but the other not till 6 o'clock next morning (Monday). During Monday, 11th February, the normal train service was restored on the P P & W main line, and also on the Girvan line.

So ended a brief but outstanding episode in the story of the steamers and the railway; one likely to be long remembered by those who were involved in it.

We have already been able, in our story so far, to learn something of the people, at all levels, who worked on Galloway's railways. History is very much about people, and a railway history needs to be at least as much about the people as about the machines that served the raileay. Our next chapter is devoted to some of the men who made the P P & W Railways go.

## CHAPTER THIRTEEN

### "Poorly Paid and Worried"

"POORLY paid and worried" was the cynically humorous interpretation that the J C's employees sometimes put on the initial letters of the undertaking for which they worked. In tracing the story of the P P R and W R we came across several examples of low wages and long hours of duty. A list prepared for the J C's officers gives interesting information about the traffic staff's wages in 1886, when the J C had just taken over. Stationmasters' wages then ranged from 30/- at Newton Stewart (where the "goods agent" received 33/-), Wigtown and Whithorn, to 20/- at Palnure, Dromore and Crossrnichael, and 18/6 at Colfin. Porters' wages were between 19/- for men, and 9/- for the boy at Colfin. Adult porters often acted as signalmen, too. The signalmen at Loch Skerrow and Newton Stewart earned from 16/- to 19/-. Wages of clerks ranged between 33/- for the chief clerk, traffic manager's office, Stranraer, to 6/- for the junior at Creetown.

Comparing these figures with the few that we have for the earliest years of the P P R, we can see that there had been wage increases which, however modest in most cases, were not negligible, considering the much greater value of money in those days, and the fact that the cost-of-living fell at least 25% between the 1860s and the 1880s. Other lists of wages show that improvement continued, slowly but steadily, until about 1900, while the cost-of-living continued to fall. In 1912, by which time all the stationmasters were salaried, they were getting between 25% and more than 50% above the wage-levels of 1886, though at this date retail prices had reached a higher level than at any time since the early 1880s, and were about 10% above that of 1886. The highest-paid station-masters in 1912 were those at Stranraer and Newton Stewart, at £140 per annum, while the lowest-paid were at Colfin and Palnure, at £75. Porters' wages now ranged up to 20/-. The "passenger foremen" at Stranraer and Newton Stewart got between 22/- and 24/-. Signalmen received about 20/-. The chief clerk in the manager's office at Stranraer had now a salary of £200 per annum, the first passenger clerk at Newton Stewart had £65 and the first goods clerk there £70.4.0, and juniors at various stations had £18.4.0 (Stations with clerical staff in 1912 were Stranraer Harbour, Castle Kennedy, Dunragit, Glenluce, Kirkcowan, Newton Stewart, Creetown, New Galloway, Wigtown and Whithorn).

In June 1891, the officers had agreed that "a reasonable holiday", without pay, should be granted to the porters. In November 1899, porter-signalmen were granted three days' leave annually without deduction of pay. Signalmen received six days' paid leave annually from 1908.

Over-long hours of work had led to a fairly serious strike on Scottish railways at the end of 1890, particularly on the C R and the N B. This had little effect on the P P & W. The drivers, firemen and guards employed by the C R and G S W on the Joint Lines received a gratuity of a week's pay for their loyalty during the strike, and the J C rewarded all their employees similarly. But the extent of railwaymen's dissatisfaction induced the House of Commons to appoint a Select Committee to investigate their hours of duty, and Sir Herbert Maxwell of Monreith, Wigtownshire's M.P., was a member. In March 1891, a correspondent according himself the comprehensive title of "Democrat" wrote in the *Free Press* that the J C had "seen fit to lessen the hours of some of their more overworked servants". Expressing the view that they had done this to hoodwink the Committee, he continued (eventually, in his earnestness and bitterness, falling into the trap of bathos):

"I will call upon him (Sir Herbert) to give particular attention to the following stations: Garliestown, Millisle, Sorbie, Whauphill and Kirkinner. Without fear of contradiction, I say that men at some of these stations work, on an average, sixteen hours daily ... let the railway companies take warning, for as 'Remember Tipperary' has become proverbial, so has 'Remember Whauphill'."

There are numerous references in the records during succeeding years to measures to avoid particularly long hours of working.

In the summer of 1899, however, officers of the C R and G SW, with Hutchinson, met at C R headquarters in Glasgow to consider the following petition:

We, the P P & W Railway Company's employees of the Traffic Department, beg most respectfully to apply for a general increase of 2/- per week, irrespective of grade. The reasons why we ask this application are as follows:

Firstly, that we consider that we are not sufficiently remunerated for the amount of duty we have to perform.

Secondly, the amount of responsibility connected with our daily avocations is very great.

Thirdly, our hours are much longer and pay considerably under the average of the agricultural labouring classes.

Fourthly, that it would be to the advantage of the committee to comply with this request, as the men would remain longer in the service if their pay was increased.

Thus, the men evidently found their wages and hours to compare unfavourably with those on the land, the main alternative source of work in Galloway, where there was little industry. This is rather surprising, especially as regards wages; farm wages in the province were certainly never notably high. And the implication that their wages were so unattractive as to lead to considerable turnover of staff contrasts with the familiar argument that security of employment was a great advantage of railway work, compensating for low wages to a notable extent.

The officers, reflecting the paternal attitude of the J C towards their employees, always gave petitions serious attention, and in this case they went over the wages paid at each station, comparing them with those paid on the C R and G S W lines. In the result, however, they declared that they could not recommend a general increase, favouring advances of pay to four individuals only! Yet they soon had to acknowledge facts which tended strongly to bear out the petition's claims. Early in 1900, Hutchinson drew their attention to the "very serious difficulty in getting efficient men to act as porter-signalmen", and they agreed to increase the maximum wages payable from 17/- and 18/- to 19/- per week. About this time the stationmaster at Newton Stewart, Robert Mirrey, induced them to grant him a small increase in staff by complaining of serious difficulties which show that their parsimony had been considerably obstructing the working of their second busiest station. A report prepared for them in 1903 shows that the same thing was happening at several other places on their lines, notably at Stranraer, where it was especially important to have sufficient capable staff. Once again they obviously investigated carefully, but equally clearly they intended to relieve only the worst features, at minimum cost, and they were going to continue to practise very strict economy in the matter of wages. Yet the increase in traffic at this period made an increase in staff essential. The number of uniformed staff employed on the P P & W, 100 in 1899, was 117 in 1906. In 1905 the officers noted "the difficulties in satisfactorily staffing the line".

From 1910, with prices rising steadily while wages for the most part stayed the same, there was a great deal of trade union activity, and the railwaymen's unions took a prominent part. In many parts of England, railways were seriously affected by a two-day strike in August 1911. This activity is reflected in the numerous petitions the J C received between 1911 and 1914 about wages and conditions, though the unions are never explicitly mentioned in the records, no doubt because the railway companies would not negotiate with them directly.

In 1912, the signalmen and porter-signalmen petitioned for higher wages and reduced hours. They got a general increase of 1/- per week early in 1913, but their hours of work were to remain twelve per day, as previously. A supplement of 1/- per week was to be paid to the two porter-signalmen at Gatehouse-of-Fleet (as, at the request of Gatehouse Town Council, Dromore station was renamed in 1912) and the two signalmen at Loch Skerrow "in consequence of the difficulty of getting men to stay at these isolated places". This difficulty, which was to worsen with the passage of time, began owing to the concern of railway people for their children's education. If young people from homes in remote places were to attend higher grade schools they would need to "board" in town during the week, and most railway families would find it very difficult to meet the cost of this, the bursaries available being very small. The number of signalmen and porter-signalmen on the P P & W lines is given as 37 in 1913.

In 1914, the J C's signalmen, numbering 14, petitioned for a minimum wage of 25/- and a working week of 60 hours. By the time the officers reported in October, war had broken out. It was "inexpedient at present", they said, "to contemplate any alteration in the rates of wages or hours of duty", but overtime would be paid at time-and-a-quarter, back-dated to 3rd August. The officers had recently considered also petitions from porters (totalling 28), shunters and yardsmen, the two passenger foremen at Newton Stewart, and the platelayers and surfacemen. They granted some selective increases, mostly of 1/- a week.

The wages of platelayers and surfacemen on the P P & W lines were given as 21/- and 17/-, respectively, in 1899. In reply to their request to be paid at the G S W rate of 22/- and 19/-, they got 22/- and 18/-. Soon after, they were granted their first holidays with pay - two days each year, as on the C R and G S W. In 1902, their request for free holiday passes was granted. The passes, covering the P P & W lines, were to be issued to them, their wives and children once a year. By 1908, surfacemen at Dromore and Loch Skerrow were getting an extra shilling a week in recompense for living at these "isolated posts". The platelayers and surfacemen numbered 89 in 1911. They must certainly have been out-of-pocket due to the rise in prices since 1899, so that it is not at all surprising to find them petitioning for improved wages and conditions in 1913. Agreement was reached through one of the conciliation schemes arranged by the Government to settle disputes between railway companies and their employees. It gave the petitioners the following terms:

> Standard hours, 53 per week, Monday to Friday, 7-5.30, 1 hour meal.
> Saturday 7-12.30, no meal.
> One man in each squad of surfacemen to be on duty till 5.30 on Saturday to inspect the "length" of the line, according to rota.
> An advance of 2/- per week to all platelayers.
> An advance of 1/- per week to all surfacemen.
> Overtime on weekdays at time-and-a-half.
> Saturday p.m. inspection of line not overtime.
> Sunday duty at double time.

Holiday passes over systems of Scotch working companies for self, wife, children on occasion of annual holidays at present allowed without loss of pay.

On a small undertaking like the P P & W, opportunities for promotion were inevitably limited, but that a career with the J C was to some extent "open to the talents" is shown by the examples of Hutchinson and McConchie, who rose from junior clerkships to be successive managers. Both got early promotion in P P R days. Hutchinson was station-master at Stranraer at the age of 29, while McConchie was put in charge of Dromore when only 20, transferred to Wigtown - making him one of the J C's three first-class station-masters - four years later, and appointed traffic inspector at the age of 26. Robert Mirrey began his career at his father's station, Parton, as a boy of 12 in 1871, became a clerk at Kirkcowan and New

Galloway, and was appointed first station-master at Stranraer Harbour when aged 19. After service as relief station-master, he was given charge of Newton Stewart in 1892, and occupied this very responsible position for the rest of the J C's rule.

A clerkship was the usual first step on the road to the position of station-master, but it was not necessarily so. There were numerous instances of porters and guards who gained this kind of promotion. John McGaw, porter at Creetown, at 18/- a week, in 1886, was soon after made station-master at Crossmichael, a post that he filled for about 40 years. It is true that porters, etc., were usually given charge only of minor stations, but such was the standing of a station-master, even at a little village or hamlet, that to reach such a position can hardly have failed to be a source of considerable satisfaction to them, apart from the increase in pay. William McJannett, awarded a wage increase from 12/- to 14/- as porter and pointsman, Crossmichael ("Angry Mick", to quote his later reference to the village), on reaching the age of 21 in 1888, was in later life given charge of Dunragit, one of the J C's busiest stations, and when Robert Mirrey died in 1923 he succeeded him at Newton Stewart, until he retired in the 1930s.

An example of a promising career in the later years of the J C, tragically cut short, is that of John McKnight. Son of a gardener employed on the Barholm estate at Creetown, he was getting 7/- a week as a junior clerk at Creetown in 1903, whence he moved to Newton Stewart as a telegraphist. In 1910, he was earning a wage of 22/- as clerk at Dunragit, and by 1918 he was chief goods clerk, Stranraer, with a salary of £95 per annum. He then became station-master at Whithorn, but with this achievement his career was to draw to an early and sad close. His predecessor, John Gordon, had died in the influenza epidemic that followed the Great War and McKnight had been only a little while at Whithorn when he too became a victim, and passed away. Mr. Cathcart, station-master at Sorbie, died at this time also. It is likely that these very conscientious men refused to go off duty until they had become very ill.

To those employees entitled to wear uniform, its provision free of charge was an important advantage of railway work. Station-masters' uniform was dark blue, with white metal buttons in most cases. The J C's three first-class station-masters, at Newton Stewart, Wigtown and Whithorn, and the Stranraer station-master, also first-class but coming under the P P & G J C, had buttons of yellow metal. During the summer months, some station-masters wore a uniform of dark grey trousers and swallow-tailed coat, though others wore the dark blue "winter" uniform issue all the year round. To the end of P P & W days there were always some who wore the grey uniform regularly during the appropriate period. From 1887, overcoats were supplied to the station-masters. These presumably were the frock-coats, the issue of which, at the latter's request, was replaced with that of jackets in 1909.

Overcoats were supplied also to the three guards on the W R line, and monkey-jackets were supplied to the W R drivers and firemen every two years. In

1899, exactly 100 P P& W staff were entitled to uniform, and henceforward new uniforms were issued yearly. Porters' and signalmen's uniform was dark green. For many years the material was corduroy. In 1911, however, the J C granted the request of their porter-signalmen to be supplied with jackets and waistcoats of pilot-cloth instead. Back in 1895, the pointsmen (signalmen) had successfully applied for pilot-cloth instead of corduroy jackets to be provided, in accordance with C R and G S W practice. Clearly, the J C and their officers were by no means insensitive to the wishes of their employees on the subject of uniform.

To many railway workers, however, the chief advantage of their occupation may well have been the provision by their employers of a house, at a low rent or rent-free. By 1900, most of the J C's station-masters had houses provided, and though it was now decided that all must pay rent for these, the rents were only 3/- a week, and those who had hitherto lived rent-free had their wages increased sufficiently to leave some money in their pockets after they paid the new rents. In 1890, the officers had noted that on the W R line - whose impecunious previous owners had never put themselves to the expense of providing houses for their station-masters - the latter were having great difficulty in finding suitable dwellings, and some were having to live "at very considerable distances from the station", whereas it was clearly desirable that they should live near at hand. Houses were therefore built, by direct labour as far as possible, at Wigtown, Kirkinner, Whauphill and Sorbie, at an estimated cost of £350 each. But the station-masters protested at the rents of 3/- per week. A few years later, J. A. Smith,. stationmaster at Portpatrick, very hard put to it to get a home for himself and his family at a rent he could afford, appealed to the J C to build him a house, and his request being refused, about the end of 1896 he killed himself, a tragedy almost certainly contributed to by his housing problem. A house was built for his successor, W. McJannett, the cost being estimated at £285, at a weekly rent of 3/-. This left Stranraer as the only place on the P P R line with no house for the station-master, and here as late as 1908 the J C seriously contemplated providing one, eventually deciding otherwise, however, probably on account of the anticipated cost, £600.

The houses were certainly small. Some tenants found them decidedly "too wee". The houses at Sorbie and Wigtown contained, respectively, "two rooms, a kitchen and a scullery" and "a kitchen and back kitchen, a small parlour and a smaller bedroom". In 1903, the J C heard of the plight of John McGaw, whose house at Crossmichael was built by the P P R. It "consists of two rooms and a kitchen, one of the rooms being a very small one. His family consists of himself, his wife, and five children, and his father also lives with him". They responded promptly. Enlargements expected to cost £160 were carried out, in consideration of which McGaw's weekly rent was raised from 2/6 to 3/-. Similar improvements were made at Colfin soon after.

Numerous employees other than station-masters lived in houses belonging to the J C. A list dated 1908 shows that some of them were living rent-free then. The station-masters' houses that were rent-free for many years were those provided in the early years of the P P R, and it is likely that the cottages in which these other employees lived were provided by the P P R at the same period, and by the W R. The house at Portpatrick where Matthew Davitt, platelayer, lived, was an ancient dwelling - "an old cottage when the Portpatrick Company had to take it over on the construction of the line in 1862"; and it may well be that some other employees occupied cottages which the P P R and W R had acquired when the railways were built. At Loch Skerrow, dwellings must have been provided for the pointsmen, needed when it was made a passing-place in the 1860s. Platelayers' dwellings were built at Dromore and New Galloway in 1876, and in 1908 a platelayer still lived rent-free in Viaduct Cottage, the house at Big Fleet originally rented by the P P R from Sir William Maxwell. The cottages at Cairntop, between Kirkcowan and Glenluce, where in 1908 two platelayers lived at an annual rent for each house of £4, were built in 1894. In the same year, cottages were built at Challoch Junction and Dunragit. At Dunragit in 1908, W. McIlwrick, signalman, paid £12 a year for his house, by far the highest rent paid by any P P& W employee. His was the "new house at Dunragit station", built in 1907 at an estimated cost of £349, following a request by McIlwrick to the J C to enlarge his existing cottage. The new house had two more rooms; his former home was given to a porter. Certainly, if some station-masters found their living quarters very cramped, humbler employees would experience even greater difficulties of this kind. In this respect, however, they would not be different from many other people in similar circumstances of life, and they doubtless found some compensation in living close to their work, without payment, or in return for rents of usually about 1/3 or 1/6 a week. "The people were very thrifty", writes one who knew Dromore and Loch Skerrow in the early part of last century, "and they had comfortable homes in spite of the low wages".

Employees in moorland places might well have an independent source of house fuel. We may recall, for example, Harper's mention of "Dromore Station ... where the station-master can very conveniently secure his supply of peats for the season at his very door". All the railway people living at Dromore could have peat for their fires in return for the considerable trouble of getting it, the landowners and farmers readily granting them permission to help themselves free of charge, provided only that they left the ground in reasonable condition. By a notable instance of the J C's paternalism, the families at Loch Skerrow, in consideration of the extreme remoteness of their homes, were each allowed six tons of free coal yearly. It usually arrived in May, being unloaded by the platelayers and stored in bunkers made from sleepers. The Loch Skerrow people had a further concession that other workers living in very remote places might well envy them, in the "market tickets" whereby they or members of their families could travel free to Castle Douglas once each week to buy provisions. Similar tickets were issued to the employees at Dromore, available to and from Creetown.

# Rails to Portpatrick

Throughout the J C's rule, free passes were issued for the railway children at Dromore to travel to and from school at Mossdale, beside New Galloway station, where the pupils were mainly children of railwaymen, shepherds and estate workers, and at Parton. Not until about 1912, however, would the J C agree to trains calling at Loch Skerrow to meet the needs of employees' children going to and from school, and until then the children were taught by their mothers. Elsie Carradice and John Kee were so taught to the age of 12, and effectively, as they were then able to go to the Higher Grade School in Castle Douglas, staying in the town during the week and returning home at week-ends.

Trains had always called at Loch Skerrow for the benefit of fishermen and shooting parties, and catering for these visitors, by providing food and occasionally lodging and in other ways, was a useful "sideline" to the residents, though it seems likely that the visitors took unfair advantage of their old-world hospitality, getting their services decidedly "on the cheap".

As the "Glorious Twelfth" drew near, the Loch Skerrow platelayers organised an ingenious perquisite. They would collect grouse killed by collision with the telegraph wires, reassembling dismembered bodies by skilful use of needle and thread, and hang them in "creeps" under the line. When the great day arrived, the fireman of a goods train would, for a small commission, take them to Dumfries and an appreciative dealer in game. The platelayers' resourcefulness was sometimes thought excessive - a note from a game dealer on one occasion reading, "One good, healthy grouse, 10/-, one tailor-made bird, 6d." - but with better luck a man might make himself as much as £5 from these proceedings.

Another curious and resourceful "perk", also not without its humorous side, is referred to in the complaint of "Insulted Passenger", in the *Free Press* during June 1891, that card-playing was rife on P P R line trains and that "some guards carry 'the pack' with them and get sixpence or so for the loan of it". This statement was refuted, however, by "Aude Alteram Partem" in the following issue.

To some porters and, to some extent, station-masters also, gratuities were a valuable part of their remuneration. Station-masters not infrequently received gifts in kind - e.g., game, farm produce - in return for services willingly and obligingly rendered, and in some cases the local laird would make such gifts regularly at Christmas. The usual "tip" to railway porters in acknowledgment of ordinary services in pre-1914 days was 2d., but people of means, travelling with their families and servants, commonly took a lot of heavy luggage with them, and in such instances a porter might well get 2/6 or 3/- as reward for courteous and efficient attendance. At Portpatrick in the holiday season the porters found it considerably to their advantage to carry visitors' luggage from the station to their lodgings in the village.

The J C continued their predecessors' custom of letting station-masters earn money in other ways, provided these did not interfere with their railway duties and that they did not compete with established trades-people. Several dealt in coal. In 1889, the Dromore station-master received permission to sell sand. In 1890, Robert Galloway was authorised to run a post-office about to be opened at New Galloway station. He is said to have found the post-office as remunerative as the station. John McGaw was granted permission to act as sub-postmaster at Crossmichael in 1922, using the station premises. Station-masters would need help to run post-offices; that at Crossmichael was carried on by one of McGaw's daughters, who continued it, from premises in the village, long after his retirement.

The J C's paternal attitude found expression in payments they made on numerous occasions when they wished to acknowledge particular length and quality of service, and when special misfortune struck employees and their dependants. A notable example was James Campbell, porter at Kirkcowan, who broke a leg in an accident in April 1898 - "exchanging tablets with the fireman of a stopping train, he, in some unexplained way, lost his footing and fell, sustaining a compound fracture of the leg". Campbell was taken to Dumfries Infirmary. He was a married man, with nine children; his wage had been 17/6 a week, and he was now entitled to a G S W Friendly Society allowance of 10/6. The J C agreed to make up his wage to the end of June if necessary. June came, and he was "progressing favourably, but likely to be confined to the infirmary for a considerable period". They continued his allowance. September came, and February and April of the following year, and they noted similar prognoses and renewed his allowance. Not till 3rd July 1899 did Campbell return to duty. Many contemporary, and later, employers would, in the case of much less protracted illness, certainly have dispensed with a man's services, even though he had similar family responsibilities.

How did the J C react when any of their staff gave serious offence? Only a few instances are recorded, and doubtless only a few occurred. Let it be admitted that most of the railwaymen of Galloway were scarcely supporters of the great temperance movements of the time. A cottage by the roadside close to Rory's Bridge, over the cutting of the same name between Creetown and Dromore, was known in P P & W days and later as "The Teapot". The story went that, in the early years of the P P R, the presence of a teapot in a window of this cottage signified that whisky (whether legally distilled or no) was available within for a small sum. The crews of goods trains, steaming slowly up the bank from Creetown or drifting down from Dromore, would look out for the teapot, and on sight of the welcome symbol of abstinence would stop the train, enter the cottage, and indulge moderately; returning, they proceeded doubtless more cheerfully on their way. Numerous P P & W men shared their taste and indulged it. Long hours, monotony, and lack of other means of relaxation, combined with whisky at around 3/6 a bottle to bring this about. Only very rarely, however were there extremely serious consequences. In March 1887, Thomas Carter, recently-appointed station-master at Crossmichael, was dismissed for drunkenness. The station cash had been found short to the considerable extent of £28.4.10, which loss was to be recovered from the L N W Guarantee Fund. The J C were not vindictive, deciding not to prosecute Carter. An unnamed procedure was agreed upon for dealing with similar cases in future.

The records are silent as to future cases, but there were some. Over the years several P P & W station-masters were transferred to a smaller station, or reduced to signalman, through over-fondness of the bottle, deficiencies in their cash, incompetence in keeping their accounts, or a combination of these offences. There were instances of misappropriation in which the J C agreed not to prosecute, provided the deficiency was made good in a stipulated time. In a few cases a satisfactory term of performance as signalman resulted in a fallen station-master's restoration to grace and a station. But one such reduction in rank led to a very tragic result.

Near the end of 1905, a signalman named John McMaster was killed in an accident at Loch Skerrow. A native of Stranraer, he had worked at the tiny outpost in the wilderness for several years, but previously he had had charge of several stations on both the P P R and the W R lines. Through drink (to some extent) and inefficient book-keeping (more particularly), however, he found himself in the comparatively humble post of Dromore at a time of life when he might have been a senior station-master, and here also the state of the books resulted after a while in his transfer to Loch Skerrow as signalman.

On the very dark, wintry night of 28th December 1905, McMaster sat in his cabin waiting for the up mail, 10.3 from Stranraer, due at Castle Douglas at 11.27, and the exchange of tablets as it passed. He booked it as having left Dromore, the previous block post. On reaching Loch Skerrow, however, it missed the exchange of tablets. The driver brought the train to a stand and the fireman walked back to investigate. A horrifying experience awaited him. Some distance from the box he came upon the dead body of the signalman, his face gruesomely marked. His back was later discovered to be broken.

D. Litterick, ganger, Loch Skerrow, thus related the story of the accident:

"It was the practice for the signalman to go to his residence for his supper after the 4.35 p.m. goods train from Stranraer to Dumfries 'cleared' New Galloway shortly after 9 p.m. On his way home, he took with him the Manson catcher from the signal box and affixed it on the post concerned, but not in the extended position, this in preparation for the passing of the express from Stranraer Harbour to Carlisle, which would pass Loch Skerrow about 11 p.m.

"Some of the platelayers had been in the signal box with Mr. McMaster prior to his going for his supper and, I think, had actually accompanied him home, but it seems that Mr. McMaster had forgotten to take the Manson catcher with him on this occasion. He evidently did not discover his mistake until he actually left the box with the pouch to place in the catcher, after the express had left Dromore.

"Mr. McMaster returned to the signal box to get the Manson catcher, and was actually in the act of affixing the catcher on the post when the extended catcher on the engine of the express struck him on the side, with fatal results.

"No mention was ever made of any drink being involved, and the unfortunate accident would seem to have been the result of a lapse of memory on Mr. McMaster's part."

McMaster was 62 at the time of his death. His family brought a claim for £150 under the Compensation Acts, settling, however, for half that amount. The *Kirkcudbrightshire Advertiser* in its obituary notice spoke of him and his long railway service with warm respect, and awarded him the mythical title of "Station Master and Pointsman, Loch Skerrow".

McMaster's successor at Dromore was John Stitt. Stitt had similar limitations, and had served a period of "probation" at Loch Skerrow, but he was to spend the remainder of his career undisturbed at Dromore/Gatehouse, retiring in early L M S days, and the story we have to tell of him is a very pleasant one. Aware of Stitt's old-established difficulty with book-keeping (not helped by his habit of using invoices to light his pipe), Mr. Agnew, the Creetown station-master, and his young clerk decided to pay him a visit one evening, and offer their assistance. They found Mr. Stitt seated in the station office reading, the picture of contentment. He assured his visitors that his books could not be in better order, and though unconvinced they had perforce to leave the matter there. The three then chatted pleasantly and long of this and that, till at last the guests had reluctantly to say that they must begin their walk home. But Stitt would not hear of it; they could not possibly be allowed to leave without supper. He would tell his wife, and she would soon prepare it for them. This said, he opened the door in the partition between office and house in the little one-storey building to reveal a table neatly laid for four. Mrs. Stitt had long since learned from the voices in the office that her husband had two guests; she had prepared places for them, and supper was ready and waiting. The clerk has remembered with unfading pleasure the geniality and homely thoughtfulness of the old station-master and his wife.

The dissatisfaction of the J C's staff over wages and conditions in the years before 1914 did not result in low morale, or in low, or indifferent, standards of service. There is an almost complete absence of the kind of criticism in the local press that would suggest this. On the contrary, there is a good deal of evidence that standards were distinctly high. We saw some of this evidence in the previous chapter, and may now notice a little more.

Shortly after midnight on 14th October 1913 - a wet, wild night - the 10.37 p.m. "Fish" from Stranraer, running late, went through the passing-loop at New Galloway station too fast, and was wrecked just beyond. The train, with "fish, game, poultry, meat and other perishable goods from Ireland to the English markets", consisted of seven heavy vans, all of which were derailed. Breakdown gangs arrived from Dumfries and Stranraer towards five in the morning, when there was a "deluge" of rain. A steam crane came from Hurlford, near Kilmarnock. The down mail, foreshadowing the practice of the distant future, was sent round by Mauchline, Ayr and Girvan, reaching Stranraer 143 minutes late. The 7.30 a.m. passenger from Stranraer ran to New Galloway as usual, however, and here another train was provided to carry the passengers forward, the horse-buses from Dalry and New Galloway being used to take the passengers from one train to the other, past the obstruction. Passengers got to Castle Douglas about 90 minutes late. The passenger service seems to have been kept going throughout the day, but the goods trains were cancelled. The rain came down in unrelenting torrents as the officials and workmen strove to clear the track. A welcome access of strength was the arrival at 2.30 in the afternoon of a larger, 40-ton steam crane from Hurlford. The foul weather continued throughout the day, hampering the operations and causing extreme discomfort, but by 9.20 in the evening the line was reopened, and the up mail went through as usual. The *Kirkcudbrightshire Advertiser* had strong praise for the workmen and officers:

"No one who saw them will forget the plucky and cheerful labours of the breakdown gangs and the railway officials in the work of clearing the line under a storm of rain, which soaked the majority to the skin before their work was well commenced."

Only a few weeks previously, the same paper had spoken equally favourably of the railway staff in another connection - that of the annual inspection, on 18th August. The report they published following this event makes very pleasant reading, though the nostalgia which it inevitably arouses at the present day is likely to bring touches of sadness also. The "inspecting gentlemen" - Dr. Dawson, M.O.H. for Galloway, and Mr. Breckenridge, solicitor, Newton Stewart, judges of the "stations, platforms, waiting-rooms, and tidiness of the staff", and Mr. Cruden, Lochinch, Castle Kennedy, and Mr. Chapman, Stranraer, judges "for the flower gardens and borders", accompanied by Hutchinson, Martin (locomotive superintendent), Haining (permanent way superintendent) and McKain (traffic inspector) - are described as "highly pleased". They called special attention to "the exquisitely trim and tidy condition of the flower plots at Crossmichael" and the display of sweet peas at Stranraer.

"The general sanitary state of the waiting-rooms, etc., was noted to have greatly improved in recent years, and the condition of the approaches to several of the stations also merited the warm approval of the judges.

"A subject of remark was the fine condition of the Joint Line, the journey over the whole of the line being performed with perfect smoothness, and this, together with the neat condition in which the permanent way and grass slopes are kept, reflects the highest credit upon the 'Way' Department."

A very outstanding railway career had come to an end early in 1907, with the death at the age of 81 of James Mirrey, in charge of Parton since February 1863 - the P P & W's oldest and longest-serving station-master. Remarkably active for his age, despite the handicap of chronic bronchitis, he had been at his post till the last day of 1906, when he was forced to go off duty by the influenza that was to result in his death. We can imagine the anxious inquiries after him that would be made during the next few days at stations cast and west, and the general feeling of sadness and loss, extending to many people not connected with the railway, which must have followed the news, on January 8th, that that long, distinguished career was closed. In recommending a gratuity of £25 to his widow, the officers spoke of his .'excellent character and long and faithful service"; this, from them, was praise indeed. The *Kirkcudbrightshire Advertiser* described him as "a most reliable and diligent servant, and strictly conscientious in the discharge of all his duties". Mirrey could undoubtedly have won promotion to more responsible and better-remunerated positions in the railway service; but it is clear that he was content to pass the years as model custodian of a little wayside station. He received the premium for freedom from accidents each year throughout the period during which it was paid - until 1900 - and towards the end of his career he could look back on more than 40 years at Parton without any fatality occurring there. Very proud of the beautiful situation of his station, by river and wood and hill, he always did his best to make it worthy of its surroundings. It was noted for the magnificent display of flowers each summer, while the station buildings were "models of cleanliness", so that it was several times awarded first prize for the neatest and best-kept station on the P P & W lines. His four sons followed him into the railway service. Two of them became station-masters: Robert, who gave over 30 years' excellent service at Newton Stewart, and John, who, like his father, preferred a quiet country retreat, and was many years at Lochanhead, on the Dumfries to Castle Douglas line (compared with which Parton must have been quite busy!); the others were passenger guards - Joseph, on the Carlisle-Stranraer "Paddy", and James, on the G S W.

    An example of fine service extremely unobtrusively given was provided by Alexander Cowan, many years senior signalman at Loch Skerrow. Born at Colmonell, Ayrshire, where his father was a shoemaker, he began his railway career as a porter at Newton Stewart in P P R days, when his hours were from 4 a.m. till 11 p.m., with a break during the day when there was little or no traffic. He subsequently became a signalman, and he and James Allison were the first to man Newton Stewart West Box when it was opened in 1875. Early in 1906 he succeeded John McMaster at Loch Skerrow. His reasons for moving probably included the house at 2/6 a week rent, the free coal allowance, and the 5/- a week for looking after the steam pumping-engine in connection with the water tank. At Loch Skerrow, he and his wife spent many very hardworking but obviously also very happy years. In his leisure he took care of boats, kept records and generally helped to make arrangements for the visitors who came to fish and shoot, and Mrs. Cowan frequently provided afternoon and high teas. One who knew Alex. Cowan well writes of him:

"He did any necessary clerical work, wages, etc., and was a most intelligent man, and conscientious to a fault. Looking back, I sometimes wonder why he did not get himself moved to a little station, but he may not have liked to ask for promotion!"

This would have been typical of the humility that was one of his strongest characteristics; it may well be also that he would have been sorry to leave Loch Skerrow, where he stayed till January 1924, when he retired at the age of 70 and went to live in Castle Douglas.

It would be almost impossible to overestimate the value of the long, unbroken service of consistently high quality given by the Mirreys, Cowan and others like them. The stability they provided, the confidence they inspired, must have done much to foster the loyalty, the courteous, willing service, and the friendly community spirit characteristic of the P P& W.

The rapid rise in prices following the outbreak of war in 1914 affected lower-paid workers such as most railwaymen particularly badly. In February 1915, the strong representations of their unions led to the grant of a war bonus. This marked the end of the period when railwaymen's wages and hours were arranged on a local basis. The era of national negotiations and settlements had begun. With the continuing steep rise in the cost-of-living, new bonuses were necessary. These bonuses, or war wages, were in effect flat-rate wage increases, benefiting the lower-paid workers particularly. Thus, at the end of 1918, with the cost-of-living 120% above the pre-war level, the wages of the lowest-paid porters were over 180% more than they had been five years previously, while those of express passenger guards were about 80% more, and those of express drivers less than 70% more. This reflects the influence of the N U R, formed by the amalgamation of three railway unions in 1912.

The war had brought railwaymen a great deal of additional work and responsibility, and in 1919, with prices continuing to rise, the benefits from war wages spread unevenly among them, and anxiety about their financial position in the future, it is not surprising that they should have shared largely in the widespread dissatisfaction which followed so swiftly on the brief spell of relief and optimism that accompanied the Armistice of November 1918. The Government, still in control of the railways, had plans for wage reductions (to accompany the expected return to "normal" of the cost-of-living), which could mean the poorest-paid men of pre-war days losing over 10/- a week. In protest, the N U R called a national strike, to begin at midnight on Friday, 26th September. ASLEF supported the strike; the Railway Clerks' Association did not.

The strike brought the railways throughout Britain to an almost complete standstill. Galloway, it is true, was scarcely a centre of militant enthusiasm. Among wages grade staff, union membership had been growing steadily, but there were few active members. Some feared lest the management should find out that they had joined; older staff might fear loss or reduction of their expected ex gratia pension if they took part in a strike. To most P P & W men it must have seemed a very drastic step indeed, and even among those who felt strong sympathy with the strike's objects, some may well have been sincerely troubled in conscience about supporting it. In the event, however, most of the wages grade staff, including the locomotive men, joined the strike, and trains stopped running in Galloway for its duration.

On the evening of Friday, 26th September, the fish train went only as far as Castle Douglas. It was carrying only a modest quantity of perishables, and most of the dead meat - fowl, game, etc. - was sent by road to Carlisle on Sunday, while the remainder was disposed of locally, housewives being delighted to find a large number of rabbits offered for sale at reduced prices. From Saturday the town was "almost cut off from the outside world", no daily newspapers or mail arriving. The *Kirkcudbrightshire Advertiser* described all classes as sharing in acts of co-operation to overcome the effects of the strike; "motorists and others who had vehicles at their disposal" gave every help; services were freely rendered, though "often involving much trial and hard work".

In the Stranraer district the wages staff came out "practically to a man" during Saturday. Pickets were placed at stations, bridges and other places, but the following Thursday the *Free Press* commented that "So far the conduct of the strikers has been admirable, and no incident of an unseemly description has been reported." Here also motor transport was much in evidence; while P. McMeekan, jeweller, of Whithorn, gave at the age of four score years a noble example of the response of an individual when confronted with ruthless collective action. Stranded in Glasgow by the strike on Saturday, he bought a bicycle, and set out that afternoon to pedal his way home.

Reaching Ayr, 33 miles, by evening, he rested there overnight, and on Sunday completed the remaining 69 miles of rolling road to Whithorn.

The steamer service to Larne was suspended from Monday, 29th September, to Friday, 3rd October, inclusive. On Saturday, 4th October, the *Maud* made a special trip for passengers only, taking home a large number of Irishmen who had been in the Rhins district for the harvesting, and some of whom had been hanging about the streets of Stranraer for nearly a week.

The strike was settled on Sunday, October 5th, by a compromise, the terms of which were favourable to the men. But the most important result of Britain's first national railway strike was its demonstration of the feasibility of motor transport as an alternative (the outstanding example being the provision of adequate daily milk supplies in London), and the strong stimulus which this gave to the future development and use of the alternative.

The period of post-war prosperity was soon over. In the autumn of 1920 the cost-of-living reached a peak of 176% above the 1914 level, but thereafter prices and wages fell, and heavy unemployment rapidly set in. Scottish railways were specially hard hit by the depression. During 1921 the volume of goods traffic they carried fell by over a third. Trade union-negotiated wages had meant the end of the free houses still available to some employees on the P P & W, and of free coal for the people at Loch Skerrow; these were withdrawn in 1920, and under an Act of Parliament of that year, the rents payable for the J C's houses were to go up by 40% from July 1921. In general, however, railwaymen did not fare by any means so badly as the deteriorated economic situation might seem to have implied. The eight-hour day, conceded by the Government in March 1919, remained, and by an arbitration award of January 1922 affecting many wages staff, wages were not to be reduced below a standard rate of 100% over the average wages of July 1914. By this time, the cost-of-living had fallen to much less than 100% above the 1914 figure, and under this agreement railwaymen were to fare considerably better than many other workers during the years to come.

THE SEAFARERS

In 1887, the Steamboat Company noted that £593 had been paid the previous year in wages, described this sum as "large in proportion to the traffic", and contemplated a general wage reduction. Deciding against this, as they already paid lower wages than those paid on the majority of steamers trading with the Port of Belfast, they instead discharged a luggageman (25/-per week), a fireman (25/-per week) and a coal trimmer (22/- per week), reduced the wages of a second engineer, a carpenter and watchman by the large amount of 5/-, and cut the "bullockmen"'s remuneration from 4/- to 2/- per night. They claimed that these measures "will not impair the efficiency of the service", but two years later Captain Campbell was warning them that it was very difficult to get a certified engineer to act as second at the wages they paid, and that there was great dissatisfaction among the bullockmen. In the matter of the engineer, they authorised him to "do what he thinks fair and right". The bullockmen were members of the steamer's crew appointed to help look after cattle when there was a cargo of 150 head or more. They had to attend to the cattle from the time the latter came on board till they were all put on shore, and this left them with only a little time for rest before starting their regular duties in the morning. Campbell asked to be allowed to pay them 4/- a night as previously, adding that he "had never a complaint of any importance re injury to the cattle on board". The company granted his request.

We saw earlier the wages paid from 1892 to the staff attached to the steamers when they were laid up in port. When Captain McCracken died in 1899 and First Officer W. McNeill succeeded him, the latter was paid £5 a week when in charge of "a running steamer", but at other times received 45/- as first officer. C. Henderson, a veteran of the passage, got £3.3.0 as chief engineer in 1904. About this time it was the practice for second officers, first and second engineers, and carpenters to pay 6/- weekly for meals aboard ship. Most crew-members seem to have had free meals. It was noted in 1909 that "about nine months of the year the greater number of the meals prepared (on board) are consumed by the steamer hands themselves, either free or at a low tariff".

In 1904, Captain Cumming gave the complement of the new steamer *Princess Maud* as 39: there were 2 engineers and 12 men in the engine-room, 14 on deck, including the master, and 11, including stewardesses, in the steward's department. He told the S C this was "the least that we can do with". He drew a comparison with a similar-sized ship, the Queen (she was the first cross-channel turbine steamer in the world, built by Denny for the South Eastern & Chatham Railway, and entering service in 1903). The Queen had, for example, one additional engineer and two additional men in her engine-room.

The chief stewards, complained the S C in 1906, were getting too much remuneration - "far in excess" of their counterparts on the other steamers of the owning companies. William Armstrong, chief Mail Service steward, had 33/- a week and 5% commission on the gross receipts of the catering department on the steamer, making 65/- a week in all. J. A. Coleman, chief steward on the Second Service. received 30/-, plus 10/- for acting as storekeeper to the catering department and 2½% commission, a total of 49/- per week. (Coleman was kept in employment while the steamer was laid up, his hours of duty on shore being from 5.30 a.m. to 6 p.m.). The S C abolished the commission in both cases, substituting allowances of 17/- per week to the chief Mail Service steward and 5/- to his counterpart on the Second Service. These were to apply only to the present holders of the posts; the pay of their successors was "not to exceed 40/- per week as a maximum rate". Coleman's successor, Peter Keane, received 30/-, which was then made the maximum for the post, the 5/- in lieu of commission being duly terminated. Coleman's duties as storekeeper were taken over by the station-master at Stranraer Harbour, at the same remuneration of 10/- per week. The records mention that in 1912 the basic wage of J. Allan, second steward on the Mail Service, was only 17/-.

There were numerous wage increases between 1911 and 1913, some of those in the latter year being substantial, and showing the effects of pressure from the S C's staff for removal of the differential which seems always to have existed hitherto between the wages paid on the Mail Service and those on the Second Service:

|  |  | Former Pay | | Increased Pay | |
| --- | --- | --- | --- | --- | --- |
| Name | Rating | Sailing | Reserve | Sailing | Reserve |
| Hamilton, A. | Master (2nd Service) | £5 | £2. 5.0 | £5 | £3 |
| Brown, V. | 1st Mate (Mail) | £2.10.0 | £2. 5.0 | £2.12.6 | £2.12.6 |
| Munro, J. | 1st Mate (2nd Service) | £2. 5.0 | £1.12.0 | £2.12.0 | £2 |
| Hollis, R. | 2nd Mate (Mail) | £1.18.0 | £1.12.0 | £2 | £2 |
| Montgomery, H. | 2nd Mate (2nd Service) | £1.12.0 | £1.12.0 | £2 | £2 |
| McGowan, J. | Carpenter (Mail) | £1. 14.0 | £1.10.0 | £1.16.0 | £1.16.0 |
| Carmichael, L | Carpenter (2nd Service) | £1.10.0 | £1.10.0 | £1.16.0 | £1.16.0 |

Like the J C, the S C paid gratuities and allowances to some of their former employees. in 1909, they granted John McLean and James Hollis, retired seamen, 1/- a week as supplement to their old age pension of 5/-. When Chief Engineer Henderson retired at the age of 71 in 1911, they granted him £1 per week, in acknowledgement of his "long and faithful service". John Watt, lately fireman on the *Victoria* and with 22 years in the S C's service, had to retire at 57 in 1917 owing to ill-health; they made him a gratuity of £10. Following the death in 1918 of Chief Officer Vans Brown, aged only 43, after 9½ years' service, they granted a sum equal to six months' salary to his widow and family of four.

In April 1915, the S C's sea-going employees received a War Risk bonus, ranging from 10/- a week to the *Maud*'s captain to 2/6 for boys. Later that year, following "a strongly-pressed demand", all the S C's staff were granted a wage increase of 5/- per week. Until now, a general increase of this size would have been unthinkable, but in the new conditions of the war it would not meet the rise in the cost-of-living. The seamen, firemen and stewards applied for holidays also, and near the end of 1915 the S C announced the first annual holidays with pay for their employees: three days after one year's service, five days after five years' service. They noted in April 1916 that wages were based on a six-day week, six double sailings making the standard week's work. Unspecified overtime was paid for Sunday work and for extra sailings. During this month, the service was interrupted by a strike.

The strike was called by the Sailors' and Firemen's Union in pursuit of a demand for a weekly wage of 55/- for the *Maud*'s crew. It began on 8th April and continued for the rest of the month. Similar disputes had stopped the Mail Services to Ireland via Fleetwood and Heysham, and the passenger service via Liverpool, and now the only means of reaching the North of Ireland from England was via Holyhead and Dublin. The union's Scottish district secretary, T. H. Walsh, said in the *Free Press* that whereas before the war the sailors and firemen on the Larne passage had received 30/- per week, compared with 32/6 on cross-channel boats from other ports on the west coast of Scotland, now the minimum wage in all the Scottish ports was 55/-, while the wages and bonus on the *Maud* came to only 40/-. Experienced seamen were, of course, at a premium during the war; the Government were willing to pay 60/- a week for their services, and the men on the *Victoria*, on Admiralty service for the duration, were now getting this amount.

There was a good deal of hostility to the strikers among local people for the very fact of striking in wartime. It was pointed out what precious advantages the *Maud*'s crew had in being home-based, with regular working hours and a regular day off, and the Larne passage free (so far) from U-boats. And "Indignant" submitted in the *Free Press* that ...

". . . the men on strike are nearly all unskilled workers. Only a year or so ago, some of them were employed driving milk to the creameries, others on railway lorries, some thinning turnips and doing odd work on farms, and others masons' labourers, etc. They would be earning on average £1 per week - when they worked.

Then they donned jerseys and took up stokers' shovels, and ultimately received as wages £2 or more per week."

No doubt patriotism and the prospect of better pay had drawn away many of the crew who had manned the *Maud* at the outbreak of war, and it is in any case likely that the S C had always a considerable turnover of staff, owing to low wages and the very long day, starting work in the early morning and not finishing till late evening. But it was always easy to raise a "scratch" crew at Stranraer - Campbell could do so at a day's notice in 1889 - and now even in wartime the S C could replace many of the *Maud*'s crew with no great difficulty. On 1st May the service resumed, "twelve of the old hands having re-engaged and the necessary number of new hands having been taken on, all at the rates of wages prevailing prior to the strike".

With the continuing steep rise in prices, early in 1917 the officers and crew of the *Maud* again applied for increased pay. The S C refused, granting them instead a war bonus. This was additional to their war risk supplement, but it took into account the 5/- a week they had received from mid-1915. The new bonus was 15/- per week to men, and 7/6 to boys and stewardesses. The staff can hardly have been very pleased with this arrangement; their morale, however, was high, for about this time Cumming spoke thus of them in a report to the S C about the *Maud*'s annual survey and overhaul at Belfast:

"The ship's hands in the engine department were fully employed in the work of the overhaul; and when the shipyard hands struck work near its completion they carried on and finished it, so effecting the completion of all necessary work in the limited time available. Those in the deck department cleaned scaled and painted the holds and the stewards cleaned out the saloons and passenger accommodation. In every way the officers and crew were most helpful."

And on a similar occasion a year later he commented:

"The ship's hands in all departments were very fully employed while the ship was in Belfast, and did their part very creditably."

Cumming clearly continued the tradition of leadership so well established by his predecessor, Campbell, and it may well be that goodwill and a spirit of service among officers and crew were strengthened by the extension of U-boat activity in 1917-18, which brought greatly-increased danger to the Larne passage. Their unfavourable wage differential compared with other routes was abolished towards the end of the war when, on Government instructions, their pay was "approximated to the National Maritime Standard". Details of the new rates are not given in the records, which state, however, that in May 1921, following the collapse of the post-war boom, standard pay was cut by 8/6 per week in the case of officers, except masters, and crews, 4/6 in that of ordinary seamen, and 4/3 in that of boys.

We have thus come to the closing years of the rule of the S C and J C, and to the final chapter of our story.

# Rails to Portpatrick

**CHAPTER FOURTEEN**

Parting

TO many people in Britain in the summer of 1914, civil war in Ireland was an imminent probability. The Ulster Protestants seemed likely to resist by force the Government's attempts to impose Home Rule, their preparations including the smuggling of weapons at Larne. A major foreign war, it is true, had been anticipated and prepared for for many years and had threatened seriously in the recent past; but this danger appeared to many people to have receded. Yet it was now that the Great War burst suddenly upon Europe.

On the first day of war, 5th August, the Government, acting under a statute of 1871, took possession of the country's railways. They were put under the control of a Railway Executive Committee, formed of the general managers of some large English railway companies; the Committee's members came under military discipline - with the rank of Colonel. All the country's railway companies were guaranteed the net revenue they had earned during the prosperous year 1913. As early a casualty of the war as truth was the J C's newly-introduced Saturday Auxiliary Service between Dumfries and Belfast, which ran for the last time on August 1st. The Second Service of steamers and express trains was discontinued at the end of the month. One or two minor P P & W local trains were also taken off; in the earlier part of the war, however, the nation believed that a speedy victory was most likely to follow if they practised, so far as possible, the principle of "Business as Usual", and a normal winter service was operated from 1st October, while the J C's tourist guide for 1915 duly appeared, with scarcely a hint of the terrible change in the country's circumstances since the previous issue.

In the first months of war, the J C lost the services of two of their three ships. They would have disposed of the *May* in any case. Commander Holland, the L N W's Marine Superintendent, made a survey of her, and reported that she would cost £28,000 to put in proper order; he recommended that she be sold, and a new ship, similar to the *Victoria*, obtained. The Shipbreaking Company, London, bought her for £3,150, and under the command of Captain Hamilton she sailed away on 10th December, reaching Swansea next day after a stormy voyage. In the case of the *May*, however, the war prolonged life: the Admiralty purchased her, and employed her on special duties for the duration; after the war she was laid up in Holy Loch, and survived till 1921, when she was broken up at Garston. The *Victoria* was requisitioned in October 1914, and used as a fleet messenger for a few months, following which she became a military transport, based at Southampton.

The *Maud* was thus left to carry on the service alone. The L N W, however, "without any question of hire or chartering being raised", agreed to lend their steamer *Galtee More* to relieve the *Maud* for docking and annual survey and overhaul. She maintained the service during most of May 1915. As they had no spare ship, the J C did not run a Second Service at any time during the summer of 1915. They considered getting the *Maud* to make a second run on the busiest days of the Glasgow Fair Holidays if all the intending passengers could not be accommodated on one sailing, but decided against out of regard for their obligations under the mail contract. The winter service on the P P & W lines in 1915 was introduced on 1st September.

On 28th December the 6 a.m. steamer was delayed at Stranraer till 4.15 p.m., and on 12th January 1916 till noon, on Admiralty orders. Zeppelin raids on England delayed the steamer's sailing until 1.4 p.m. on 1st February 1916, 5.27 p.m. on 1st April, and 9.15 a.m. on 3rd April, the late departure on 1st April from Stranraer delaying the 7.15 p.m. sailing from Larne until 9.40 p.m. Trains were stopped when air-raids took place long distances away. "... even in Galloway", wrote C. H. Dick, "trains halted and lay low at the warning of Zeppelin airships approaching Britain, as birds crouch in their coverts when a hawk appears on the horizon".

By early 1916 there was great concern over the delays to traffic caused by lack of crane power at Stranraer Harbour. The steam crane erected in 1896, with its original lifting capacity of 5 tons at a radius of 35 ft., had been modified in 1904 when turbine-steamers were introduced on the passage, its 45 ft. jib being altered to 60 ft., reducing its lifting power to 3½ tons at 45 ft., 3 tons at 50 ft., and 2½ tons at 55 ft. At the same time, the coaling of the ships was added to its work, as with a turbine steamer this could no longer be done manually. In the pre-war years when the Second Service was operated, it handled about 13,000 tons of coal per annum; in 1915 the quantity handled was about 10,500 tons. We saw earlier the steady increase in the quantities of goods sent by the Larne route during these years; including the coal, the crane handled a total of 23,328 tons in 1915. It had needed major repairs. With so much depending on efficient crane-power, McConchie now urged the provision of a modern crane of greater power and speedier manipulation. The officers made a full investigation.

They reported that the old crane, erected in 1878, lifting capacity 30 cwt. at 28 ft. radius, was now almost worn out. The 1896 crane was in fair order after its recent overhaul, but age and constant use made it liable to breakdowns, and there had been several delays to traffic from this cause. At Larne the crane-power available was much greater; yet whereas the ship was alongside the quay at Larne for 11 hours, at Stranraer it was there for only 8 hours, with coaling occupying the crane completely for about 3 hours. Stranraer thus had only 5 hours for cargo work compared with 11 hours at Larne, and "the broad position is that Larne can ship about twice as much as Stranraer can discharge". As a result, goods were frequently carried backwards and forwards for several days before there was time at Stranraer to unload them. During the winter of 1915-16 it had been quite common for quantities varying between 3 and 40 tons to go to and fro for the best part of a week. Through this traffic being thus delayed, other goods could not be accepted.

# Rails to Portpatrick

The officers supported McConchie's request for a new crane, "of powers and speed not inferior to that of the 1896 crane". The two cranes could then work together, perishables could be more quickly despatched and a larger volume of goods cargo handled. McConchie anticipated a further expansion of traffic if better despatch from Stranraer could be organised. Additional perishable traffic should yield about £1,000 per annum more to the "joint interests". Goods cargo, acceptance of which was at presented limited by the quantity that could be handled at Stranraer, had averaged 30 tons nightly in 1915; with another crane, this could be 90 tons, and the increase in through goods traffic ought soon to yield another £1,000 per annum to the joint interests. The officers concluded their report by recommending the purchase of a new crane, with a lifting capacity of 5 tons at radius 40 ft., and 31 tons at radius 50 ft., as soon as possible, the price to be about £2,200.

Wartime conditions made such equipment difficult to get, and in the meantime the J C tried to hire a suitable crane, but they applied to all twelve principal English and Scottish railway companies without success. Stranraer harbour eventually got its new 5 ton crane in June 1918; its makers were Ransome & Rapier, Norwich, and it cost £2,319.13.9.

The *Maud*, which had steamed 13,969 nautical miles in 1914, steamed 19,807 in 1915 when she maintained the service alone. The *Galtee More* was on the passage for most of March 1916, and from 9th to 23rd October. By the end of 1915, the S C were having to use some higher-priced coal, owing to difficulty in getting a satisfactory quality for the *Maud*; the supply they ordered in August 1916 cost 25/- and 31/- per ton, delivered in trucks at Stranraer Harbour. They kept up the bing they had established at Stranraer before the war, and it now contained 1,453 tons.

As the war continued, there was a considerable increase in the numbers of members of the armed forces moving about Galloway. The stationing of two small naval vessels at Stranraer harbour led to an increase in the coal traffic passing over the P P R line. There was an increase in the quantity of round timber and pit props dispatched from the province, particularly by way of New Galloway and Creetown stations, while from some of the stations there was a considerable hay traffic, mainly for the use of army horses. As younger members of the P P & W staff not in "key" positions went into the Services more clerkesses were employed, and in a few instances women took the places of junior porters. Some curtailment of services became necessary, the winter service operating on the P P & W lines throughout the summer of 1916. The officers revived the project of a turntable at Newton Stewart, noting that if this were now to be provided, "One of the goods engines which presently work from Dumfries to Stranraer one day and back the next could be made to work from Dumfries to Newton Stewart and back in a day, thus releasing an engine and a set of men, while still leaving a sufficient goods train service as between Newton Stewart and Stranraer". The total saving would be about 12,200 goods train miles per annum; the cost of the works about £2,300. The plan included a small water tank near the engine shed, so that engines could be "turned out watered and fully ready for work", instead of having to use the present facilities which were placed for the running lines. The latter were usually already occupied when an engine was called from the shed to give urgent assistance. Owing to the scarcity of material, the plan was deferred, but to make an immediate saving in engine power the officers recommended fitting some engines with double cabs; this, they stated, had been done already on "certain engines" running on the W R line. They could then run tender-first in all weathers, and instead of going to Stranraer and coming back next day, a goods from Dumfries could stop at Newton Stewart and return the same day. Train mileage would be reduced by about 240 per week, and an engine and "a set of men" would be saved. This suggestion seems, however, not to have been put into practice.

No tourist guide had been published for 1916, the printer being unable to take it on, and the guide, in fact, never appeared again. The number of holiday-makers visiting Galloway had greatly declined, and shooting and fishing parties no longer came for the respective seasons. At Loch Skerrow, the railway people who had catered so well for the latter now transferred their efforts to the humane and patriotic cause of collecting sphagnum moss from the nearby moors for use as dressings. This was organised by Jenny Galloway, daughter of the veteran station-master at New Galloway, the work of extracting the moss being done mainly by Alex. Cowan, the senior signalman, with the help of his grandson, and sometimes of the junior signalman also. It was hard work, as the best moss grew in the deeper bogs, and had to be dragged out with long rakes; following this, the moss, which was, of course, likely to be extremely wet therefore very heavy, had to be taken to higher ground and scattered to dry, when it became pale-coloured and feathery. Often on Saturday afternoons, Miss Galloway and other members of the family would come up the line to help, and the party would be rewarded for their labours with one of Mrs. Cowan's celebrated high teas. The dried moss was put into sacks and sent by goods train to New Galloway station, whence, after further treatment by Miss Galloway and her helpers, it was finally dispatched to the hospitals.

At the close of 1916, consequent on the need to send 300 locomotives to France, big reductions and other alterations in passenger train services were introduced throughout Britain. On the P P & W, the mail trains and steamers were retimed to suit altered connections at Dumfries and Carlisle, the up mail running about half-an-hour earlier, and the down mail about an hour later. The duplicate of the down mail was withdrawn. The mail train in each direction now carried only one sleeping car, and on the up train two berths only were available for passengers joining at Stranraer, Newton Stewart or Castle Douglas, the other nine being reserved for passengers from Ireland. The 9.30 a.m. up train from Stranraer was withdrawn, and the 3.40 p.m. up - the last slow train of the day to Castle Douglas and Dumfries - retimed to leave as early as 2.35. The 6.45 a.m. down and 9.20 a.m. up trains on the

## Rails to Portpatrick

W R line were withdrawn and some other times altered, "to effect economy in engine power and at the same time give a new train Stranraer-Newton Stewart at 11 a.m.". The Friday market train from Whithorn to Newton Stewart was also withdrawn. At the same time that these alterations took effect, passenger fares were increased by 50%. The object of this was to discourage people from travelling. Taking the country as a whole, it had only very temporary effect, a result attributed to wartime prosperity.

Reverting to the steamers, Cumming was well satisfied with the results of the *Maud*'s annual survey in March 1917, particularly the state of her engines:

"In general, it may be stated that everything in the engine department appears to be in good condition, considering that the ship has practically been in constant work for nearly the whole of the past three years."

The *Galtee More* maintained the service from 12th to 24th March and 1st to 12th October 1917, and from 27th May to 14th June and 14th to 25th October the following year. In 1916 the *Maud* had burnt 9,055 tons of coal, steaming 1.99 nautical miles per ton of coal burnt, compared with 10,276 tons, 1.93 nautical miles per ton of coal burnt, in 1915. For the 12 months from August 1917 the S C ordered coal at 24/6 and 30/- per ton, delivered in trucks at Stranraer Harbour. During that year, however, there were continued increases in the price, by order of the Government Coal Controller, totalling 7/- a ton, and the prices in the S C's 1918 contract were 31/6 and 37/6 per ton. In the closing months of the war, "temporary hitches" at Messrs. Waldie's Hirst colliery led to deterioration in the coal supplied, with loss of time on the passage and complaints from the *Maud*'s engineers, so the S C ordered 500 tons of Bredisholm navigation coal from United Collieries Ltd., Glasgow, at 38/1½ a ton.

During 1917 and 1918, intensified U-boat activity was a steadily increasing danger on the Larne passage, and a series of precautions was taken in an attempt to safeguard the *Maud*. In June 1917, wireless was installed, at a cost of £397.16.3. An operator was temporarily engaged from the Marconi Company at £100 per annum, plus 5/- a week War Risk bonus and free food and quarters, but meanwhile a P P & W clerk, David Broadfoot, was sent to the Marconi school for training, and he was subsequently appointed the *Maud*'s wireless operator, at a starting salary of £35, plus 7/6 War Risk bonus, 15/- war bonus and "uniform and victualling when sailing". John Maxwell, another P P & W clerk, was sent to the Marconi School also, getting a first class certificate of proficiency in radio-telegraphy, and was transferred to the *Maud*e at the end of September 1918 as reserve wireless operator, with £30 per annum "plus the usual bonuses and victualling when sailing". In July 1917 the naval authorities mounted a machine-gun and smoke-apparatus on the *Maud*, providing a gun-layer and second hand, and paying all expenses. Soon after, Captains McCalmont and Hamilton and Chief Officer Brown took Admiralty courses on the U-boat menace.

Cumming reported thus on the *Maud* following her annual survey in May 1918:

"Boilers appear to be in very good condition internally and externally, there being no sign of pitting, corrosion, or wastage in the furnace crowns, combustion chamber tops or sides, and after 14 years pretty constant steaming they do not appear to have deteriorated to any extent.

"Turbines - Starboard low pressure cover and rotor were lifted and found in good condition, no sign of pitting or corrosion apparent.

"Steward's Department - Most of the paintwork in the passengers' accommodation was recoated, and a general overhaul of lavatories, etc., carried out and the upholstery repaired. The fittings in the Steward's Department suffer a good deal from the heavy military passenger traffic. The carpets are very far through, having been fitted in 1910 and 1912."

He went on to list anti-submarine precautions taken on Government orders:

"Crow's nest in fore mast for look-out.
Dimming switch for regulation lights.
Plain lenses in lieu of dioptic for regulation lights.
Removal of reflectors, side and mast head lamps.
Wood screens fitted at front of deck-house doors opening on weather deck.
Automatic switch on deck cabin doors.
Screening by painting, etc., all side posts and windows.
Dazzle-painting all outside work, including hull, masts, funnels, boats, etc.
Spars fitted between boats' davits for securing boats.
Screens on gun platform.
Wood chocks fitted above and below rubber belting in way of each of the 7 boats."

In conclusion, he noted that gun practice had taken place while the ship was on her way from her survey at Belfast to Larne.

As a further precaution, the *Maud* followed zig-zag courses, and in August 1918 the Admiralty recommended that she make the crossing in daylight all the year round, a view strongly endorsed by Cumming. The L N W said they could not give a London connection at Carlisle earlier than by the present 9.35 p.m. from Stranraer Harbour without running a special train, which would be difficult in view of coal shortage and pressure of wartime traffic. On 1st November, however, a revised Belfast-London service began, by which the evening steamer would reach Stranraer at 5.15 during winter months.

But now the war was, at last, all but over. The *Maud* had previously been escorted by airships; latterly destroyers had provided the escort. On 5th November, the destroyers were withdrawn; on the 7th, direct course sailing was resumed; normal navigating lights were allowed to be used.

THE STEAMERS AFTER THE WAR

From 1st December 1918, the evening steamer and the up mail express went back to their previous timings. On 1st March following, several trains were restored, and the officers reported that the P P & W service was "practically what it was in pre-war days". The *Maud* continued to maintain the passage alone throughout 1919; the *Victoria* returned early the following year, but the Second Service was not restored that summer, or in the two summers following. Since 1916, Ireland had been convulsed by terrorist activities, this villainy being at its worst between 1919 and 1922.

The Admiralty released the *Victoria* at the end of 1919, and she was taken to Stephen & Sons, Govan, for reconditioning. Cumming supervised, assisted by Captain Nash, the L N W's marine superintendent, and Mr. Harris, his superintending engineer. Nash received an honorarium of 100 guineas, and Harris one of 50 guineas. Cumming reported to the S C:

"It was evident from the work found necessary in reconditioning that the wear and tear of war service had been excessive. Throughout the ship, in decks, deck fittings, passenger accommodation, and equipment generally, it was found that she was much more the worse for wear than the sister-ship, the *Maud*, which is 8 years older and had to maintain the service between Stranraer and Larne alone during the whole period of the war."

The *Victoria* came back to Stranraer on 22nd April, 1920, and took up the Mail Service on 29th, releasing the *Maud* for her annual survey. She stayed on the service till 31st July, when she was relieved by the *Maud*, Cumming intending to divide the service equally between them.

The *Galtee More* had maintained the service from 31st March to 14th April and 14th to 25th October, 1919. In his report on the overhaul of the *Maud* during the latter month, Cumming made the following reference to the *Maud*'s wireless equipment:

"As had been arranged, Mr. Russell, of the Telegraph Department of the G & S W Railway, was notified and the wireless installation was inspected; and it was found that everything was in very good condition and reflecting great credit on the care and attention given to the apparatus by the operator, Mr. Broadfoot. The aerials were taken down and the insulators thoroughly cleaned, as is our practice each time that opportunity offers."

After her survey in May 1920, Cumming mentioned the high cost of overhaul, including renewal of the saloon upholstery work and a general overhaul of the passenger and officers' accommodation and the life-saving equipment, "which has suffered a good deal during the war period". Extra repairs had been necessary in the engine department.

He continued:

"Now that we have a steamer in reserve, we hope to overtake a great deal of work with our own people at Stranraer, which we have been compelled during the past 6 years to get done by shipyard people; and we hope that the reduction in cost of repair will be apparent in future overhauls. Unless necessity compels, it is intended to try and forego the autumn docking for a time until costs of labour and material come back to something considerably less than they are at present."

In the summer of 1921, he described measures to ensure regular wireless communication between the *Maud* and the *Victoria*.

"An emergency set having been fitted in the *Victoria* while in Government Service, and in order to complete the installation in this ship to enable us to make full use of the wireless and to maintain communication between the reserve and mail steamer throughout the passage, it was found necessary to procure from the Marconi Company and fit an emergency set and storage battery on board the *Maud* at a cost of £100. It is obvious that without this equipment the wireless on board the *Victoria* when she was on service was of no use as a means of communication with us unless steam was up and the dynamo was kept running in the *Maud*, which would have been out of the question in ordinary circumstances, whereas now there is no extra expense involved and we can keep in constant touch with the mail steamer throughout the passage, morning and evening; and I am now in a position to report that the wireless installation is complete in both ships."

The *Victoria*'s wireless had been installed in June 1916; it was 1½ kW. power, and rented by the Government from Marconi International Marine Communication, the makers. The rental for the period January 1920 to July 1922 inclusive amounted to £477.15.2. This set being more powerful than was necessary, the S C now decided to replace it with a new ¼ kW. apparatus, to be bought outright. They purchased a Quenched Gap set, price £375.

The *Victoria* and the *Maud* each being out of commission for six weeks in 1922 for survey and overhaul, the *Duchess of Argyll* was again, as in 1910-12, retained as reserve ship. She was equipped with wireless, the combined cost to the S C of wireless and retainer being £294.7.1.

During the post-war boom period, the tremendous demand for British coal at home and even more in Europe, forced prices up to unheard-of levels. For the 12 months from August 1919 the S C contracted for prices of 37/6, 47/9 and 51/6 a ton, and for the following 12 months for between 39/9 and 55/4 a ton. The miners, apart from seeking and gaining increased wages, subsidised by the State, and shorter hours, seized the opportunity to try to force the Government to nationalise the mines, a measure which the miners interpreted as giving control of the industry to themselves. They went on strike in October 1920, and Stranraer-Larne sailings were suspended for five days, beginning from the 25th of the month, on Ministry of Transport instructions; several reductions and alterations in the train service were made at the same time.

By now, however, the boom was over, and in the spring of 1921 a prolonged strike took place as the miners resisted reductions in their wages. The shortage of coal led to serious curtailments of railway and steamer services, Stranraer-Larne sailings being suspended from 15th April till 11th July. The S C sold 1,092 tons from their bing at Stranraer to the C R and G S W, and some to local workplaces also. Henceforward, coal prices fell steadily, and for a time the S C bought their requirements in fortnightly quantities. At the end of 1922, numerous coal-owners tendered eagerly for their needs, and they agreed to purchase 6,000 tons in trucks at the pits: 2,000 of Muirkirk from William Baird & Company at 20/6 a ton, 2,000 of Afton from the Clydesdale Coal Company at 19/6, and 2,000 of Killochan from South Ayrshire Collieries, also at 19/6. It was, they noted, now unnecessary to bing a reserve.

Shortly before the S C's rule ended, there came some changes among their senior staff. In October 1921, Captain McCalmont, their senior sailing captain, resigned, and was granted a retirement allowance of £250 per annum. Captain Andrew Hamilton, hitherto reserve master, was appointed in his stead, at a salary of £560, and John Munro, first officer, became reserve master, at £473. A year later, Cumming, his health declining, retired also; he was granted an allowance of £300 per annum. Probably because of the imminent railway amalgamation, the S C did not appoint a successor, permanent arrangements being deferred. Pending these, the G S W's marine superintendent was to "take oversight" at Stranraer.

THE TRAINS AFTER THE WAR

In April 1913, the J C had ordered improvement of the junctions to the crossing-loops between Castle Douglas and Stranraer, to give smoother running for express trains. This would be expensive - nearly £7,000 - and the cost was to be spread over five years, but it was resolved to carry the work through at once. It was not carried through, however, and in September 1916 the officers decided to introduce long-section tablet working from Stranraer Harbour Junction to Castle Douglas instead. This would save £1,920, and give the advantages of long-section tablet working "combined with the saving of wages effected if it should be necessary at a future time to reduce the hours of duty of the signalmen". In April 1920, the officers noted that installation of the apparatus would soon be completed, ready for opening, but in fact it was not until 1924 that long-section working was introduced for night trains, the block-posts being Stranraer Harbour Junction, Challoch Junction (soon to be replaced for the purpose by Dunragit), Newton Stewart West, Loch Skerrow and Castle Douglas No. 2. The Manson tablet exchange apparatus went out of use at the same time. The boxes that were not block-posts were now closed from 10 p.m. to 6 a.m., and at each of them a signalman was dispensed with. At the switched-out points, up trains avoided the curved loops and used the down lines, which, except at Palnure, were straight. This "running straight line", combined with the avoidance of reductions of speed for the uplifting of tablets at the switched-out places, resulted, of course, in a saving of time. Loud-sounding bells were installed in the stationmasters' houses at switched-out points, so that they could be called out in the event of train failure or other emergency. The bells could be operated from the box at any of the block-posts, and they rang in each station house simultaneously. By the use of special apparatus it was possible to revert to short section working, provided that the station-masters at switched-out places were all on duty.

Some major works were carried out at Newton Stewart in 1920-21. In March 1919, the wooden engine shed there had been completely destroyed by fire, "believed to have been originated by a collier lamp set down by an engine cleaner on a wooden bench much saturated with oil". The J C ordered the building of a new shed of brick, and improvements to the locomotive yard, chief of which was to be, at long last, a turntable. In April 1921, they noted that a second-hand 50 ft. turntable previously offered by the G S W would not now be available, and a new one was to be purchased, the estimated cost being £1,350. Improvements were made at Stranraer Harbour Junction about the same time, a shunting head and two crossover roads being provided and the signal cabin reconstructed. McConchie had complained that delays to engines due to shunting at the junction cost upwards of £900 per annum. Other large works undertaken at this period were urgent and extensive repairs, costing over £1,100, to the viaduct over the Bladnoch on the P P R line between Kirkcowan and Newton Stewart, and the installation of a Blake hydram, estimated cost £550, at Loch Skerrow in place of the steam pumping engine there, which was worn out. In April 1922, the new machine was reported not only to have been cheaper to buy than a steam engine, but also to be proving much less costly in working. Part of the saving would be the weekly payment of 5/- hitherto made to the senior signalman for looking after the steam engine. The "Blake Ram" was usually efficient, but there were occasions when it was put out of action, the cause being the jamming of its small outlet jets by the moor grass. This grass, coarse and broad in the blade, was called "blaw-grass" by the local people. In dry periods when there was a strong wind it got blown about everywhere, including the Loch and the streams. When the ram was installed, frames covered with fine netting were erected to prevent grass carried by the stream that fed it from interfering with its working. These were usually effective, but not quite always, and perhaps because of the exceptions the ram was in the course of time itself superseded by another steam engine.

The high prices of labour and materials, coupled with the great amount of work needing to be done to make good the extreme wear-and-tear of the war, presented railway companies in the immediate post-war period with a formidable problem. There was a danger that, in this situation, Joint Lines would be neglected as their owning companies concentrated on their individual requirements. In the case of the P P& W, whose permanent way became very badly run down during the war, renewal may well have been delayed from this cause. On 30th January 1918, a van had become derailed near Glenluce, resulting in considerable damage to the track as well as to the van itself. G SW engine No. 67 was hauling the 5.30 p.m. passenger from Dumfries to Stranraer, consisting of:

> G S W 8-wheeled 3rd class carriage
> G S W 8-wheeled 3rd class carriage
> G S W 6-wheeled composite carriage
> G S W 6-wheeled brake van
> N E R 4-wheeled perishables van
> L N W 4-wheeled open fish truck

About 1¾ miles east of Glenluce station the N E R (empty) perishables van left the rails and ran 2,057 yards before the train stopped, breaking 2,330 chairs and 159 sleepers. A remarkably similar mishap occurred on 15th August 1921. Again, an evening train from Dumfries was involved: a train now left Dumfries for Stranraer in the early evening during summer as well as winter, as Hutchinson had so earnestly but vainly striven to arrange before the war; its departure time was 5.40. Hauled by G S W No. 385, it consisted of:

> L N W 8-wheeled brake van
> G S W 8-wheeled 3rd class carriage
> G S W 8-wheeled 1st class carriage
> G S W 8-wheeled 3rd class carriage
> L N W 8-wheeled brake van
> L N W 6-wheeled brake van
> L N W 6-wheeled brake van
> L N W 4-wheeled meat van

Again, about 1¾ miles east of Glenluce station, the L N W (empty) meat van left the rails. It ran about 147 yards, when it fell over on its right side, released itself from the train, and "came to rest in an upright position obliquely across the line".

The officers were understandably very concerned at this second mishap; it was "discussed at length" and they "agreed further investigation should be made". The minutes do not record the results of the investigation, but on 28th December 1922 a third accident happened, and brought to a head the matter of the condition of the permanent way. This time the train concerned was the 3.40 p.m. from Stranraer to Dumfries, drawn by C R No. 1069 and consisting of:

G S W 4-wheeled meat van, loaded poultry, butter,
one can milk, general parcels.
G S W 4-wheeled meat van, loaded milk.
M R 6-wheeled fish van, loaded game.
M R 6-wheeled fish van, loaded game.
G S W 4-wheeled fish van, loaded milk.
L N W 8-wheeled brake van.
L N W 8-wheeled brake van.
C R 8-wheeled brake 3rd class carriage.
C R 8-wheeled composite carriage.
L N W 8-wheeled brake van.
C R 6-wheeled milk van.

As the train was crossing the Cree Viaduct, between Newton Stewart and Palnure, one of the vehicles became derailed: very soon the first five vehicles were all off the rails, and went tumbling down the embankment just beyond the viaduct; the next five were also derailed, but stayed upright on the top of the embankment. This section included the passenger carriages and brake vans, and the 30 passengers and three guards on the train were unhurt. The C R milk van was not derailed. Following the Ministry of Transport inquiry, a 45 miles per hour speed restriction was imposed on the P P & W lines.

The final years of the J C saw a brief revival of two of the schemes for new railways in Galloway that appeared earlier in our story. In 1918, a Government-appointed committee recommending improvements in communications in rural areas of Scotland after the war suggested light railways through the Glenkens from Dalmellington to Parton and through the Rhins from Stranraer to Drummore. These recommendations were not followed up, but in 1920 the Rhins scheme was revived again in the district itself. On 1st July, Sir Mark McTaggart Stewart chaired a meeting at Sandhead, where a motion was carried in favour of a railway connecting with the P P R line near Dunragit. The age of Government subsidies had now arrived, and it was hoped that the recently created Ministry of Transport would support the project. Failing this - but only as the last resort - they were to be asked to subsidise "a number of four or five ton lorries". The times, however, were unfavourable; prosperity was soon to give way to depression; the new Ministry was to be threatened with extinction under the "Geddes axe" of the following year: not surprisingly, therefore, yet again a scheme for a "Rhins Railway" came to nothing.

The Government relinquished possession of the country's railways on 15th August 1921, paying the companies £51,000,000 in part compensation for their services during and since the war. The Railways Act of the same year, providing for amalgamation, came into force on 1st January 1923. On 20th March 1923, a meeting of proprietors of the P P & W lines was held in the railway offices at

# Rails to Portpatrick

Stranraer, to consider the Preliminary Scheme under the Railways Act for absorption of the J C by the L M S Railway Company. A total of 16 people, six of them proxies, responded to the invitation extended by newspaper advertisement and circular. The chairman of the J C, the L N W's C. J. Cropper, and other members sent apologies. Stair McHarrie, as chairman of the meeting, explained the Preliminary Scheme, and moved a resolution in favour of approval. The veteran Fred. Hutchinson seconded, and the tiny meeting carried it unanimously.

To some extent, the P P & W benefited from the amalgamation. This was particularly evident in the permanent way, which was greatly improved, with the laying of longer rails and the provision of more metal ballast, so that greater engine power could be used; bridges were strengthened. Numerous members of the staff, both salaried and wages, benefited considerably through the opening of a very much wider field for promotion, and during the years which followed some P P & W men won their way to senior positions in Scotland's principal railway centres. Galloway's railways continued to play an important part in the life of the province for many years, despite increasing road competition, to which rural lines such as the P P & W were, of course, particularly vulnerable. Nevertheless, the amalgamation brought some very real changes for the worse, whose effect was heightened by the fact that they followed the period of unsettlement formed by the years of war and its immediate aftermath, with their very abnormal conditions.

Until 1923, the P P & W Railways were very much a local undertaking, run from a local headquarters, two of the three managers of P P & W days being men of long and close local connections who consistently did their best to make the railways serve the province as well as was compatible with the larger, different interests of the big owning companies. In spite of dissatisfaction over wages and conditions, there was a spirit of community among the staff, which expressed itself in high standards of service and won the goodwill of the local people. This happy state of things was seriously marred by the amalgamation. Stranraer ceased to be a railway headquarters. McConchie, as manager, became redundant and left Galloway altogether, a very disappointed man. The management staff were dispersed, either by transfer or retirement, the only exceptions being a traffic inspector and two telegraph clerkesses. For a time, management of the P P & W lines was undertaken by L M S headquarters at Glasgow; later, again for a time, it was transferred to the District Superintendent, Carlisle. The change of control inevitably damaged the relationship between the railways and the area they served. Though the good feeling that had been such a clear and welcome distinguishing mark earlier never completely died away, a sad feature of the years following the war was the gradual fading of the friendly spirit that had existed previously. This was probably partly due to the evil influence of the war, as men who had served in it returned to their railway duties deeply and permanently unsettled by their experiences, and unable again to feel the comparative ease of mind they had taken for granted before. The decline was undoubtedly contributed to also by the

# Rails to Portpatrick

changes consequent on amalgamation, and as the years passed people able to remember the P P & W before the war, though by no means forgetful of railwaymen's difficulties and grievances then, came to think of those days as a kind of Golden Age. Looking back over 50 yrars across a lifetime of earnest and enthusiastic service to his early years on the P P & W, a retired railwayman commented, "It was practically a family concern."

# Rails to Portpatrick

# APPENDICES

## APPENDIX ONE

### The Building of Loch Ken Viaduct

From The *Dumfries Courier*, 1st September 1859

THE Ken at this point, a little beyond its junction with the Dee, is 36 feet deep, and the works here are the most extensive on the Portpatrick line, the Ken bridge being the subject of a separate contract. The main structure will consist of three arches, each of a span of 130 feet clear, besides two small arches on each side of the bank. The stonework of the piers on the land sides is well forward and progressing rapidly. These piers are elegant in form and are substantially built of reddish sandstone from Cove and Cumberland, the stones being blocked out before being despatched to the Dee. There will be two piers in the deep waters of the river and, owing to the great depth of water, these piers will be partially built within cylinders of iron. These cylinders have been brought to the spot, and those intended for one of the piers placed in the river. The cylinders are each 6 feet in height, and about the same in diameter. Six of them placed one above the other reach nearly to the top of the water, which is at present small, the lower sinking down from the superincumbent weight into the sand and gravel of the bed of the stream. The cylinders are firmly joined together and form an elongated coffer dam which will be permanent. On Friday, workmen were engaged in surrounding the bottom of the lowest with clay; a pump driven by steam power is placed on the staging above and ready to commence clearing the cylinders of water. As soon as this has been effected, a foundation of concrete will be laid and building within the cylinders commenced. It has been already mentioned that there will be two piers in the water; but each of these piers will be double below the water, and for each, two sets of cylinders will be required. When the piers within the cylinders have been filled with masonry, they will be joined by an arch, and a single large pier, resting on the arch which will rest on the two sunken piers, be raised above the water line. The cylinders will remain around the lower piers and under the water, so that the piers will appear to be wholly of stone. Rising from the summit of the piers, which will be 50 feet high, semicircular iron girders will stretch their huge arms high above the water, to which they will be concave, and from them will be suspended the iron tramway for the railroad, braced together by all the resources which science can command. The diameter of the main piers will be 8 feet, and the span of the girders 130 feet clear. This promises to be not only a stupendous but a most elegant erection, and must prove an ornament to the beautiful scenery around the Boat of Rhone, where wood, mountain, water and classic ground unite to form a most interesting landscape.

# Rails to Portpatrick

**APPENDIX TWO**

The Stranraer-Drummore Bus

ON 23rd May 1892 a new horse-drawn coach service began between Stranraer and Drummore, via Lochans, Stoneykirk, Ardwell and Port Logan, leaving Stranraer Post Office each weekday at 7.20 a.m. and due at Drummore at 10.5, and leaving Drummore at 4.50 p.m. and due in Stranraer at 7.25. This coach carried the mails, the contract being held by Adam Henry of Ardwell. When the mail-coach service started, there was already a coach running every weekday, but in the reverse direction, leaving the Queen's Hotel, Drummore, at 7.30 a.m. and returning from Meikle's Hotel, Stranraer, at 4 p.m., the fare for the whole journey being 2/6 single and 3/6 return. This was presumably the service which Henry referred to in 1899 as run by Mr. MacRobert. W. MacRobert, who was Provost of Stranraer in that year, was a job-master, and kept the King's Arms Hotel in Stranraer.

As early as July 1905 the operation of the Mail Service by a motor bus was being seriously considered. A limited company was contemplated, with a starting capital of £3,000 in £1 shares, 100 shares to be a director's qualification. Nothing came of this plan, but on 28th September 1906 the J C agreed to provide "two Steam Motor Cars (constructed to carry at least 30 passengers each)", estimated cost £1,000 for each vehicle, for the Stranraer and Drummore service. The chief credit for the considerable achievement of persuading the J C to commit themselves to the venture seems to belong to Hugh Mayberry, the Glasgow business man and native of Drummore, who had been so enthusiastic a promoter of the light railway scheme of 1899.

By the early months of 1907, preparations for the new service were well advanced. The County Council spent considerable sums on widening the road. The Officers recommended that there should be no half-fares for children; that a notice be printed on the tickets warning passengers to see that their tickets were torn from the pack in their presence; and that a fare table be exhibited in the cars. Two drivers and one conductor would be required. The two cars arrived in Stranraer on Friday, 26th April, and were placed in a shed reserved for their use near the traffic manager's office. The *Free Press* thus described them.

"Built in the workshops of the G & S W Railway at Kilmarnock, the bodies of the new cars have a most massive as well as elegant appearance. Measuring 25 feet in length and 7 feet 6 inches in breadth over all, they are designed to accommodate no fewer than thirty passengers, the seats, which are of the folding deck-chair type, patented by Mr. Lees, of Girvan and Ballantrae, being arranged transversely, leaving a clear passage between for entrance and exit. The large

# Rails to Portpatrick

windows at the front and sides of the cars may be opened or closed as required, and a number of acetylene lamps will brilliantly illuminate the interior of the cars after dark. The rear wheels are fitted with twin solid rubber tyres, an arrangement which greatly lessens the tendency to side slip when the roads are in a greasy condition. The method of propulsion adopted is the invention of MM. Darracq and Serpollet, of Paris. Steam has many advantages as a motive power, and in the case of heavy road vehicles it has proved both safe and reliable. The motion of the piston being produced by the direct application of steam pressure, a strong starting force is given, and this is of great utility in ascending hills. Then, steam is rapidly got up and easily maintained. In the generator, instead of the volume of water being heated to boiling-point, a certain quantity is injected into a heated coil at each stroke of the piston, and instantaneously converted into steam, and superheated. Moreover, no mechanical speed change gear is necessary, as with petrol motors, the variation being obtained by a throttle valve, while to drive the car in a backward direction it is only necessary to reverse the engine. An automatic regulator feeds the petrol of the burner at a determined rate so as to keep the steam pressure at the desired limit, and as all the steam generated is condensed, there is great economy in water and fuel. The new cars which cost about £1,000 each are driven by engines developing between 30 and 40 h.p. and they are capable of reaching a high rate of speed, but in an ordinary service the limit will be 15 miles an hour."

On a trial trip the cars were claimed to have run at over 20 miles per hour "for considerable stretches"; if the weather was dry, they must have raised spectacular, and inconvenient, clouds of dust. The newspaper, in welcoming the new service, which began on 1st May, expressed renewed hope of a light railway to meet all the district's transport needs.

The following time table was issued for the opening of the service:

|            | dep. | a.m.  | * noon | p.m. |          |      | a.m.  | p.m. | * p.m. |
|------------|------|-------|--------|------|----------|------|-------|------|--------|
| Stranraer  | 7.15 | 12.00 | 4.00   | Drummore | dep  |      | 9.30  | 2.00 | 6.00   |
| Lochans    | 7.30 | 12.15 | 4.15   | Logan Toll |    |      | 9.55  | 2.22 | 6.25   |
| Stonykirk  | 7.45 | 12.30 | 4.30   | Ardwell  |      |      | 10.02 | 2.29 | 6.32   |
| Sandhead   | 8.01 | 12.46 | 4.46   | Sandhead |      |      | 10.15 | 2.42 | 6.45   |
| Ardwell    | 8.14 | 12.59 | 4..59  | Stonykirk |     |      | 10.29 | 2.56 | 6.59   |
| Logan Toll | 8.21 | 1.06  | 5..06  | Lochans  |      |      | 10.44 | 3.10 | 7.14   |
|            | arr. |       |        |          |      |      |       |      |        |
| Drummore   | 8.40 | 1.25  | 5.30   | Stranraer |     | arr. | 11.00 | 3.25 | 7.30   |

*The 12.00 noon 'bus from Stranraer and the 2.00 p.m. from Drummore will run during July and August only.

# Rails to Portpatrick

In his report to the Officers on the first month's operation of the cars, Hutchinson said that the service appeared to be giving great satisfaction to the public, and had received gratifying support. The "horse-drawn buses" were still running, but fares by them had been lowered considerably. There had been difficulties owing to breakdowns, but these were being overcome. "The comparative frequency of break-downs may, to some extent, be due to the motormen being new to the work and the route. Only one of our men had previous experience of steam-propelled motors. Both men now appear to be pretty well trained in respect of the mechanism and the manipulation of the motor, and I look for improvement as regards the future".

Month of May:

| No. of pass | Receipts for pass | Luggage and parcels Receipts | No. of trips run | Mileage | Receipts per trip | Receipts per car mile |
|---|---|---|---|---|---|---|
| 1,812 | £113.5.9 | 18/10 | 110 | 1,922 | 20/9¼ | 1/2¼ |

The Officers considered several matters connected with the motors, and made recommendations:

1. Conveyance of newspapers by motor car, by contract or otherwise.

   Newspaper parcels to be accepted for conveyance at the usual train rates applicable on Scotch lines.

2. Proposed revision of motor car passenger fares, in view of the reduced fares quoted by the horse omnibus proprietor.

   Question of motor car fares to be reviewed at end of 12 months' experience of the service.

3. Cleaning of the cars.

   Deferred for joint report from manager and locomotive superintendents.

4. Proposed additional stations (i.e. stages at Dystersbrae., between Sandhead and Ardwell; and Tirally, between Logan Toll and Drummore.

   Approved. Fares to correspond with existing scale.

5. Spare motor car driver, months of July and August.

   Deferred for further report.

6. Rates for season tickets by motor cars.

   Not agreed.

265

# Rails to Portpatrick

At a meeting of Hutchinson and Robert Martin, the C R and G S W's locomotive foreman at Stranraer, with McIntosh and Manson, locomotive superintendents of the two companies, it was decided that when the drivers were too busy with the engines to be able to attend to cleaning the cars, P P & W traffic staff (porters, presumably) should do this work – "... the time to be charged to the P P& W motor car account". Hutchinson urged the need to train a third man as driver in case of emergencies, especially during July and August, when there were three journeys each way daily, and this was agreed to. A man now employed by the C R at Stranraer shed was to be trained "as a spare motorman", and to get a retainer of 3/- per week; if he was needed to drive a car he was to be paid 4/6 a day, but the retainer would cease. Martin was granted an allowance of 5/- per week, backdated to 1st May, for supervising the care and maintenance of the cars. Hutchinson reported that he had "found it necessary" to pay the two regular drivers wages of 36/- per week. At about this time the J C noted that the cars had cost £2,022.0.4, the cost of the bodies accounting for £338.15.0 of this sum.

When the service had been running for six months, it appeared to be making a loss.

Earnings for 6 months ending 31st October 1907:
Number of passengers 10,854.    Miles run 13,075.
Passenger receipts              £730.5.7
Luggage and parcels             £16.1.8
                                -----------
                         Total  £746.7.3

Receipts per car mile                                  1. 1¾
Estimated expenditure per car mile,
including interest and depreciation                    1. 2¾

This was ominous. If it ran at a loss in the summer months, it was likely to prove even less profitable in winter. The figures for the year ending 31st July 1908 showed a loss of about £550, and seeing no prospect of making the service remunerative the officers recommended that it be withdrawn. The J C ordered it to cease after 30th November, and the cars to be sold. It proved difficult to find purchasers for them; in spite of widespread advertising, they were not disposed of till the following May, when Martins Motors Ltd., London, bought them for only £100 each.

It was a very disappointing result for a public-spirited enterprise. It seems that Hutchinson's optimism after the first few weeks had not been justified, and that breakdowns - the bane of early motor services - continued to be a major problem throughout. In the last week of operation, a correspondent, "Forward", wrote in the *Free Press* that "the motors were not running to time, breakdowns were too frequent, with the inevitable result that the public lost confidence in them". He added, however, that there would be "great hardship" if the buses were allowed to cease running, and, in fact, though the J C's service was withdrawn, almost immediately new operators took over. They were the Scottish & Irish Motor Service Company, Edinburgh, who ran numerous buses in conjunction with railways in the South of Scotland and North of Ireland. Fares for the whole run were 2/- single and 3/6 return (day of issue only). The newcomers, in their turn, soon withdrew, and thereafter, for a great many years, the service was maintained by local enterprise. In December 1908, MacRobert, of Stranraer had been reported to be arranging for "a motor brake, with cover" to run on the route, in place of his horse-drawn service. Nothing seems to have come of this, and MacRobert's service drops from our story. In 1910, however, McHarries, motor engineers, of Stranraer, came on the scene with their Stranraer & Drummore Motor Bus Company Limited, and in 1912 this service was carrying the mails. Rival operators in the latter year were Reliable Motors, Stranraer, the proprietor being the Mr. Henry whom we met earlier in connection with the mail coach. Later the route was maintained for a very long time by Messrs. Murray, of Stranraer. They kept the service going into the midd-1960s, when it passed to Western S M T. It is now once again in the hands of local operators.

# Rails to Portpatrick

**APPENDIX THREE**

Motive Power on the P P & W

IN early P P & W days, seven of the eight P P R locomotives taken over by the C R under the Working Agreement in 1864 still survived. The exception was P P R No. 3, withdrawn after being involved in the Dalbeattie collision in 1874. Among the survivors was No. 7, a Sharp, Stewart 2-2-2, designed by McConnell, in its later days given the affectionate nickname of "Fluff"; and No. 5, the ex-L N W Ramsbottom 0-6-0 goods, nicknamed "Aul' Jean". Driven by Edward ("Ned") Cogie, it used to work the ballast train; it was reputed also to have worked the Portpatrick Harbour Branch during the latter's brief period of activity. By 1890, however, all the ex-P P R engines had been withdrawn.

As until 1892 only a 40 feet turntable was available at Stranraer, the C R used 2-4-0 tender locomotives, with a small 0-4-0 tank for the pier - presumably "the small engine now at Stranraer" whose use on the pier was authorised by the P P R in 1873. A few of the 2-4-0s earned themselves a place in the "Officers' Minutes". Thus, on 26th June 1892, C R No. 551 was working the 9.5 p.m. from Newton Stewart to Whithorn when, between Millisle and Whithorn, its driving axle broke; it left the rails, but its train was not derailed, and no one was hurt. The mishap was found to have been due to "an old flaw in the axle, which external examination would fail to reveal". On 10th August 1897, No. 472 was on the 8.1 p.m. Castle Douglas- Stranraer passenger when its trailing axle broke about two miles east of Kirkcowan, the line being blocked for six hours; while on 8th May 1899, moorland and pasture were "alleged" to have been burned by sparks from 591A, working the 8.10 a.m. passenger from Stranraer.

In later P P & W days C R Drummond 2-4-0s worked some of the passenger trains, e.g. No. 67 the 8.30 a.m. ex-Dumfries, returning with the 3.40 p.m. ex- Stranraer, and No. 69 the 9.30 a.m. ex-Stranraer returning with the 5.30 p.m. ex-Dumfries. No. 69, by this time renumbered 1069, was working the 3.40 p.m. ex-Stranraer, however, when it was derailed near Palnure on 28th December 1922. C R Nos. 65, 68 and 70 also remembered on the P P R line during this period.

The "Midday Paddy" expresses operating the Second Service in summer were hauled by C R locomotives, in both directions, the engines working from and to Dumfries.

C R engines working goods trains in later P P & W days included 0-6-Os Nos. 321 and 409. Like all C R ordinary goods locomotives, they were painted black. 321 was a Dumfries engine, its regular driver being William Roney; 409 was at Stranraer, and its regular driver was Sam Young.

For their period of supervision of the W R line in 1914-16 the C R sent three

Drummond 4-4-0s, Nos. 195, 197 and 198, instead of the hitherto usual 2-4-0s. The newcomers were provided with tender-cabs for running tende- first on the W R line, with its lack of turntables.

Among G S W locomotives at Stranraer in 1885 were three James Stirling 0-4-2s. The engines derailed while working the snow-plough near Newton Stewart in February 1895 were of this type, and in early L M S days engines of this type did shunting duties at Stranraer. In 1885 there was an 0-4-0 saddle-tank also at Stranraer; this presumably would be able to work on the pier if required.

During most of the P P & W period the chief expresses were hauled by G S W engines. For some years from 1887 the "Paddy" was worked to and from Carlisle by No. 18, whose regular driver was John Shankland. It was a 2-4-0 locomotive, one of Smellie's "Twelve Apostles". The P P & W men called it "The Eagle". It was succeeded on the "Paddy" by Smellie's "Big Bogie" 4-4-0s Nos. 87 and 88. No. 88 proved remarkably accident-prone wherever it went; an instance of this occurred on the P P & W on 2nd April 1901 when, working the up "Paddy", it ran into a fall of rock between Dromore and Big Fleet. It was quite badly damaged, but there was no derailment, and it was able to take its train forward as far as Castle Douglas. It was superseded on the "Paddy" by 4-4-0 No. 189, displaced from the G S W main line expresses by Manson's new 4-6-0s.

From 1905 the "Paddy" was worked by Manson's "big-boilered" 4-4-0 No. 249, one of the '240' class of fifteen built in 1904-6. Its drivers included William MacEwan, James Murray and Agnew Skimming. In 1915 it was succeeded by No. 152, a superheated 4-4-0 designed by Peter Drummond, which proved remarkably efficient, its coal consumption being only half that of its predecessor. But it was a heavy engine for the P P & W track, and in little more than a year, following the breaking of some chairs, it was withdrawn. In March 1919, a Manson 4-4-0, No. 214, is recorded as working the "Paddy"; this engine was heading the fish train on the night of the accident at New Galloway in October 1913.

No. 18 was still a familiar feature of the railway scene in Galloway in the P P & W's later years, as it regularly hauled other passenger trains. Usually it worked the 7.30 a.m. ex-Stranraer and returned with the 2.50 p.m. ex-Dumfries. On a stormy night in October 1907, however, it was heading the 6.39 p.m. from Castle Douglas: between Kirkcowan and Glenluce, with the train running at about sixty miles per hour, a connecting-rod broke; the engine was considerably damaged and driver Agnew Skimming and his fireman had an extremely disturbing experience. About this time it was renumbered 18A, the first of Manson's large-boilered '18' class appearing in 1907. It may well have been about this time, also - after repairs following the mishap just described - that it caused great concern to the permanent way ganger at Loch Skerrow by repeatedly breaking chairs at a point between High Change and Wee Fleet; the ganger believed the track to be in perfect order and the source of the trouble to be that 18A's wheels were too tightly coupled. (High Change was the "hump" between Big and Wee Fleet viaducts; so called because of the change in the direction of the gradient at that point.)

Towards the end of the J C's rule, the train leaving Dumfries in the early evening for Stranraer was hauled by a G S W engine, not a C R as had once been the practice. It returned from Stranraer with "The Fish". When on 30th January 1918 the 5.30 p.m. ex-Dumfries was derailed near Glenluce, it was worked by No. 67, a 4-4-0 of Smellie's '153' class. On the 15th August 1921, the occasion of the second derailment of this train in the same locality, it (now 5.40 p.m. ex-Dumfries) was headed by No. 385, formerly 250, a Manson "big-boilered" '240' class 4-4-0.

The two engines badly damaged in the fire that destroyed Newton Stewart shed on the night of 24th March 1919 were G S W Nos. 130A and 181. 130A was working the Wee Train at this time; it was a Smellie "Wee Bogie" 4-4-0. 181, one of the W R line engines, was a very small Stirling 0-4-2, originally No. 205, rebuilt by Manson as 181. It had a tender-cab. The other two engines on the W R line at this time were Nos. 113 and 114. First sent there during the period of G S W supervision 1905-7, they also were Stirling 0-4-2s, rebuilt by Manson and fitted with tender-cabs.

G S W engines had also a share of the goods traffic. They worked the 4.40 a.m. Dumfries-Stranraer goods and returned with "The Midnight", a goods train which, until the opening of the cattle lairage at Stranraer in 1913, left Stranraer about that hour for Dumfries, carrying livestock brought over from Ireland by the steamer. When the lairage was opened a 12-hour quarantine period was introduced, so "The Midnight" ceased to run and was replaced by a train leaving Stranraer Harbour usually about 11 a.m.; the G S W engines now probably returned to Dumfries with this train. When there were very busy sales of livestock at Newton Stewart special trains were run, taking empty cattle and sheep trucks from Dumfries, loading and marshalling at Newton Stewart and returning to Dumfries; these trains were worked by G S W engines. Other special goods trains from Newton Stewart, also worked by G S W engines and men from Dumfries, were those run during the new potato season in Wigtownshire, carrying potatoes either in bulk or in barrels.

Until 1919 the enginemen on goods trains did one trip daily, Stranraer-Dumfries or vice versa, and returned the following day. The enginemen on passenger trains did the double trip daily. Under this system men had the same engines in their care for long periods and took intense pride in them, looking after them as if they were their own. Engine cleaners were usually youths, who, in view of the employment situation, would probably always be in adequate supply. As the local goods trains would work at almost every station between Stranraer and Castle Douglas and vice versa, the enginemen were unlikely to have much spare time in the course of their shift. However, if a goods was delayed at a crossing-place the driver would have his fireman cleaning and polishing the engine, while he himself was occupied in oiling it. When working hours were reduced, "change-over turns" were brought in, the men changing engines at Newton Stewart or some other place where trains crossed.

# Rails to Portpatrick

Enthusiasm for the romance of steam was not restricted to little boys collecting train numbers on wet Saturday mornings at Clapham Junction. Throughout the land people of all ages followed the trials and tribulations of the rail system. One of those enthusiasts was Dr. M. F. Brewster, a G.P. from Wigtown. Over the years he ammassed an enormous library of photographs of the activities of the railway in his own area - Wigtownshire. His written observations of the closure of the railways, are included along with a selection of his photographs.

## **TRACK-LIFTING**
(Dr. M. F. Brewster)

Newton Stewart to Whithorn.

British Rail left the dismantling of the Newton Stewart to Whithorn and Garlieston branch line to an independent contractor.

Lifting started at Newton Stewart and proceeded quickly towards Whithorn. The bullhead rails and chairs (there was no flat-bottom "modern" rail on the branch) were dealt with by a team of three or four men using a privately-owned four-wheeled motor shunter type of locomotive hauling two condemned BR standard steel coal trucks. The first wagon contained oxyacetylene cylinders and cutting gear. The second contained a wheeled air-compressor which provided the air to drive two pneumatic power tools for unscrewing the bolts holding the chairs to the sleepers. The procedure was that, preceding the train, one man with a wooden measuring bar walked the line for a section of three to four hundred yards at a time. The measuring bar approximated to the length of rail that could be easily handled weightwise, and the rail running surface was marked with chalk where it should be suitably cut. The rail was cut with the acetylene torch, supplied forwards from the first wagon gas cylinders. The train was moved forward in short steps, the distance of each move being dictated by the length of the pneumatic hose available backwards from the second wagon, which was roughly equal to the length of gas hose available from the first wagon to cut the rail in front. Using one power tool for each rail two men unscrewed the chair bolts from the sleepers of the track behind the train, while behind them, a third man hammered out the wooden "keys" or chocks and freed the cut rail sections from the loosened chairs. By this means, with four men working, the rail-cutting in front, with bolt and chock removal behind, could proceed simultaneously and quickly.

Behind this activity, the salvaged material was cleared separately by road haulage along the trackbed, accessed at the nearest suitable station yard, level crossing, or farm/field road gate.

# Rails to Portpatrick

According to local lore, the salvage team had strict instructions to remove and dispose of everything. This rule apparently extended to buildings, telephone poles and ballast where present in usable condition. Everything was demolished. The only survivals were the stone (standard plan with brick extension) cottages originally built to house the stationmasters at Wigtown, Kirkinner, Whauphill and Sorbie, along with the more substantial combined station building/house at Millisle and some level crossing gatekeeper or worker cottages such as the ones at Carslae Crossing and the unique oblique ungated Garlieston Crossing. These were already under separate occupation, having been disposed by the railway following the end of passenger services in 1950. Apart from Millisle, the only other station building to survive was at Sorbie, where it was close enough to the station cottage for it to be incorporated as an additional extension of the cottage.

When tracklifting was finished, the condemned wagons, now marooned in Whithorn, were also cut up. Engineering structures, including the Bladnoch viaduct, and also some of the other smaller over and under bridges, were then removed separately at a later date.

The Main Line from Dumfries to Stranraer.

The track-lifting of the direct Stranraer-Dumfries link from Challoch Junction to the factory at Cargenbridge outside Dumfries (the factory rail-link was retained) was carried out under the aegis of British Rail. This track had been maintained to express train standards with speed cambering on curves, and routine track maintenance renewals had continued right up to the time of closure. Manufacture dates were stamped on rails and most, if not all, of the track was less than ten years old. Major sections had been laid with modern flat bottomed rail. There was no continuous welding at that time.

British Rail had decided that the track sections could be used for relaying elsewhere, and that they should be lifted as far as possible intact.

After the fishplates had been unbolted at the rail joints, the uncut rail lengths, complete with sleepers still attached, were lifted out by a large caterpillar mobile crane and stacked four or five sections high on three coupled standard fourwheel flat wagons, this formation of three being the length of a standard track section..

A four-wheeled diesel shunter was used to propel a three flat truck train towards the track-ending one section short of the front of the crane. The crane could then lift the track section on to the trucks. The train reversed one section length, the crane "walked" forward to it over the newly emptied track bed, and the process was repeated until the three wagons were fully stacked. The loaded wagons were hauled to the next eastwards station yard where a further coupled group of three empty flats were collected and propelled back up to the crane. When the yard had accumulated sufficient numbers of loaded three wagon flats units to marshal into a full train load, a new train of empties was sent up the line from the Dumfries end and the loaded train hauled back.

After disconnection from the retained Glasgow-Stranraer line at Challoch junction, the closed line was treated as one long siding entered from Dumfries, with only one train allowed in. The BR track-lifting trains were diesel locomotive hauled. Despite what has been written elsewhere, to my knowledge steam traction reigned supreme until the railway closed, and the only diesel locomotives ever seen on the line were used on the track-lifting freight specials which ran after the official closure date.

Thus, lifting started at Challoch Junction and proceeded eastwards towards Castle Douglas and Dumfries. As lifting progressed eastwards, each successive passing loop in turn became the full train-load assembly yard, with Glenluce, Kirkcowan, Newton Stewart, Creetown, etc. successively becoming the termini for the diesel workings.

# Rails to Portpatrick

### **THE LAST DAY**

Dr. M. F. Brewster.

There was very little local interest in the Whithorn branch closure and evidently none from elsewhere. The Machars must have been too far away from civilisation for "foreign" gricers and "last train" buffs to attempt the arduous journey to a happening 100 miles beyond Carlisle. Perhaps, the enthusiast fraternity of the national scene did not know about it or did not care.

Officially there were two passengers with permits on this last scheduled freight train. These were Mr David Gladstone, a keen railway enthusiast and previously a local farmer at Carsenestock, who had a permit to ride on the locomotive, and Mr. Bert McCreadie, a steam model maker from Newton Stewart, who apparently travelled at least some of the journey in the guard's van.

It had become apparent to the train crew that there was going to be no official presence of "bowler hats", (foremen or railway management), and on the train's down journey to Whithorn, another local enthusiast, Dr. M. F. Brewster, who was taking photographs in Garlieston, was invited by the driver to ride the engine from Garlieston to Millisle. Once in Millisle, the driver suggested that while the train went to Whithorn, he (Dr. B.) should return home to get old clothing, and that, provided no officialdom turned up at Whithorn or Wigtown, he could rejoin the engine in Wigtown as an unofficial guest of the train crew on its run to Newton Stewart.

The writer has no personal knowledge of what happened in Whithorn itself, but the Galloway Gazette reported that only a few local people, including railway staff and old employees, along with a couple of crews from the adjacent bus depot and two holiday-makers, turned up to watch this last scheduled freight train leave the station.

On the train's return journey from Whithorn, Mr. Alex Muir from Kirkinner, one of the linesmen, used the last of his detonators on the rails at Whauphill station to give the last departure a noisy send-off with several loud explosions.
At Wigtown station, Mr. James Allan, who had worked at Wigtown's station in his youth, and Mr. William McGowan, whose grandfather had ridden on the first train, were there to witness the last departure. After these two posed for photographs with the train crew and guard, the last train departed from this, its last scheduled stop, to the accompaniment of long whistle blasts. No official British Railways management personnel had appeared, and from Wigtown, through

# Rails to Portpatrick

the two stops necessary for the crossing gates at Carslae, and up to the outer branch signal at Newton Stewart the driver and fireman supervised their two unofficial "students", Mr. Gladstone who drove the engine and Dr. Brewster who shovelled the coal. After arrival at Newton Stewart, the train's last passengers alighted on the station platform and watched sadly when the train finally left for Stranraer.

Even so, this was not really the last train on the line. The last scheduled train had delivered loaded wagons to the branch and the empties had to be removed before the branch's connection at Newton Stewart was finally severed.

Eight days later, on the following Saturday, a train came down the line to collect the rolling stock which had been left behind. It followed the usual pattern of working, first at Wigtown and then onwards to Whithorn, before working back along the line after picking up "strays" from Whi±horn itself, as well as from Garlieston, Sorbie and Bladnoch siding. It truly was the last proper train

Within a year the line was completely dismantled.

However, the last railway wheels to pass along the line belonged to the three vehicles of the lifting contractor's train, comprising a blue privately-owned four wheeled motor rail-tractor pulling two condemned British Railways standard steel coal wagons containing the equipment required for the track salvage operation.

Starting from Newton Stewart and having the track cleared behind it as it moved south, this train took many weeks before it finally reached Whithorn.

"The last shall be first and the first last" is probably the most appropriate epitaph to apply to this final "San Fernando" operation.
It was the real "last train" from Newton Stewart to Whithorn.
It was the slowest train ever to make the journey.
It made the most stops.
It was, sadly, the first branch train to travel from Newton Stewart to Whithorn and not come back!
It was the first train on the line to be hauled by an internal combustion engined locomotive.

It was sad for the little boys from Wigtown and Bladnoch who, (in those far-off days before modern "health and safety" spoiled children's fun and prevented childrens' tragedies), played on the Bladnoch bridge rails as the train jerked its wagons along the tracks in its lifting mode movements of some 20-30yds at a time.

It was, sadly also for them, the first and only train to Whithorn hauled by an engine that could not go "choo-choo" and could not crow-whistle to mark its passing.

# Rails to Portpatrick

## FREIGHT TRAIN OPERATION ON THE WIGTOWN BRANCH BEFORE CLOSURE

## DR. M. F. BREWSTER

Freight trains for Whithorn normally came from Stranraer and shunting operations at stations on the branch line were often complicated and difficult to understand.

Trains destined for Whithorn were always hauled from Stranraer to Newton Stewart with the locomotive travelling backwards, tender first, and would continue past the trailing branch line connection into one of the loops at Newton Stewart station. After shunting at Newton Stewart, which included moving the brake van to the other end of the loose-coupled trains, the locomotive would run round the train. After leaving Newton Stewart by the way that it had arrived, the train could now proceed chimney first on to the branch line through the now facing junction.

On the actual branch, wagons were shunted, left or picked up at each station or siding according to whether the points made facing or trailing connections. Thus, Wigtown, Whauphill, Sorbie and Millisle were dealt with on the down run to Whithorn. Wagons for return to Newton Stewart and beyond were left in the loops, where present, for collection on the return up-run, or taken south to Millisle, e.g. Sorbie.

At Millisle, there was an operational signal box with a full-time signal man employed to the last. According to the local grapevine, (which waxed red hot when it was announced that the local railways were being closed because they were making a loss), British Rail paid him the standard wage for a full five-day week. He never had to work on a Tuesday or a Thursday because trains never ran on these days. It was alleged that he got double-time pay for working on a Saturday when it was not uncommon for an extra working to be scheduled at short notice. Furthermore, the rail unions would not allow the train guards to work the points at Millisle after the whole system had become unnecessary - because there had never been more than one train at a time on the branch since passenger services ended around 1950. Such expensive follies were said to be widespread in the railway system and deliberately maintained to justify unnecessary line closures.

When a train arrived at Millisle with its numerous signals and points, the engine, under the control of the signal man, would detach any wagons for Garlieston from the rest of the Whithorn train and the guard's van would be redeployed at the rear of the new formation (a necessary manoeuvre - see below). The new subdivision was then pulled down the branch until the loop at the old Garlieston station platform was reached. The guard would wind on his van brakes and the locomotive would then detach from the train and set into the platform, leaving the wagons with the guard's van attached at the rear, standing on the slight incline behind the station. With the driver or fireman keeping the ungated road crossing clear of cars, the guard would then release the van brakes. The train wagons and van would then roll past the engine and across the road using gravity. Once clear of the loop points and the road crossing the guard would stop the train and the engine would pull forward and couple to the back of the brake van to shunt the two harbour sidings, - rearranging, picking up or leaving wagons as required. Delivered wagons were normally left in the covered loading area underneath Wyllie's mill building at the faraway end.

Once shunting was completed, the train would be pulled back to Millisle with the brake van still between the wagons and the locomotive, which now had to run backwards, tender first. At Millisle the train met the previously-detached wagons for Whithorn which now became wagons in front of the rear of the engine. These were propelled out of the branch line on to the main line loop, once the engine and brake van had been detached from Garlieston wagons. (These latter were left behind on the branch line end to be collected again when the train returned from Whithorn.) After further shunting and run-around on the Millisle mainline loop in order to get the brake van repositioned to be at the rear of the train, the train would proceed, the engine now chimney first, in normal formation forwards to Whithorn.

On the return journey the engine had to run tender first again as there were no turning facilities at Whithorn. Return wagons left in the loops were picked up, for example, the Garlieston wagons left at Millisle. Traffic at Bladnoch siding was always delivered or picked up on the return journey because of its up direction trailing connection.

At Newton Stewart after further run-round and shunting, the train, with its formation now reversed for the fifth time, would proceed with to Stranraer with the locomotive heading the train chimney-first.

# Bibliography

**Primary Sources**

In the Scottish Record Office, Edinburgh.
Minutes of meetings of directors of the following companies:
- The Portpatrick Railway.
- The Wigtownshire Railway.
- The Portpatrick & Wigtownshire Joint Railways.
- The Caledonian Railway.
- The Glasgow & South Western Railway.

Letter Books of the Wigtownshire Railway Company.
Minutes of Meetings of Officers of the Portpatrick & Wigtownshire Joint Committee.
Minutes of Meetings of Directors of the the Larne & Stranraer Steamboat Company.
Minutes of Meetings of the Larne & Stranraer Streamship Joint Committee.
Copies of papers relating to the sale of parts of the Cally estates by H. G.. Murray Stewart to the Portpatrick Railway Company.
Copies of papers relating to the claim of H. G. Murray Stewart against the Portpatrick Railway for damage to his property.

In the Public Library, Stranraer:
*Tours in Galloway*, the PP&W tourist guide, published annually 1898 to 1915.

In the *Free Press* Office, Stranraer:
Files of the *Galloway Advertiser & Wigtownshire Free Press*.

In the *Galloway Gazette* office, Newton Stewart.
Files of the *Galloway Gazette*.

In the *Galloway News* office, Castle Douglas.
Files of the *Kirkcubrightshire Advertiser*.

contd.

**Secondary Sources**

Dick, C. H.: *Highways & Byways in Galloway & Carrick*
    (Macmillan 1st ed. 1916; 1st pocket ed. 1924; revised 1938;
    Special Memorial Edition with biographical introduction,
    G.C. Books, Wigtown, 2001.)
Harper, M. McL.: *Rambles in Galloway.*
    (R. G. Mann, 1st ed. 1876; 2nd ed. 1908.)
Duckworth, C. L. D., & Langmuir, G. E.: *Railways & Other Steamers.*
    (T. Stephenson & Sons Ltd., 2nd ed. 1968.)
McNeill, D. B.: *Irish Passenger Steamship Services. Vol. 1*
    (David & Charles, 1969.)
Coleman, T.: *The Railways Navvies.*
    (Hutchinson, 1965.)
Smith, D. L.: *The Little Railways of South West Scotland.*
    (David & Charles, 1969.)
Smith, D. L.: *Tales of the Glasgow & South-Western Railway.*
    (Ian Allan, 2nd ed., 1970.)
    The former of these works provided very helpful information about the early locomotives on the PPR line, and Wheatley's engines on the WR, while the latter yielded some interesting items about motive power in PP&W years.

I found it interesting and helpful to place the information I collected about the builders of the Portpatrick Railway against the background of the more general picture provided by this book.

H. D. T.